CRAWFORD COUNTY ARKANSAS

BIOGRAPHICAL
AND
HISTORICAL MEMOIRS

Goodspeed

Heritage Books
2025

HERITAGE BOOKS

AN IMPRINT OF HERITAGE BOOKS, INC.

Books, CDs, and more—Worldwide

For our listing of thousands of titles see our website
at
www.HeritageBooks.com

A Facsimile Reprint
Published 2025 by
HERITAGE BOOKS, INC.
Publishing Division
5810 Ruatan Street
Berwyn Heights, MD 20740

Previouly published:
Mountain Press
Signal Mountain, Tennessee
2005

International Standard Book Number
Paperbound: 978-0-7884-9830-5

1

CRAWFORD COUNTY, ARKANSAS - BIOGRAPHICAL AND HISTORICAL MEMOIRS
****

HISTORY OF CRAWFORD COUNTY

BOUNDARY, GEOLOGY, NATURAL FEATURES, ETC.

The Terraces.—Crawford County is bounded north by Washington County, east by Franklin, south by Sebastian and west by Indian Territory. It is generally understood to be a "mountain region," but that is "a misnomer," says an Arkansas *Gazette* writer, "if it includes not the idea of a system of five great terraces, the rise of which in elevation, the one above the other, is at the rate of fifty-seven feet to the mile.

"As due to the difference in the altitude of the terraces, the uppermost being 1,620 feet above the lowest, and, therefore, as is due to the topography of the country, and to protection against the storms of winter afforded by the Boston range, the meteorology is not the least remarkable condition upon which is founded the general difference from other counties of the State.

"In the immediate valley of the Arkansas, south of the Little Rock & Fort Smith Railroad, the track of which approaches the base of the third terrace, the annual mean temperature is 66° Fahrenheit. This is the maximum of the county. Throughout the third and fourth terraces, or the belt of country inclosed in the parallels bounding Townships 10 and 11 north, the annual mean temperature is 62° Fahrenheit. While not so indicated in the annual mean temperature, this given belt of country has been declared, after careful hygrometrical measurement, to have the dryest atmosphere of any scope of country in the State.

"The annual mean temperature of the highest terrace, which is also strictly the mountain region of the county, is 58° Fahrenheit.

"The superficial area of the five great terraces of the county is in square acres 390,000. From this 79,430 acres are to be deducted as the aggregate area of a system of creek valleys, the head-waters of which are in the Boston range, and the course of which toward the Arkansas, in general, intersects the terraces at right angles. The effect of the valleys subordinated to the terraces has been, not only to build up in the interior of the county a system of extraordinary creek lands with material derived from the upper levels, but it has brought about a drain system which, as a whole, is the best so far encountered in the State. The area of creek valleys is 79,430 acres."

Water.—"The county is well watered by numerous streams, all running from north to south, and the large ones emptying into the Arkansas River. On the west is Lee's Creek, running the entire length of the county, from Boston Mountain on the north line of the county, and emptying into the Arkansas; about the center of the county is Big and Little Clear Creek, rising in Boston Mountain and traversing the county, the latter joining the former, which empties their combined waters into the Arkansas; on the eastern boundry of the county Big and Little Mulberry, rising in the Boston Mountain, running nearly through the county, join and empty into the Arkansas. These are all clear and beautiful streams, and all abound in the very finest fish. In addition to these are several smaller streams. Water for family use is easily obtained by digging, and there are many fine springs in the northern portion of the county. Cisterns are used to a limited extent, and principally in towns."*

Natural Dam.—One of the most remarkable features in the scenery of Northwestern Arkansas is the "Natural Dam." Prof. Owen says it is formed by a solid bed of sandstone, from six to eight feet in thickness, which runs entirely across the bed of Lee's Creek, forming a natural barrier to the descent of the water, in consequence of the gradual dip of the rock *up stream* toward the northeast, at an angle of four to five degrees, being just the proper inclination to dam the water back, and throw it to a sluice, that might be solidly and permanently fixed to this rock wall near where it runs into the northwest bank.

Stone.—Close to the spring, at the foot of the mountain over which we passed from the Barren fork of the Illinois to Lee's Creek,

---

Argus, February, 17, 1876.

3

CRAWFORD COUNTY, ARKANSAS - BIOGRAPHICAL AND HISTORICAL MEMOIRS
****

the Archimedes limestone is in place, 260 feet below the level of the principal mass of corresponding limestone in the section of the northwest slope of the mountain. There is, no doubt, a dislocation of the whole of the rocks of the mountain, with a subsidence to the southeast, which causes so sudden a depression of this limestone.

Half a mile below Alfred Smith's farm sandstone was observed dipping ten degrees to the southeast, the Archimedes limestone being no longer visible above the bed of Lee's Creek.

The high cliffs along Lee's Creek " are composed of sandstones, shales and limestone, belonging to the age of the millstone grit and sub-carboniferous group, the strata gradually dipping down stream toward the south." The heights at Van Buren are composed of similar rocks, the exposed strata being sandstone, grey shale and shaly sandstone, with ferruginous segregations, 30 feet; black and reddish shales, 15 feet; blackish grey shale, with segregations of carbonate of iron, 15 feet; shales, including 18 inches coal, passed through in the steam-mill well below the town of Van Buren, 110 feet.*

At the "Phillips Bank," in Section 18, Township 19, Range 30 west, from which coal was mined to supply the blacksmith trade of the region in 1858, the following section is given: Top of the hill, soil and subsoil; thin bedded sandstone, alternating with red marly clay (base of millstone grit), 25 feet; blue agillaceous shale, with segregations of carbonate of iron, 60 feet; black bituminous shale, with fossil plants, 1 foot; semi-bituminous coal, 1 foot; fire clay, .6 foot.†

Mineral Springs.—The Pennywit sulphur water was tested at the fountain head. Its principal constituents are bicarbonate of lime, bicarbonate of magnesia, chloride of sodium or common salt, chloride of magnesium, trace of sulphate of soda (Glauber salts), trace of sulphate of magnesia (Epsom salts), a trace of free sulphuretted hydrogen.* A spring thirteen miles from Van Buren, and about one mile north of the old stage road, is of similar composition.

The following mineral springs are located in the county:

---

*Prof. Owen.
†Dr. Elderhorst.

White Rock Springs and Sulphur Springs, north of Alma; Three Rock Springs and Chalybeate Spring, north of Uniontown; Oliver Springs and Sangster Springs, near Van Buren; Tapp Springs, near Rudy, and others of lesser note.

Mines.—Interest has been manifested in developing coal, iron, zinc, copper and fire clay, but so far two coal mines are the only effects of this interest.

Products.—The timber embraces gum, cotton-wood, oak, elm, hackberry, walnut, paw-paw and pecan, on the bottom lands; on the uplands, post oak, red oak, white oak, black-jack, black oak, hickory, and some pine and walnut. Cotton: 4,000 to 6,000 bales are shipped annually. Wheat, oats, rye and barley grow finely; corn, forty to 100 bushels to the acre; sorghum does well; Irish and sweet potatoes unsurpassed; entire millet family, timothy, red and white clover, red-top, blue, Bermuda, orchard grass (the favorite); tobacco on the uplands; broom-corn; apples (Peerless, Shannon, Dwight, Ben Davis, Arkansas Queen, Wine Sap and Shockley); pears (Bartlett, Duchess D'Angouleme, Seckel, Virgaliens, Bergamot and Winter Niels); peaches (Hale's Early, Amsden's June, Alexander, Early Beatrice in June, Amelia, Crawford's Early in July, Great Eastern, Lemon Cling in August and Heath's Cling or Eaton's Golden in September); quince, plum, cherry (Morello varieties, Early Richmond, English and Red Morello); grapes (Concord, Ives, Hartford Prolific, Delaware, Herbemont, Clinton and Norton's Virginia, a fine wine grape); fish (black bass, bream, speckled cat, rock bass, sun perch, blue and yellow cat, buffalo, drum, red-horse and suckers).*

The shipment of posts, timbers and ties, and the culture of fruits, particularly apples, peaches and berries, are the leading industries in all but the bottom lands, where "cotton is still king."

Stock.—The chief new breeds of cattle introduced have been the Durham, Holstein and some Jerseys; ordinary work horses and mules are bred; the favorite hogs are the Berkshire and Jersey Red, while Merino sheep represent that class of stock.

---

*Immigration Society articles, by D. Dickson, L. Graf, W. L. Taylor, R. Thruston and G. Wilcox.

ERA OF SETTLEMENT.

Earliest Inhabitants.—It is uncertain whether ancient earth-works now found are those of Indians or Mound Builders; the probabilities place them among Indian remains. "Uncle" Peter Kuykendall, whose keen observation and life as a hunter since 1835 enabled him to know the territory of the county very thoroughly, found in several different places ring-like mounds similar to the rings used in a circus. On the southeast side of Vine Prairie Lake crockery was dug up also. On his own land he plowed up a rock weighing about thirty pounds, which was almost perfectly hollowed out as a basin, capable of holding a gallon of water; afterward many others of various sizes were found and used by the settlers as wash-bowls. The rocks were sometimes round and sometimes square. In the eastern part of the county is a mound of an elongated oval form, somewhat tapering at one end, and is composed of all sorts of rocks and covered with soil and very old trees growing upon it. At its highest point it has an elevation of six feet, and at that point is about thirty yards wide, while its length is given as about fifty yards; it is not impossible that this may have been a monument-al mound erected by that ancient race which preceded the Indian occupation of the Mississippi valley. This is on the land of Mr. W. Bollings, on Frog Bayou (Clear Creek). In Section 35, Town-ship 10, Range 31, and on a mountain, is a peculiar rock struc-ture almost solid, and very regular, its dimensions being prob-ably ten feet by six feet by ten feet, and concaved on top in a very regular form. Crockery was found in it by Mr. James Tapps, it is said. There are evidences of abandoned small mines also, from one of which "Uncle Peter" sent ore to St. Louis, which produced in silver, $17.50. In the northwestern part of Cedar-ville Township, about three miles from that village, are remains of an old fort, with mounds in the interior. Its arrangement is quite regular and gives evidence of some engineering skill in defenses. In some of its walls the stones are set perpendicularly and in others horizontally. From the branch of the creek two parallel walls extend about fifty yards apart. The right one is given as about 450 feet, and from its middle extends another

6

CRAWFORD COUNTY, ARKANSAS - BIOGRAPHICAL AND HISTORICAL MEMOIRS
****

wall toward and almost to the left wall, with a wing to the left making a passage way. This 450-foot wall, after leaving a passage way, is continued for over 150 feet farther, and from its end a wall extends at right angles to the left, over to where the left wall would be if it extended far enough; but the left wall comes only far enough to leave a passage way between its end and the branch of the right wall, and from this end, at right angles, extends a wall toward the right wall and almost to it, and parallel to the end wall, thus protecting this entrance in an excellent manner. This makes a form of about 600x150 feet, using the creek as one end, but an enclosure of about 400x150 feet, using the wall extending from the middle of the 450 foot wall as one end. At the passage way in the right wall is a peculiar arrangement of walls; you may enter the inclosure, but you find you are only in one part, for to your right, two walls, extending from the right and left walls toward each other, and presenting an acute angle toward you, leave a passage way between their ends into the farther apartment. There are numerous legends concerning this fort; one considering it a work of Mound Builders; another that of Indians, and the one most fondly held relegates it to the intelligence of the famous De Soto.

The Indians who are first known to have occupied Crawford County territory are the Osages, a savage nation; but their treaty of 1825 caused them to remove, and only occasionally return for a hunting expedition. During the following years the Creeks, Choctaws and Cherokees came through, and many of the Cherokees settled and were given right of title to their land. They were a largely civilized nation, and had orchards and log cabins equal to their white neighbors. A tradition says that the Cherokees and Osages had a fight just over the Crawford County western line, and a white man with the former, named Lee, was wounded and crawled back to the creek and there died; from this the Indians gave the creek the name " Tu-yah-ho-sah," meaning "where something dies." Lee's name was afterward used. Trails generally followed the water courses. The buffalo seems to have been pretty thoroughly killed off, as the skeletons of them were very commonly seen by the settlers of 1828. The exodus of the Cherokees, following the treaty of 1828, was followed by an influx

7

CRAWFORD COUNTY, ARKANSAS - BIOGRAPHICAL AND HISTORICAL MEMOIRS
****

of white settlers, and all of the possible sources of information give the Indian relations with the whites of Crawford County as peaceful. The white people simply came in and occupied the deserted Indian settlements, and welcomed the Indian hunter when he chose to return.

First White Settler.—David Boyd first set foot on the site of Van Buren in 1818, when cane-brake covered it, and bear, deer and wild turkey were to be seen. Thomas Martin, in his opinion, built the first house there. He saw the overflow of 1833, and witnessed, at Crawford old court-house, the punishment of a criminal, by Sheriff Joshua Brown, by means of public whipping.

The first permanent settlements* in the original county of Crawford were made in 1818-19-20, in what are now the counties of Sebastian, Scott, Franklin, Logan, Johnson and Yell; on Big Creek and the Arkansas River by the Billingsleys, Buchanans, Newtons, Joys, Sumners, Robinsons, Olivers, Wilsons, Howards, and Moores, Dillards and McGees a little later, together with many others; and between Big Creek and Fort Smith, by the Maxwells, Simpsons. Shannons, Marrs, Putnams, Knoxes, Ratcliffs, Saunders, Alexanders, Featherstones, Stagners. Larrimores, Moodys and others; and on the Upper Petit Jean by the Carthrons, Tumlinsons, Arringtons, Frenches, Perkins and others; and at McLain's Bottom (now Roseville), by the McLains, Titzworths, Forts, Marshalls, Scotts, Hixons and others; and about this time a few settlers were scattered along the river at various points from Fort Smith to the mouth of the Petit Jean, among whom were the Cravens, Clarks, Stinnets, Johnsons, Peeveys and others. These early settlers of Crawford County were mostly, it is believed, from the States of Kentucky and Tennessee, and were a most substantial body of yeomanry. It jis no disparagement to others to say, speaking of them as a whole, that in point of character, worth and intelligence, they have not been surpassed by any succeeding tide of emigration that ever set toward Arkansas, from that day to this. Many of their descendants are now living in Western Arkansas, some in this and some in adjoining counties. Of this early emigration few are now alive. The Rev. John Buchanan and Maj. John Billingsley, of Washington County (both mere striplings at that day) are among the few survivors.

Soon after the present county of Crawford was attached to and made a part of the original Crawford, many of the settlers removed across the river into the newly annexed territory lying north of the river and south of the Boston Mountains. The first permanent settlements made in the annexed territory were in 1828-29 in what are now the counties of Pope, Johnson, Franklin and Crawford—Crawford embracing them all at that time. I regret that I have only data to give a few of the names of the early settlers of Crawford and Franklin. There were on White Oak the Russells, Gilbreaths, Merideths, Meltons, Huggins, McLaughlins, Lanes and others; the Bourlands followed a few years later. On Mulberry, the Beans, Quesenburys, Russells, Hendersons, Maxeys, Moores, Jesse Miller, Simpsons, Snodgrass, Reeves, Mosses, Williams and others. On Frog

*Address of Hon. Jesse Turner, 1876.

Bayou the Corders, Larrimores, Smoots, Scotts, McPhails, Prices, Trammells, Howards, Bashams, Orricks, Mooneys, Peters and others. On Lee's Creek the Moores, Peevehouses, Harrells, Howells, Forristers, Dodges, Blacks, Martins, Paynes, Smiths, Mobleys, Swearingens, Shannons, Barkers, Olivers and others. Among the early settlers of Crawford County may also be mentioned David Thompson, John Drennen, John Henry, Edward Cunningham, the Hindes, the Prices, Whitfield Bourne and others.

The settlers on the north side of the river were very similar in character to those who had settled on the south side; being, in fact, in some instances the same persons, and in others recruits from Lovely County who had been compelled to abandon that county upon its cession to the Indians.

Sparsely scattered over a wide extent of country, these early settlers could not enjoy all the advantages and conveniences of an older and more densely populated country, and yet they did not neglect schools, nor the moral training of the people.

The Cumberland Presbyterians, Methodists and Baptists — those earliest missionaries of Christianity in the Southwest — made their advent into the country with the first settlers, and their labors bore abundant fruits in moulding and giving tone to the moral sentiments of our people.

At that early day buffalo, bear, deer, turkey and other game were abundant in Crawford County, and although our pioneers were agriculturists and relied on the cultivation of the soil for a living, yet for awhile they were to a considerable extent dependent on game for a support. Their tastes were simple and their wants few. Maj. Bradford, of the United States Army, who had in 1817 established a military post at Fort Smith, was supplied by them plentifully with buffalo meat, and he in turn supplied the settlers with luxuries to which they had long been strangers, particularly the article of flour, and they for the first time for years enjoyed the supreme felicity of eating biscuit shortened with bear's oil. While the limited supply of corn lasted, to use the expressive language of Maj. John Billingsley, "they had *pound cake* every day," the meaning of which was that the corn was pounded and reduced to meal in a mortar, and baked into a very palatable bread, which was facetiously called "pound cake." This primitive style of mill for manufacturing meal was soon succeeded by the steel-mill and the horse-mill.

I would here observe that while these early settlers were subjected to some of the hardships and inconveniences of frontier life, they were also exempt from some of the burdens and vexations which a more advanced stage of society has entailed upon their descendants. They were comparative strangers to taxation for the support of government. A small tax of one-fourth or one-half per cent. for county purposes was all they were called upon to pay, the other expenses of the territorial government being paid by the United States. What a contrast between that day and this!

The following description of a pioneer "camp meeting" (from a paper by Hon. Benjamin T. Duval) will serve as an excellent specimen:

In the midst of the forest, the neighbors built log huts for the accommodation of their families and visitors; these were arranged so as to form a hollow square. In the center was a large shed covered with clap-boards, and seats were made of split puncheons laid upon logs; a rude stand or pulpit was erected at one end; around, at convenient distances, scaffolds covered with dirt were put up to make pine knot fires to light the night services. Early in the fall people would gather there from a distance even of fifty miles, with their families and an abundant supply of provisions. The preachers, from four or five to ten or more, would also come from all parts, and meeting would hold a week. At night especially the scenes were impressive and exciting; after a sermon replete with startling appeals to the consciences and fears of the congregation, an invitation would be extended for mourners to come forward to be prayed for, while preachers and congregation were singing. The preachers and older members would go around exhorting, and urging sinners to come forward; after the whole congregation had become excited, members would crowd up around the pulpit, where straw had been strewn; here the mourners would kneel and crouch down, while the preachers would pray over and exhort them; the sobs and moans of the mourners, the sweet melody of the simple hymn, sung with heartfelt energy by the members, the prayers and exhortation of the preachers, with the shouts of those who "got religion," formed a scene at once striking and impressive, and especially with its surroundings. The flickering of the pine-knot fire, as it was stirred by the night breeze, caused the trees, shed, and mass of beings, swaying to and fro under an apparently invisble feeling, to give the picture a weird and unnatural appearance.

The services often continued until a late hour at night, and I have seen a large portion of the congregation shouting and exhibiting the wildest actions, in their subjection to an uncontrollable emotion. Those scenes were repeated night after night, and large numbers were admitted into the church. The opportunities for going to church in those days were rare; the circuit rider could not visit the distant settlements oftener than once a month, and these camp-meetings were seasons of refreshing, not only spiritually, but for social intercourse and friendship.

Here, as elsewhere, a generous hospitality gave the stranger and wayfarer a hearty welcome to the table of all the campers. "Uncle Buck" in those days, as I have said, was a man of might; he braved the dangers of the forests and streams; endured the vigors of the seasons in carrying the gospel tidings, as he understood and believed them, to the people scattered throughout the territory; undaunted by perils, he served the people in the cause of his Master.

A somewhat noted *ante-bellum** institution of Crawford County is thus neatly described by an *Argus* correspondent:

Imagine yourself on a high bluff on Lee's Creek, a thousand feet above its low valleys, in a small log house with a side room, on an Indian trail, with no house in sight, and nothing to cheer your midnight hours save the owls and the Sah-wah-loh (hoe-bird), a peculiar kind of bird that utters one of the most lonely cries a little after dark, which bird can be heard a great distance. Then look a little northwest, a few hundred yards, and see a growth of wahoo, intermixed with some underbrush, witch-hazel and some tall water-oaks, across the Cherokee line, together with some moss-covered rocks on the brow of the hill, and you have something of a description of (Jonathan Roder's) Pike's Peak Saloon on the Cherokee line in Arkansas.

*About 1853.

Land Entries.—Land entries do not always indicate actual settlers, but the following list of entries, in chronological order, and giving sections, names and date, will serve to show the ownership of the present territory of Crawford, and in most cases the settlement: December 18, 1828, J. Clark, 1–8–30; January 2, 1829, Charles Kelly, 35–9–30; January 9, 1829, J. McLaughlin, 1–8–30; December 2, 1830, B. L. Moore, 12–8–30; May 14, 1831, Nancy M. Hill, 25–12–32; June 30, 1831, James Campbell, 9–8–30; same date, John Hardin, 10–8–30; December 31, 1831, Fanny Ramsdale, 23–9–30; January 31, 1832, M. Mayes, 13–9–30; January 31, 1832, Jeremiah Smellgrove, 7–9–30; November 26, 1834, Jacob Niderer, 18–9–30; December 2, 1834, George Couch, 6–9–30; December 15, 1834, Thomas Phillips, 18–9–30; December 16, 1834, H. Oliver, 6–9–30; February 25, 1835, Simon Miller, 36–10–29; April 9, 1835, James M. Randolph, 20–9–30; July 2, 1835, Andrew Morton, 6–9–30; October 2, 1835, James Ramsey, 17–9–30. In 1836 entries were February 22, G. W. Knox, 17–8–30; April 13, Mary Snodgrass, 36–10–39; John Drennen, 6–8–31; Berry H. Oxford, 1–9–31; D. B. Collins, 2–9–31; Thomas W. Norwood, 30–9–31; Richard Turner, 30–9–31; April 20, John O. Nick, 20–8–31; M. Lieper, 23–8–31; April 22, Silas Colville, 11–8–31; April 25, John Howell, 2–9–31; April 26, James Woodson Bates, 14–8–30; John Bell, 29–9–31; Jonathan D. McGee, 19–9–31; May 10, Leander Lock, 20–9–30; May 18, Dennis Tramell, 7–9–30; May 31, J. S. Scott, 33–9–30; May 16, King Fisher, 5–8–31; Thomas Ratcliff, 7–8–31; May 21, Edward Carney, 35–9–31; May 28, Robert Henderson, 19–9–31; June 23, James Heard, 1–9–30; June 20, James K. Polk,* 36–9–30; June 22, Whitfield Bourn, 7–9–31; June 23, John Knight; June 13, David McClellan, 30–9–31; June 6, George Y. Latham, 11–8–31; July 27, Moses Sanders, 6–9–30; July 6, George C. Pickett, 19–9–31; August 3, Hugh A. Anderson, 9–8–30, and Ira Smoot, 8–9–30; August 10, W. M. Givin and S. Davis, 21–9–30; August 1, Henry H. Enlows, 10–8–31; April 22, 1837, W. Robinson and John Lewis, 6–8–30; April 21, Isaac Harrell, 6–8–30; April 10, Robert Stewart, 27–9–30; April 21, W. Copps, 11–8–31; April 15, R. C. S. Brown, 19–9–31; September 23, J.

*The President.

11

CRAWFORD COUNTY, ARKANSAS - BIOGRAPHICAL AND HISTORICAL MEMOIRS
****

B. Powell, John Rose and Hugh Pierce, 24–9–32; September 25, Benjamin Weaver, 15–9–32.

Later Settlers.—The greatest influx of settlers was after the Territory became a State. The settlements were chiefly along the bottoms, Frog Bayou, Lee's Creek, and the Fayetteville and Little Rock roads. The old steamer ".Kentucky" brought more Indians from the east, but they passed on through. William Neal came with them. "Old Uncle" Peter Kuykendall was here on Frog Bayou in 1835, and voted on the organization of Arkansas as a State; he voted at Amstead Smoot's, where about forty votes were cast, covering a radius of about five miles. "Uncle Peter" thinks those the balmy days of hunting, when he could in a single day see 120 deer or 300 wild turkeys, and bears, panthers, wild-cats, foxes, wolves, all through the canebrake and upon the mountains. Rude farming and hunting were the occupations of these early settlers, and they were good marksmen; almost every Saturday there would be a shooting match. "We'd put up a big beef, and shoot sides for it," said "Uncle Peter," and one of the largest stakes to be won was $100 (about 1839), at a match between the Lathams, Couches, "Uncle Peter" and others, in which "Uncle Peter" won in seven shots. It is not known whether "Uncle Peter" took his defeated comrades over to Couches' "still" and cheered them with some of the peach and apple brandy that was to be found there; he didn't say. If he didn't then it would not be improbable if they had some "reels and square dances" that night, for the settlement had a "sucker fiddler" by the name of "Bill" McLaughlin, from Illinois. He might have proposed an old-fashioned "North Carliny corn-shuckin'" or a "quiltin'," but probably not, for he remembers the dances better, although it is said he was but a spectator; an observant one, too. "They wuz a heap uh perty wimmen thar," said "Uncle Peter," "and a dod-blamed perty black-eyed widder." He tells of a new-comer at one of these dances, in which it seems that the local swains looked with disfavor on intruders; but the new-comer was courageous, and concluded to win them by a frank confession of his abilities; he made a conciliatory appeal and ended up with the clincher: "I can dance as good *serviceable* dancin' as any man on the floor," after which, it is presumed, he

12

CRAWFORD COUNTY, ARKANSAS - BIOGRAPHICAL AND HISTORICAL MEMOIRS
****

had no trouble in winning the hand of the "dod-blamed perty black-eyed widder" for a reel. "Yes, that wuz the way, son," said "Uncle Peter." James Kuykendall and Ira Smoot were here the first justices.

Keel boats and canoes were used upon the river and creeks. Capt. Pennywit owned two steamboats, "The Little Rock" and "The Arkansas." The oldest road was probably that from Old Crawford court-house up Frog Bayou, on to Cedar Creek and Lee's Creek to Washington County. Mails were carried on horse-back to Van Buren, and there distributed to Fayetteville, Fort Gibson and Fort Smith. Travel to Little Rock was often done by caravan, horses or mules packed, and four or five tied together, the second being tied to the tail of the first. Phillips' Tavern at Phillips' Point was a place for travelers. It was a two-room log house, and often, it is said, "Uncle Johnny Buck" (Buchanan) would be holding services in the front room, while a game of faro was in progress in the back room. Travelers would often have to frequent John Bostick's blacksmith shop to have their horses shod; and upon one occasion he did such a job for "Uncle Buck," but assured the reverend old gentleman that he made "no charge except to be remembered in your prayers;" whereupon the practical "Uncle Buck" rejoined, "Come right back here and kneel down; for I don't want to be indebted to anybody!" It is said that the blacksmith withdrew his exception.

Indian trading was a considerable business, and small stores were scattered all over the county; large droves of cattle were raised in the canebrake; fine fish were caught, and beaver and other trapping was followed.

Soon after 1836 William G. Shannon and Hezekiah Taylor were on Cedar Creek, and not far distant was William Hargraves and William Whitehead. George Miller, a Mrs. Crim and her sons, and George Nettles were all on this creek.

On Mountain Fork of Lee's Creek a Mr. Larrimore owned the first mill at Natural Dam. Andrew Morton, W. Duval and another gentleman bought out Larrimore about 1838–39, and opened a store. Near Main Lee's Creek were Mr. Black, David Allen, Mr. Elmore, a merchant, Jack Hargraves, Clementine Mobley, David Mobley, John Shannon, Hiram Brodie, a Mr.

Hart, and Joe Bryant; and on the creek were Eli, Richard and William Oliver, Mr. Blackburn, Mr. Courtnay. Below Natural Dam were the Widow Fort, "Bob" Harris, Jim Black, George Foster, H. Foster, Parker F. Stone, Andrew Lester, Daniel Pevyhouse, I. B. Vinsant, G. S. Foster, Thomas Walden and George Stone. On the Cedar Creek road to Van Buren were Gooding's Mill, Jesse Stewart, Abe W. Jackson, the Widow Walters, Mr. Hancock, Mr. Taber, Lucretia Mayes, Mr. Forester, "Old Man Miller," D. P. Collins and William Mussett. Old Mr. Shannon's place and Mr. William Neal's place, not far from the present site of Cedarville, were settlements, and there were but about sixty in the township. Mr. Shannon was the first justice there after the State was admitted, and Mr. Matlock was a constable. One of his cases was a levy upon the wagon of a man about to leave the county, and owing "Uncle Billy" Neal for a steer. In "the forties" a store at Henry Elmore's, on the Fayetteville road, and one at Natural Dam, were probably the only ones outside of Van Buren, and no post-offices except that of Van Buren in the county, until late in that decade at least. There were but two grist-mills—that at Natural Dam and Stewart's old mill, near the present site of Lancaster. Natural Dam is probably the oldest settlement in the county, and probably the Shannon settlement, about Cedarville's site, the next, although this is not certain. Logtown (Collinsville or North Van Buren) is an old settlement dating to the arrival of the Widow Powell, who came there from Lovely County in 1828. A Mr. Locke was the first settler about Dripping Springs, and George Matlock opened the first store there. The debts of these days were paid in trade or "peltries;" these were deer-skins with the hair shaved off, and were valued at about $3 apiece. The honesty—said to be peculiar to those times alone—is illustrated by the following custom: There would be several in a hunting party, each of whom would secure a number of pelts. These would be hung together on a tree near some frequented place to cure; one danger to the hides was bugs, so that any one who passed would feel it his duty to "bug" every hide, whether he owned any of them or not, and none were ever stolen. One little feature might be added to show that these honest settlers were human, namely, that as the peltries were sold by weight there would be an occasional forgetful memory which would leave some flesh on the hide, and work sand into it to keep it from spoiling ! Bee trees were considered public property, and no honey was wasted; a hole would be cut in the tree, and all that was needed for a sugar substitute was taken out, and a plug placed in the hole.

ORGANIZATION.

County Formation.—It is uncertain who was the first white man to enter Crawford County territory, but it is certain that only a comparatively few miles prevented that man from being the great discoverer De Soto in April, 1541. That it was a part of French Louisiana until 1762, Spanish until 1804, when it was transferred to the French and the same day became our own, affected it only in name. In 1812 it was included in the District of Arkansas in the Territory of Missouri, and on March 2, 1819, became part of the Territory of Arkansas. It can hardly be said that Crawford County was created by the first legislative body of Arkansas Territory, for the first, held at the Post of Arkansas in July and August, 1819, was composed of the governor and supreme judges; a special session, composed of the council and House of Representatives, convened in February, 1820, at the same place, and it was a special session of this body, held in the following October, in which "an act to divide Pulaski County" was passed and approved October 24, 1820. This act created a new county, composed of most of the territory now embraced in Yell, Logan, Johnson, Franklin, Scott and Sebastian Counties, and part of Indian Territory, and it was named in honor of William H. Crawford, secretary of the treasury under President Monroe. It is seen that no part of the present county of Crawford was included in this new county; by a treaty in 1809, between the Indians and the United States, the present territory of Crawford County was a part of Indian Territory.

The first seat of justice of Crawford County* was located temporarily at the house of John Jay, on the south side of the Arkansas River, half a mile above the point on the river now known as Crawford Old Court House. The commissioners appointed by act of the General Assembly of October 22, 1821, to

---

* Hon. Jesse Turner's address at Alma, July, 4, 1876.

15

CRAWFORD COUNTY, ARKANSAS - BIOGRAPHICAL AND HISTORICAL MEMOIRS
* *

make permanent location of the seat of justice, were Clark Sanders, John McLain and John Wilson, who, it is believed, made the location near the present residence of Mrs. John D. Arbuckle, about three miles west of Crawford Old Court House. An act of the General Assembly of October 24, 1821, enlarges the boundaries of the county on the southwest, and an act of October 30, 1823, made some changes of boundaries in what is now the Cherokee Nation, but did not materially enlarge or diminish the area of the county. By an act of October 30, 1827, all that portion of the county of Crawford known as "Lovely's Purchase," and certain adjacent territory not previously apportioned to any county in the territory, the boundaries of which were particularly described, was created into a separate county of "Lovely." The county of Lovely embraced the greater part of the Cherokee Nation, and (it is believed) the present counties of Washington, Benton and Madison, and must at that time have contained nearly or quite 5,000 inhabitants. The Western Cherokees, by treaty with the United States of 6th of May, 1828, having ceded to the latter their lands north of the Arkansas River, included in the treaty of 1817 and convention of 1819, embraced mostly in the present counties of Pope, Johnson, Franklin and Crawford, for which the United States ceded to the Cherokees the county embracing Lovely County and some other territory adjacent thereto (the present Cherokee Nation), the General Assembly, by act of October 22, 1828, attached the Indian country thus acquired from the Cherokees to and made it a part of Crawford.

A paper by Hon. Ben. T. Duval, read before the State Historical Society in 1882, says: "By treaty made at St. Louis on the 25th of September, 1825, between William Clark, governor of Missouri Territory, and a full and complete deputation of considerate men, chiefs and warriors of the Great and Little Osage Nation, the territory within the following bounds, to wit: 'Beginning at Arkansas River, at where the Osage boundary line strikes it, at the mouth of Frog Bayou; then up the Arkansas and Verdigris to the falls of the Verdigris; thence eastwardly to the said Osage line at a point twenty leagues north from the Arkansas River, and thence to the place of beginning,' was added to the United States. Lovely's name does not appear in the treaty. For this cession of territory the United States agreed to pay their own citizens the full value of such property as could be legally proven to have been stolen and destroyed by the Osages, not exceeding the sum of $4,000. This ceded territory was included in the limits of Lovely County—in fact, was Lovely County.

By an act approved October 20, 1828, it was made the duty of the "clerk of the circuit court of Lovely County to transmit to the clerk of the circuit court of Washington County all records, dockets, vouchers and other papers remaining in his office."

Since Lovely County covered a part of the present Crawford, the following letter from Col. Thomas Moore, of Franklin, Tenn.,* may throw some light on it:

I moved with my father's family to Crawford County, Ark., in 1821, and settled five miles above Crawford Court House The names of the lawyers that I remember, who practiced in court at that time, were Col. William Quarles, William Oden, William Cummins and Robert Crittenden. Alexander McLean

*To Hon. Ben. T. Duval.

was clerk;* and I believe James Woodson Bates was judge of the court.† The name of the Cherokee agent was Loveless (not Lovely), and the purchase, I suppose, was made by him and named for him. His widow lived many years near the old Dwight Mission, in the Cherokee Nation, not far from Dardanelle.‡ After the white people commenced settling in the Purchase, commissioners were appointed to lay off a county seat, Gen. John Nicks being one of them. The town was laid off and named Nicksville in honor of him. I was appointed sheriff by the governor of the Territory, and John Dillard, Esq., appointed county clerk. My brother Benjamin was my deputy. We, with our families and my brother, also Dr. J. D. McGee, moved up from Crawford County in March, 1828, and settled in Nicksville (the exact spot where new Dwight Mission was founded). Not long after we moved there court was held there, and only one. I do not recollect the names of the lawyers, except Mr. Robert Crittenden, of Little Rock, and Col. Franklin Wharton. Judge James W. Bates presided. Mr. Wharton Rector was there. I don't know whether he was a lawyer or not. In May, of the same year, an edict came from the authorities at Washington City, that all settlers must leave, for the purchase had been exchanged for the Cherokee lands below, on the north side of the Arkansas River, and all males over twenty-one years of age, who had made an improvement, would be entitled to 320 acres of land to remunerate them for their losses. A rush was made by speculators and others to Loveless County to buy all the claims that they could, etc. So the newly acquired county was soon settled, and Nicksville was short-lived. I fear I have given you but little satisfaction, but it is the best I can do.

The following is taken from the address of Hon. Jesse Turner, at Alma, July 4, 1876:

By an act of November 2, 1829, the county of Pope, embracing the present county of Johnson, was formed out of the eastern part of Crawford. By an act of November 5, 1833, the county of Scott was formed out of the southern and southwestern part of Crawford, and by act of December 18, 1837, the county of Franklin was formed out of the eastern part of Crawford. The county of Sebastian embraces all that part of the county of Crawford which remained on the south side of the river, and was created into a separate county by an act of the General Assembly of 1851.

Thus we see the United States acquired the present territory of Crawford County in 1825 from the Osage Indians; that the Cherokees seemed to have been given rights of settlement in the same before 1828; that on May 6, 1828, the Cherokees relinquished this right; that it became a part of Crawford County on the following 22d day of October, and that it became the entire county in 1851.

While the boundaries of the county were undergoing repeated changes from the formation of new counties out of its territory, the seat of justice was far

*The date 1821 or name Alexander McLean is wrong; for Henry Bradford was clerk in 1821 -23.—Ed
†Bates became judge in 1833.—Ed.
‡The name "Lovely" in one of the treaties settles that question.—Ed.

from being stationary. After its temporary location, it was located about the year 1823 near the present residence of Mrs. John D. Arbuckle, but was afterward at Fort Smith, McLain's Bottom (now Roseville, Crawford Old Court House, Whitsontown, on Big Mulberry, and finally at Van Buren, where the courts have been held since 1838.*

The public square † was donated to Crawford County by David Thompson and John Drennen, the original owners of the town site in the year 1839, on condition that Crawford County should locate the seat of justice at Van Buren. The county, by a vote of the people, in that year did locate the seat of justice at Van Buren upon the public square. The proposition to donate this ground for public purposes was in writing, and is probably still in existence, but it is believed no formal deed to the county for the property was ever made by the donors. In 1844 or '45 the county court deeming it best to procure from the court of chancery a decree for title to this property in pursuance of said donation, employed me to institute suit for that purpose. Suit was brought, John Drennen and the Thompson estate being defendants, and they at once admitted the charges; upon this hearing the court decreed absolute title. The following is the proposition, brought to light by the efforts of Alma to secure the county seat:

To Messrs. Brown, Gibson and Knox, Commissioners of the County of Crawford and State of Arkansas for Locating the Seat of Justice, etc.:

Gentlemen: We, the undersigned, will make as a donation to the county of Crawford, Block 14, in the town of Van Buren, containing sixteen lots. Each lot contains thirty-three feet front, and 127 feet back, with a ten-foot alley running through said block. The block of lots, No. 14, agreeable to the town of Van Buren, is well situated to make a public square, and an eligible site for a court-house. According to a correct calculation, the donation will contain something upward of three acres of ground. We, the undersigned, will make a deed in fee simple for the said block of land (No. 14), provided said commissioners will place the court-house and jail of said county of Crawford, on said block of land.

Given under our hands, at Van Buren, March 15, 1839.

David Thompson.
John Drennen,
    By his attorney in fact.
David Thompson.

The actions of the county court, previous to 1838, would properly be treated in the histories of counties in which the county seat was then located. The destruction of the records from 1838 to 1877 make the acquirement of information concerning the organization of civil townships, polls, issuance of scrip, bridge warrants, and other county actions of importance, practically impossible. Under Judge Sangster a large amount

---

* Address of Hon. Jesse Turner at Alma, July 4, 1876.
† Jesse Turner.

of ten-year scrip was issued, and soon this was redeemed by bonds bearing 10 per cent, but all of these were redeemed previous to 1878. In 1873 bonds were issued for ten years bearing 8 per cent to the amount of $13,000, but these were also redeemed within five years or thereabouts. These are the most important issuances. The custom of issuing scrip or warrants for bridge building and other county purposes has long been in vogue by the county, and is still the method in use. The county has no poor-farm; land was bought for one previous to the war, but it was soon afterward sold.

On the night of the 23d inst.*the Crawford County court-house, at Van Buren, was destroyed by fire, nothing remaining but the outer walls. The fire was discovered a short time after midnight; the alarm sounded. * * * * Efforts were made to save the records locked up in the county clerk's office, in the northwest corner of the building, second floor, but of no avail. No ladder was at hand, and the window could not be reached. When a ladder was secured and raised to the window, the flames had reached the rooms and rendered it impossible to effect an entrance. All the papers and records of the county, together with about $4,000 in county scrip, allowed by the county court, and issued by the clerk, but which had never been called for, were consumed in the flames. * * * * The loss of the court-house sinks into insignificance when compared with the loss of the records of the county. * * *

It was supposed to be an incendiary's work. Mass-meeting's were held and rewards offered for the offender; the city council voted a two and a half mill tax for two years, to build a joint court-house and city hall. The county court, in April, 1877, also ordered the court-house built on the old walls on the citizens' plan, and ordered a tax of one and one-half mills on the dollar for that purpose. This was not done, however, before Alma, headed by Col. M. F. Locke, had petitioned for a vote on the question, which was granted, and after an exciting fight the election was decided for Van Buren, by a vote of 1,042 to 842.

The first record of the Crawford County Court now in existence reads as follows:

APRIL 16, A. D. 1877.

WHEREAS, On the morning of the 24th day of March, A. D. 1877, the court-house of the county of Crawford, in the State of Arkansas, was burned, together with all the records, books, papers, etc., belonging and pertaining to the county court of said county, on file in the clerk's office of said court, and, WHEREAS, On the 4th day of September, A. D. 1876, J. C. Chapin was

*Argus, March, 1877.

duly elected county and probate judge of the county of Crawford, in the State of Arkansas aforesaid, and afterward was duly commissioned by the governor of said State as such judge, which commission is in words and figures as follows, together with oath of office of the said J. C. Chapin, to wit: [Here both are inserted.—Ed.]

And now on this 16th day of April, 1877, the day as established by law for holding the regular term of the county court of said county of Crawford, at the town of Van Buren, which is the county seat of said county, in a room in the Pennywit Block of said town, the said J. C. Chapin, as judge aforesaid, appeared at the hour of 9 o'clock, A. M., together with the clerk of said court and the sheriff of said county, and, by the order of said judge, said sheriff then and there proceeded to, and did in that place, open the county court of Crawford County, Ark., for the April term, A. D. 1877, whereupon the following proceedings were had, to wit: [Here follows allowances for destitute persons, preliminaries for the rebuilding of the court-house, and the provision of a court-room to be used until the new building was erected.]

A half-mill tax was levied, and Samuel Martin with A. B. and Josiah Howell were appointed commissioners for the erection of the building on the old walls, and $6,500 was appropriated for that purpose. F. Adams was the architect, and R. L. King was the first contractor accepted, but he failed to file a bond.

SOCIETIES, ETC.

The Crawford County Immigration Society was organized May 3, 1877, at the court room in Van Buren, by Hon. H. F. Thomason, a county vice-president of the State Immigration Society. J. C. Chapin was chosen secretary. The members were as follows: Jesse Turner, Sr., L. C. White, Henry Pernot, M. Lynch, D. C. Williams, W. H. Gill, J. G. Peevey, C. F. Brown, W. L. Taylor, E. A. Scott, A. M. Bourland, A. O'Brien, A. Smith, S. D. Daugherty, C. F. Harvey, P. Richards, John Brodie, A. J. Ward, D. Dickson, L. Graf, Henry Shibley, George C. Thayer, J. D. Hawkins, D. W. Moore, Levi Chapman, G. Wilcox, G. Wood, J. Chapman, F. R. McKibben, W. J. Neal, J. B. Ogden, H. F. Thomason, J. M. Baxter, C. Reeve, N. F. Cornelius, J. A. Wade, J. W. Cary and J. C. Chapin. "The object of the society is to induce and facilitate immigration, by collecting and transmitting reliable information to capitalists seeking investment, and also to parties in other States desirous of seeking new homes, regarding soil, climate, different branches of business to be pursued with profit in the county of Crawford."*

* Constitution.

This organization has been one of the greatest instruments in Crawford County development. From time to time they have shown up the resources of the county in the local and Little Rock papers, corresponded with other societies, issued pamphlets, etc., and encouraged every enterprise tending to augment the county's development.

The Patrons of Husbandry, so famous in its short life, grew to goodly proportions in Crawford County, and withered away, as it did elsewhere, and at about the same time. Crawford County Council was organized at Alma February 6, 1874, by five granges, represented by the following masters: M. F. Locke, of Alma; D. Michael, of Van Buren; C. C. Holland, of Arizona; R. Hill, of Lafayette, and J. Winters, of Prairie Grove. Van Buren and Alma were chosen as alternate places of meeting. The order was at the zenith of its prosperity and size in 1874, when the complete list of granges in Crawford County was as follows: Crawford Grange, James Sangster, M.; Mulberry Grange No. 137, Z. Hopper, M.; Sarah Grove Grange No. 61, J. S. Matlock, M.; Alma Grange No. 29, M. F. Locke, M.; Prairie Grove Grange No. 178, J. Winters, M.; Shamrock Grange No. 74, F. C. Oliver, M.; Van Buren Grange No. 38, D. Michael, M.; Lafayette Grange No. 40, R. Hill, M.; and Oliver Springs Grange No. 347, J. S. Boatright, M.

The Crawford County Agricultural Society was organized September 10, 1859, at Van Buren, Isaiah Vinsant, chairman; secretary, Gran. Wilcox. Messrs. Burrow, Hays, Woosley, Kuykendall, Brown, Thruston, Stevenson, Matthews, Heard, Walden, Dibrell, Brodie, Maxey, Southmayd, Scott, Steward and Foster were present, and the officers chosen were president, N. B. Burrow; vice-presidents, Jesse Turner and Isaiah Vinsant; treasurer, R. Pernot, and secretary, G. Wilcox. The war, of course, closed the career of this society.

The Crawford County Agricultural and Mechanical Association was organized July 10, 1869, at Van Buren. M. F. Locke was chairman and John B. Ogden, Sr., secretary. Among the organizers were J. Baxter, R. Thruston, B. J. Brown, Gran. Wilcox and C. F. Harvey.

The Crawford County Horticultural Society was organized

in January, 1887, with the following officers: E. Arkbauer, president; F. Smetzer, vice-president; H. A. Meyer, secretary; H. C. Miller, treasurer. The object of the society is the encouragement of fruit growing and berry culture, and for the protection of those engaged in such culture. At their meetings reports are made as to the condition of plants, trees and vines at various seasons. There is no doubt that the society has been, and will be, a powerful influence in the promotion of this new industry.

The Crawford County Medical Society has had a variable existence, and has been organized under different names at different periods. The original society had a meeting in May, 1847, and had the following officers: President, Dr. R. Stevenson; secretary, J. H. T. Maine; censors, J. H. Bailey, J. A. Dibrell and C. F. Brown.

The Van Buren Board of Health might be mentioned in this connection. It was established in April, 1866, with the following members: Chairman, H. Pernot, and Dr. White, Dr. Bourland and Hiram Brodie as sanitary committee.

The Crawford County Medical Association was organized November 15, 1875, at the court-house, by Drs. H. Pernot, A. M. Bourland, W. T. Black, L. C. White, C. F. Brown, J. H. Decherd and W. L. Cathey. The officers chosen were President White, Vice-President Black, Treasurer Pernot and Secretary, Cathey. Resolutions were passed against quacks and non-graduates. The society afterward gave way to others.

The Van Buren Medical Society, successor to the Crawford County Medical Society, was reorganized in April, 1886, at Van Buren, by the physicians of the city: Drs. Dibrell, Brown, Hynes, White, A. M. and O. M. Bourland and Coryell. The following officers chosen are still the incumbents: President, C. F. Brown; vice-president, G. F. Hynes; treasurer and secretary, O. M. Bourland. The society have but eight members, but have had delegates to represent them in the State and national associations of their profession.

RAILROADS.

The Little Rock & Fort Smith Railway was organized in 1853, the first president of the company being John Drennen, of Van

Buren. The growth of the enterprise was very slow, but the large number of stockholders in Crawford County were persistent, and the company complied with the terms of the congressional grant, and secured an immense amount of land, not only in Crawford County, but all along its line, gaining alternate even sections for six miles on each side of the track. After Col. Drennen's presidency the Hon. Jesse Turner, of Van Buren, held the office until about 1866. It is well known that Presidents Converse and Gould have since been the executives. Judge Turner became vice-president, in 1874. The first vice-president, George W. Clarke, and Secretary John B. Ogden, were Van Buren men. During the fifties Capt. Barney surveyed the route, and the bed for twenty miles south of Van Buren was prepared. The citizens of Crawford County had invested about $15,000. Work was not begun again until in 1869, and in August, 1871, 120 miles were completed, and the total stock, bonds, etc., were valued at $9,400,000. At 8:30 P. M. on June 24, 1876, the first train entered Van Buren. The road continued up the river to opposite Fort Smith, and used transfer there until the erection of the present Frisco bridge. The road has had a considerable effect in Crawford's development, but chiefly as a better substitute for river conveyance.

The Kansas & Arkansas Valley Railway, although of a later date than the Frisco, may be mentioned here, for it is really an extension of the Little Rock & Fort Smith Railroad. It runs directly from Van Buren to Wagner, I. T., and was completed, and the first train run from Van Buren over its line, on August 13, 1888. Its repair shops will be at Van Buren, and its control of the Indian country trade will add greatly to the business of the Crawford County seat. Judge Jesse Turner, of Van Buren, is a prominent director and stockholder. This company was first given fifteen acres by the citizens, and afterward the Van Burenites gave land on the south side of its track, 132 x 1,288 feet.

The St Louis & San Francisco Railway was the first successful effort of a great many to open a line from Van Buren to the trade of St. Louis and Kansas City. The Van Burenites took $10,000 of stock in this road. It was practically completed in the middle of 1882, and this led to the building of a union depot at

23

CRAWFORD COUNTY, ARKANSAS - BIOGRAPHICAL AND HISTORICAL MEMOIRS
****

the crossing of the roads, although the freight depot is situated at the upper end of Main Street. About the same time their splendid steel bridge, across the Arkansas River near the old ferry, was completed, at a cost of probably $400,000.

The first passenger train over the Arkansas division of the St. Louis & San Francisco Railway rolled into this thriving and important trading center at 6 o'clock this evening. Nearly half the 1,500 population of the city awaited the arrival of the train at the handsome new depot. * * When the train, drawn by an engine, brave in garlands and floral decorations, pulled up at the depot, a battery stationed on the summit of the neighboring bluff boomed forth a deep-mouthed welcome, and the bells in every church tower united in a jubilant peal, announcing that the long waited and worked for hour had arrived, when St. Louis and Van Buren were united in the iron bands of free and uninterrupted commerce. *

Large numbers of excursionists from all points to Spring-field were aboard, and these were welcomed by a committee composed of Hon. Jesse Turner, Sr., Hon. B. J. Brown, Capt. R. S. Hynes and Capt. H. C. Hayman, who escorted them to a banquet at the court-house. So, probably, the most important commercial event in the history of Van Buren and Crawford County's career was ushered in, and from that moment dates a remarkable revival and development in not only Van Buren and Crawford County, but all Northwestern Arkansas. It was a transformer; made the region a fruit and vegetable region equal to any in the United States; made it a sought-for home, where before it was almost unknown.

The Arkansas Northern Narrow Gauge Railroad, organized under State laws, was surveyed in 1882, from Van Buren, up Lee's Creek and bearing off toward the western State line in the direction of Joplin. Work has been attempted several times in grading, but for some reason it is still suspended.

The Northwestern Border Railway Company, chartered in March, 1867, was one of the futile efforts to open a railway taking the general course of the "Frisco Line," and several thousand dollars were subscribed. Its successor, The Arkansas Western Railway Company, chartered in May, 1870, suffered the same fate, and many other efforts came to naught.

---

*Van Buren special (November 15, 1882) to St. Louis *Globe-Democrat.*

ELECTION RETURNS.

OCTOBER, 1844.

OFFICERS.	Big Creek Township.	Sugar Loaf Township.	Jasper Township.	Mountain Township.	Richland Township.	Lee's Creek Township.	Ft. Smith Township.	Van Buren Township.
Democratic.								
Governor, Drew..............	21	24	53	74	49	55	120	110
Byrd................	1	1	4	2	6	3	10	16
Congress, Yell.................	23	24	56	76	54	53	129	125
Tully.............. ..								
State Senate, Smith...............	23	23	55	69	57	53	115	99
Representatives, Mayes...........	21	17	57	75	57	50	127	
Roane..........								
Duval								
Sheriff, Bell.....................	22	25	73	81	54	70	92	158
Circuit Clerk, Gibson	8	16	47	42	31	45	73	65
Whig.								
Governor, Gibson................	18	8	33	20	26	40	118	126
Congress, Walker..........	18	9	34	19	26	45	119	128
State Senate, Turner	16	8	35	24	25	45	127	147
Representatives, McKinney......	18	6	27	16	4	32	117	113
Simpson	18	6	34	20	28	41	113	130
Collins.	19	6	43	19	35	46	95	131
Sheriff, Kannady	19	6	15	13	28	23	141	84
Clerk, McLean......	30	14	41	49	48	48	163	167

NOVEMBER, 1848.

Democratic electors: J. S. Roane, 447; John Martin, 452; James Yell, 452. Whig electors: Jesse Turner, 345; J. W. Cocke, 343; John Preston, 343.

NOVEMBER, 1860.

TOWNSHIPS.	Bell.	Breckenridge.	Douglas.
Van Buren............................269		116	121
Richland............................ 8		19	16
Lafayette............................ 16		29	40
Mountain.......................... 4		3	54
Cedar Creek.......................... 10		4	18
Lee's Creek.......................... 19		10	36
Jasper............................ 23		12	24
Upper............................ 2		14	18
Vine Prairie....................... 23		8	29
Sheppard.......................... 0		20	1
Totals........................374		245	357

REGISTRATION OF VOTERS, 1867.

TOWNSHIPS.	White.	Colored.	Total.
Van Buren..............................255		115	370
Lee's Creek............................ 46		10	56
Upper............................ 30		0	30

TOWNSHIPS.	White.	Colored.	Total.
Sheppard	33	0	33
Mountain	44	0	44
Jasper	50	0	50
Cedar Creek	81	0	81
Lafayette	88	0	88
Vine Prairie	21	19	40
Richland	56	3	59
Totals	704	147	851

CONSTITUTION, 1868.

TOWNSHIPS.	Against.	For.
Van Buren	246	139
Mountain	41	9
Sheppard	13	27
Lafayette	38	38
Jasper	44	33
Upper	1	30
Lee's Creek	18	26
Vine Prairie	15	19
Cedar Creek	18	56
Richland	83	9
Totals	517	386

NOVEMBER, 1868.

TOWNSHIPS.	Grant.	Seymour.	For Railroad.*
Van Buren	209	176	371
Richland	13	73	86
Vine Prairie	18	24	43
Lafayette	51	41	92
Cedar Creek	62	14	76
Jasper	41	27	56
Upper	44	—	44
Mountain	8	23	31
Sheppard	13	4	17
Lee's Creek	27	9	36
Totals	486	391	852

The Crawford vote, for and against $100,000 aid to the Little Rock & Fort Smith Railway, was—Van Buren, for, 204, against, 2; Jasper, for, 7, against, 9; Cedar Creek, for, 4, against, 9; Upper, for, 6, against, 10; Sheppard, for, 6, against, 2; Mountain, for, 13, against, 0; Lafayette, for, 25, against, 1; Vine Prairie, for, 11, against, 0; Lee's Creek, for, 0, against, 7.

---

*But one vote against railroad.

NOVEMBER, 1872.

President—Greely, 589; Grant, 938. Governor—Brooks (liberal), 587; Baxter (radical), 932. Congress—Hynes (liberal), 586; Bradley (radical), 935. State Senate—Brown (liberal), 693; Arbuckles (radical), 913. Representatives—(liberals) Fishback, 577; Stevens, 569; Felker, 584; Alden, 579; (radicals) Davie, 922; White, 893; Strong, 943; Berry, 935; Devilbiss, 29. Sheriff—Grady (radical), 919; Carson (liberal), 541; J. C. Grady, 14; Singleton, 37. Clerk—Shibley (liberal), 607; Bowlin (radical), 903. Judge—Meadows (liberal), 612; Harrell, 887. Surveyor—Alexander (liberal), 622; Chastine (radical), 900. Treasurer—Ward (liberal), 601; Kirnes (radical), 911.

Crawford's vote on the amendment in March, 1873, was—for, 444, against, 98. The vote in July, 1874: Thomason, 827; Sangster, 774; for convention and no delegate, 14; for convention and delegate, 1,596; against convention, 5. The vote on the constitution in April, 1876, was—for, 1,444; against, 209.

VOTE OF 1880.

President—Hancock, 1,138; Garfield, 974; Weaver, 48. Governor—Churchill, 1,387; Parks, 1,135. Senate—Thomason, 1,366; Creekmore, 1,153. Representatives—Nettles, 1,295; Robertson, 1,240. County Judge—Hale, 1,404; Lamb, 1,174. Sheriff—Houck, 1,285; Taylor, 1,282. Clerk—Southmayd, 1,612; Scott, 967. Treasurer—Ward, 1,297; Renfroe, 1,262; Amendment—for, 1,821; against, 441.

COUNTY OFFICERS.

The first officers of Crawford County were a clerk and sheriff, the former being Henry Bradford, and the latter, Jack Mills, who died and was succeeded by Mark Beane. This term was from 1821 to 1823. The next term of two years Clerk G. C. Pickett and Sheriff Mark Beane were accompanied by the first coroner, J. C. Sumner. From 1825 to 1827 Mr. Pickett and Mr. Sumner were retained, James Wilson became sheriff, and Alfred Oliver became the first county surveyor. These officers seem to have held over until 1830, when all were reinstated, except Mr. Sumner, whose successor was Elihu Joy. At this date, too, Crawford, had her first county judge, in the person of Robert Sinclair. From 1832 until 1836 the terms embraced but one year only, the two-year term continuing from 1836 onward, however. Messrs. Pickett and Sinclair were continued in 1832, but the sheriff's office was held by J. E. Brown, the coroner's by D. A. Williams, and John Harrell took charge of the tripod and chain to use them until 1842. In 1833 James Woodson Bates became judge, and that veteran clerk, Alex. McLean, picked up the clerk's quill to relinquish the same after twenty-three years of service. Messrs. Brown and Williams were retained, the latter for two more successive terms. Judge Bates retained his office until 1840, with the exception of one year, 1834, when the office seems to have been vacant. R. C. S. Brown, W. P. Moore, Jesse Miller and J. M. Randolph were the successors of J. E. Brown as the " mine host " for criminals up to 1840. On the organization of the State William Hull became the first county treasurer, and his successors up to the long service of A. J. Ward were D. P. Collins, D. R. Looney, W. Duval and W. R. Heard. Mr. Ward served from 1846 to 1860. The office of coroner found few incumbents who held it for a second term; the sucessors of Mr. Williams were Isaac Shannon, Thomas Hazen, D. L. Looney. Moses Kahoe, T. A. Brooking, G. W. Hawkins, H. W. Bell, T. J. Powers, D. Dickson, G. R. Bell for two terms, W. I. K. Meadows, J. Bentley, Joel Dyer, William Stovall* for two terms, Calvin Phelps, J. S. Rainwater, J. J. Hinson, Sr., H. C. Hayman, A. C. Turman, S. Pernot, W. W. Brodie, H. B. Manes and J. P. Mack in 1888. After John Harrell's long term and two terms held by John Carnall, the most persistent holder of the transit and chain is D. Dickson. This gentleman began in 1846, and has held it ever since with the following exceptions: E. G. Cader (1850 to 1852), R. C. Hattaway (1854–56), H. Bushong (1860–62), R. Allen for three terms on account of the resignation of James Bushong, George Kilgore and M. Kelleher, who divided the long term of 1868–72 between them, and J. S. Chastain. From 1868 to 1872 is the only four-year term in the history of the county. The first assessor, of which the report of the secretary of State makes mention, is D. D. Dickson; Hiram

---

* A vacancy seems to have occurred between his two terms.

Brodie succeeded him in that office for the next two terms, and the "long term" was divided between M. W. Warden and T. G. Singleton. George Gross gave property owners opportunity to answer questions for three successive terms, and was succeeded by J. B. Vincent for two terms. J. Q. West, for two terms, was the predecessor of the present incumbent, R. B. Winfrey. The treasurer's office and the name of A. J. Ward seem almost synonymous, for his service altogether covered a period of a score and four years. George Austin served from 1860 to 1864. W. L. Meadows served one term, and the "long term" was occupied by E. Coleman and J. S. Shannon, who was followed by M. Kimes. Mr. Ward's second long service was followed by the incumbency of B. L. Orrick, for two terms, and W. T. England, who now serves. The duties of sheriff have been performed by many different persons since J. M. Randolph's term ended in 1840; Eli Bell held the jail keys for three terms, and John Carnall for two terms. S. F. Cottrell served four terms, but two terms of J. M. Brown intervened between his third and final terms. Martin Thomas came next. The term of 1864–66 was filled by William Sills, James Allison and E. G. Whitesides, and the last mentioned gentleman was retained for the succeeding term. W. S. Anderson occupied the long term, and was followed by J. P. Grady, J. F. Winfrey for two terms, W. L. Taylor for three terms, although a term by J. S. H. Houck intervened between his first and second terms. J. D. Hawkins is the present incumbent. The clerk's office has been held by but few different persons; after Mr. McLean's extended service I. W. Talkington served two terms, and then began that other veteran clerk's, E. A. Scott's, six terms of service, which were divided by the long term filled by George Devilbiss and J. A. Lockhart, also his own successor for one term. L. C. Southmayd served for three terms, beginning in 1878, and the present incumbent, Benjamin Decherd, was preceded by J. Neal. Few county judges have been their own successor since the days of Judge Bates. Judge R. S. Gibson served from 1840 to 1842; then Judge R. P. Pryor serves between two unoccupied terms, according to the report of the State secretary, and afterward served two terms more. N. A. Pryor was the incumbent from 1852 to 1854. The next incum-

29

CRAWFORD COUNTY, ARKANSAS - BIOGRAPHICAL AND HISTORICAL MEMOIRS
****

bent, G. J. Clark, resigned, and D. N. Collins served the unexpired term. J. W. Sangster was the next judge, but for some cause R. C. Hattaway served the part of the term from November, 1856. W. B. Robinson was the next chief executive of the county, and Judge J. A. Wright followed him. R. C. Hattaway served from 1862 to 1864, and Judge Sangster again assumed the duties of the office, which he held for two terms longer. Joseph Harrell served the long term, and another of those unexplained vacancies occurred, which in one case may have been occupied by Isaiah Vinsant, who seems to have acted in the capacity of judge for a short time. D. H. Creekmore was judge in 1874–76, and Judge J. C. Chastain followed next. Ben Decherd, H. B. Hale, J. W. Matlock, W. T. Morgan and H. B. Hale were the latest occupants of the chief office of the county.

Judge Ben Johnson presided over the circuit court of Crawford County in 1831–32–33; Judge Archibald Yell, in 1834–35, and Judge R. C. S. Brown up to 1840. In 1840 it was in the Fourth Circuit under Judge J. M. Hoge; in 1844, Judge S. G. Sneed; in 1846 in the Seventh Circuit under Judge W. W. Floyd; in 1851 in the Fourth again under Judge A. B. Greenwood; in 1853 under Judge F. I. Batson; in 1859 under Judge J. M. Wilson; in 1860 under Judge J. J. Green; in 1868 in the Fifth Circuit under Judge E. D. Ham; in 1874 under Judge B. J. Brown; in the same year under Judge W. W. Mansfield, and in 1877 under Judge Rogers in the Twelfth Circuit.

In the constitutional convention of January, 1836, Crawford County was represented by J. W. Bates, John Dennen and R. C. S. Brown. The constitutional convention of March and May, 1861, had H. F. Thomason and Jesse Turner as Crawford delegates. In January, 1864, L. C. White, J. Austin, J. Howell and C. A. Harper were delegates to the constitutional convention. Crawford was represented by Thomas M. Bowen, who was president of the constitutional convention of January, 1868; and in that of July, 1874, H. F. Thomason was their delegate.

The first mention of Crawford County representation in the Legislature of Arkansas was in the Third Territorial Legislature of October, 1823, John McLean in the council and John Nicks in the House of Representatives. William Quarles in council, and John Nicks as representative, were chosen by the county for the Fourth Territorial Legislature. In the Fifth Assembly John Dillard and Mark Beane spoke for the county. The Sixth Assembly received Gilbert Marshall into the council, and three members, Mark Beane, J. L. Cravens and R. C. S. Brown, were representatives of Crawford. Robert Sinclair, with Representatives C. Wolf and R. C. S. Brown, were sent to the Seventh Legislature of the Territory; and the Eighth received Councilman Sinclair and Representatives William Whitson and B. H. Martin. The Ninth Territorial Legislature records are lost.

On the State organization in 1836 R. C. S. Brown was senator and John Drennen, John Lautor and A. Morton entered the Lower House for Crawford. Senator Brown and Representatives J. Turner, W. Duval and J. Miller were in the Second Assembly; Senator J. A. Scott and Representatives W. Duval and Tyree Mussett in the Third; Senator J. A. Scott and Representatives A. G. Mayer and William Reeves in the Fourth; Senator H. Smith and Representatives A. G. Mayer, J. S. Roane (speaker) and W. J. Duval in the Fifth; Senator Smith and Representatives Eli Bell, R. C. S. Brown and G. W. Clarke in the Sixth; Senator G. W. Clarke and Representatives G. J. Clarke, D. C. Price and T. E. Wilson in the Seventh; Senator Clarke and Representatives A. Martin, W. Russell, Jr., and H. Stewart in the Eighth; Senator Clarke and Representatives A. Morton and J. D. Shannon in the Ninth; Senator J. J. Green and Representatives J. M. Brown and A. Morton in the Tenth; Senator J. P. Humphrey and Representatives R. C. Oliver and M. B. West in the Eleventh; Senator Humphrey and Representatives J. J. Green and S. M. Hayes in the Twelfth; Senator Jesse Miller and Representatives J. M. Brown and Andrew Morton in the Thirteenth; Senator H. F. Carter and Representatives J. Harrell and R. C. Oliver in the Fourteenth; Senator L. C. White and Representatives J. Austin and J. G. Stephenson in the Fifteenth; Senator Carter and Representative R. C. Oliver in the Confederate Legislature; Senator Jesse Turner and Representatives H. F. Thomason and Gran. Wilcox in the Sixteenth; Senator Valentine Dell and Representatives J. B. C. Turman, D. H. Devilbiss, A. J. Singleton and A. Gunther in the Seventeenth; Senator Dell and Representatives

J. M. Pettigrew, C. B. Neal J. B. Stevens and J. P. Grady in the Eighteenth; Senator J. D. Arbuckle and Representatives J. A. Davis, C. E. Berry, L. C. White and S. L. Strong in the Nineteenth; Senator B. J. Brown and Representative J. F. Wheeler in the extraordinary session convened by Gov. Elisha Baxter in 1874; Senator Jesse Turner and Representative James Greig (who resigned and was succeeded by M. C. Moore) in the Twentieth; Senator H. B. Armistead and Representative J. J. Warren in the Twenty-first; Senator Armistead and Representative D. H. Creekmore in the Twenty-second; Senator H. F. Thomason and Representative R. E. Nettles in the Twenty-third; Senators Thomason and T. Comstock in the Twenty-fourth; Senator J. M. Pettigrew and Representative J. H. Huckleberry in the Twenty-fifth; and Senator Pettigrew and Representative H. F. Thomason in the Twenty-sixth Legislature.

THE COURTS.

The history of the courts of Crawford County must ever remain an uncertain quantity; the fire of 1877 destroyed the records of over a half century.

Circuit Courts.—The first circuit court was held in a little log house, having one room and a shed-room for the clerk's office. It was located near the site of the Van Buren Canning Factory, and had been hauled up from Columbus and remodeled, and was used for a few years until the present court-house was built, *i. e.*, the walls. The first case, according to Mr. E. A. Scott, who was a juryman, was a civil case between an Eastern merchant and a citizen. The jury retired to a big cotton-wood log about fifty yards distant, and failed to agree as to the amount of damages. The judge was R. C. S. Brown.

The present court-house was built about 1842, probably, and the jail was built during the same decade. Both buildings have had the wooden parts of them burned out, and have been rebuilt on the same walls.

Under the first judge, R. C. S. Brown, was a case of gambling, and, although it occurred at Old Crawford Court-house, the chief witness was a unique old settler, John Oliver. Mr. Oliver was a witness against the players, and it was rumored that the honorable judge had a hand in the game, which, of course, lent interest to the cross-examination. The judge asked: "Mr. Oliver, did you see anyone playing cards?" "Yes, by ——, I did," replied the profane old farmer. "Mr. Oliver, you must not swear in court," said his honor. "No, by ——, I won't, but I'll tell you all I know," was the rejoinder. "What game were they playing?" was asked. "Don't know, Judge; one-to-me—one-to-you—one-to-me" (with the appropriate gestures), "what do you call that, Judge?" said the witness. "Mr. Oliver, I know nothing about cards," replied the Judge with some dignity. "By ——, neither do I," said the wrathy witness, "but ace is master card in the deck, bet on 'im 'n' yer bound tu win." "Address yourself to the jury, Mr Oliver," interrupted his honor. "Hold on, Judge, I'll make it so plain that the biggest fool on that jury 'll understand!" said he. "Mr. Oliver, did they bet bones or money?" inquired the composed judge. "Clean truck, by ——, 'n' once 'n awhile the'd say: 'Hocksplits, hocksplits, rake 'er down boys, but don't snatch!'" Mr. Oliver was dismissed.

About 1842 a peculiar case was tried under Judge R. C. S. Brown, with Judge Turner and William Walker for the prosecution, and J. S. Roane, W. S. Oldham and S. G. Sneed for the defense. It seems that James Robinson and Emily Bishop had some trouble over a "still," and Bishop's boy and dog had either purposely or accidentally injured a cow owned by Robinson. The two men were sitting on a log quarreling about the affair, and it is said that Robinson shot Bishop. Robinson was tried and convicted, but the charge stated that he was justly provoked, and the sentence was made one year in the penitentiary. The feeling in Robinson's favor was so strong, that officers and lawyers sent him *alone* to Little Rock, with a petition for pardon, and with his sentence. Gov. Samuel Adams received him in the evening at his home, but said: "I can't pardon you out until you get in." So the papers were arranged, and the two walked down to the prison and went through the form of locking in and pardoning, and Mr. Robinson hunted up a hotel to remain until the next morning, when he set out for Van Buren a free man.

But few cases of execution have occurred within the limits

of Crawford County by order of the circuit court. In 1843 Jeduthan Day and two negroes, Frank and Dennis, were convicted of rape on a white woman, and sentenced to be hung June 9, 1843, but, by a technical point of a repealed statute, Day was released and the negroes were hung. Great indignation was expressed against such clumsy legislation.

John Kennedy was tried for the murder of John Hurley, in April, 1843, at the September term, under Judge R. C. S. Brown. William Walker was prosecuting attorney, and John F. McKinney, S. G. Sneed and James A. Simpson were counsel for defense. The result was conviction for manslaughter and fifteen years imprisonment.

In "the fifties" a case of justifiable homicide created considerable excitement. Dr. R. Thruston killed a man named Harger, and a coroner's jury returned the above verdict, but the enemies of the old hunter persecuted him until his friends asked for trial. Two grand juries refused to make an indictment, but finally, at the request of Dr. Thruston, H. F. Thomason secured a trial, and he was acquitted without argument.

During this decade two men, Proctor and Skilley, killed a man, and during the trial a false interpreter caused some trouble, but the men were convicted and hung.

About the same time W. Baldridge, with others, killed James Matoy, and was convicted, but escaped. Also "Big Nitz" killed a Mr. Benge, but, even with sworn evidence on both sides (!), there was a failure to convict.

A noted case, said to have been the instigation of the notorious Mountain Meadows massacre, occurred during the latter part of the same decade. Parley P. Pratt, a Mormon preacher proselyting in Crawford County, influenced a Mrs. McLean with her child, to go to New Orleans at the same time he did, with the ostensible purpose of going to Mormon quarters. So Mr. McLean thought, at least, and he traced them, and had them arrested on a charge of stealing the child's clothing, merely in order to get hold of him. A preliminary trial released the man, but the McLean party followed him, and found him in front of Tealy Wynn's blacksmith shop, across Frog Bayou, and shot him; McLean was arrested, but escaped. The Mountain Meadows affair occurred afterward, and many Crawford people were in the massacred party.

A Mr. Shannon and one Dobbins, at Shannon's home, were talking over plans to steal some hogs, while near them in the room was a Mr. Williams lying drunk, and unconscious to all appearances. Williams reported the plans, and even made up some doggerel verses on the plan, which roused the ire of the Shannons and Bells (relatives), and the latter attacked Williams and his sons with pistols and knives on the streets of Van Buren. The Williamses fought with brick-bats and rocks, and one of the Bells was killed. Williams was tried and acquitted. This was about 1858.

In 1859 a slave named Willis was convicted of larceny, and was punished by private whipping, and being fastened for an hour by hands and neck in a pillory erected on the public square.

On October 13, 1860, a muster-day, Benjamin and Silas Edwards were the murderers of Jackson Covington and his son, and Rufus Covington, at Van Buren. It was some feudal trouble; Benjamin stabbed Jackson Covington, and Silas stabbed his son, and then made for Rufus and stabbed him, leaving the three dead bodies in a pile. The Edwards were imprisoned, and, when brought out for trial, and witnesses not being ready, they were being taken out of the court-yard gate, the infuriated mob shot at them and killed one and wounded the other. He was imprisoned, but later on burned his way out of jail with a candle and escaped.

On January 18, 1861, Robert Davis was executed at Van Buren, for the murder of a man and his son on the Fayetteville road.

During "the sixties" a man named Pope killed a Mr. Gregg, near the site of Mountainburg, and after trial he was convicted, but the decision was reversed by the supreme court.

In this connection might be mentioned a noted jail delivery in December, 1868, when thirteen prisoners escaped. The guards were Messrs Morse, Dabbs and O'Bryan. It appeared to be a lack of precaution on the part of Morse.

In January, 1870, James Brodie, a deputy city marshal of Van Buren, in the discharge of his duty shot Jesse Q. Morton.

The circumstances were so evidently justifiable to the deputy's action that the coroner's jury acquitted him without letting it go to the circuit court.

In November, 1870, two negroes became involved in a difficutly over an abandoned woman named Ellen Anthony, who was living with one of them, Robert Monroe. The other, Jerdon Grinder, as he said in his confession, wishing to frighten Monroe, shot into his cabin one night and killed him. Grinder was tried, and sentenced to be hung February 3, 1871, at high noon. He confessed to Rev. Rutherford, his spiritual adviser.

On May 3, 1871, was a jail delivery of seven men, who escaped by prying off rafters and climbing out and letting themselves down by rafters.

In April, 1883, William Purse, a bigamist and convict, was living near the mouth of Frog Bayou, and at the instigation of his former wife he was ordered arrested. A small posse of men found him in his field, but he was armed and drove them off. A larger posse returned and found that he had barricaded his house and run up a black flag. The men made a portable fort and moved on the house, whereupon Purse, fearing they would burn him out, escaped by the back door to the water. On dragging the river his body was found.

First Recorded Term.—The first circuit court in Crawford County of which any records exist, is that of the March term of 1877. The record in part reads:

CRAWFORD CIRCUIT COURT, MARCH TERM, A. D. 1877.

STATE OF ARKANSAS, ⎱
COUNTY OF CRAWFORD. ⎰

Be it remembered that on the 27th day of March, 1877, at the spring term, as fixed by law, for holding the circuit court in and for the county of Crawford, State of Arkansas, at the court-house, in the town of Van Buren, present and presiding the Hon. William W. Mansfield, judge of Fifth Judicial Circuit. * *

Since 1877 the circuit docket has increased so greatly that measures are being agitated to divide the circuit.

The Bar.—The bar of Crawford County has been a talented one almost from the first. Certainly in *ante-bellum* days there was no bar outside of Little Rock, probably, in Arkansas that stood higher. In its courts the greatest legal minds of the State frequently practiced. This chapter deals only with resident attorneys.

Previous to 1831 were a few resident lawyers. James H. Lucas was among the very first, if not the first. He soon removed to St. Louis, of which city he afterward became mayor. Franklin Whorton was probably the next. He was a good advocate, capable of making a strong impression on a jury. He was especially successful in criminal practice. A Mr. Quarles was another resident of Crawford county seat, and was chiefly a lawyer devoted to civil cases. John Houston, a brother of the famous Texan, Sam. Houston, was located for a time, but did little practice. One of the ablest orators and advocates of the Crawford bar was William H. Parrott, who resided in the county for a short time. His usefulness was injured by his inability to inspire moral confidence. He was well educated and had a large criminal and civil practice.

In 1831 there were but three resident lawyers at Van Buren: The Hon. Jesse Turner, Judge Richard C. S. Brown and Bennett H. Martin, and the most prominent of these is the subject of the following remarks:

"Jesse Turner is also one of the notable men of these times who still live, honored and beloved," says the Hon. Ben T. Duval, writing of famous Arkansans. "He came from North Carolina to Crawford County in 1829, and settled at old Crawford Court House, and has followed the county seat in its various changes until it finally rested at Van Buren. He now occupies the same office he built in 1840, where for more than forty years he has day by day studied and given counsel to his numerous clients.

"His culture in legal lore, his stern integrity and his undaunted courage have placed him always in the front rank of the profession. His career has been eminently successful. As a judge of the supreme court he has settled some of the most intricate questions of law. His opinions are recognized as leading authority."

*R. C. S. Brown, who resided for many years at Van Buren, and presided over the circuit court, was a man of mark and exerted great influence. His learning as a lawyer was said not to have been profound, but he had good common sense, and was prompt in his decisions. He did not seek to become an eminent jurist while judge of a circuit court. He was popular with the bar and the people. He was a Tennesseean, a grandson of the famous Gov. Sevier. He was especially successful in civil law, and afterward became very prominent in State affairs. He also became agent for the Pottawottamie Indians.

Bennett H. Martin, it is thought, was a Kentuckian, who spent his early manhood as a brick-mason. It is uncertain when he began the study of law, but

---

* Hon. Ben. T. Duval, before the State Historical Society.

it was probably as late as his thirtieth year. He was one of those naturally strong-minded men who have a capability of independent study under even the most adverse circumstances; he never became more than fairly informed, however, but became a very respectable lawyer and a good advocate. His practice, too, was such as his ability and popularity deserved. In about 1842, or thereabouts, he moved to Texas, and became a district judge.

It was about 1835 (approximately) that William H. Wisner became a resident member of the bar at Van Buren. He remained probably a year only, when he returned to Tennessee.

But a few years later (about 1839) Royal T. Wheeler swelled the legal list of local Van Burenites. He was a "Hoosier," and spent but a year or thereabouts at Van Buren, and then located in Texas, where he became a supreme judge.

It was about this time that George W. Paschal, a Georgian, who had married a Cherokee lady, a member of the well-known Ridge family, located at Van Buren. He was fairly educated, and a man of more than ordinary ability. He became a supreme judge at an early age. He began practice in the supreme court at Washington after the war, and became the author of several law books, among which are "Paschal's Annotations on the Constitution." He also arranged the code of Texas.

Gov. John S. Roane, after serving one term in the Legislature from Jefferson County, went to Crawford and located as a lawyer at Van Buren. [ED.— This was, according to Judge Turner, about 1840]. He soon engaged in politics, was elected again to the Legislature, and afterward governor of the State to fill out the unexpired term of Gov. Drew, who resigned a short time after being elected a second term. He was talented, ambitious, patriotic, genial and popular. He was a brigadier-general in the Confederate States army, and died soon after peace. He raised a company of volunteers for the Mexican War, and was elected lieutenant-colonel of the regiment commanded by Gov. Archibald Yell. After the death of the latter, at the battle of Buena Vista, he became colonel of the regiment. A difficulty grew up between him and Albert Pike, who commanded a company, which resulted in a duel. They fought, in 1846, with pistols, on the sand-bar opposite Fort Smith. Luckily, neither was hit, and the reconcilation, which took place on the field, was permanent, and they were ever afterward good friends.

About 1840 W. S. Oldham, a Tennesseean, moved to Van Buren. He was a man of good capacity and rather brilliant, with a thoroughly legal mind. He was a good general, rather than special, lawyer. It was about the same time that Mr. Pryor, of Nashville, located. His death soon occurred.

A few years later John B. Ogden came to Van Buren. His business abilities as an accountant, and his information and ability in using statistics, have made a splendid business lawyer of him. As a speaker he is striking and incisive. He has been prominent in the business affairs of the county and in its courts and offices. He was a partner of George W. Paschal for a time, and served as United States Commissioner.

Andrew Campbell was a popular man, and a partner of G. W. Paschal. The firm did a large collecting business, and Mr. Campbell, from his live, social characteristics, had charge of this department of the business. In May, 1843, he was assassinated about twelve miles north of Van Buren, for his money.

Among the lawyers of "the forties" was James H. Simpson, who was for some time a partner of Judge Turner. He was somewhat brilliant as an orator, and was an impressive advocate and pleader,

Henry Wilcox was a contemporary of Mr. Simpson, and a political rival of Judge Turner. He was one of those naturally sturdy, shrewd-minded men, who began law somewhat late in life. His strong common sense, and his keen knowledge of human nature, coupled with his ability as an advocate and speaker, made him successful.

About 1859 or 1860 Granville, a son of Henry Wilcox, entered the law. He had been educated under Robert Graham, and at Princeton, N. J.; he was one of the finest orators the county ever produced. It was his ability as a writer and editor, that gave the *Argus* its standing throughout the Northwest, and his oratorical powers which gave him the popular title of "The Little Giant." He represented his county in the Legislature, and was district prosecuting attorney for a time. His death occurred in the early part of the present decade.

William Walker came to Van Buren about 1842. He is a fine lawyer, of a highly analytical mind, and is a genius as a special pleader; no flaw in legal papers can escape his microscopic vision, and his own papers are faultless. He is an effective speaker, of intense earnestness and feeling, and has many other strong characteristics. He is a fair writer and an aggressive worker.

Thomas McKinney came late in the forties, and for a time had some practice.

About 1850 John T. Humphreys began a fair practice in Van Buren, and could then be called a good "all around" lawyer with many excellent characteristics. He afterward went to Fort Smith.

Not far from the same time Hugh F. Thomason became a

member of the Crawford bar. He is still practicing. He has a naturally strong legal mind, and is a fine, fluent, forcible orator. He is a good advocate, and is a good lawyer in all phases of the law, but is especially able as a criminal lawyer. He has been a powerful influence in State politics, and has few equals as a political speaker. He represented the State in the Montgomery Congress, and was a Union delegate to the famous Little Rock convention of 1861, in which he was prominent.

John B. Luce came about 1850, and became a partner with John B. Ogden. He remained two or three years, engaged chiefly in general collection business. He was a remarkably well-informed man.

A partner of William Walker was J. J. Green, who came about 1848. He was a fair speaker and was a man of excellent information. He was the Confederate circuit judge of Crawford.

It was about 1858 or thereabouts when B. J. Brown, still of the Van Buren bar, located there. Judge Brown has a strong natural mind, of prompt, energetic characteristics, and which, with more extensive educational advantages, would have made him still more prominent. He is a good lawyer and strong advocate.

William Alexander was a partner of Hugh F. Thomason for a time. He was well educated and a fair lawyer, but soon abandoned the profession.

Samuel Miller was a student under B. J. Brown, and grew to have a good civil and criminal practice. He was largely a self-made man.

J. H. Huckleberry came in about 1870, and has made a reputation as a good, safe, successful lawyer. His partner, a Mr. Jay, was a member of the bar for a time.

John J. Warren, a former editor of the *Graphic*, arrived about the same time, and has been devoted chiefly to claim and homestead cases. He has also been an influential figure in Republican politics.

Among the younger members of the bar is the son of Judge Turner, Jesse Turner, Jr. Mr. Turner has been well prepared for his profession, and has many of the cultivated social graces and natural appointments of manner, which always smooth the way for ability. He is a young man of keen mind and excellent executive capabilities.

Nimrod Turman is a self-made young lawyer of fair ability, who has grown up in the county and is becoming active in its affairs.

Mr. Pierce is another gentlemanly young member of the bar, and is arranging to make a specialty of abstracting titles and doing a loan business.

William Taylor turned to law rather late in life, but is a good business man, and is especially successful as a pension and claim lawyer. J. P. Mullen has a large practice of a civil character chiefly. J. W. Frederick is a fair speaker and a good general lawyer. W. F. Willey is a fluent speaker. E. A. Tabor practiced a short time. J. C. White did some business also.

Berkley Neal, another pupil of B. J. Brown, is a good lawyer and very successful. He has a large colored practice.

The United States District Court of the Western District of Arkansas was the result of too great a demand on the National Court at Little Rock. The jurisdiction of the latter, including the Indian Nations, was so large that its docket was always full to overflow. Congress passed "An Act to Divide the State of Arkansas into two Judicial Districts," which reads as follows:

Be it enacted by the Senate and House of Representatives of the United States in Congress Assembled, That from and after the passage of this act the counties of Benton, Washington, Crawford, Scott, Polk, Franklin, Johnson, Madison and Carroll, and all that part of the Indian country lying within the present district of Arkansas, shall constitute a new judicial district, to be styled "The Western District of Arkansas," and the residue of said State shall be and remain a judicial district, to be styled "The Eastern District of Arkansas."

Section 2. *And be it further enacted,* That the judge of this District Court of Arkansas shall hold two terms of said court at the town of Van Buren, the county seat of Crawford County aforesaid, on the second Mondays of May and November in each and every year, and shall continue in session until all the business shall be disposed of; and he is hereby authorized and directed to hold such other special sessions as may be necessary for the dispatch of the causes in said court, at such time or times as he may deem expedient, and may adjourn such special session to any other time previous to a stated term.

Section 3. *And be it further enacted,* That the District Court of the United States for the Western District of Arkansas hereby established, in addition to the ordinary jurisdiction and powers of a district court, shall, within the limits of its respective district, have jurisdiction of all causes, civil or criminal, except appeals and writs of error, which now are or hereafter may by law be made cognizable in a circuit court, and shall proceed therein in the same manner as a circuit court; and an appeal or writ of error shall be prosecuted from the final decree or judgment of said district court to the supreme court of the United States, in the same manner that appeals and writs of error now are, by law, from a circuit court of the United States.

SECTION 4. *And be it further enacted,* That the President of the United States, by and with the advice and consent of the Senate, shall appoint a district attorney and marshal for said Western District of Arkansas, who respectively should receive the same salary and perquisites as the present district attorney and marshal of the State of Arkansas have by law; and the said district judge shall appoint a clerk of the said court hereby established. Approved March 3, 1851.

According to the best information obtained, since the records are destroyed, the May term began at Van Buren in the circuit and county court room, then in the lower story. Daniel Ringo was judge, and George W. Knox the first marshal, while Jesse Turner was appointed by President Fillmore as district attorney, and Alexander McLain was made the first clerk. The county donated the upper story of the court-house to the district court in 1854, and Judge John B. Ogden was made commissioner to furnish the room, which he did in an elegant manner, equalled by few other courts in the Southwest. Before 1861 the successors to the marshal's office were Samuel M. Hayes, Benj. J. Jacoway, and James M. Brown; and Attorney Turner's successors (his appointment being unsolicited and not desired by himself) were Alfred M. Wilson and Granville Wilcox up to about 1858. Clerk McLain was succeeded by John B. Ogden, who held office up to the convention of May, 1861. By the action of this convention Judge Daniel Ringo felt it his duty to resign his office, and the convention ordered the records into the keeping of Clerk John B. Ogden, and the court ceased to be for the period of the war. The records of the proceedings of a decade were kept by Judge Ogden, and were held by him in February, 1863, when a raid was made on Van Buren by a company of Federal soldiers under Lieut.-Col. Stewart, from the Fayetteville post, and the clerk's office was rifled, and the records and papers torn out and destroyed with one exception—namely, the records from 1855 to 1860.

This term of the court closed December 6, 1855. The following May term S. F. Cottrell was made crier, and George Gross and

Elias H. Gilbert were made constables, and the grand jury embraced the following persons: G. J. Clark, foreman; I. Ripato, (?), D. Chandler, W. H. Alexander, P. V. Ray, W. T. Dollins, Allen Prasher, Isaiah Vinsant, G. S. Turrentine, A. H. Kuykendall, Andrew Panby, J. B. Strout, John Odell, Henry Powell, I. B. Huston, William B. Robinson and James S. Foster.

The chief causes during the years of this record were larceny, introducing spirituous liquors into the Indian Nation, bribery, contempt of court, assault with intent to kill, mail robbery, murder and negro stealing, the first two being largely in the majority. Among the lawyers admitted during the time covered by this record were H. Thomas Brown and B. J. Brown, in 1860. The last record, previous to the war, now extant is that of December 15, 1860, in which two cases of assault with intent to kill, two cases of murder and one of larceny were had.

At the special term of the district court of the United States, begun and held at the court room in the city of Van Buren, within and for the Western District of Arkansas, on the 31st day of August, 1865, present the Honorable Henry C. Caldwell, judge of said court. The following rules of court were adopted and ordered to be spread on the records of said court, viz.:

RULE 1. Whenever the district attorney shall file in the clerk's office a libel of information against any property, under the Revenue Confiscation laws of the United States, it shall be the duty of the clerk to issue to the marshal of the district a warrant of arrest, in the usual form, returnable on the first day of the next ensuing regular term.

RULE 2. Whenever the marshal shall receive a warrant of arrest it shall be his duty to give notice of the time and place of hearing such cause, by publication in some weekly newspaper, published in the city of Van Buren, for two weeks successively, the last of which publication shall be made at least ten days before the day of trial, and shall also post a copy of said notice in some public place in the vicinity of the place where the court is to be held, twenty days before the trial. In case no paper be published in the city of Van Buren, then the publication herein provided for shall be made in some weekly newspaper published in the city of Fort Smith, and in case no paper is published at either of said cities, the notice shall be given by posting in some public place in both of said cities, and in the county seat of the county where the property libeled is situated, or was seized, at least twenty days before the day of trial; and thereupon court adjourned until the next regular term.

HENRY C. CALDWELL, *District Judge.*

Luther C. White was made marshal, and E. D. Ham, Esq. became district attorney. The first regular term after the war was the May term, A. D. 1866, Judge Caldwell presiding.

43

CRAWFORD COUNTY, ARKANSAS - BIOGRAPHICAL AND HISTORICAL MEMOIRS
****

On motion of E. D. Ham, Esq., it is ordered that Augustus N. Hargrove, Esq., E. J. Searle, Esq., Marshall L. Stevenson, Esq., and John M. Oliver, Esq. (it appearing to the satisfaction of the court that they are attorneys-at-law in this State) be admitted to practice as attorneys in this court on taking the oath as prescribed by act of Congress of July 2, 1862, which was then taken and respectively subscribed [to] and placed with the files of this court.

The court continued to hold regularly at Van Buren until by an act of Congress it was removed to Fort Smith in 1871. The last district court held at Van Buren was the November term of 1870. The court was then reorganized at Fort Smith by order of "an act authorizing terms of the United States district courts to be held at Helena, Arkansas, and for other purposes," approved March 3, 1871.

United States Commissioners held their courts at Van Buren whenever the business of the district court made it necessary. Judge J. B. Ogden and Judge J. O. Churchill were among the commissioners.

The lawyers that are mentioned in connection with the circuit court all practiced in the Federal court while it was located at Van Buren.

It is estimated by Judges Turner and Thomason that probably but one or two over a half dozen executions took place while the court remained in Van Buren, and previous to the war there were but few cases of any kind, and nothing like the stupendous proportions now assumed by the docket of the court now at Fort Smith. The little county jail now used at Van Buren was large enough for the prisoners of both courts; the executions took place near the present site of the *Graphic* office, and near the cemetery.

One interesting case in "the fifties" was that of the United States *vs.* Willis Beard, who murdered a man in the Indian county. He was executed.

Another case was that of Maj. Elijah Hurst, who killed Jack Rector with a pen-knife. He was convicted, but afterward pardoned by President Buchanan. A. M. Wilson was prosecutor, and Judges Turner and Thomason were for the defense.

A case in 1869 was that of Dave Ross for the murder of John Lytle. Messrs. Wilcox and Robinson were for the prisoner, and Messrs. Ham and Huckleberry for the United States. He was convicted, and sentenced to be hung on September 3, 1869.

John Roper was convicted of the murder of John Rogers, and sentenced to be hung on the last Friday of April, 1860. The sentence was commuted by President Buchanan.

Amos McCurtain was convicted of murder in 1869.

A case against J. S. Bostick for perjury in the " Kersey case" was *nolle prose'd.*

A case against Nail Randall and Dean occupied over a week in November, 1869. The indictment was for the murder of a negro called " Buck " or " Jefferson." Messrs. Rogers, Brown, Walker and Wilcox appeared for the defense, the first two speaking on Friday and the last two on Saturday. The prisoners were acquitted.

The greater number of cases were for introducing spirituous liquors into the Indian country, larceny, etc.

CITIES, TOWNS AND VILLAGES.

VAN BUREN.

The Town Site.—About 1817, when the second war with Great Britain had closed, and the Government was pushing the control of her western domains, Maj. Stephen H. Long, United States Army, was sent out to locate a fort to cover the territory of the Upper Arkansas River; his choice fell upon the bluffs that overlook the river, just above the present site of Van Buren, as the most suitable the county possessed, and he offered the owner a large price, far more than has ever since been offered. Two explanations are given of the failure to purchase the site: one gives the owner as raising his price exorbitantly far above the offered price of the Government, because the site was so desirable that he thought he would be given his own price, and thereby disgusted the Government agent, Maj. Long, who proceeded to locate at Belle Point, as is more fully set forth in the sketch of Fort Smith in this volume; the other reason given by the parties interested in the land is that the result was a mere accident, contingent on some complicated negotiations with the Washington authorities caused by the long time required to travel between this point and Washington. Whatever the reason,

45

CRAWFORD COUNTY, ARKANSAS - BIOGRAPHICAL AND HISTORICAL MEMOIRS
****

the result has been two cities within five miles of each other, when they would have otherwise been one, under some suitable name, which would probably not have been either Fort Smith or Van Buren.

First Residents and Business.—Thomas Martin was the first white settler on the site of Van Buren, about 1828 or 1829. He was a mere "squatter," with no title to his land except the claim of settlement. A few half transient people gathered about him, and the place became a landing, and in 1829 was dignified as a post-office, the name of which was made Van Buren, in honor of Martin Van Buren, a secretary of President Jackson, and afterward the well known President of the United States himself. In 1830 Thomas Phillips bought Mr. Martin's claim for a small amount and perfected his title otherwise; the place even then went by the name of Phillips' Landing, or Phillips' Point, for some time after. His purchase included a large tract of land extending down beyond the foot of the great sand-bar below Van Buren. There was no white woman in the settlement, and river gamblers and roughs were the larger part of the frequenters of the place. The river at this time was a much narrower one, and deeper, the north bank having since then receded many feet along the present Van Buren frontage, and many rods down where the largest part of the sand-bar rests at present. But one or two years after Phillips' purchase, the landing, now washed in the river and composing the above sand-bar, was bought by Mr. David Thompson, a land speculator of Little Rock, formerly of Nashville, Tenn., and who owned large tracts of land along the river on both sides, and his associate, Mr. John Drennen, a younger man. They established a landing and store, and gave it the name Columbus. The enterprise of these men soon made the new place rival Phillips' Point, and in 1836 they bought out Mr. Phillips. The admission of the State at this time would indicate a growing population, and Van Buren post-office gained with the rest. Dr. Mahon was the first postmaster, and Squire Henry Mahon was a merchant. The Trimble family were here at that time; Edward Cunningham was a merchant, also, and the firm, Henry & Cunningham, built the brick block now occupied by the wholesale grocers, Shibley, Bourland & Co. James A.

Scott, Turner & Chapman, and Foster & Medley were among the first merchants. Judge Jesse Turner passed through the place on his way to Fayetteville as early as May, 1831, but did not settle until the location of the county seat. Drennen & Scott had a stock in the building near the river, now owned by Robert J. Hynes. The place was growing so fast that in 1837 Messrs. Thompson & Drennen laid out the first plat of the town.

In 1839 Peter Hanger (now of Little Rock) built a large house on the river bank, and which was long used as a hotel; it is now owned by Mrs. H. Massey. A branch of the famous Arkansas Real Estate Bank was opened in it also. The Indian trade grew to be enormous, and the place became a shipping point even for Springfield, Mo. The permanent location of the county seat there, in 1838, through the influence of Messrs. Thompson & Drennen, was a great influence in its growth. The great influx of people into the territory surrounding it in the years immediately succeeding the admission of the State made its growth solid and certain; it was destined to become one of the first commercial centers of the Southwest and the greatest in all Arkansas; and its trade was especially wholesale in its character; its buildings were of good quality, many of them brick, which still stand. In 1842 the first newspaper was established— the Arkansas *Intelligencer*. Dr. R. Stevenson and Dr. Dibrell were there in 1843. George W. Paschal was a lawyer with Andrew Campbell, and the firm that year became (Andrew) Campbell & (Alfred W.) Arrington. W. C. Scott, Turner & Simpson, William Walker and Elkins & Linton were also legal lights. John Austin & Co., Scott, White & Co. and Henry & Cunningham were wholesale grocers. The Columbus Hotel was kept by J. S. Gross, and the Van Buren House by John Dillard (the Hanger House). John Taylor and J. S. Freeman had tailor shops. Dry goods were sold by John G. Rohr. Thomas A. Brooking dealt in farm implements, and did blacksmithing. John Drennen was postmaster. Dr. W. Richards hung out his sign about the same time. W. C. Robinson sold dry goods. Oldham & Roane came in as new attorneys, and John B. Ogden also. Whig and Democratic campaigns enlivened the burg, and in 1844 two newspapers were in the fight. The town had grown

47

CRAWFORD COUNTY, ARKANSAS - BIOGRAPHICAL AND HISTORICAL MEMOIRS
****

so as to become incorporated. Now churches began to be built. Austin & Clegg were a wholesale grocery firm during this year. S. G. Brownfield was a painter. Wallace & Ward opened up a general merchandise stock in 1844. Henry Wilcox was enrolled among the attorneys. The wharf business was crowded. In 1845 Mrs. E. C. McClellan opened the Hanger House. Dr. James Forman comes in. Reagan & Wilson, J. M. Terretts were attorneys. J. W. Washbourne became postmaster; Dr. D. L. Saunders in 1845. Forman & Sprott opened a drug store. Stevenson & Bell did likewise. John Bostick took charge of the Van Buren House. E. B. Bishop and Torras & Foggs had general stores. Van Buren became the meeting place of conferences, presbyteries, and other State and secular societies. Says the *Intelligencer* of March 1, 1845:

> The place has recently become a city; has its commissioned mayor and aldermen, and in this respect is better off than Boston; second, new houses of substantial brick are constantly going up, and more are in prospective; third, this place is a great thoroughfare already for the emigration to Texas, and will become greater if that country is annexed; here these emigrants cross the Arkansas, one of the ferries even now renting at auction at $1,325 per annum.

The travel was so great that the Van Buren Bridge Company was incorporated, but they never built. J. H. Roberts appears as a jeweler in 1847. The city was prolific in societies, among which was the Van Buren Hunting Club, of 1847, of which Jesse Turner was president; George W. Clarke, vice-president; H. W. Bell, secretary, and J. J. Green, treasurer. Among other businesses Eli Newland had a saddlery depot, Marshall & Powell were a new grocery firm, and D. T. McCollum was a draper and tailor. W. R. Simmons had a hardware store. In 1848 R. P. Pryor became a Van-Buren attorney. In February of that year an internal improvement convention was held at Van Buren to take measures for a turnpike to Fayetteville, and stock subscriptions were soon made up. Books were also opened at the office of John B. Ogden to start a cotton spinning factory. The Sons of Temperance was a popular organization of those years. In 1849 California emigration was agitated, and companies formed. Abbey & Doubleday opened a patent churn manufactory. The need of a market house was discussed. Willhaf, Glass & Co. had a bakery. J. J. Ogden and John B. Luce formed a law firm. Philip Pennywit's steam flouring mill was opened with a capacity of forty barrels per day. The value of merchandise taxed in the city at this time was $192,758. An editorial of September 29, 1849, says:

This place certainly has the most flattering prospects of any in the southwest. * * It now contains a thousand or twelve hundred inhabitants, and is increasing in population and business daily. There are now two brick churches, and several large brick houses for business and private residence in process of erection. On Monday, April 18, 1849, the Van Buren Emigration Association, the Washington City Mutual Mining Company, Capt. E. B. Robinson, the Louisiana California Trading Association, Capt. Pibron, the St. Joseph's California Emigrants, Capt. Shackleford, a pack-mule company, the Empire Mining Association, Capt. Hammond, a pack-mule company, left Van Buren on Gregg's route to Santa Fe.

The next decade witnessed a steady increase in the wealth and business of Van Buren. In 1859 Ward & Southmayd had a full line of general merchandise, also W. B. Heard. J. J. Green was a partner of William Walker. The new paper—the *Press*— said on October 21st of that year: "No town in Arkansas can boast the same number of extensive mercantile establishments, more solvent and wealthy merchants, or more substantial edifices both as stores and dwellings." In 1860 Drs. R. F. Colburn, L. C. White and M. O. Davidson were at Van Buren. Burrow & Brown was a law firm. S. J. Adler had a store, also Heard & Vinsant, P. Perkins and Frank & Eastburn. Martin Simon had a notion trade; W. Coleman sold boots and shoes; Daugherty & Glass dealt in furniture; S. Harrington and Fellmer & Graff were jewelers; hardware was handled by R. S. Roberts; S. Thompson was a tailor, and Iredell Jones was a tobacco merchant. Thursday, July 12, 1860, the first telegram was received in Van Buren over the Stebbins Western Telegraph Line. It was a message from Fayetteville, and a salute was fired in its honor. The following administrator's sale of negroes on July 2, 1860, will illustrate a species of Van Buren wealth: "Sam, twenty-nine years, $1,525; Bob, twenty-three years, $1,355; Ned, twenty-seven years, $1,376; Ned, seven years, $730; Jim, six years, $608; Angeline, twenty-seven years, and child, two years, $1,475; Betsey, twenty-five years, $1,182; Lizzy, nine years, $715; Sally, fifteen years, $1,252." W. B. Beard was postmaster during this

49

CRAWFORD COUNTY, ARKANSAS - BIOGRAPHICAL AND HISTORICAL MEMOIRS
****

year. Railway agitation was very considerable in the city during the year. In 1861 Hiram Brodie owned the Planters' Hotel, and Geo. W. Pendergrass, the Globe Hotel. Slack & Holman had carriage works; C. H. Drake, a brick-yard; J. A. Noble & Co. had a merchandise establishment during the decade; also Drs. C. F. Brown and J. H. Decherd were there in the latter part of the decade. In the thirteen years ending in 1860, Van Buren mortality was 464 deaths.

The war found Van Buren exceedingly flourishing. Upward then was commerce, education and society. The war almost utterly destroyed the town, as well as the adjacent country. For long years before the war Van Buren was the pleasantest, politest, richest and most attractive town in the Arkansas Valley. But the war emptied its warehouses and stores; owls and bats took possession; grass grew in its streets, and its churches and schools were ruined. * * * To-day I again tread its streets and see more evidence of recuperative power than I have seen in a thousand miles travel."*

Later Business and Events.—F. Miller & Bro. had a bakery in 1866; J. Felmer, a grocery; A. M. Calahan & Co. and E. C. Powell, stocks of merchandise. Dr. H. Pernot was located. Hayman & Scott opened the Van Buren Agricultural Works; G. W. Newland erected a new steam flouring mill and cotton gin. C. T. Ward, White & Hanley and C. F. Harvey had stores. Dr. A. B. Hoy was a dentist. Of H. C. Hayman's improved cotton plows and scrapers (invented in 1867) the *Press* said: "In order to make cotton raising profitable and remunerative hereafter, inventions have become necessary;" and on reconstruction feeling it urged, "Let us get strength and wealth first, and perhaps by that time everything may be 'fixed.'" Van Buren mortality for eighteen years previous to and including 1866 was 722 and 247 soldiers, making 969 as the aggregate. Immigration began to be agitated. C. G. Scott was proprietor of the steam ferry. H. L. McConnell was a lawyer, and F. M. Neal a new merchant. In November, 1871, was the first really successful fair probably ever held in the county; the best trotting was done by A. H. Carson's "Old Tom." A successful one was held in 1872, also. William Whitfield & Co. dealt in merchandise during the year 1872. Harmony Council, No. 27, Temperance Reform, was one of the societies of the year.

---

* Oct. 26, 1866—a *Press* correspondent.

50

CRAWFORD COUNTY, ARKANSAS - BIOGRAPHICAL AND HISTORICAL MEMOIRS
****

Our cotton lands yield from three-quarters to a bale and a half per acre, and our cotton ranks high in the New Orleans market. All the grasses do well here, and the farmers are beginning to find out the advantage of raising grass, and many acres are being seeded down.

The Fort Smith & Little Rock Railroad is now complete to within thirty five miles of Van Buren, and work is being pressed forward. The road will be completed to this town by the 1st of July next. With this road and the Askansas River as our trade channels, Crawford County will soon rank among the foremost counties in the State.

In Van Buren we have four churches, two good schools, two newspapers, the various mystic fraternities, and a temperance society of some 130 members.

* * * We have two large steam flouring mills, two steam cotton-gins, a steam cotton factory and a steam planing-mill.*

A complete list of business in 1878 is: General merchandise, 12; grocers, 5; furniture, 2; saloons, 7; hotels, 4; drug stores, 2; bakeries and confectioners, 2; hardware, 1; wagon factory, 1; saddlery, 1; blacksmith shops, 3; news stores, 1; newspapers, 2; gallery, 1; livery, 1; barbers, 2; butchers, 2; cooper, 1; jewelers, 1; upholsterers, 1; tailors, 1; milliners, 1; broom factory, 1; planing-mill, 1; steam cotton-gins, 2; steam flouring-mills, 3; hominy-mill, 1; shoe-shop, 1.

In 1876 a dramatic society was one of the organizations of the city. M. W. Drewery was a contractor; P. T. Devany sold boots and shoes; Dr. R. Thruston had the Van Buren nurseries; Thomas Edmondson had a bakery; F. M. Neal, a meat-market; Johnson & King, dry-goods; also D. C. Williams; J. M. Wood & Son, merchants; M. Lynch, dry goods; B. B. Thayer, grocer; A. Smith, grocer; J. S. Brodie, grocer; G. T. Maddox, grocer; J. W. Cory, hardware; E. Wall, drugs; Wilcox & Southm ayd F. Adams & Co., builders and architects; Austin, Martin & Ward general merchants, and Lizzie Lockhart, postmistress. It was the Little Rock & Fort Smith Railway that caused this improvement in business. A horticultural society was organized, and the agricultural association held another successful fair. The taxable property of 1877 in Van Buren was given as $400,000, and the receipts of the city treasurer were $4,871.74. Adams & Anderson had a planing-mill and furniture factory; Shibley, Moore & Co. became merchants in 1879. The Murphy temperance work of the year was a feature of interest. In 1880 the census gave Van Buren as 1,087 in population. On January 15,

---

*Christmas initial number of the *Argus*, 1875.

1882, at 2 o'clock in the morning, six buildings on the corner of Main and Thompson Streets were burned—the old Whitfield Block, the Eagle Block (a two-story brick), and a dwelling owned by G. Wilcox. In these were the furniture store of Mr. Glass, rooms of the athenæum, F. & A. M. and I. O. O. F. orders. The origin of the fire was never known, and of the $15,000 loss but $2,000 was insured. The completion of the "Frisco Railway" about this time gave a considerable impetus to business, and it is grown to what is given as follows:

Banking.—The Citizens' Bank of Van Buren was organized May 1, 1886, as a stock company under the State laws. Their officers have been president, B. J. Brown; cashier, U. H. Park (deceased), and cashier *pro tem.*, O. P. Brown. Their nine directors are as follows: B. J. Brown, L. C. Southmayd, Josiah Foster, George R. Wood, B. Neal, O. P. Brown, J. D. James, W. Bowlin and J. D. White. Their capital stock at the beginning of business was $40,000, but its present proportions were assumed in May, 1887. Their statement of July 2, 1888, is as follows: Resources, loans and discounts, $127,006.48; overdrafts, $797.31; due from other banks, $16,574.18; current expenses, $20.70; furniture and fixtures, $1,476.82; cash on hand, $17,243.61; total, $163,119.10; liabilities, capital stock, $75,000; undivided profits, $83.64; notes rediscounted, $7,500; individual deposits subject to check, $80.535.46; total, $163.119.10. Their correspondents are as follows: Boatmen's Savings Bank, St. Louis; Importers' and Traders' National Bank, New York; German National Bank, Little Rock; Bank of Commerce, Memphis, and the Merchants' Bank of Fort Smith.

The Crawford County Bank, the oldest bank in the county, now organized under State laws, was opened in April, 1882, as a private bank, by William Vickery. Its capital stock was then $30,000. Mr. R. S. Hynes purchased it, however, in February, 1884, and has since been in control of its affairs as cashier. On February 15, 1887, it was incorporated by R. S. Hynes, D. W. Moore, Jesse Turner, Jr., W. T. Merrill, H. P. King, J. M. Weaver, T. M. McGee, A. Smith, J. H. Huckleberry, R. Oliver, Jacob Yoes, H. F. Meyer, F. R. McKibben, A. Gooding, Jesse Turner, Sr., and W. H. Shibley. The officers chosen were Jesse

Turner, Sr., president; J. Yoes, vice-president; R. S. Hynes, cashier, all of whom are retained. Mr. S. A. Pernot is assistant cashier. The capital stock of the bank is $50,000; surplus, $6,031.88; undivided profits, $4,395; earnings, $5,162.06. An indication of their conservative policy is seen in the fact of the following firms having been their correspondents for eight years: Chase National Bank, New York; Laclede Bank, St. Louis; First National Bank, Little Rock, and the First National Bank of Fort Smith.

Associations.—The Van Buren Building and Loan Association, Perpetual, was organized in February, 1884, by sixty stockholders. The officers chosen were president, F. R. McKibben; vice-president, L. H. Southmayd; secretary and attorney, Jesse Turner, Jr., and treasurer, P. D. Scott. The directors chosen were F. R. McKibben, George Wood, A. Smith, D. W. Moore, B. Neal, J. Foster and L. H. Southmayd. The company first authorized a capital stock of $25,000, divided into 10,000 shares of $25 each, and began business with $47,700 subscribed. The company has been the means of advancing the building interests of Van Buren very materially. Their present officers are as follows: President, L. C. Southmayd; secretary, S. A. Pernot; treasurer, W. H. H. Shibley; directors, J. J. Warren, D. W. Moore, R. S. Hynes, T. M. McGee, R. W. Funk and L. H. Southmayd.

The Van Buren Building and Loan Association, Perpetual, No. 2, is one of the most thriving companies of its kind in Northwestern Arkansas. It was organized June 17, 1887, by about sixty stockholders, from whom the following officers were elected: President, A. H. Colgrove; vice-president, C. W. Jones; secretary, R. P. Allen; treasurer, George H. Williams; attorney, L. P. Sandels; directors (including the foregoing), Jesse Turner, Jr., H. F. Meyer, W. C. Lee, M. Lynch, J. P. Mack. The same officers are retained with the following exceptions: Treasurer, R. W. Quarles. The directors (including the officers) are H. C. Wood, T. S. Cox, H. F. Meyer. The company first authorized a capital stock of $500,000, with $58,000 subscribed, with which to begin business; the present subscribed stock is $68,000. Their last dividend was 50 per cent., and premiums range from 25 per cent. to 32 per cent.

53

CRAWFORD COUNTY, ARKANSAS - BIOGRAPHICAL AND HISTORICAL MEMOIRS
****

Industrial Standing.—The Van Buren Canning Company was organized in February, 1877, by a number of stockholders. The firm employs about seventy-five persons, and has a capacity of about 10,000 cans daily. They began business with $7,000 paid in, but in 1888 their stock was increased to $15,000. The first annual dividend was 20 per cent. The following list of officers has been retained from the first: President, W. H. H. Shibley; vice-president, F. R. McKibben; secretary and treasurer, R. S. Hynes; directors (including the foregoing), A. Smith, Jesse Turner, Jr., J. J. Warren and D. W. Moore. The superintendent of the works is Samuel Sheets.

The Van Buren Ice and Coal Company is a local stock corporation, organized April 19, 1887. They manufacture ice in summer and deal in coal during the period of demand for that article. Their ice is formed by the De Coppett absorption system, with a capacity of five tons in twenty-four hours. They supply not only the Van Buren market, but ship up and down the railways centering here. Their officers are president, George R. Wood; vice-president, O. P. Brown; secretary, P. D. Scott; treasurer, T. W. Edmondson, and superintendent, P. D. Scott. Their paid-in capital stock is $13,000.

The Barnes Lumber Company Planing Mills, although owned by Little Rock capital, is one of Van Buren's most important enterprises, furnishing employment for a large number of persons, and a market for the timber of the surrounding country. The mills and dry-house were built in 1885, in the northern suburbs of Van Buren. They have a capacity of 80,000 feet of lumber per day. Their work is exclusively dressing all kinds of lumber for shipment. The officers of the company are L. W. Coy, president; Logan H. Roots, treasurer, and D. H. Barnes vice-president.

The Shibley, Bourland & Company Wholesale Grocery and Commission House is one of Van Buren's leading business houses. Wood Bros. & Southmayd, McKibben & Pape, Meyer, Hodges & Co., are the leading general merchandise houses; the firm of McKibben & Pape also deal extensively in furniture. Among other general merchants are C. J. Murta, N. F. Cornelius, Smith & Scott, J. Hinkle & Bro., Max Lyons and E. Gilbert, who also are large firms. The grocery trade is well handled by Wood, Edmondson & Britt, J. Fritz & Co., W. A. Briscoe, T. C. Ribling, C. F. Ward, G. T. Maddox, T. M. McGee, F. Laurent, J. F. Mathews, John Pew and J. M. Harshaw. McKinney & Kerr, W. H. Ross, W. B. Allen, H. C. Johnson and Reed & Daniel mould the drug interests of the city. The jewelers are C. C. Montague and C. M. Beard. Lynch & Hattaway have the finest cotton-gin in the State, it is said; W. J. Kerr also has a good one. The Callahan Flouring Mills, by J. R. McLean, represent that branch of business, while the Van Buren Planing Mills, by Lynch, Colgrove & Co., and the Miller & Jones Planing and Saw Mills and Wooden Box Factory fill the list in that line. J. L. Rea and C. J. Smetz are produce shippers. The marble works are owned by T. M. Mitchell, and the undertaker's establishment by Birnie Bros. Lillard & Ogden, D. Dickson and D. W. Moore deal in real estate, and C. F. Harvey in insurance. The freight agents are C. Hays and R. W. Littlejohn. Jacques Bros. have a general book-store. J. P. Hollingsworth, C. Ribling and H. C. Miller attend to the custom shoe trade. Harness and saddles are furnished by John Kerwin. Lunch rooms and restaurants are represented by Albert Logan, B. L. Orrick, J. K. P. Howell and Frank Steward. Meat markets are kept by W. T. Merrill and R. C. Rees. R. S. Roberts handles stoves, tin-ware and hardware. B. C. Covey deals in sewing machines, pianos, organs, etc. The telephone and telegraph agents are W. B. Allen, S. P. Humphrey, W. E. McKinney and Miss Annie R. Dell. The hotels and boarding houses are as follows: The Broadway Hotel, by Mr. Wentworth; the Collins House, by Samuel Collins; Central Hotel, by C. A. Campbell; St. Charles Hotel, by N. C. Cagle; Mrs. J. Williams' and Mrs. Charles Ward's boarding-houses. Col. J. M. Weaver is the Little Rock & Fort Smith Railway land agent; J. L. Rea is express agent, and P. W. Furry the Union ticket agent. T. C. Murphy is a dealer in Jersey cattle. Livery and carriage works are owned by McIlvaigh & Son, and Pernot's Livery and Sale Stables are popular. L. M. Speaker is a barber, and the Jarvis Barber-shop is another representative of that art. M. W. Drewrey and R. B. Allen have brick-yards. M. F. Reber is a contractor. Millinery is handled

55

CRAWFORD COUNTY, ARKANSAS - BIOGRAPHICAL AND HISTORICAL MEMOIRS
****

by Mrs. R. V. Knight, Mrs. A. H. Lacy and Mrs. E. Rea. Ward & Cummings are photographers. F. E. McCullough and Beardsley & Bro. are painters. The Van Buren Bottling Works promise to be an important industry. Among the blacksmiths are A. K. Davidson, T. M. Laws and W. Haden. H. H. Huston is a gunsmith. The legal fraternity is very large: Turner & Turner, Brown & Sandels, J. B. Ogden, Sr., H. F. Thomason, Taylor & Neal, E. B. Pierce, Bryan & Cooper, J. P. Mullen, J. R. Reeves, J. W. Frederick, N. Turman, Huckleberry & Jay, S. A. Miller and D. N. Moore. The medical profession is also well represented: Bourland & Bourland, C. F. Brown, Dr. Dibrell, H. D. Hammack, Dr. Coryell and Dr. Smith. The dentists are R. W. Quarles, H. C. Stone and E. F. Burson. The Queen City Commercial College is managed by President F. G. Delano. The Highland Fruit Farm is owned by H. C. Miller. Mr. Arkebauer is also an able nursery-man. C. E. Taylor has a billiard hall. The liquor trade has six representatives: W. T. Wallace, S. Collins, T. Wallace, L. A. Bing, J. Carson and P. R. Cravens.

Incorporation.—The first incorporation of Van Buren was, according to Mr. D. Dickson, a temporary affair in 1842, and the recorder, a Mr. McMillan, became improperly hilarious and threw the books into the river. The *Intelligencer* mentions " An act to incorporate the town of Van Buren, approved January 4, 1844," but the first reliable information to be found is the act of January 4, 1845. A Dr. Herrick is thought to be the first mayor, but the *Intelligencer* mentions A. McLean as mayor in 1845, and W. J. McMillan as recorder. About this time the council issued scrip, which was given the euphonious name " shin-plasters," and which were so largely counterfeited that it caused considerable excitement. Mr. D. Dickson and Reuben Pryor were mayors of " the forties." John B. Ogden served in 1847–48, and A. J. Ward in 1849. The records previous to 1854 are lost. It is said that about 1852 or 1853 a tax of $2.00 per foot on Main Street was levied to put down the stone pavement from Scott's store to the river. In 1854 the officers were as follows: Mayor, John Austin; recorder, J. A. Eno; aldermen, S. F. Cottrell, E. B. Bishop, George Austin, John Bostick, D. C. Williams, W. F. England and D. Dickson. At that time forty-five men were annually chosen as night patrolmen, who served in squads. Mayor Austin was followed by A. J. Ward (1855), S. F. Cottrell (1856), W. F. England, A. J. Ward (1859), Thomas Walden (1860–61), W. F. England (1862—war period), D. Dickson (1866), John T. Lytle (1869), James O. Churchill (1869–70), J. M. Wood (1871), L. C. White (1872), J. M. Wood and P. R. Johnson (1873), J. J. Burrow (1874), C. F. Harvey, F. M. Neal (1875), W. J. Alexander (1876), John B. Ogden, L. H. Southmayd (1877), F. M. Neal (1878), E. A. Scott (1879), Jesse Turner, Jr. (1880–86), J. D. Hawkins and Jesse Turner, Jr. (1886), F. M. Neal (1887), and Alvis Smith (1888).

One of the early acts of the council, said to have been as early as 1846, probably, was the leasing of the river front of John Drennen. They built a wood and rock wharf, and established wharf receipts as a fund. Mr. Drennen also gave the city ten acres for a cemetery. In 1861 the council ordered forty Hall's rifles, and the patrol were organized, into seven squads under Capt. S. F. Cottrell. On August 28, 1862, the council voted the expiration of police duties, as the city then came under martial law. After the war the council elect first met February 22, 1866, and adopted all the old laws except those referring to negroes, and soon after the first board of health was established. At a meeting of November 14, 1870, Van Buren, being less than 2,500 in population, was reincorporated under the general " Incorporation Law" of April 9, 1869, and James O. Churchill became mayor. The original city maps had been lost, and John B. Ogden was authorized to make new copies.

The Railroad.—In 1876 the Little Rock & Fort Smith Railroad were contracted with, to "rip-rap" a large section of the river bank. In 1880 an ordinance was passed, issuing scrip to the amount of $8,000, for the purpose of benefiting and improveing said town; this was paid to citizens who had bonded themselves to aid the Kansas & Arkansas Valley Railway.

Statistics.—Van Buren handles 15,000 bales of cotton and does an annual business of about $1,000,000. The K. & A. V. Railway is making a marked improvement in her trade in the Indian country. Lots vary in price from $50 each in the suburbs to $130 per front foot on Main Street.

The indebtedness of the town November 1, 1887, was $11,150.92, and November 1, 1888, $7,422.28. The net revenue for the year 1888 was $3,728.64. The present officers are Mayor Alvis Smith, Marshal R. Creekmore, Recorder A. M. Orrick, Aldermen A. Hays, A. H. Colgrove, James O'Kane, John Thayer and F. Laurent.

Societies.—The Secularist Society at Van Buren has a following, if not membership, of thirty-eight persons about Van Buren. They are also known as Liberals, Agnostics, and the Society for Aesthetic and Ethical Culture. They are philosophic, rather than religious, and their members hold almost all shades of philosophy, from the plainest materialism up to the purest idealism; but materialism prevails. Their definition of " pure religion," as given by their most prominent representative, Dr. A. M. Bourland, is as follows: "Pure religion is that inspiration, resulting from conscientious loyalty to truth, which fills one with a sincere, earnest, abiding desire to adjust oneself wisely to the conditions of our being." By the same gentleman Virtue is thus prettily described: " Every faculty and passion of the human mind is for good; the right use of which is virtue, the abuse, vice." The first two most prominent representatives of the movement in Crawford County were D. C. Williams and Louis Graf, but it was not until after the arrival of Dr. A. M. Bourland, about 1867, or thereabouts, that anything of a society nature was attempted. An organization has recently been formed by Mr. Henry Shibley, their chief lecturer, formerly a follower of the teachings of Alexander Campbell, and lectures are held monthly at " School-house 64." Henry Addis *et. al.* also lecture.

Ivanhoe No. 2, K. of P., was the first lodge of this order organized in Van Buren, the date being November 20, 1872. Col. Robert Newell, D. G. C., of Arkansas, under jurisdiction of the Supreme K. of P., established it, with the following charter members: A. W. Ward, G. P. Gross, C. T. Ward, W. V. Whitfield, D. W. Brodie, John B. Ogden, Jr., S. W. Daugherty, F. M. Neal, J. D. Hawkins and Robert Newell. The first officers chosen in December were P. C., E. G. Whitesides, and William Whitfield as C. C.; Granville Wilcox was V. C.; F. M. Neal, Prelate; G. P. Gross and Charles T. Ward were respectively M. of E. and M. of F. The offices of K. of R. and S. and M. at H. were held by S. W. Daugherty and W. V. Whitfield, while Q. G. and O. G. were the titles of D. W. Brodie and John B. Ogden, Jr., respectively. The C. C.'s were W. Whitfield, G. Wilcox and J. B. Ogden, Jr. Those who have borne the title P. C. are E. G. Whitesides, J. D. Hawkins, D. W. Brodie, W. T. England, A. W. Ward, W. Whitfield, G. Wilcox, G. R. Wood and J. B. Ogden, Jr.

The next lodge was Ivanhoe 27, organized April 20, 1885, by G. C., Frank M. Thompson, with the following grand officers present: *W. E. Barnes, P. G. C.; *Robert Newell, G. V. C.; *S. M. Rutherford, G. P.; M. Jessup, G. M. of E.; J. M. Taylor, G. K. of R. and S.; *J. A. Mayer, G. M. at A.; *J. S. Fielder, G. Q. G., and *G. B. Needles, G. O. G. There were twenty-four charter members, and the following officers were elected: S. A. Miller, P. C.; G. R. Wood, C. C.; J. W. McKinney, V. C.; H. H. Pernot, Prelate; J. D. Hawkins, M. of E.; D. T. Reynolds, M. of F.; F. O. Knight, K. of R. and S.; J. B. Ogden, Jr., M. at H.; W. F. Langley, Q. G., and M. L. Weaver, O. G. Messrs. G. R. Wood, J. W. McKinney, L. H. Southmayd, L. P. Sandels, John Archer and H. C. Pernot have served as C. C. Those who have borne the title P. C. are J. D. Hawkins, W. T. England, J. B. Ogden, Jr., G. R. Wood, J. A. Stevenson, S. A. Miller, J. W. McKinney, L. H. Southmayd, H. C. Pernot, W. H. Dyer, W. F. Langley, L. P. Sandels and John Archer. Their membership is eighty-two, and their total assets, $675.

Van Buren Division No. 5, K. of P., was formed November 8, 1887, by Col. Thomas M. Gibson, with twenty-nine members. The officers elected were G. R. Wood, S. K. C.; U. H. Park, S. K. L. C.; H. C. Pernot, S. K. H.; R. W. Funk, S. K.; Treasurer, C. W. Jones, S. K. R.; J. B. Ogden, Jr., S. K. G., and J. Archer, S. K. S. They now enroll thirty-three members.

Queen City Lodge No. 24, A. O. U. W., was founded at Van Buren, August 3, 1887, by J. C. Byers, D. D. G. M. W.; J. W. Frederick, P. M. W.; L. P. Sandels, M. W.; John Archer, F.; E. G. Arkebauer, O.; W. L. Gullett, R.; John B. Ogden, Jr., Recorder; U. H. Park, Financier; T. W. Davis, G.; H. C. Miller,

---

* Pro tem.

I. W.; D. Lile, O. W.; W. L. Gullett, Medical Examiner; A. Hays, J. L. Rea and E. G. Arkebauer, Trustees. Henry Perry, T. W. Davis, John Alton and M. B. Roby were the first organization as to members and officers. The lodge have, in their meetings at I. O. O. F. hall, increased their membership to twenty-three. The following persons are the present incumbents of the various offices: L. P. Sandels, P. M. W.; W. L. Gullett, M. W.; M. H. Johnson, F.; S. T. Jackson, O.; W. B. Allen, R.; J. B. Ogden, Jr., Recorder; E. G. Arkebauer, Financier; S. P. Mitchell, G.; H. C. Miller, I. W.; D. Lile, O. W.; W. L. Gullett, M. E.; L. P. Sandels, A. Hays and H. C. Miller, Trustees. This is the only lodge of this order in Crawford County.

William A. Britton Post No. 48, G. A. R., was organized at Alma in October, 1887, by Deputy Commander S. K. Roberts. The charter enrolled the following names: E. B. Hassett, James Johnson, Mack Franklin, A. H. Huckleberry, J. P. Settles, Baron D. K. Martin, James Clark, J. H. Erby, M. Magness, Elisha Hartridge, John Sergeant, Richard Phillips and William Bowen. The order then chose the following officers: E. B. Hassett, P. C; James Johnson, S. V. C.; M. C. Franklin, J. V. C.; D. K. Martin. Q.; John Gregory, Adj.; W. T. Morgan, Asst. Adj.; — Alexander, O. of D., and J. P. Settles. There has been no change in officers except in the office of Post Commander, the present incumbent being James Johnson. Their present membership embraces twenty-six persons. The Masonic hall is their place of rendezvous.

The Van Buren Local Assembly No. 6307, K. of L., was organized April 15, 1886, by D. F. Thompson, State organizer, with twenty-four charter members. The first officers chosen were J. H. Farrow, M. W.; Charles Bell, W. F.; W. H. Mitchell, W. I.; Levi Bowen, A.; W. L. H. Couch, F. S.; Horace Addis, R. S.; J. M. Harshaw, Treas.; J. Buel, Statistican; J. F. Arnold, U. K.; William O'Bryan, I. E.; S. Hunter, O. E. M. W. Drury succeeded Mr. Farrow as M. W., and was succeeded by W. F. Stoecker and J. H. Cunningham, who now officiates. A. M. Orrick is the present R. and F. S., and H. H. Dill, the district organizer. The lodge has a membership of sixty-two persons, and hold their meetings at Eugenie Hall.

The Van Buren Lodge No. 6, F. & A. M., was chartered December 3, 1840, and organized by William Stirman, M.; Henry Starr, Sr., S. W., and John Gregg, J. W. The charter and record were burned, it appears, about 1850, the minutes of meetings in 1850 appearing as copied from reports to the grand lodge, and the charter likewise being a duplicate of the original. Meetings were held under a dispensation from December 21, 1850, to February 1 of the following year, when regular meetings began. From the minutes of July 11, 1850, the following are found to have been officers: T. H. Johnson, W. M.; Jacob S. Grove, S. W.; C. F. Brown, J. W.; W. F. England, Treas.; D. C. Williams, Sec.; J. B. Ogden, S. D.; R. S. Roberts, J. D.; Henry S. Wilson, Tyler. Mr. Johnson was succeeded in the Worthy Master's functions by W. O. Chilton; then came W. F. England at several various times, as he seemed to be a very desirable executive; then came C. F. Brown, H. F. Thomason, who served three various terms; John Ingram succeeded him; H. C. Hayman served two terms at non-successive times; R. S. Roberts served in a similar manner, and likewise Granville Wilcox; J. C. Kennedy came next; W. H. H. Shibley was twice honored, and was followed by H. C. Norton and D. Spencer; A. H. Colgrove, the present incumbent, has served twice, and was preceded by L. H. Southmayd. The various offices are now filled as follows: George R. Wood, S. W.; John B. Ogden, Jr., J. W.; H. C. Johnson, Treas.; N. Turmon, Sec.; W. H. H. Shibley, S. D.; A. A. Clinkscales, J. D.; H. C. Miller, S. S.; C. C. Brown, J. S.; Jas. R. Hewitt, Tyler. The lodge has used various places of meeting; its rooms in the Eagle Block were burned January 15, 1882, and their next home was in the Hinkle Hall. They rent from the I. O. O. F. order at present, but are negotiating for room in the new Lynch's Hall.

Van Buren Chapter No. 3, R. A. M., was chartered May 22, 1874, by the Grand Chapter R. A. C. of Arkansas, to H. F. Thomason, J. C. Kennedy, Charles F. Harvey, Hiram Brodie, J. A. Dibrell, Gran. Wilcox, Pearson Mayfield, Robert H. Love, Louis Graf, H. C. Hayman and B. J. Brown. Gen. Thomason was chosen H. P., while J. C. Kennedy and C. F. Harvey served as the first K. and S. respectively; the C. of H. was Gran. Wil-

61

CRAWFORD COUNTY, ARKANSAS - BIOGRAPHICAL AND HISTORICAL MEMOIRS
****

cox, and B. J. Brown became Prin. Soj., while H. Brodie bore the title R. A. Capt.; the M. of Second V. and of Third V. were J. A. Dibrell and H. C. Hayman, respectively, and Louis Graf cared for the records. Gen. Thomason was succeeded by J. C. Kennedy; then followed C. F. Harvey, R. S. Roberts, A. H. Colgrove and their present honored officer, W. H. H. Shibley. With the last-named gentlemen are associated, as officers, L. Graf, K.; H. G. Haines, S.; John Hinkle, Treasurer; Henry Shibley, Secretary; A. H. Colgrove, C. of H.; S. A. Pernot, Prin Soj.; E. Arkebauer, R. A. Capt.; H. C. Hayman, J. W. Frederick and R. J. Miller are respectively M. of Third V., Second V. and First V., and John Archie, Guard. The chapter was one of the lodges burned in 1882, since which time they have occupied Hinkle's Hall, rooms in the Whitfield Block and the Edmondson Hall. Their property is estimated at about $200. They number about thirty-six members.

Newspapers.—The *Arkansas Intelligencer* was the first paper founded in Crawford County and probably the first in Northwestern Arkansas. At so early a date as February, 1842, one would hardly expect to find a newspaper of a high literary character so nearly on the Indian border as was Van Buren, but those were the golden days of American literature, and the people of the border, without the railway and the telegraph, took great pride in giving finished expression to their ideas in their local paper, and the *Intelligencer* is stamped with that leisurely literary finish not always seen in these days of the *news*-paper. The earliest known issue now preserved was No. 4, Volume 2, on "a small sheet, as we have not yet received our paper," the editor explains. The next full-sized folio was No. 8, Volume 2, issued April 18, 1843. Thus it must have been and was established February 19, 1842.* It seems to have been established by Francis M. Van Horne & Thomas Sterne, for they dissolved partnership December 16, 1842, and the latter continued alone. Messrs. Sterne & Wheeler were editors and proprietors in 1843, but in July George W. Clarke's pen became the chief, with Mr. Sterne as manager. Its policy was then neutral, but in March of the succeeding year Mr. Sterne withdrew to found the *Western Frontier*

---

* Files of most of the '40s are owned by Mrs. A. J. Ward, of Van Buren.

Whig, and the *Intelligencer* became Democratic. In April, 1845, J. W. Washbourne and C. D. Pryor assumed control, the former as editor, and so continued until March 21, 1847, when Mr. Clarke resumed the quill. During his control he had a remarkably excellent corps of contributors, that being a prominent feature of the paper, and one, a young thirteen-year-old girl of Fayetteville, sailing under the cognomen "Clementine," deserves mention as one who ought to have afterward made a literary name. The *Intelligencer* continued until September, 1859, when it was purchased by W. H. Mayers, of Fort Smith, and merged into the *Thirty-fifth Parallel* at the latter place.

The *Western Frontier Whig* was founded in May, 1844, as an advocate of the party whose name it bears, by Messrs. Sterne and Logan. Thomas Sterne had withdrawn from the *Intelligencer*, and with his new partner as chief editor expected to make a successful rival of his old paper. Among their chief contributors were the Hon. Jesse Turner, Sr., and James H. Simpson. Judge Turner tells an incident which will illustrate the editorial wars of that day: Editor Logan was a calm, imperturbable, self-possessed man, while his rival, Mr. Clarke, was brilliant, impulsive and forceful; these conditions, together with the irritation resulting from political rivalry, led the editor of the *Intelligencer* to christen his rival with the name of a certain comical Indian chief, "Big Mush;" Mr. Logan returned the compliment, and spoke of "Toady" Clarke. The "honorable code" was called in play forthwith, and on the "field of honor," near Fort Smith, two rifle-shots were exchanged, but the smell of powder and bad marksmanship led to reconciliation. According to Judge Turner, the paper was moved entire to Victoria, Tex., about 1845, and finally located in San Antonio.

The Van Buren *Press* was the third paper established in that city. On July 6, 1859, was issued its first number, by its founder, publisher and editor, J. S. Dunham, of Middletown, Conn. The fact of its more extended existence than any other paper in Crawford County, and during her most vital experience, makes it, from a historical point of view, the most valuable. In its first editorial is the following: " We believe in extending our territory peacefully by annexation, or purchase, if we can, but in any event we go for *our country right or wrong.*" Being the only paper in the county for some time, its influence was not small, and its course seemed remarkably consistent with the principles upon which it acted. On the whole, too, it was, during a trying period, a very fair mirror of the public mind and feeling of the county. Late in 1861 and at the beginning of the following year scarcity of paper led to partial issues, until a half-sheet, issued January 23, 1862, was the last. During the chaotic period that followed that date no paper was issued in the county until the *Press* reappeared February 3, 1866, with the following editorial comments: "After a lapse of nearly four years, we with this number resume the publication of the *Press*. * * * * It is the part of wisdom to set about in earnest repairing, so far as we are able, the evils our country has suffered. * * * * We shall warmly support the reconstruction policy of the President. * * * This class (negroes) of our people have been suddenly thrown upon the community as free men, being utterly unprepared for the boon. The only question for us to discuss now is, what can we do for them to make them good citizens, and prevent them from becoming an element of strife and disturbance? Their *status* as free men gives them certain rights that under our form of government we cannot deny them. The privilege of voting we believe they ought not to enjoy at present, certainly, and we feel that the State has a perfect right to withhold it, because it is a *privilege*, and not a *right;* for the reason that by giving them this privilege we would introduce an element of corruption that would be highly injurious, if not ruinous, to the country by placing it in the power of wicked and disigning demagogues to eventually rule the State. The public mind, and the negro, are not yet prepared for this dangerous innovation." This gives not only the editor's ideas then, but the prevailing temper of the county at that time. Mr. Dunham has had continuous control of the paper ever since, and has at brief periods been assisted by Hon. Granville Wilcox and the editor's son, who for a short time was a partner, under the firm title J. S. Dunham & Son. Its policy on public questions has generally been characterized by conservatism, in the better sense of that term; and generally represents the more progressive wing of its party. It is ably edited and active in the county's development.

The Van Buren *Argus* was a child of the Brooks and Baxter War. The *Press* had espoused the Baxter cause, and the Brooks leaders of the county, in order to have an organ advocating their position, encouraged Messrs. George Thayer and John Cass, of Hillsboro, Ohio, and Danville, Ills., respectively, to establish the new paper, and Hon. Granville Wilcox was installed as its able editor. It made its first issue, a seven-column folio, on Christmas day of 1875; times were changed, and although ably edited, in a literary sense, it became essentially a *news*-paper, and exponent of the new development of the county. Mr. Wilcox's connection with the *Argus* was severed in 1885, a few months previous to his death, and the Thayer Brothers assumed control of all departments, as at present. The publishers and proprietors, following Thayer & Cass, were G. C. Thayer, in 1879; John A. Thayer, in 1880; Thayer & Ibbotson, in 1882, and since that the Thayer Brothers. In 1887 the Messrs. Thayer issued a daily *Argus* for a few months also; it was a six-column folio.

The Van Buren *Graphic* was founded in 1881, its first issue, a seven-column folio, bearing the date January 28, and for its title the *Graphic*. Its founder and editor, J. J. Warren, and its publisher, Frank Ibbotson, were associated until the latter was succeeded on September 2, 1881, by W. N. Bradbury, and the paper assumed its present full title. After Mr. Bradbury's withdrawal Mr. Warren had exclusive management of the paper until its purchase on March 12, 1888, by its present editor and proprietor, Mr. Z. Wells. The *Graphic* was the first effort to supply the Republican element of the county with a local organ, and its continued existence indicates a demand for it. Its course has been especially characterized as aggressive and spirited, and its life is identified with what might be called the "Frisco Period" of Crawford County's History. It published the *Peoples' Protector* during the brief existence of that paper.

The Arkansas *Agitator* was established at Van Buren in June, 1883, by the Davidson Publishing Company, with Maj. F. B. Davidson, of St. Louis, as editor. Its purpose was chiefly industrial and agricultural agitation. It was a semi-monthly, and issued but a few numbers.

The *Daily Optic* was another short-lived Van Buren paper, issued for a few months in 1885, by Messrs. Frank Ibbotson and G. N. Callahan.

The *People's Protector*, a paper managed in the interests of the colored people, ran for about eleven weeks in 1888. It was printed at the office of the *Graphic*, as a six-column folio. H. H. Wilburn, its first editor, was succeeded by E. W. Merchant, who soon retired in favor of G. H. Hill, under whose management it was suspended.

ALMA.

First Residents.—Alma is a beautifully situated town—the second of Crawford County business centers. Its land was entered August 3, 1836, by Ira Smoot, and continued merely farm land afterward, under the ownership of John Henry, until it was bought by Col. M. F. Locke about 1872, although this gentleman had bought other land near by in 1869. The log cabin now back of W. W. Smith's drug store was the only house on the site of the town in 1869, and but ten acres were cleared. Col. Locke built his present house the same year (1869), and also his gin. A Mr. A. W. Griffin kept the first store, and acted as postmaster for the settlement. Renfroe & Byars next built a store on Main Street. In 1870 a residence, now the McKinney House, was built by J. D. James, who also kept a livery stable and stage stand. Renfroe, L. B. Byars, J. E. Smith, followed next in building. The school-house and Masonic hall combined was the next structure erected. The land was deeded to representatives of the Methodist, Presbyterian, Christian and Baptist Churches and the Masonic order, and Col. Locke, president, and B. P. Renfroe, secretary, of a voluntary building committee of fifteen, proceeded to erect a structure at a total cost of about $1,700. After the societies erect buildings of their own this house reverts to exclusive school uses of the public schools.

The King Hotel, managed by a Mr. King, was built by Col. Locke, on the corner of Railroad Street and Fayetteville Avenue (also called Main Street), but it was burned about December, 1884, in the greatest fire which ever visited Alma, and which destroyed about seven buildings—a loss of probably $300,000. One other occurred in January, 1886, in which three or four buildings were burned by an incendiary, it is supposed, at a loss of about $25,000. Col. Locke's and also W. R. Bolling's steam mills and cotton gins, likewise a saw and flouring mill, were erected about 1874.

Later Growth.—After August, 1876, when the Little Rock Railway was completed, Alma showed the greatest signs of growth. The original roadway was a half mile south of its present bed, but through a grant of some land and $1,500 by Col. Locke the survey was secured to its present position. From this time until about 1882 Alma grew to its present proportions, since which time its development has not been so marked. The cotton trade is the controlling one, although black walnut, locust, cedar and sweet-gum timber and lumber are largely shipped. Hay is a large shipment, too, and some oats and corn. The Alma Canning and Evaporating Company was incorporated in August, 1888, by about thirty stockholders and $25,000 in stock. The officers are president, J. D. Rheinhardt; vice-president, M. F. Locke; secretary, W. Nunnally, and J. D. James, treasurer. The works are to be erected in the spring of 1889, about 100 yards east of the depot, and this is expected to draw a considerable fruit trade to Alma.

In general merchandise J. D. James does an average annual business of $120,000, and ships about 3,000 bales of cotton every year; W. R. and S. B. Locke are a large firm in this line; McKibben & Pape (a branch house), A. C. Seale, G. J. McNeely & Bro., Fry & Ford, McFall & Orme, J. G. Orme & Co. and Mrs. A. B. Sloan also represent that line. The grocery trade is managed by M. L. Wright, R. C. Lytal, A. Broome and J. A. Robertson. W. W. Smith and W. F. Baker control the drug trade. Drs. L. J. Wilson, R. H. Alvis, W. T. Black, J. C. Chaney and W. L. Wynne represent the medical fraternity, while the legal lights are J. P. Byers, W. H. Byers, W. L. McFall, J. M. Wright and D. B. Locke. Besides the mills of Mr. Bolling and Col. Locke, before mentioned, H. S. Lewers & Co. and J. K. P. Douglass have corn mills and cotton gins near the town. B. F. Thompson, M. C. Bowlden, F. J. Knight and John Richardson are blacksmiths, and R. F. Hamer has a livery and feed stable. The Howell House, by Mrs. S. E. Howell, the

London Hotel, by the London Bros., and the McKinney House, by Mrs. M. E. McKinney, are the homes of the traveling public. S. Wright and M. L. Wright have restaurants, and the ladies of the churches have shown enterprise in establishing ice-cream rooms. B. P. Renfroe deals in insurance. E. R. Lee is express agent. Mr. James, the Lockes, Fry & Ford and L. B. Byars are cotton buyers, and timber is shipped by J. M. Dick. The lumber yard of the Van Buren Planing Mills is managed by Chas. Faber. O. N. Baldwin, L. T. Benton and F. J. Dorshay are builders. Miss Annie Higginbotham manages the millinery department of J. D. James, who also has an implement, wagon and undertaker's department. John London cares for the meat and ice trade, while John Maffitt and Thomas Maxwell deal in hardware and harness, respectively. The barber is H. J. Miller.

Since A. W. Griffin's postmastership his successors have been B. P. Renfroe, W. A. Britton, E. B. Hassett, Noble Bolen and H. S. Lewers.

Newspapers.—Newspaper life has been a variable thing in Alma. The Alma *Herald* was founded in 1877 by M. L. Yeatman, with whom a Mr. Bell was afterward associated. It was a seven-column Democratic sheet. Two years later a stock company, composed of M. F. Locke, J. T. Hollowell, L. C. Locke, D. W. Brodie, W. T. Black, B. P. Renfroe and E. B. Hassett, bought the office, and George Thayer (of the Van Buren *Argus*) leased it, and for two years it was independently Democratic, under the name Crawford County *Democrat*. John Renfroe and R. R. Wood were the next lessees, under the name of *The Arkansas Farmer*, and two years later a Mr. Stonecipher gave it the name Alma *Leader*, and Frank Ibbotson was its publisher for a few issues. It might be mentioned that Eugene Douglass and P. H. Hillyer were connected with the paper a short time in its first years, under the name Alma *Independent*. J. S. Renfroe used the name *Leader* while he had charge, and again, B. P. Renfroe had control of it under part of its present name, the Crawford County *Democrat*. Col. Locke took charge of it in March, 1887, and replaced " Crawford County " by " Alma," and in June, 1888, D. B. Locke and J. A. Garner assumed control.

Incorporation.—Alma has a population of over 800, located

on Sections 5, 6, 7 and 8, Township 9, Range 30. It is estimated that about 15 per cent is colored population. In 1872 it was incorporated, with W. P. Brown, mayor; J. C. Betton, recorder; J. H. Gill, M. F. Locke, J. D. James, J. M. Wright and L. B. Byars as aldermen. The mayors have been G. W. Smith, J. D. James, J. C. Betton, J. M. Wright, J. A. McNeely, B. Caraway, W. C. Bostick and W. S. Byars. The present officers are mayor, J. A. McNeely; recorder, L. Black; aldermen, W. W. Smith, Joseph Ford, D. J. McNeely, R. F. Hamer and W. R. Bolling. The marshal is T. T. Byars.

The excellent churches and schools of Alma will be treated in the chapter devoted to those subjects. Alma has frequently taken the lead in such county societies as the Agricultural Association, the County Immigration Society, etc. It has three fraternities, the F. & A. M., K. of H. and G. A. R.

Lodges.—Alma Lodge No. 43, F. & A. M., was organized August 14, 1875, the date of charter being October 12, 1875. The original members and officers were H. G. Haines, W. M.; W. R. Bolling, S. W.; J. F. Bushman, J. W.; J. M. McGuffey, S. D.; J. E. Smith, J. D.; T. W. Bolling, Treas.; W. H. Byers, Sec.; T. T. Byars, Tyler; R. M. Thurston, H. C. Hill, L. Byars, R. P. Morrow, A. Toole and J. M. McKinney. Mr. Haines' successors have been J. M. McGuffey, J. A. McNeely, J. M. McKinney, S. Bolton, H. S. Lewers, E. M. Lowery, J. E. Smith, W. R. Bolling and Dr. L. J. Wilson, the present W. M. The remaining officers at present are G. J. McNeely, S. W.; J. E. Smith, J. W.; L. Nunnally, Treas.; J. H. Bolling, Sec.; William Hanners, S. D.; J. M. Hardin, J. D., and J. P. Settles, Tyler. They have forty-seven members.

Alma Lodge No. 3166, K. of H., was chartered May 26, 1888, by Mr. Futrell, of Little Rock, Ark. The charter members were J. E. Smith, James N. Patton, W. R. Bolling, O. Echols, J. M. Bates, John Matthews, A. C. Seale, Joseph Balentine, R. H. Alvis (medical examiner), W. W. Smith, G. O. Alvis, S. H. Reed, A. J. Harrell, Edmond Burton, E. T. Reed, M. M. Rinegar, John Sharp, J. D. McKumon, R. N. Anderson. The first dictator was W. R. Bolling, who was succeeded by J. E. Smith and O. Echols. The membership is now thirty-one persons.

69

CRAWFORD COUNTY, ARKANSAS - BIOGRAPHICAL AND HISTORICAL MEMOIRS
****

CHESTER.

Its Early Life.—Chester is the third town in Crawford, and is located on Sections 27 and 34, Township 12, Range 30. The land was entered by Samuel Rush December 9, 1850, and Solomon Basham January 12, 1852, and by Capt. J. C. Wright in 1853. Messrs. Rush and Wright were the first settlers, and the first man to make any real improvements was Abner Scrimpshire, who located at Capt. Wright's spring about 1839. He still lives in the neighborhood. Charles Howard bought the land about 1849, but since 1853 Capt. Wright has owned it, and his home was the only buildings on the site of Chester up to September, 1884.

Later Business.—Jacob Yoes followed the completion of the Frisco, and built, in 1884, a frame store, 20x50 feet, now standing near his fine two-story brick block, built in February, 1888. Capt. Wright had a little room in April, 1882, in which the post-office was opened by him, and some groceries kept. In July, 1887, the Frisco Railway opened a station, and built the present commodious depot in September. The new Yoes Block contains a dry goods store and hotel, the Chester House, which was run by W. C. Douthett and F. M. Wilhoit before the present proprietor, Mrs. M. E. Crowe, took charge. Capt. Wright built his present grocery and post-office rooms in 1887. In 1884 he put up a blacksmith shop, and employed workmen until he sold out to Jacob Yoes. He then built another in January, 1888. He also erected a barber shop, and rented it to W. Stokes and Mr. Harris, the present manager.

In July, 1887, the "Frisco" round-house and repair shops were completed, with coal-chutes and timber yard, giving employment to about 100 men. George W. Mooney built a general merchandise store in 1887, and in 1888 sold to Butler Bros. They now run a billiard hall. In 1887 was established a drug store by Dement & McGinnis, but the firm sold out to Dr. L. G. Friday, who had, in January, 1888, put a dry goods stock into the old post-office building. Dr. J. L. Dement had bought land adjoining Capt. Wright's in 1884, and has been the chief physician in Howard's Fork Valley. J. F. Parker began the family grocery business, and built his store in January, 1888, and soon after

Mrs. Mary Kindrick built a boarding house. J. W. Emerson started a saw-mill in the fall of 1887 to supply the railway company. This is what is left of the extensive lumber trade of the White River Lumber Company and the Arkansas Lumber Company during the early half of "the eighties." Ties are still a great shipment, but strawberries and produce are the leaders. Capt. Wright had four acres of the berries at one time. A. P. Brooks manages a lumber yard. J. R. Stewart has built a boarding house, and Dr. Friday has a neat new drug house. Lewis Flatoe has a dry goods store.

Capt. Wright laid out the town in March, 1887, on the east side of the railway, into nine blocks, 300x300 feet, with Front Street as the principal thoroughfare.

Lodge.—Chester Lodge, F. & A. M., No. 459, was organized in April, 1887, by the following members and officers: J. D. Hoffman, W. M.; E. P. Stafford, S. W.; J. M. Rogers, J. W.; J. M. Carter, Secretary; Capt. J. C. Wright, Treasurer; W. H. Ranken, J. D.; O. Ross, S. D.; John Furlow, Tyler; Samuel Eddy and Dr. Dement. The present officers are Dr. Dement, W. M.; Mr. Stafford, S. W.; J. R. Wilson, J. W.; F. M. Butler, Secretary; Capt. Wright, Treasurer; Mr. Hoffman, S. D.; Mr. Ranken, J. D., and Mr. Furlow, Tyler. The fraternity own half of a two-story school-house, District 65, built at a cost of about $400. The present membership is twenty-four.

MOUNTAINBURG.

Mountainburg, like other offshoots of the "Frisco Railway," is beautifully located among the mountains on Section 15, Township 11, Range 30, and its population is estimated at about 250. Its present site was entered by George Dyer about 1845, and by James C. Wright about 1883. It has sprung up in the last few years around a store and station started by Jacob Yoes, the town builder along the "Frisco" in Northwestern Arkansas. Round this has clustered a blacksmith and wagon shop, a good gin and mill, and the shipments of lumber and fruits, which have come to characterize these local points along the St. Louis & San Francisco Railway. The place also has one physician, Dr. Bushong; a Masonic hall and school-house also are institutions

71

CRAWFORD COUNTY, ARKANSAS - BIOGRAPHICAL AND HISTORICAL MEMOIRS
****

of the place, the latter serving also the purpose of a church, in which the Christian, Baptist and Methodist societies and others hold occasional services.

Clear Creek Local Assembly No. 9259, K. of L., was organized December 22, 1886, at Mountainburg, Ark., by D. F. Thompson, State Organizer. There were thirty-six charter members, from whom were chosen the following officers: H. B. Reamy, M. W.; Joel Miller, R. S.; H. C. Reamy, F. S.; J. W. Hatfield, Treasurer; James S. Bushong, W. F. The lodge is young, but prosperous, enrolling 100 members in good standing. The present incumbents of the various offices are as follows: J. R. Galaway, M. W.; Isaac Gilstrap, R. S.; J. H. Reamy, F. S.; W. R. Peter, W. F.; M. E. Wagner, Treasurer.

CEDARVILLE.

This is a picturesque inland village of (it is estimated) about 200 people, and is located on Sections 2 and 11, Township 10, Range 32. It was laid out in March, 1879, by Palmer and Lee Neal, Charles Crowell, Archibald Hays, James O'Bryan, Philip Howell and W. G. Nipper—the surveyor being Davidson Dickson. Eight blocks, four on each side of Main Street, was the form that spread out over the beautiful cedar-adorned Webber Valley of Lee's Creek; its boundaries were: " Beginning 32 rods east of the southeast quarter of Section 2, Township 10, Range 32; thence due south 40 rods; thence due west 110 rods; thence due north 120 rods; thence due east 110 rods; thence due south 80 rods to the place of beginning."

The most reliable information obtainable gives the first house erected as a log one, on the site of Mr. Maxey's home, by Valentine Matlock. This was in " the thirties."

Dr. Young was among the next residents. After the war H. S. Anderson secured the land under a tax title, and built the Maxey house, and gave the place its present name, Cedarville. His brother-in-law built a house also. Dr. Young's widow was enabled to secure the place next, and from her a Mr. Crowell bought it. This gentleman sold parts of the land from time to time to Palmer Neal, Jacob Shelly, Robert Crowell, Henry Crowell, Lee Neal, and others, all of whom erected business houses or homes, or both. Mr. Shelly had a shoe-shop and store during the war, and afterward James O'Bryan, a saloon and grocery; Palmer Neal, a general store; H. C. Crowell, a store, and Lee Neal & Bro. opened a drug store. At present J. F. Neal has a general store; Lee Neal & Bro., Maxey Bros. and Neal & Purcell have drugs and groceries; John Trewhitt and Robert Rowell have blacksmith shops; Mr. Shelly has his shoe-shop; The C. W. Neal estate own a mill and gin; and Dr. R. G. Harrison attends the sick. Among the postmasters have been Robert Crowell, Lee Neal, C. W. Neal and M. J. Purcell. The place has one union church, in which several societies hold services, and one of the finest Masonic halls in the county. The town was incorporated in 1881, the first meeting of the council being held on October 2. W. A. Ives, Palmer Neal, Lee Neal and Dr. R. G. Harrison have served as mayors.

COVE CITY.

This is an enterprising inland village of about 150 inhabitants, situated on Section 36, Township 12, Range 32. It has two live merchants, R. C. Oliver and Isaac Briscoe; a blacksmith and wagon-shop, owned by J. J. Beale, and a grist and saw mill and cotton gin combined, the property of R. C. Oliver. Dr. P. B. Swearingen is the only physician. The town was laid out in 1880 by W. B. Shoemaker, and covers thirty acres in the form of a square, with 108 lots. The residents at that time were J. R. Reed, F. W. White, H. G. Shoemaker, C. D. Gilliam, D. P. Cox, J. J. Beale, Dr. E. G. McCormick and Albert Rainwater. The land was entered at an early date by Clem Moberly, and the first store was established about 1854, and later on a blacksmith shop and post-office, the postmaster being a Mr. Hill. Oliver and Gilliam were the merchants. Cotton and corn are the chief shipments, and Van Buren is their market. The village has a school-house erected in 1882, and D. P. Cox has charge of their schools. Cove City Lodge, F. & A. M., No. 268, and Cove City Eastern Star Chapter, W. D., are two flourishing fraternities. The place has about twenty-seven buildings.

UNIONTOWN.

This is another inland village of probably 150 people, located

73

CRAWFORD COUNTY, ARKANSAS - BIOGRAPHICAL AND HISTORICAL MEMOIRS
:

on Section 31, Township 11, Range 32, and Section 6, Township 10, Range 32. Its land was entered by I. Vinsant in "the forties," and by the Howell family. A mill and cotton gin was erected by Alexander Thompson before the war, and a church and school-house was built. Mr. Wood afterward opened a store, and is now the leading merchant.

Uniontown Lodge No. 395, F. & A. M., was chartered November 28, 1882. The original members were Thomas Comstock, James A. Burress, L. H. Oliver, R. G. Harrison, Henry Howell, William S. Williams, Adam Howell and William H. Remy. The officers were Thomas Comstock, W. M.; James A. Burress, Sr. W., and L. H. Oliver, J. W. The present membership of the lodge is twenty-nine.

PORTER.

This is a " Frisco " village of considerable vigor as a shipping point for lumber and fruits. It contains about 150 people, and is twenty-nine miles north of Van Buren, on Section 10, Township 12, Range 30. Edward Lee received a patent for the land on which the place is located, in 1886. The first building in the village was a store, moved there from a mill below by John Rutherford, but this is now destroyed. Mr. B. F. Strong's residence was next, and that was followed by Thomas Testament's store building. The depot was located and erected in 1882, and in 1885 the land was laid out in lots, which were arranged in the form of six blocks. Porter has developed rapidly, so that there are now three stores owned by Messrs. Edward Lee, Thomas Testament and M. M. Saylor, respectively; a hotel, managed by Mrs. W. T. Kimbew; railway agent, operator and postmaster, Mr. J. W. Scobey; a school, taught by Prof. H. P. Johnson, and twelve residences.

RUDY.

This is one of the most picturesquely located villages in Crawford County, and is one of the " Frisco Railway's" considerable shipping points for cotton, strawberries, peaches, apples and wild berries. Its population has been estimated at possibly 125 persons. It is located on Section 23, Township 10, Range 31. The land on which it is situated was settled by a Mr. Green about

1830, but a Mr. E. Bell entered it in 1835, and the first few buildings were of the rude log variety. It was made a station after the completion of the railway, and was laid out by Maj. Hinckley, the chief engineer of this division of the Frisco Railway. Two stores, a blacksmith shop, cotton-gin and grist-mill, embrace the business of the place. The Farmers' Alliance is a local secret order, and the Fine Spring Masonic Lodge, about two and one-half miles east of Rudy, serves as a fraternity for this village also. The Methodist Episcopal Church, South, is the only organized religious society in the place, and a fine district school building, about one mile to the east, serves as their public school.

SMALLER VILLAGES.

Dyer is a station on the Little Rock & Fort Smith Railroad, and a shipping point of importance. The land was railway land, bought in 1870 by S. M. Dyer, whose name it bears. W. U. Casey built the first dwelling, store and shop, and W. A. Dyer and Frank Hays also built homes. J. W. Moss and G. E. Dyer laid out the place in lots in 1884. The present business embraces two stores, a blacksmith shop, cotton-gin, grist-mill and saw-mill. Cotton, cotton-seed, timber and fruit are the chief shipments. The station house was recently burned. They have one public school, and the Methodist and Christian Churches are represented.

Dora is a border village on the Kansas &'Arkansas Valley Railway of, it has been estimated, about 100 people. It is located on Sections 18 and 19, Township 9, Range 32. The land was entered by John Harrell at an early date. Vinsant and Hood are the leading merchants. The town is on the State line, and is the result of the railway.

Graphic is a young inland village embracing a population of about twelve families. The first store was started in October, 1886, by Isaac Smith, and the following year J. H. Walker put up a general store. Dr. E. M. Dowry opened a stock of drugs about the same time. Moore & Yoes established a general store in 1888, and were soon followed by Leonard Dyer & Bros., grocers. C. W. Smith & Son opened a dry goods store, and general merchandise received an addition to its trade through Lawry &

Son. George Weeks is the blacksmith. Lewis and Ellis Peters have a saw and grist-mill and cotton-gin. A two-story frame building, 28x50 feet, is occupied by the Masonic lodge in the upper story, and the first is used for church and school purposes. Frank Dyer is postmaster.

Lancaster is a station on the St. Louis & San Francisco Railway, located on Section 6, Township 10, Range 30.

Lilly is a considerable shipping point for fruit on the "Frisco Railway," and is located on Section 35, Township 10, Range 31. The depot and a single store include its buildings.

Cross Lanes is a settlement located on Sections 4, 5, 8 and 9, Township 8, Range 30.

Natural Dam is an old and small settlement located about the noted Natural Dam, elsewhere described in this volume, and is situated on Section 9, Township 11, Range 32.

Belmont (Post-office) is located on Section 10, Township 10, Range 30. John R. Meadows is its leading spirit.

Sulphur Springs, or White Sulphur Springs, is located on Section 32, Township 11, Range 32, about the popular mineral springs there.

Eads and *Anna* are post-offices in the northern part of the county.

Armada ships timber and fruits. It has a store, blacksmith shop, and is headquarters for the White River Lumber Company. It is located on Section 16, Township 12, Range 30.

London Town was first started in 1853. A saw-mill, blacksmith shop and one store, a cotton-gin, and grist-mill also, includes the business. M. L. London is the leading spirit of the place. Judge H. B. Hale is their trader. They have a lodge of F. & A. M.

ADDENDUM.

Fruit.—The fruit shipments of Crawford County points along the "Frisco Railway," between April 20 and July 31, 1888, were as follows: From Van Buren, strawberries, 9,200 crates; peas, 900 boxes; beans, 1,300 boxes; apples, 1,250 boxes; tomatoes, 3,300 boxes; peaches, 3,700 boxes; raspberries, 1,108 crates; grapes, 900 crates. From Lilly, strawberries, 1,000 boxes; peaches, etc.,

****

2,500 boxes. From Rudy, strawberries, 900 crates; peaches, etc., 1,400 boxes. From Mountainburg, peaches, etc., 1,500 boxes. Many were also shipped from Chester and other points.

MILITARY ANNALS.

The Mexican War.—The first notice of Crawford County's interest in the Mexican War was an editorial in the *Intelligencer* favoring the annexation of Texas.* In August, 1845, was the first mention of war, and on June 1, 1846, pursuant to the call of Gov. Drew, the "Van Buren Avengers" were organized as a mounted company, which was afterward accepted as Company—, Sixth Arkansas Regiment. The officers were as follows: Captain, John S. Roane; first lieutenant, George S. Foster; second lieutenant, Alexander Steward; first sergeant, B. F. Ross; second sergeant, George Y. Latham; third sergeant, John Sprott; fourth sergeant, J. W. B. Davis; first corporal, John Rudy; second corporal, D. Steward; third corporal, J. Pierce; fourth corporal, D. D. Thompson; musicians, W. Quesenbury and F. A. Rector. Col. Drennen was active in furnishing the company with supplies. This was the first Arkansas company mustered in at Washington.

The Crawford Guards, organized in 1845 for frontier protection, about the same time became a cavalry company, with the following officers: Captain, John Drennen; first lieutenant, R. Stevenson; second lieutenant, George Turner; orderly-sergeant, I. M. Marshall; secretary, J. W. Washbourne. Capt. Price's mounted gun-men in Jasper and Lee's Creek Townships, Capt. Brook's in Big Creek Township and Capt. Orme's general company were other companies used chiefly for frontier protection.

The battle of Buena Vista was reported quite fully in the *Intelligencer*, one writer† saying: "We paid dearly for our glory. In the few minutes of the conflict Col. Yell had fallen, Capt. Porter, John Pelham, Richard Sanders, the standard bearer of Independence, and several others. Darwin Stewart rode perhaps 200 yards before he fell. I passed him, but did not know him at that time; he was upon his face, and many of

---

* May 11, 1844.
† William Quesenbury.

our men wore similar dresses." Capt. Dillard succeeded Capt. Roane after the latter's appointment as lieutenant-colonel. The "Avengers" were in the Taylor Campaign in Northern Mexico, and rendered distinguished services. The following is a statement of the company after the campaign:

Captain, Dillard; first lieutenant, B. F. Ross; lieutenant, G. W. Foster; second lieutenants, A. Stewart and L. Willhaff; G. Y. Latham, J. W. B. Davis, D. Thompson, W. Allen, J. S. Boyd, R. B. Chew, A. Dale, O. Fogerty, J. L. Haynes, S. Knous, J. W. D. Lasater, W. R. McFarlaine, J. C. Roberts, W. F. Houck, J. Pearce, D. E. Lewis, G. R. Bell, A. J. Boyd, G. A. Chew, R. Foster, F. Houck, A. C. Ingram, M. Kelley, J. W. Little, I. Patty, W. Quesenbury, W. Stinnett, W. Capps, G. W. Peyton, B. Smith, W. C. Thomas, S. White, S. Johnson, J. H. Smith, M. Thomas, M. A. Worley, J. Story, M. H. Parker, R. Price, L. Moore, J. A. Hagwood, W. Duty, John Rudy, D. Hart, R. Smith, J. W. Taylor, D. Atkins, J. B. Compton and J. Sprott.

On the return* of the volunteers, with the body of Col. Yell, impressive ceremonies were held in the transferring of the remains to a committee from his home, Fayetteville. A barbecue reception was also prepared, and on the 29th of July, although inclement weather interfered, a successful demonstration was held. The Hon. George W. Paschal delivered an oration, and all the conviviality that attends the barbecue was indulged in thereafter, and the " Van Buren Avengers " were citizens again.

THE CIVIL WAR.

Forebodings.—Time enough had hardly passed for dust to gather on the arms of the Mexican soldier before the faint rumblings of the Civil War began to be heard. The first notice of the Abolition movement to be found in the Van Buren journals is a caustic squib on William Lloyd Garrison in the *Intelligencer* for February 1, 1845, and in that for June 14, of the same year, appears significant comments on the separation of Northern and Southern branches of various denominations. On June 2, 1849, a strong editorial appeared discussing the "Emancipation movement," and in several other issues are remarks on the mission-

---

*July 25, 1847.

aries sent South by the Northern branch of the Methodist Church, which plainly gave evidence that the Southern branch viewed the movement as an Abolition propaganda. The probabilities of abolitionism and colonization were also discussed, as if there was a presentiment that all possible solutions of a great question must be tried. An anti-slavery convention at Batesville in December, 1849, was also criticised. Then, July 6, 1859, comes the first issue of the Van Buren *Press*, that powerful organ of war times and reconstruction days, speaking in decisive tones, "in any event we are for our country right or wrong." The *Press* represents the Crawford County of those days in so masterly a style that its columns are freely quoted in these pages.

Crawford County was as unlike Washington County in their main political characteristics on this question as in the physical features of the two counties. Washington had a large element that was decisively national in its sympathies, while that element in Crawford assumed considerably less than the same proportions, although the first Northwest Arkansans, probably, to join the Federal forces were from Crawford County, as the following from the pen of Col. A. W. Bishop witnesses: "On May 10, 1862, there came to its pickets* a band of eleven Arkansans, led by Thomas J. Gilstrap and Furiben Elkins, of Crawford County," and these men gave Col. M. La Rue Harrison the first idea of a sufficient latent national following in Northwest Arkansas to warrant the organization of regiments among them. Still, within the borders of Crawford County decisive nationalists were far fewer than the followers of the Confederate cause, in comparison with her northern neighbor, and far less concerted in their action.

In Crawford, as elsewhere in the Southern States, the Brown Harper's Ferry raid seemed to be the brand that set the Southern cause aflame.

Comments of the Press.—The August issues of the *Press*† record the news of Abolition incendiaries in Texas and other surrounding States, and also gives evidence of a systematic Abolition party secret propaganda for arousing insurrection among the slaves in the various Southern States, a movement of which John

---

*At Cassville, Barry Co., Mo.
† August 10, 1860, *et al.*

79

CRAWFORD COUNTY, ARKANSAS - BIOGRAPHICAL AND HISTORICAL MEMOIRS
****

Brown was considered an intelligent member. Public meetings were held, one on September 15, 1860, at Van Buren, to organize a county police force to ferret out horse-thieves and incendiary or insurrectionary Abolitionists. S. M. Hays was chairman and I. B. Riley, secretary. The meeting chose 117 police for the county service, thirty-eight for Van Buren Township and four for Sheppard, with others varying between. A later number of the *Press* says: "We are requested to give notice that hereafter all slaves found at large after the 9 o'clock bell rings will be lodged in jail." * * * It also says:* "Let it be remembered * * that Yancy, an avowed disunionist and a bold traitor to the Union, is the father and the soul of the sectional party south. That the Democratic party is pledged to resist the Abolition doctrine of Congressional intervention in the States and Territories. That the whole power of the present corrupt and tyrannical administration has been wielded in vain, to destroy the great champion of popular sovereignity, Stephen A. Douglas, of Illinois. That Caleb Cushing, of Massachusetts, who presided over the Bolter's Convention, which nominated Breckenridge and Lane, voted, when in Congress, against the admission of Arkansas into the Union because she tolerated slavery. That the object of the Yancy–Breckenridge–Lane faction is to 'fire the Southern heart, instruct the Southern mind, and at the proper moment, by one organized, concerted action, to precipitate the cotton States into a revolution.' " The *Press* was the leading Douglas organ of Northwest Arkansas. On October 15, 1860, by order of Col. J. T. Humphrey, the Fifth Arkansas Militia met and drilled at Van Buren, and often thereafter. It comprised about 1,000 men.

The *Press* says†: "From our telegraph reports, which are quite full, it is certain that Abraham Lincoln, the 'rail-splitter,' is elected President for the next four years, from the 4th of March.

"With both houses of Congress opposed to him, as they are, by large majorities, we do not see, for the life of us, how he can carry out his Abolition doctrines, if he is so disposed. Give him a trial, and then, if his administration is so obnoxious that we can

---

* August 10, 1860, *et al.*
† November 9, 1860.

not honorably live under it, let us cast it off. Let us ponder well before we give up a good government, without the certainty of bettering ourselves. Examine well this subject of a Southern Confederacy, fellow citizens—carefully and practically, without prejudice, and we are willing to abide by your decision."

The Clarksville Conference, in session at Van Buren, in November, 1860, " *Resolved*, That we appoint the Friday before Christmas to be observed by our church throughout the bounds of our Conference as a day of fasting and special prayer to Almighty God for the preservation of our political Union." Rev. R. W. Hammet, P. E., Rev. G. A. Schaefer, of Van Buren, and Rev. P. Basham, of Van Buren Circuit, were among the prominent members.

" Let Arkansas, as well as every other Southern State, make preparations for any event that may transpire—let us be prepared for any and every emergency. Common prudence should dictate such a course. We cannot say what Northern fanaticism and Southern exasperation combined may bring about—but let us as a State be prepared—willing to concede, for the sake of and preservation of the Union, all that we can in honor do—but submitting to nothing beyond. Again, then, we say, let us be 'prudent, firm and conservative,' " says the *Press*.*

The following editorial in the *Press*, so well represents the general public pulse at the close of 1860 that it is given entire:

ARKANSAS AND HER DUTY.†

We are in the midst of a time, and are surrounded by events, which will form one of the most important and interesting passages in future history ever submitted to the eyes of an earnest and inquiring public. They will then see the bearings of events more clearly than we possibly can; their eyes will be freed from the vail of prejudice and passion; their reason unclouded by excitement or fanaticism. We are preparing our cause for the bar of the future. They must try us; they must acquit or condemn us. We are entrusted by our fathers with institutions and privileges attaching thereto, hallowed by events long passed, made sacred by their blood and treasure, purchased at the expense of untold sorrow, trial and privation. Our fidelity to this trust is about to be tried. The events which have occurred in the last few days speak too plainly of the trouble which is in the great womb of the future, soon to be cast upon us. At such a time as the present it is worse than useless for men to speculate—worse than useless for us to descant in long essays, or argue in wordy speeches,

---

*November 23, 1860.
† *V. B. Press*, November 23, 1860.

81

CRAWFORD COUNTY, ARKANSAS - BIOGRAPHICAL AND HISTORICAL MEMOIRS
****

upon the abstract right of a State to secede from the Union. It is wholly immaterial to us now which is right—the doctrine announced by Calhoun and Haynes in their great speeches on the floor of Congress upon the legitimate significance of the word *compact*, or the opinion promulgated by the immortal Webster in his reply. We have to deal with abstractions no longer. As in all resolutions, abtractions are lost, and the mind naturally and necessarily seeks the tangible, the practical, the expedient. The abstract moral or legal right of our State to secede from the Union is gone for the present, and we can deal only with the other division of the question, namely, the practical. We cannot wait to solve the first part of the question, for one or two States *have* put in practice the thing itself, call it secession or revolution, names cannot effect the truth. The only question now in issue is, would it be expedient for Arkansas to follow in the wake of the other States that have taken it upon themselves to withdraw from the compact heretofore entered into by these sovereign States? Shall we assist in demolishing the government which is the wonder of the world—the pride of Americans? Shall we, too, retrace the bloody steps of our revolutionary heroes? Shall we undo all that a wisdom little short of inspiration has done for us, and emerge into the dark clouds of an anarchy too terrible to be even contemplated without a shudder of horror? Shall we assist in demonstrating to the civilized world that Republicanism is a whim, a folly, which only has a being in the brains of speculative politicians? Shall self-government and free liberal institutions prove a disgraceful failure? And shall we assist in bringing about the failure? These are the questions which press themselves home upon us now. And *now* they *must* be answered—their solution must be given quickly. The election of Mr. Lincoln has passed from doubt into certainty, and we behold in him a President elected by only one character of States. The free (?) States alone have had a voice in his election; but he goes into the presidential chair checkmated; he is a naught, powerless, impotent. So long as he fulfills the constitutional obligations of the oath he will take, all will be well enough, but the moment he attempts to overstep them he becomes justly ridiculous, and exhibits himself to a mocking people as an impotent puppet clothed in the robes of royalty. It is said that Mr. Lincoln intends to promulgate his line of policy, and make known the members of his future cabinet as soon as he is certain of his election, and especially intends to announce his views upon the slavery question. If this be true let us hear him, for the presumption is, and to my mind it is a violent one, that he intends to modify his hitherto expressed sentiments on that important subject, so that they may fully comport with the views entertained by the Southern people, and with the Constitution; if not, then why issue any address at all, for we certainly are fully advised as to the opinions he has heretofore held. Now if he chooses to retract his former opinions on this subject, and this is the apple of discord, and thereby turns a cold shoulder upon his radical and insane brethren, and shows every disposition to abide by the Constitution, especially the Fugitive Slave clause, and by the laws already enacted, we certainly cannot object to his going on, and to giving him a fair chance, particularly when disunion and anarchy are the alternatives. The most sensible opinion certainly is that he cannot, at all events, maintain himself in the presidential chair six months unless he does abide by the Constitution. And if he does so abide, then he will plant seeds of undying contention in the bosom of his party, and these, co-operating with the innate elements of destruction, will soon entirely destroy the Republican party. And so unblushingly corrupt is the party, that when it does go, no other party of a

82

CRAWFORD COUNTY, ARKANSAS - BIOGRAPHICAL AND HISTORICAL MEMOIRS
****

similar character can rise upon its ruins. All these things being true, would it not be better for Arkansas to keep perfectly cool, and not allow herself to be hastened on to destruction and treason by scheming and designing men? Let her citizens reflect upon the condition in which she will place herself by so mad a step as secession from the Union. Let the masses, the tax-paying masses, reflect that upon them and their property will fall the burdensome weight of supporting the new government, even if they succeed in forming one. They must pay taxes sufficient to keep the wheels of their government in motion—to keep up the post-office department—new and additional duties on imports, and more than likely be compelled to assist in maintaining a standing army, that instrument and companion of despotism, which will be able at any day to raise a military despot over them. These are the legitimate offshoots of revolution. There is talk of calling a convention.

If a call is to be made, let the people be on the lookout, and have their members in that convention who will express their sentiments. If they are unwilling to hazard a secession, let them elect men who are opposed to secession, and let the convention reflect the true sentiment of the people. Circumstances may become such as to force Arkansas to go with the Southern States or abolish slavery. If Alabama, Mississippi, Louisiana and Texas should secede, then, of course, but two paths are open to Arkansas. She will then be forced to secede, also, or abolish slavery. It is, of course, too great a pecuniary sacrifice for her to do the latter; she must adopt the former course. And in that case she will have nothing to regret. She will then have acted wisely by keeping quiet, and allowing the current of events to take their course, and when nothing else is left her, she will fall into the tide and become a creature of destiny, for the step once taken, events become greater than men, and we all are forced to trim our sails to suit the storm, and sail onward to safety or ruin. Let us do all our thinking before we get into the power of the political maelstrom, for we may rest assured but little opportunity will be afforded us to do so afterward.

" Garrison tells us," says the *Press*,* " he is in for ' *meddling with slavery everywhere, attacking it by night and by day, in season and out of season*,' in order to finally effect its overthrow; * * well knowing, also, that Abraham Lincoln is a perfect exponent of the party expressing such views, we should no longer doubt as to the expediency of immediate action." Commercial boycot on the North was recommended.

On January 5, 1861, a mass-meeting was held at the court-house in Van Buren. Henry Wilcox was made chairman, and John B. Ogden, secretary. A committee on resolutions were chosen, embracing Jesse Turner, Samuel Harrington, C. A. Carroll, Jacob Meadows, Josiah Harral, Robert Sutherland, Jesse Marshall, James Heard, Whitfield Bourne, Andrew Couch, Hiram Brodie, Thomas Walden and J. S. Dunham. After an eloquent

---

* December 21, 1860.

83

CRAWFORD COUNTY, ARKANSAS - BIOGRAPHICAL AND HISTORICAL MEMOIRS
****

address by Gen. Thomason, this committee reported the following resolutions:

Resolved, In view of the alarming crisis which is upon us, that the rights and institutions of the slave-holding States ought to be maintained and defended at every hazard, and to the last extremity.

Resolved, further, that we view the personal liberty bills of certain non-slave-holding States, passed for the purpose of defeating the fugitive slave law, not only as unfriendly in spirit, but as palpable infraction of the Federal Constitution, and gross violation of the plighted faith of these States, and that we insist on their speedy repeal, and a faithful execution of said law, as one of the conditions of fraternal relations between the slave-holding and non-slave-holding States of the Union.

Resolved, further, in view of impending dangers to our beloved country, that it is our ardent desire to preserve this Union, if it can be preserved consistently with the honor, rights and interests of the slave-holding States; and that, for the purpose of deliberation upon this momentous subject, we are in favor of a conference of all the slave-holding States, to be held at Nashville, at such a time as may be agreed upon, and if need be that a convention of all the States be held at such a time and place as may be agreed upon, in order that an effort be made to adjust and settle on a satisfactory basis all the disturbing controversies which have arisen between the slave-holding and non-slave-holding States.

Resolved, further, that in the event of a failure of the slave-holding States obtaining such guarantees of their rights in the Union as may be compatible with their honor and interests, that they then insist upon a fair and equitable division of the public property, including the common territory of the United States, they assuming their proportionate share of the public debt, and that, if this cannot be obtained, they separate from their northern confederates, not peaceably, but that they draw the sword and fight for their rights to the bitter end.

Resolved, further, that we are opposed to separate State action, and especially to the secession of Arkansas from the Federal Union, without co-operation with her sister States of the South.

Resolved, further, that in a spirit of conciliation, and in view of the calamities which, we believe, would attend a dissolution of the Union, we are willing that time should be given to the non-slave-holding States to retrace their steps, to repeal their unconstitutional laws, to depose their unprincipled leaders, and to give the South such satisfactory guarantees as will secure their rights and equalities in the Union.

Resolved, further, that while we deplore the election of Abraham Lincoln to the presidency, upon a purely sectional issue, and upon the ground of his hostility to Southern institutions, as an event justly calculated to excite our alarm, and a sufficient cause to warrant us in demanding additional guarantees for the protection of our rights and equality in the Union, yet we unhesitatingly declare that, in our opinion, it is not in itself a sufficient cause for the dissolution of the Union.

Resolved, further, that we heartily tender the thanks of this meeting to Messrs. Crittenden, Butler, Bigler, Rust and others for their patriotic and unwearied efforts in Congress to heal the unhappy dissensions which have arisen between the North and the South, and to preserve our Federal Union consistently with the rights and honor of all the States.

Resolved, further, that we are in favor of a State convention, to be held at an early day, with power to appoint delegates to a Southern conference or convention, with such other powers as legitimately belong to such a convention.

William Walker then offered resolutions recommending an increase in *ad valorem* tax to 45 cents on $100, to provide for State defenses. C. A. Carroll offered a minority report of a more radical tone, but it was not adopted. Isaiah Vinsant offered resolutions commendatory of Hon. Albert Rust.

Believing the conflict to be probable, local State companies were organized forthwith. In January, 1861, the Van Buren Frontier Guard was organized, with the following officers: Captain, H. Thomas Brown; first lieutenant, J. P. King; second lieutenant, Alex Lacy; third lieutenant, Granville Wilcox—from among the flower of Van Buren chivalry. The following month Minie rifles were shipped to them from Little Rock.

Little Rock Convention.—Then came the Little Rock convention, that pivotal point in the history of Arkansas. Public expression was not uncertain as to the desire of the people to have the proceedings of this body passed upon, finally, by popular ballot. Senator R. W. Johnson's and T. C. Hindman's "Address to the People of Arkansas" was published, in which they were urged to join the confederacy. A "Private Column" in the *Press*, controlled by D. C. Williams, of Van Buren, was a standing pathetic plea for moderation and reconciliation; it also urged the people to vote for no delegate who would not vote to refer to the people. The Hon. Jesse Turner and Henry Wilcox, Esq., the most prominent candidates, were requested to express their intention publicly; whereupon Judge Turner appeared in the *Press* of February 8, 1861, saying: "Denying, as I do, the constitutional right of a State to secede from the Union, and utterly denying that any adequate cause exists, justifying a resort to the extreme and original right of revolution, I should the more earnestly insist on submitting the ordinance to a direct vote of the people, before the same shall become final." He also speaks thus of the Union, saying: "It may endure for ages and ages yet to come, blessing and blessed of all our race."

In the same issue Mr. Wilcox said: "Unless some apparent injury might result to the interests of Arkansas by delay, I shall vote on a resolution to refer (to the people) in the affirmative." The election followed with no unusual incidents; and the *Press* announced the results exultantly in the issue of February 22d: "The People 10 to 1 for the Stars and Stripes!!! Glorious victory! Western Arkansas all right for the Union. Crawford County 740 majority for the Union candidates." The Hons. Jesse Turner and Hugh F. Thomason were the Union candidates.

Volunteers.—Meanwhile other events were happening. The Independent Light Horse Guards were organized in Richland Township and officered as follows: Captain, P. Perkins; first lieutenant, P. H. Hoyle; second lieutenant, John Ross; third lieutenant, J. Stevenson. The feeling seemed to be: "Union as long as we can, then Arkansas for herself." On Washington's birthday anniversary happened an almost pathetic incident, that in the light of succeeding events made the action of both Crawford County and the National Government seem paradoxical. It was a public mass-meeting held at the court-house in Van Buren, memorializing the United States Secretary of War *not* to withdraw troops from the Fort Smith garrison. It was signed by John B. Ogden, chairman, and William Whitfield, secretary. In March Capt. Jasper Pevyhouse organized a cavalry company. Many of these companies were organized with no particular purpose, except to be prepared for any emergency. It was the withdrawal of the Fort Smith garrison that precipitated the action of Crawford County in taking up arms for protection, and on April 20 the secessionist, Hon. R. W. Johnson, spoke at Van Buren, and for the first time a Confederate flag was flaunted from a pole in the court-house square. This was followed on May 1 by the appearance of the *Press* with its editorial column adorned with the stars and bars. The Home Guards, a company of old men, was organized April 20, 1861, with the following officers: Captain, Davidson Dickson; first lieutenant, A. J. Ward; second lieutenant, R. S. Roberts; third lieutenant, J. T. White. An organization called the "Daughters of the South" was formed in April, with Mrs. A. J. Ward as president, Mrs. George Austin, vice-president, and Mrs. William Walker as secretary. The society did some noble work in supplying their soldiers with clothing and other necessaries. Capt. Charles A. Carroll's cavalry company was organized in May, with the following subordinate officers: first lieutenant, N. O. Davidson; second lieutenant, L. N. Hollis; third lieutenant, A. J. Hayes.

President Lincoln's inaugural address was received with most contradictory opinions; some thought it threw down the gauntlet, and some that it betokened no danger whatever. The convention of Little Rock at its first session chose Judge Turner as chairman of the committee on Federal relations, and the well-known result of that session, the vote of thirty-nine to thirty-five against secession, was hailed at Van Buren with a salute of thirty-nine guns, and flags innumerable, and a demonstration and serenade was tendered Judge Turner on his return. The May session followed, and events had crowded in thick and fast; during the February session, everything was resting on a pivot; during the May session, secession was sweeping the South, and the tide seemed to sweep men off their feet; the convention tale has been told; the *Press* of May 15, 1861, says: "One of the delegates from this county writes that 'the scene at the capitol was solemn and impressive—some rejoiced, while others wept—to me it was the saddest hour of my life, and yet a stern necessity demanded my vote for revolution.'" Gen. Hugh F. Thomason was chosen by the convention as a delegate to the Montgomery Confederate Congress. The die was cast.

First Troops.—Capt. Carroll's cavalry started for the frontier May 25, and Capt. H. Thomas Brown's "Van Buren Frontier Guards" were tendered a touching farewell at the court-house by the spirited mothers, sisters and maidens of its members. Other organizations followed fast. Brig.-Gen. N. B. Pearce took charge of the western division May 16. During the month Capt. James M. Stewart organized the Crawford Artillery Company, and Col. John T. Humphreys organized a company of riflemen, with the following subordinate officers: First lieutenant, Dupee Sadler; second lieutenant, W. R. Turner, and third lieutenant, William Rosson. Capt. Joel H. Foster's company was fitted out with complete suits by a few ladies and gentlemen, and Dr. Colburn presented each with a New Testament.

"We venture to say," reads a *Press* editorial,* "that no county of the same population as Crawford (being in territory one of the smallest in the State) has turned out so many volunteers for the war as ours. We now have four companies in camp, and one, the 'Crawford Artillery,' awaiting orders to march, viz.: Capt. C. A. Carroll's company of mounted riflemen, the 'Pope Walker Guards,' numbering eighty-four rank and file, well mounted, armed with Sharp's rifles and sword-bayonets— a most effective weapon. This company is made up of the best young men of the county, who have been on horseback from their youth up, and well trained in the use of arms. 'The Van Buren Guards,' Capt. H. Thomas Brown, numbering about eighty, composed mostly of young men of this city, armed with Minie muskets, is probably the best drilled company in the State. Their ranks are composed of the very *elite* of the city—'gentlemen all'—and one to be depended on in all situations in which they may be placed. The above two companies are now in camp in Benton County. Capt. P. Perkins' company of cavalry, numbering about sixty-five members, armed with sabres and pistols. This is a stalwart company of horsemen, now stationed at Fort Smith, and should they be so fortunate as to get into action with the enemy will give a good account of themselves. Capt. J. H. Foster's company of infantry, numbering sixty-four members, armed with good muskets, which is about as good a weapon as can be used. This is a good company, and from their gallant captain down are itching for a fight; they are stationed for the present at Fort Smith, but will soon, no doubt, be under marching orders for the Kansas and Missouri line. Last, but not least, Capt. J. M. Stewart's company, the 'Crawford Artillery,' but recently organized, is now awaiting marching orders. They have two pieces of the celebrated 'Bragg's battery;' and all who know the men of whom this company is composed, know the cry with them will be 'a little more grape, Capt. Stewart,' should they come into action. From their captain down to the lowest in ranks—if there are any lowest—they are warriors all."

Other Companies.—The Van Buren Frontier Guards, at the first organization, were officered as follows: Captain, H. Thomas

*June 5, 1861.

Brown; first lieutenant, James P. King; second lieutenant, Alex. H. Lacy; third lieutenant, Granville Wilcox; orderly-sergeant, Samuel Martin; second sergeant, John W. Wallace; third sergeant, Thomas J. Allen; fourth sergeant, J. Neal; fifth sergeant, Madison Shannon; first corporal, James Whitfield; second corporal, J. H. Hill; third corporal, B. Frank Hinkle; fourth corporal, Eli D. Oliver; fifty-six privates. The Van Buren Brass Band were the musicians for the company.

The Crawford Artillery had the following officers: Captain, James M. Stewart; first lieutenant, Fenton Sanger; second lieutenant, R. M. Bean; third lieutenant, John Winfrey, and orderly, Isaac Keller.

The assumption of command of Confederate forces by Brig.-Gen. Ben McCulloch gave great confidence to the forces already organized as State forces, and inspired a large amount of recruiting. His staff was as follows: Capt. James McIntosh, adjutant general; Lieut. J. W. Lubbeck, aid-de-camp (in Texas); Lieut. Hamilton Pike, volunteer aid; Lieut. Frank W. Armstrong, volunteer aid; Lieut. Ben Johnson, volunteer aid; Maj. George W. Clarke, brigade quartermaster; Maj. W. M. Montgomery, field quartermaster; Surgeon J. Winchester Breedlove, medical director.

In regard to the simultaneous calls of Gov. Rector for State troops, and Gen. McCulloch for Confederate troops, the *Press* said: " We fear it will be some time before the ten regiments under this arrangement will be made up, all in this part of the country preferring to respond to the call of Gen. McCulloch."

Meanwhile Thomas J. Davidson was elected delegate to the Confederate Provisional Congress, *vice* Gen. Hugh F. Thomason, resigned.

Gen. McCulloch's promptness soon opened the conflict. The Crawford Guards took charge of the Fort Smith garrison in July. The various companies were organized into regiments, among which were the Arkansas Volunteers, colonel, T. J. Churchill; lieutenant colonel, C. H. Matlock, and major, James Harper. The Third Arkansas Regiment was officered as follows: Colonel, Gratiot; lieutenant-colonel, Province; major, Ward; adjutant, Granville Wilcox; surgeon, W. C. Smith; commissary, Elias B.

Moore; sergeant-major, D. W. Moore; wagon-master, B. F. Engles; forage-master, A. J. Gross.

The Federals in South and Southwest Missouri were the objective point. The first action in which Crawford County participated was a successful attack on Neosho, Mo. Success followed success, but as in many other, all other, sections of the whole domain of the United States there were those who thought a soldier's life was parade only, and the result was the following in the July 17 issue of the *Press:* "$20 Reward! Stop the Deserter!"

The Action at Oak Hill.—McCulloch was encamped at Pea Ridge in July, and on August 12 the famous action at Oak Hill occurred. Col. J. R. Gratiot's captains were as follows: Company A, Capt. J. H. Sparks; Company B, Capt. Hart; Company C, Capt. Bell; Company E, Capt. Griffith; Company F, Capt. Corcoran; Company G, Capt. Brown; and Company G's casualties: Killed, Capt. H. Thomas Brown, D. B. Carr, James Adkins; wounded, J. A. Clarke, J. Neal, H. Marean, G. R. Clarke, J. H. Deshoso, T. Davis, J. L. Whitfield, J. Wallace and R. Howard. Capt. King's and Capt. Buchanan's companies were there, and that of Capt. James M. Stewart, armed as infantry, the latter's casualties being as follows: Killed, M. West Vaughan; wounded, W. T. Vincent, L. Graf, W. Coleman, F. E. Enlow, R. Lawless, S. Montgomery, James King, Lieut. F. M. Sanger and J. M. Clem. Capt. Woodruff's artillery was also with this regiment. The total casualties were as follows: Killed, twenty-six; wounded, eighty-four, and missing, one.

In Col. De Rosey Carroll's Second Regiment of Cavalry were Capt. C. A. Carroll's company, from which Private Bush was missing after the fight; Capt. Lewis' company and Capt. Armstrong's company; in Capt. P. Perkins' company P. B. Wells, B. F. Walker and W. I. Spivey were wounded; the companies of Captains McKissick, Walker, Parks and Withers were also a part of the regiment. The total casualities of the regiment were: Killed, 5; wounded 17; and missing, 2. Capt. Perkins' company secured as a trophy the hat of the brave Gen. Lyons, who fell on that field.

Says the *Press:* "Monday (September 2, 1861) was a grand

day for Van Buren.   Saturday evening our citizens were notified by telegraph that the remnants of two companies, the Frontier Guards, Capt. King, and Crawford Artillery, Capt. Stewart, would arrive at home on Monday morning.   The young ladies, to the number of twenty-five or thirty, were astir at sunrise and in their saddles, and proceeded some four miles to meet them, and escort them to town.   At the hill, just as they came into town, they were met by the Home Guards, who escorted them all amid the firing of artillery, waving of handkerchiefs, cheers, etc., to the Planters' Hotel, where a collation was prepared for them." Capt. Carroll's company was similarly received on Tuesday, and the funeral of D. B. Carr was duly solemnized.

On September 18, 1861, Henry Wilcox was chairman and John B. Ogden, Sr., secretary, of a meeting called to organize a county committee to furnish soldiers with supplies, especially clothing. Messrs. Ward, Austin, Lynch, Woolsey, Matlock, Stewart, Harper, Simcoe, Wright, Sheppard, Jones, Sangster, Willey, Gregg, Oliver, Heard, Morris, Howell and Winters were chosen to act in their respective townships—two in each, excepting Van Buren Township, which required three.

New Calls for Troops.—The marked successes of the troops seems to have led many of the Crawford companies—like others—to virtually disband after the results of Oak Hill; and for a time they seemed to "rest on their oars." On September 25, however, Gens. McCulloch, Hindman and Pearce simultaneously called for 3,000 men for twelve months; and Crawford began again.   Capt. Dr. M. O. Davidson enlisted the "Crawford County Rangers" in September; Capt. J. T. Barlow organized the "Van Buren Rifles" in October, with the following officers: First lieutenant, Martin Simon; second lieutenant, S. Deshoso; third lieutenant, James Spooner.   The papers teemed with advertisements for army supplies.   The State troops of Arkansas were turned over to the Confederate government in November, and the first year closed with the armies in winter quarters. Brig.-Gen. N. B. Burrows became commander of the Van Buren post, which was the headquarters of the Third Brigade.   J. B. Luce, became receiver under the "Sequestration Act," and assumed the duties of his office in November of 1861.   Gen. McCulloch's staff, in charge of Col. McIntosh, made headquarters at Van Buren for a time.

With the abandonment of the publication of the only paper in Crawford County in the early part of 1862, and the meager reliable data of Confederate operations to be obtained, the succeeding events of the conflict, as far as Crawford county was concerned, are very uncertain.

The events of 1862 in Crawford that led up to the battle of Prairie Grove on the 7th of December, were born of that confidence gained in previous successes on the Confederate side, little shaken by the death of McCulloch at Pea Ridge and of less timidity among the few Federal followers. Gen. Hindman's famous "orders No. 17" appeared in June, and the bushwhacking began. Independent squads and companies began their conscription; every organization that could be was worked into the Confederate army, and the more determined Unionists among the mountains secretly stole away to the Federal pickets in Missouri and Kansas. The territory of Crawford was, of course, under the post at Fort Smith, although local commanders of a subordinate rank were in charge at Van Buren. Gen. Burrows was succeeded by Col. Monroe; and Col. Wallace and Col. Carroll were also among the commanders of the Van Buren post. Gov. Marmaduke and Gen. Price were among the number, also. S. F. Cottrell was provost-marshal for a time. All business was directed to carrying on the war; the male population of Crawford County were nearly all going or gone to active service; women and children were left and they, too, were supporting and taking care of themselves and were preparing necessaries in clothing for the fathers and brothers and husbands in the camp; some were even tearing up their carpets in after days for blankets to ship to the camp; other maidens whipped their steeds across the mountains with secret dispatches of importance. "The Yanks are coming!" was a startling exclamation.

Battle of Prairie Grove—Then came the fiercely-fought action at Prairie Grove on December 7, 1862, elsewhere graphically described in this volume by Col. Pettigrew. No regiments were organized in Crawford County, but the companies organized there were placed in the various noted regiments and battalions like the Thirty-fourth Arkansas under Col. Brooks, and the Federal First

Arkansas Cavalry. The well-known retreat of Gen. Hindman during the night after the battle was followed up by Gen. Blount and the gallant Herron, and the armies descended the Boston Mountain, and, passing over Crawford and through Van Buren, the former crossed the river. The waters of the Arkansas seemed to raise fears in the minds of both the opposing commanders, and after Gen. Hindman had shelled the town awhile and battered its walls somewhat, and Gen. Blount's batteries on the cliff had belched forth at an imaginary foe, in the words of Judge Ogden, of Van Buren: "The two —— fools run from each other." Of course almost every able-bodied male Confederate in Crawford County kept to the Confederate lines, and Crawford County was in the hands of the Federals. Gen. Blount's forces soon returned, however, and sacked the county.

Sacking the County.—To realize what that means the fact must be recalled that Van Buren had been the wealthy commercial center of Northwestern Arkansas during the previous decade, as Fayetteville had been the educational center; and Van Buren was, in wealth, the flower of this region. Houses of wealthy citizens were ransacked for silver-ware, jewelry, gold; churches were rifled of their chalice; the merchants' shelves were made bare, and their contents sometimes destroyed; slaves were told that they had made their master's wealth, "You have been proclaimed free; take all you can get and go North!" and many of them did. It might be mentioned that of the large number who followed this advice, and went to Kansas, Missouri, and other States, but few ever returned, the present negro population of Crawford County being an immigration chiefly from the south and southwest. Stock was nearly all run out of the county; furniture demolished and sometimes carried off; many fences torn down and buildings burned; probably not a house within the limits of Crawford County but was at some period of the war rifled more or less—mostly more. The Unionists' homes were rifled by the Confederates and the Southern homes wrecked by the Federals, and often no distinctions were made. It was unsafe to reside without the corporate limits of Van Buren, and that city became a great camp of destitution; home-made stuffs became necessary; and the books of the city miller, H. C. Hayman, show page after page of flour

93

CRAWFORD COUNTY, ARKANSAS - BIOGRAPHICAL AND HISTORICAL MEMOIRS
****

orders to the destitute, so lately in affluence. The forests and fields again became the homes of deer and other wild animals; no schools, churches, courts, mails, newspapers; nothing but stern hardihood, fear and anxiety, and scarcely the bare necessaries of life. Let succeeding generations dwell on such pictures, and wars will have less fascination for their hot blood.

This was not by any means wholly the result of Gen. Blount's raid, but occurred during the whole period of the war. In the Federal occupation succeeding the arrival of Gen. Blount, Van Buren was a post, and was commanded by Lieut.-Col. Wheeler, Maj. E. D. Ham and Col. Thomas Bowen. When the latter took charge the court-house was fortified, and pickets were placed just beyond the city limits. The colonel was not unsusceptible to the romance of war, and his predilections in that line led to his rashly following cupid beyond the safety of the pickets alone; a squad of "Johnny rebs" under Capt. Wright, now of Chester, one day surprised the "Fed" colonel, and carried him off and relieved him of his valuable horse and some personal effects. He was soon released, however, on a parole, whose validity was afterward questioned. The provost-marshal, Col. Johnson's office was the rooms now Dr. Bourland's office. A characteristic incident of the first "Fed" general in command may not be inopportune, since it illustrates the "bluntness" of that general. A Mr. Robinson, of Van Buren, who, before the evacuation of Fort Smith, had been a vigorous Unionist, was arrested by Gen. Blount, who had been informed that he was a prominent rebel. Mr. Robinson, wishing to prove his unionism, requested that Judge Turner might witness the fact; the Judge came, and, wishing to aid his friend, added to the confirmation asked for, " and General, this gentleman is also from Massachusetts !" Thereupon the profane old commander grew furious and exclaimed, "Some of the d——st rascals I ever saw came from Massachusetts!" Gen. Blount was from Maine. Here might follow a reference to a historic old Van Buren building, and to the picturesque situation of two important personages of Crawford County. It will be remembered that the old building now used by Judge Jesse Turner and his son is one of the oldest structures in Van Buren, and has been occupied by the venerable judge for about a half-century. The building, a low long frame, presenting its side to the street, has the judge's office in the west end, and another office in the east end; this was occupied by Henry Wilcox and his son, both of whom, it will be remembered, were decided secessionists; when to this is recalled the Unionism of Judge Turner, and their rivalry as candidates for the famous Little Rock convention, the situation is interesting.

No battles were fought on the soil of Crawford County; a few slight skirmishes and considerable bushwhacking, with a great deal of purely bandit villainy, was all that occurred, beside the Federal raids. Lieut.-Col. Steward once came down on a raid from Fayetteville to secure a lot of cotton supposed to be stored along the river; on this raid he did that unexplainable deed, the destruction of court records and papers. Five regiments of Confederate cavalry wintered in Crawford County during the winter of 1862 and part of 1863.

Summary of Troops.—The number of Crawford County men in both armies is variously estimated; Gen. H. F. Thomason however, places the Confederate representation at about 1,000 men, and Capt. William Bowlin, of Van Buren, thinks the Federal soldiers of the county ranged between 250 and 300.

The Federal troops were distributed somewhat as follows: First Arkansas Cavalry—Company A, 15; Company B, 5; Company C, 7; Company D, 28; Company E, 4; Company F, 6; Company G, 4; Company I, 4; Company K, 2; Company L, 5; Company M, 5. Second Arkansas Cavalry: Company A, 7; Company E, 7; Company F, 3; Company G, 24, having among its officers Chastain, Meadors, Rodgers and Hatley; Company H, 8; Company K, 3; Company L, 62, Capt. William Bowlin, whose other Crawford County subordinates were Second Lieut. Alvin Smith, First Sergt. John A. Davis, Quartermaster-Sergt. John Q. West, Commissary-Sergt. Benjamin Hargraves, Sergt. Charles Pense, Sergt. W. H. Bushong, Sergt. Lewis Simpson. The First Arkanas Infantry, Company I, 18, and Company K, 5. The Second Arkansas Infantry, Company F, 5, including officers London and Basham; Company G, 2; Company H, 4, and Company I, 1. Battery A, First Arkansas Light Artillery (Stark's battery), 14, including officers Alexander Thompson and Richard Dewitt. Those in the regiments of other States are not known.

The distribution of the Confederate troops of the county have been largely given in this chapter. Capt. John Ross' company of cavalry in Col. Clarkson's regiment was organized as late as 1863, so also was that of Capt. B. F. Winfrey. Capt. J. C. Wright organized Company E, of the Thirty-fourth Arkansas at Sheppard Springs; its forty-two men were officered as follows: First lieutenant, Wesley Fellows; second lieutenant, Elbert Peters; third lieutenant, Joseph Neally, succeeded by M. Vaught. The First Arkansas Mounted Infantry was officered during its career as follows: Colonels, C. A. Carroll, Rector, L. L. Thompson and A. Gordon; lieutenant-colonels, Armstrong, L. Thompson, Andrew Gordon and another; majors, Frear, L. L. Thompson, H. McConnell, Faith and Robert Wilson; captains (Company C), C. A. Carroll and J. O. Sadler; first lieutenants, J. O. Sadler, Robert Wilson and J. T. Perry; second lieutenants, Robert Wilson and J. T. Perry; third lieutenants, J. T. Perry, Jones Clark.

EDUCATION.

In educational affairs Crawford County has always taken great interest, but the excellent institutions of her sister county on the north have made the establishment of large institutions within her own territory largely unnecessary. The Far West Seminary, Cane Hill College, Ozark Institute, Miss Sawyer's school, Arkansas College, and the University have educated many of the leading men and women of Crawford County, and made no demand for schools at home much above the grammar grades, barring one attempt on the part of the Wallaces.

Private schools had for years a great hold on the minds of Crawford County, and a large and somewhat aristocratic sentiment continued for some time to delay the progress of free schools; in this respect it differed from Franklin County, where the resistance came largely from the poorest classes. The question as to when free schools were established in Arkansas is here referred to a tracing out of her school acts in connection with the history of Benton County.

First Schools.—According to the best information obtainable a Dr. Powers taught the first school in Crawford County at Van Buren, although as early as 1838 or 1839 a regular school was held on Section 36, Township 10, Range 30, by a Mr. Smith, who was succeeded by a Dr. Meyers. This was a log house, and the attendance numbered about thirty pupils. It would seem probable that the first school might have been at Van Buren, however. There were no doubt many children taught in private houses in ways that would hardly have been termed a school. Dr. E. D. Powers also taught in a private house.

Academies, Seminaries, Institutes, etc.—In March, 1842, Dr. Powers and Dr. J. S. Davis opened the Van Buren Academy, which continued a few sessions. In August, 1843, the Van Buren Seminary was opened by Rev. Daniel McManus and Thomas McKinney, and continued for some sessions. The activity of the Far West Seminary and Miss Sophia Sawyer's school at Fayetteville drew off the youth of the county largely to them during the latter part of " the forties." Between Van Buren and Fort Smith, and in Crawford, Rev. C. C. Townsend and his wife opened Prairie Female Seminary in September, 1846. This, like many others, run for a few sessions. In March, 1849, Rev. W. K. and Mrs. S. M. Marshall opened the Van Buren Female Institute, and were assisted by Miss M. C. Brigham; and in August of the same year a Dr. McCormick opened Van Buren Academy. Early in "the fifties" Mr. and Mrs. Wallace, of Van Buren, conceived the idea of founding an advanced school, which became known as the Wallace Collegiate Institute, and had a successful career during most of " the fifties " under the presidency of Rev. P. A. Moses, chiefly, and his assistants were R. W. Moses, and Rev. J. L. Denton. Mr. and Mrs. Wallace endowed the project quite liberally, but the oncoming war led to the loss of a large part of the funds, although much has been recovered and is even yet held in trust for an institution under Methodist Episcopal Church influences. None of these schools had more than ordinary school buildings, although the institute might have bloomed into a fine institution. It had an attendance of about sixty students. The Van Buren Female Academy was organized during this decade, also; among the trustees were President J. J. Green, Secretary D. C. Williams, Treasurer C. G. Scott, and J. A. Dibrell and W. F. England. The principal was a Miss Chapman; a Prof. De June assisted her in the musical phase of it. The attendance reached

97

CRAWFORD COUNTY, ARKANSAS - BIOGRAPHICAL AND HISTORICAL MEMOIRS
****

from eighty to ninety pupils. The faculty in 1859 was Principal I. N. Smith, A. M., Miss Ellen Phinney, Miss Julia A. Smalley, and Miss F. A. Chapman. During this year the Crawford County fund (Seminary) was $102.40. About this time Rev. P. A. Moses organized the Southern Literary Institute at White Sulphur Springs; its existence was not extended long. Prof. Smith became principal of the male division, and Mr. F. Leavenworth was at the head of the female division, in 1860. Rev. William Binet opened a school the same year; he was assisted by W. Salt.

Mr. C. K. Marshall, Jr., succeeded Rev. Moses in Wallace Institute, and he was succeeded by D. B. Carr. Miss Julia Smalley, assisted by Miss Mary J. Gross and Miss Laura Harrall, had charge of the female school, one session. The war closed the schools, and even in 1866 Van Buren had no schools for young ladies, and the first general school was held in the Methodist Episcopal Church by Principal W. J. Alexander and Mrs. A. S. Barbour. In May, 1867, the first colored school was opened, in the Episcopal Church, by a Miss Farrar. The old seminary building was a private enterprise, and had been used as barracks during the war, and it was unfit for school purposes. In February, 1867, the town council voted $150 for its repair, and the building was purchased. Mr. Alexander and Mrs. Barbour were assisted by Miss Sallie Alexander, during this year.

County Institute.—The first county institute under the act of 1868 was held at Van Buren during the first three days of September, 1869, under the direction of District Supt., E. E. Henderson. The enrollment embraced the following names: Henry Shibley, S. R. Cox, B. L. Orrick, L. C. Wright, E. C. Deffenbaugh, James Bryan, L. F. Bryan, W. J. Alexander, Mrs. Henrietta Hiner, Mrs. A. S. Barbour, Miss E. A. Handfield, Miss S. E. Alexander, B. H. Hale, M. C. Moore, E. Scott and W. A. Northcutt. Capt. J. O. Churchill assisted the superintendent.

Public Schools.—The first really public free school meeting held in Crawford County was that in December, 1868, at the Presbyterian Church, to consider the offer of the Peabody Educational Fund agent, Dr. Sears. This was an offer of $400 annually to a free school which should accommodate 100 pupils. The result was that it was accepted, and the high-school was held in the seminary building and the primary school in the Methodist Episcopal Church. The teachers of the previous year were retained. This brings us to the inauguration of the free-school system of 1868, when Col. S. F. Cooper was trustee of Van Buren Township. Col. Henderson, the first district superintendent, began pushing the organization of the new system, and in September, 1871, he held the Crawford County Teachers' Institute at the court-house in Van Buren, and was assisted by Mr. Harrison and Prof. Bruner, *et. al.* Prof. J. C. Helm was principal of the Van Buren schools in 1871, and in 1872 the enrollment of that school district was 248 white and 129 colored children. H. A. Pierce became district superintendent in 1873. The cost of two white schools and one colored, with six teachers in all, was for that year to Van Buren, $4,500, $800 of which had for each of two years been received from the Peabody Fund. A school was opened in Van Buren in September, 1876, under the title "Arkansas Normal and High-school." A district normal institute, sustained by the Peabody Fund, was held in Van Buren in March, 1880, and fifteen Crawford teachers were present. The Van Buren Male and Female High-school was opened October 18, 1880, by Principal A. J. McIntosh and his assistant, Prof. W D. C. Boteführ. The Peabody Normal Institute was held again in Van Buren, in August, 1882, by State Supt. J. L. Denton. It was held in the Presbyterian Church, and the attendance was seventy-nine enrolled. Prof. O. F. Russell (secretary), Prof. Burrows, Mrs. Phelps, Prof. Reynolds and Mr. Scott were among the workers. During this year four-fifths of the school districts voted the 5-mill tax. The following year County Supt. Lee Neal held an institute, at which thirty-eight were enrolled. The workers were J. Wheeler, I. P. Green, W. A. Dyer, E. Scott, Profs. R. I. Guinn, Bryan and Hardy. These institutes no doubt had a great effect in moulding the feeling regarding free schools in Van Buren, and the county judge, J. J. Burrows, was the successor of Prof. T. B. Logan as a Van Buren teacher, and Miss Maggie Wood was his assistant. One school might be mentioned here, the Western Union Telegraph College, in Edmondson's Hall, which Mr. H. H. Dill organized in 1883, and continued for a year. At the institute of November, 1884, Prof. Shinn, of Little Rock, was the instructor, and Judge Turner, Rev. W. A. Sample and Dr. Hynes were lecturers. Prof. E. B. Barnes opened the North Van Buren (Collinsville or Logtown) schools about this time. In 1885 during the construction of the present school building of Van Buren, four private schools were taught, by Misses Nannie Rea and Maggie Wood, Prof. Frank Colburn, Mrs. W. C. Bostick. A colored school was also in operation.

Van Buren School District (No. 4) was organized by election August 25, 1869. John Austin, David Williams, A. M. Calahan, B. J. Brown, C. F. Harvey, and J. O. Churchill were the first directors, and Miss Lucetta Harrall was the first teacher employed by them. The first assessment, made October 11, 1869, was 1 per cent. on $295,389—the taxable property of the county; $2,500 were to be given for teachers, and $453.89 for the building. The Van Buren Academy, before mentioned, was made public by paying the principal $60, and the assistant $50 per month. Miss Mattie L. Jarvis taught the colored school in 1870, and during the same year uniform text books were adopted. August 3, 1870, a draft for $800 was received of the Peabody agent, and male principals were employed. In 1875 the lack of funds caused the schools to be suspended. Among the principals of the schools of the city have been L. C. White, D. B. Hunnicutt, Miss M. E. McBride (two years), Lewis Bryan (two years), W. J. Alexander, T. B. Logan (two years), Frank L. Colburn and Prof. T. S. Cox. No public school was had in the winter of 1882–83 on account of the accumulation of fund for building. The Bostick House was used one year as a school-house. In 1884 T. M. McGee, George R. Wood, D. W. Moore, Alvis Smith, Frank Stewart and J. J. Warren were chosen directors, and they began the erection of the present commodious building. The old Wallace Institute grounds were first chosen, but the old seminary site was finally decided upon, and a tax of $7,000 to $10,000 was provided for. The structure was finished in 1885. It is a fine red brick of two stories with mansard roof, and is capable of extension on the east side, at the junction of Broad and Main Streets. The ample hall of the entrance shows large primary rooms to the right and left, and the stairs lead to the upper floor, at the north and south ends of which are the principal's room and the grammar school, respectively. Between these is a well-arranged recitation room, with all the advanced appurtenances of the modern school. The first teachers in the new public school were Prof. F. L. Colburn, Miss Maggie Wood, Mrs. Hattie Pernot, and Miss Rose Meyer. The principal of the colored school, J. B. Mack, was assisted by Mrs. M. A. Jones. "Rules and Regulations of the Van Buren Public Schools and the Course of Study," a pamphlet, was printed, and the school graded. On the resumption of control by Prof. Cox, in 1886, he began enforcing the grading with more vigor. Nine grades, with an attendance of about 400, was the condition of things in 1886, and in 1888 the first class of five graduated, fitted to enter the first year in the university. The attendance at present, 1888, is about 450, and active efforts are making toward a larger corps of teachers and more room, as many primary pupils are compelled to be turned away. The present teachers are principal, T. S. Cox; assistant principal, Miss Kate Findley; Mrs. Bessie Quesenberry, Miss Blanche Huffman, and Miss Doggett. Nine and a half to ten months are taught annually, and the class of 1889 will probably number twelve. The only change in the directors of 1885 is the substitution of F. R. McKibben and Jesse Turner, Jr., in the places of Messrs. Wood and Stewart, respectively. Prof. Cox placed samples of the school's work in the State Exposition at Little Rock, in 1887.

The last normal institute held in Van Buren was in August, 1887, under State Supt. W. E. Thompson, with Prof. T. S. Cox as instructor. About fifty were in attendance.

The Alma Schools originated in a log house about one and a quarter miles to the southeast, about 1870. The half-mill tax has been voted in the district for over seventeen years. The first director was A. M. McKinney, and B. P. Renfroe followed him for about nine years. Private schools have also been held more or less ever since the settlement of the county, and one institute was held here, in 1884, by Supt. Lee Neal. The second or present school building was erected, as has been mentioned in the settlement of Alma, before the district center was voted at Alma proper, and three teachers were employed. They enroll about

150 white pupils, and a colored school, conducted in a rented one-room frame house, has an attendance of about fifty, and was organized about 1876, after the entrance of the colored population following the completion of the Little Rock & Fort Smith Railway. Walter P. Brown and wife were the first teachers in the new district. Prof. P. McKay and Mrs. Fannie Echols had a daily attendance of from 100 to 120, in 1883. Prof. Carroll and Prof E. D. Cochran have since had charge of the schools. and had from one to three assistants. The corps of 1887–88 were Prof. Carroll, Miss May Carroll and Mrs. Webber.

The Chester Schools trace their beginnings to about 1844, when a log house was built at the mouth of Howard's Fork, by the citizens, for a summer school for children. John Crawford was the second teacher in that building, all his predecessors but one having taught in private houses. The citizens and the society of the Methodist Episcopal Church, South, at Pleasant Grove, built a union school and church there in 1866, and B. L. Orrick was the first teacher. In 1882 the Chester people petitioned for a new district, and a union school and Masonic hall was erected on the north side of the "Frisco Railway" tracks. Mrs. M. J. Stafford was the first teacher in the new building. The schools have so increased that the attendance warrants over two teachers, although but two are now employed.

Other Schools.—The schools of other places in the county are simply large district schools, and will be treated under the general school statistics of the county. Attempts have been made in a few cases, like that of Alexander Gooding and others at Sarah Grove, to form really graded schools, but none have won any noticeable standing. John Shannon was a pioneer teacher in the neighborhood of Dripping Springs, and among other veterans of early days who graced the school-room the county is proud to mention the noted *litterateur*, statesman, lawyer and soldier, Albert Pike.

Educational Statistics.—The earliest report obtainable showing the condition of the schools of the county is that ending June 30, 1881, but the reports from directors to their superior officers and to the State superintendent have been so unsatisfactory and incomplete that the following statistics do not tell as much as they should:

102

CRAWFORD COUNTY, ARKANSAS - BIOGRAPHICAL AND HISTORICAL MEMOIRS
****

For 1881 the white children numbered 4,505; colored, 481; total 4,986; previous year, 5,130; in orthography, 994; written arithmetic, 268; higher branches (above history) 19; whole number taught, 1,087; previous year, 2,605; male teachers, 25; female, 2; first grade, 12; second grade, 9; third grade, 6 whole salary paid, $9,777.44; previous year, $6,469.25; buildings erected during year, 5 (wooden); cost, $487; previously erected, 41; (40 wood, 1 brick); cost, $6,262 (five districts reported in 1881); total receipts, $18,952.48; total expenditures, $9,976.46; unexpended, $8,976.02.

In 1882, when probably four-fifths of the school districts voted a five-mill tax, " Flat Rock," the *nom de plume* of a teacher, writes: " The morning I began I found, in attempting to organize, that of the fifty students present I could form seventeen classes in reading, five in geography, six in grammar, and as many in arithmetic. Other studies were similar. Every book that had been used in the family since the boyhood days of their grandfathers was presented, and I soon had organized forty intelligent little classes, numbering from one to five in each class. Imagine, kind teacher, the perplexity of that moment! Labor for three teachers, and but one to perform it." The writer, a live teacher, soon solved the difficulty by securing uniform textbooks through the directors.

For 1882—White children, 5,226; colored, 462; total, 6,014; increase, 1,028; number districts, 64; number districts reporting, 24; white enrollment, 1,355; colored, 38; total, 1,393; average daily attendance, 321; number in orthography, 1,175; written arithmetic, 258; geography, 90; history, 20; higher branches, 1; white teachers, male, 36; female, 4; colored, 1; total, 41; average first grade salaries, male, $30.38; female, $34.33; second grade, male, $28.70; female, $24; third grade, male, $30.24; female, $30; number buildings erected during the year, 3 (wood); cost, $1,111; total (reported is meant), 11; value, $2,841; total receipts (including last year's balance), $19,745.07; total expenditures, $10,963.86; unexpended, $8,781.21. The county examiner was Mr. L. Neal.

For 1883—White children, 5,912; colored, 582; total, 6,494; increase, 480; districts, 68; number reporting, 32; white enroll-

103

CRAWFORD COUNTY, ARKANSAS - BIOGRAPHICAL AND HISTORICAL MEMOIRS
****

ment, 2,234; colored 129; total, 2,363; in orthography, 1,534; written arithmetic, 392; geography, 141; history, 45; higher branches, 26; male teachers, 45; females, 1; total, 46; average first grade salaries (for males), $37.85; females, $30; second grade, males, $32.22; number buildings erected during the year, 11 (wood); cost, $3,203.15; whole number in the county (reported), 31; value, $5,575.15; receipts, $16,402.50; expenditures, $5,274.07; unexpended, $11,130.43.

For 1884—White children, 6,052; colored, 645; total, 6,697; increase, 203; number of districts, 75; number reporting, 40; white enrollment, 2,820; colored, 147; total, 2.967; orthography, 1,856; written arithmetic, 603; geography, 296; history, 75; higher branches, 17; teachers, white males, 50; white females, 2; colored females, 5; total, 57; average first grade salaries for males, $37.65; females, $30; average second grade salaries for males, $28; females, $32.70; third grade, males, $27; number of buildings erected during the year, 8 (wood); cost, $3,093; whole number of buildings, 40 (wood); value, $9,298; receipts, $25,883.74; expenditures, $13,204.22; unexpended, $12,679.52. Mr. Lee Neal was county examiner.

For 1885—White children, 6,847; colored, 758; total, 7,605; increase, 908; number of districts, 78; number reporting enrollment, 56; white enrollment, 3,732; colored, 261; total, 3,993; in orthography, 2,664; written arithmetic, 717; geography, 322; history, 136; higher branches, 24; teachers, male, 75; females, 3; total, 78; average first grade salaries, males, $40; average third grade salaries, females, $22; number of buildings erected during the year, 5 (wood); cost, $1,259; whole number school-houses, 47 (wood); value, $1,314; receipts, $31,239.60; expenditures, $18,249.41; unexpended, $12,990.19.

For 1886—White children, 7,378; colored, 830; total, 8,207; increase, 602; number of districts, 83; number reporting, 53; white enrollment, 3,744; colored, 229; total, 3,973; in orthography, 3,316 written arithmetic, 945; geography, 390; history, 188; higher branches, 11 (other branches in proportion); teachers, males, 69; females, 5; total, 74; average first grade salaries, male, $45; female, $37.50; average second grade salaries, males, $32.50; female, $30; average third grade salaries, male, $27.50;

females, $20; number of buildings erected during the year, 16 (frame); cost, $3,409; whole number in the county reported, 39 (frame); value, $12,951; receipts, including balance from previous year, $30,252.19; expenditures, $21,161.84; unexpended, $9,090.35.

For 1888 the district enumeration is as follows: No. 1, 73; 2, 72; 3, 64; 4, 87; 5, 67; 6, 27; 7, 135; 8, 78; 9, 67; 10, 77; 11, 53; 12, 70; 13, 30; 14, 67; 15, 80; 16, 87; 17, 38; 18, 58; 19, 93; 20, 150; 21, 114; 22, 127; 23, 65; 24, 115; 25, 93; 26, 86; 27, 231; 28, 148; 29, 86; 30, 244; 31, 106; 32, 74; 33, 172; 34, 85; 35, 181; 36, 115; 37, 160; 38, 176; 39, 90; 40, 125; 41, 124; 42, 880; 43, 73; 44, 94; 45, 81; 46, 96; 47, 45; 48, 70; 49, 53; 50, 76; 51, 37; 52, 125; 53, 70; 54, 108; 55, 118; 56, 128; 57, 105; 58, 97; 59, 99; 60, 12; 61, 48; 62, 149; 63, 151; 64, 80; 65, 148; 66, 60; 67, 65; 68, 76; 69, 92; 70, 90; 71, 86; 72, 56; 73, 72; 74, 33; 75, 68; 76, 58; 77, 101; 78, 80; 79, 86; 80, 71; 81, 67; 82, 81; 83, 64; 84, 55; 85, 59; 86, 59; total, 8,612; white, male, 3,928; female, 3,743; colored, male, 479; female, 462. Mr. N. Turmon is county examiner.

CHURCHES AND KINDRED SOCIETIES.

Earliest Religious Observances.—The earliest known religious work in Crawford County was made by the Primitive Baptists in the region of Alma, and Rev. Moses Fisher was among the first preachers. This denomination was followed closely by the Cumberland Presbyterians from Cane Hill, who held services at the home of Daniel Pevyhouse (or Pevehouse), on Lee's Creek; this was probably in 1834 or 1835. It was but a year or so later that the Methodist Church representatives came in, and Rev. John Harrell was among the first of their ministers at Van Buren and on Frog Bayou. Following them, it is thought, were the followers of Alexander Campbell's ideas, of whom Rev. William Stirman was probably the first to begin aggressive work. This was done in the Bell school-house near Fine Spring (Tarrytown), about 1842, it is thought. He was followed by Revs. Johnson, Graham, Carrollton, Polly, Strickland and others. It is not known when the Missionary Baptists began work, and the Catholic and Episcopal Churches have been confined to Van Buren, as is given more fully

105

CRAWFORD COUNTY, ARKANSAS - BIOGRAPHICAL AND HISTORICAL MEMOIRS
****

elsewhere. The Presbyterians also began in Van Buren. The Protestant Methodists' initiative work began with the organization of that body. In 1847 the Methodists, Cumberlands and Christians had a union church and camp-meeting outfit on Cedar Creek, on land whose deed was made to the Methodist Church. The peace of the community was suddenly broken by the advent of a minister from Illinois, who told the community of the separation of the northern and southern branches of the church, and placed the matter before them to choose; twenty-five became adherents of the Methodist Episcopal Church, South, and twenty gave their allegiance to the northern branch, but the deed was gained by the Southern Church. It was then time for a camp-meeting, and each branch agreed to hold these meetings at the same place, but that the Southern branch was to begin first, which they did, continuing three weeks in camp. The Northern Church, seemingly irritated at their extended time, determined to excel, and continued for four weeks; this rivalry gained large accessions to both churches, it is said. The interest in Sabbath-schools has always been vigorous. There has been no collegiate center for the dissemination of denominational doctrines as there has been in Washington County. Accounts of various churches are given in the following pages.

The Cumberland Presbyterians.—Arkansas Presbytery of the Cumberland Presbyterian Church is treated more fully in the chapter on Washington County Churches. The complete list of congregations is as follows: Beersheba, Cincinnati, Cane Hill, Dripping Springs, Fayetteville, Lone Elm, Mount Vernon, Mount Comfort, Mount Pleasant, Mulberry, Ozark, Oak Ridge, Prairie, Rieff's Chapel, Southwest City (Mo.), White Oak, White River, West Fork, Wards, Salem, Mount Zion, Barker, Cove Creek, Rogers, Siloam Springs, Vineyard, Natural Dam, Van Buren, Main Fork, Mount Liberty, Salem Springs, Maysville, Bethel and Bentonville. Those in Crawford County are given as far as obtainable.

The Van Buren Cumberland Presbyterian Church is a member of Arkansas Presbytery. The society was organized December 31, 1882, by Rev. J. D. Boone, with Ben Decherd, H. C. and M. C. Miller, Dudley Bourn, L. A. Miller, M. S. Collins,

Delphia Harshaw and Mosetta Bourn among the original members. The society was under the pastoral charge of Rev. J. D. Boone but a few months, when he was succeeded by Rev. E. E. Morris. Bro. G. A. Henderson and Dr. F. R. Earle preached for them next, until in October, 1887, Rev. Buchanan assumed ministerial duties of the society. They have held services in the Presbyterian Church on alternate Sabbaths, but are taking steps at this writing (summer of 1888) toward building at an early date.

Dripping Springs Cumberland Presbyterian Church was organized July 11, 1840, by Rev. John Buchanan. The elders were I. Vinsant, Josiah Howell, G. M. Burris and John Shannon, and the members were W. Beach, G. Parish, J. Parish, Elizabeth Pevyhouse, Franklin Thrasher and Fata Thrasher, M. Harrall, E. R. Locke, M. Owens, Jackson Owens, J. W. Morgan, M. Butler, R. Storey, E. Reeder, Laura Copps, E. C. Batford, John Pevyhouse, Genevra Pevyhouse, Laura Killenberger, J. J. Williams, Eliza Williams, E. Block, I. Shannon, J. Shannon and Dorothy Davis. In 1841 a log building was erected, and the present frame structure was built in 1872 at a cost of $500. It was dedicated by Rev. F. R. Earle, of Cane Hill. The pastors since 1857 have been Revs. George Morrow, J. P. Russell, J. M. Brigan, P. Carnahan, Samuel Cox, John Hughes, G. Thompson, B. F. Fatten, J. W. Sullivan, F. Maloy, Allen Canada and J. T. Buchanan. The present membership is about forty persons, and the elders are A. Gooding, J. S. Matlock and B. F. Massey.

Cove Creek Cumberland Presbyterian Church has had a few scattering members, but have neither church nor pastor. About six or seven members have occasional services in the district school-house.

The Christian Church.—The Van Buren Christian Church has had a varied career, and little exact information can be gleaned concerning its history. The following letter, found in the biography of J. T. Johnson, a prominent convert of Alexander Campbell, speaks of early missionary work in Crawford County, and gives a clew to its organization:

107

CRAWFORD COUNTY, ARKANSAS - BIOGRAPHICAL AND HISTORICAL MEMOIRS
****

VAN BUREN, March 7, 1848, Tuesday Morning.

BELOVED BRO. CAMPBELL: I am here, in good health, about 1,500 miles from home, laboring in the good cause of the reformation. * * The success has been far beyond the expectations of the most sanguine. * * I reached here and labored a week. The result was twelve additions. * * I visited Fayetteville, fifty-two miles north, and labored twelve days with good success. * * I returned to Van Buren and visited Oakland—a fine population, ten miles from this place. * * I expect to start in the stage in the morning for The Rock. I had one baptism here on Lord's day. I expect to organize this church to-night. * * This is a great country. * *. J. T. JOHNSON.

The society seems not to have thrived. Services were held occasionally by the then Rev. Henry Shibley, and for a time Rev. Ezell, of Fort Smith, during "the fifties." After the close of the Civil War a few active members, among them being Mr. and Mrs. S. Wood, Mrs. H. C. Hayman, Elder William Murphy and wife, Dr. (now Elder) Stone, Thomas Murphy and wife, Mrs. Farrar, Gen. H. F. Thomason, Mr. Simmons and wife, Mr. Barnes and wife, and Mrs. Ribling, reorganized at the fair ground building. A year later they met in the old seminary, which was used until the erection of the high school building. In the summer of 1887 the society rented their present rooms, known as the Old Episcopal Church. The elders have held the services, with the exception of occasional services held by the present pastor, Rev. J. Q. West. Their membership is about thirty persons.

The Alma Christian Church was organized October 13, 1877, by Rev. George W. Owen. The first members and officers were Elders A. J. Moody and L. B. Byars, Deacon J. E. Smith and E. B. Hassett, Margaret E. Renfroe, Lucy Wright, Mary A. Smith, Nannie J. Byars, Nannie E. Reed and Mary Griffith. Rev. Owen was succeeded in the pastorate by Revs. A. G. Lucas, J. Q. West, J. T. Jones, B. W. Lauderdale, J. H. Hambleton, E. C. Gillespie, J. C. Mason, Morgan Morgan and Kirk Baxter, some of whom were only temporary evangelists. The society now has 111 members, but has so far been unable to build a house. They still use the old union church and school building.

Antioch Christian Church was organized in 1855, and was first known as the Flat Rock congregation. Among its members were G. J. Clark, Russell Allen, M. H. West, Mary A. West, J. G. Stevenson, Jane Stevenson, Louis Waddle, J. T. West, Susan

Stevenson, Elizabeth Stevenson, J. Q. West, Henry Shibley, W. H. H. Shibley, Ann Allen, Mary E. West, M. T. West, John S. Shibley, Henry Coleman, William J. Neal and wife and B. Neal. Their first building was a log one, plastered with stone and mud, and was erected about 1855. The present building is about 30x50 feet and cost about $600. Elder Stirman, Revs. M. J. Robinson, Henry Shibley, —— Polly, A. J. Moody, Eli Baker, J. W. Garrett and J. Q. West have been among the pastors. The membership now reaches about ninety persons.

Philadelphia Christian Church was organized by Rev. J. Q. West, assisted by J. F. Jones. They have a building about 20x36 feet, located in Jasper Township. The deacons are J. E. Slover and Noah Scott. They have about sixty members.

Cedar Grove Church was organized about twenty-five years ago by John West. They had a log building destroyed during the war, but they reorganized about 1866, and now have about seventy-five members, under the pastoral charge of Rev. J. Smalley. The frame building now used is about 24x36 feet, and cost about $600. In 1885 Rev. Marshall and H. C. Cradduck organized a Sunday-school, with a membership of about seventy-five; this has increased to 110. Lemuel Mullen is superintendent.

The Methodist Episcopal Church, South, held the fifty-first session of its annual Conference at Fayetteville, in November, 1887. The churches of this denomination in Crawford County are in the Clarksville District, under the presiding eldership of Rev. I. L. Burrow, ex-president of the Central Collegiate Institute, at Altus, in Franklin County.

Alma and Mulberry (Franklin County) were under charge of Rev. Frank Naylor; Dyer Circuit, Rev. H. A. Storey; Van Buren Station, Rev. D. J. Weems; Van Buren Circuit, Rev. W. D. Powell; Chester Circuit, Rev. J. D. Edwards, and Ozone Circuit by Rev. A. M. Belcher. In the whole district there are nineteen churches, valued at $20,130.

Van Buren Circuit (not including Van Buren) had three local preachers, 301 white members, five Sunday-schools enrolling 300 pupils.

Chester Circuit had 151 members; one church, valued at $230; one Sunday-school of seventy-seven members.

The Van Buren Methodist Episcopal Church, South, was organized about 1846, by Rev. J. J. Roberts. Some of the earliest members are as follows: P. A. Moses and wife, N. Colburn, S. M. Hays and wife, Miss Susan Hays, S. D. Daugherty and wife, Ellen Ward, Mary E. Ward, Susan Southmayd, Miss V. Tachett, Samuel Colburn, A. K. Foster, M. J. Foster, the Misses Harrell, Mrs. Wade Cottrell, Mrs. S. Hamlin, R. S. Roberts, William Mooney, Nancy Mooney, Eliza Mooney, Charles Heart, Mrs. E. Dickson, Mrs. M. A. Bearden, A. M. Callahan, Mrs. Kate Callahan, Mary Gillespie, J. Hattaway and wife, J. Whitfield, James Brown, Mrs. Kate Brown, Isaac Austin and Mary Austin. There was a considerable general revival in 1847. The old brick church was built in 1850, and during the Civil War was so much damaged in serving as a hospital, as to be considered unsafe. This was torn down in August, 1886, and the new church was begun during the following month. It was dedicated by Dr. John Matthews, of St. Louis, the corner-stone ceremonies being performed by the Masonic fraternity, and the address delivered by the editor of the *Southwestern Methodist*. The structure is a fine one of brick, and second to but one other in Northwestern Arkansas. Its cost was $5,000. This was very largely the result of the efforts of Rev. D. J. Weems, who has been the pastor of the society for four years. The first pastor was succeeded by others, among whom were Revs. Pogue, Lugg, Thornberry, Lively, Burrell Lee, A. R. Winfield and F. Colburn before the late Civil War. Revs. R. W. Hammetts (P. E.), S. A. Sheaffer (none during the war), N. B. Pearson (P. E.), John Harrell, J. M. P. Hicheson (P. E.), C. H. Gregory, S. S. Key, J. J. Roberts (P. E.), S. H. Babcock (P. C.), H. R. Withers (P. E.) and Rev. Babcock in 1871 and 1872, C. H. Gregory (P. E.) and W. J. Bolling (P. C.) during 1873 and 1874, J. M. Clayton (P. E.), R. S. Hunter (P. C.), I. L. Burrow and R. S. Hunter, H. M. Granade (P. E.), B. H. Greathouse, I. L. Burrow (P. E.), B. L. Ferguson, I. L. Burrow (P. E.), Dr. J. W. Kaigler, T. J. Smith (P. E.), James A. Anderson, F. S. H. Johnson, V. V. Harlan (P. E.), G. W. Hill and D. J. Weems; the pastors since 1885 embrace all the presiding elders and pastors since 1861, except Revs. William Penn (P. E.), I. L. Burrow (P. E.), J. A. Anderson (P. E.) in 1887, and Rev. I. L.

Burrow (P. E.) in 1888. This society is, no doubt, the largest in Crawford County, its membership now being 225. Steps were taken in *ante-bellum* days to found a college at Van Buren, and a donation of $10,000 was made toward that object by Alfred and Martha Wallace; this fund, however, was largely lost during the late war, but about $6,000 is now in the hands of trustees.

The Methodist Episcopal Church in Crawford County has shared the fortunes of that denomination in the State, and falls within the jurisdiction of the Fort Smith District of the Arkansas Conference. The withdrawal of that society from the State in 1857 is well known, and also its return in 1868. The first session of Arkansas Conference was held at Little Rock in 1873 by Bishop Bowman, the secretary being Mr. Bushong. Intermediate sessions have since been held there and at Batesville, Russellville, Fayetteville, Fort Smith, Harrison, Waldron, Rogers and Judsonia, while that of 1889 will be held at Eureka Springs under Bishop Warren. This society is not largely represented in Crawford County.

Natural Dam Methodist Episcopal Church was organized at the residence of John Rainwater, about twenty years ago, by Elisha Robison, Caswell Mills and David McCaslin, and then belonged to the Van Buren Circuit. John S. Rainwater was class leader. They have never had a building, but services have been held at various times since by Revs. Gilcoat, Conley, Manus, A. Hyde, Obarr, Bryant, Hunt and others. The church at one time had thirty-five or forty members, but there are very few at present.

North Van Buren Methodist Episcopal Church was organized in 1886 by Milton Z. Brown. There had been a good society before 1856, but the political exigencies of those days led to its abandonment. The society began again in 1886, and has so flourished that they now have a neat pine structure in course of erection, and have a membership of thirty-five persons. The society is a member of the Arkansas Conference of the Methodist Episcopal Church. Their present pastor is Rev. Obarr.

The Mount Olive Methodist Episcopal Church (colored), at Van Buren, is a member of the Little Rock Conference, and began its existence in 1869. It was organized by J. G. Pollard

111

CRAWFORD COUNTY, ARKANSAS - BIOGRAPHICAL AND HISTORICAL MEMOIRS
****

with thirty-eight members. In 1874 the society built a frame church two blocks west of Main Street at a cost of $900, and it was dedicated the same year by Rev. T. B. Ford. Rev. Ford has been succeeded by Revs. G. W. Taylor, W. H. Crawford, R. Boon, H. Turner, A. J. Phillips, J. G. Thompson, F. Wallace, W. S. Lanford and E. Roberts. Their membership is now ninety-five. The church is preparing to erect a commodious brick house of worship.

The Methodist Protestant Church is not largely represented in Crawford County. There are but eight congregations in all.

Cedarville Methodist Protestant Church is a member of the Fort Smith Annual Conference and of the Cedarville Circuit, which embraces Shiloh Church and Whitewater Chapel. It was organized about 1884, by Rev. Leonidas Neal and Rev. Youngs Coleman, associate pastor at Cedarville. Among the first members were F. C. Oliver, Eli Oliver and wife, Youngs Coleman and wife, L. Neal and wife, M. G. England and wife, Mrs. Rosana Neal and two daughters, Misses Ruth and Hattie J. Oliver, Richard Lollis and wife, Ellen and Jane Lynn, S. Q. McCurdy, John Hubbard and wife, and E. M. Oliver and wife. Among their pastors have been Rev. Boaz Ford, the two already named, and Rev. Hiram Kimes. They have thirty members. They have a union church building and school and Masonic Hall combined, worth about $3,000.

The Shiloh Church was organized about 1885, by Rev. Youngs Coleman, and among the original members were G. W. Pittman and wife, J. A. Standridge, M. J. Purcell, William Brazuell and wife, R. J. Brazuell and wife, *et al.* They have about twenty-five members, and use a school building.

Whitewater Chapel was organized at Gum Springs, by Rev. George O. Hickey, probably in about 1872. Many of the members were from the Cedarville congregation.

The Anna Circuit includes three churches and the Winslow Mission.

Episcopal.—Trinity Church, of Van Buren, is one of the oldest members of the Diocese of Arkansas. The society was organized about the years 1841 or 1842 by Bishop George W. Freeman. The corner-stone of the first church was laid April 5, 1844, and the membership reached about twenty-five persons. It began under the rectorship of Rev. D. McManus, whose successors were Revs. O. Townsend, William Binet, —— Littlejohn, —— Matthew, and the present rector, Rev. L. F. Guerry. The society has been independent and earnest, and although without a pastor for a time succeeded in building a brick edifice valued at $5,000 (including the cost of site). This was completed in 1887, and will be dedicated in the winter of 1888–89 by the first pastor. The present number of communicants is sixty-nine, while the congregation numbers about 150.

The Presbyterians.—The Van Buren Presbyterian Church (O. S.) is a member of Washburn (or Washbourne) Presbytery, whose organization is mentioned elsewhere in this volume. It was formerly a part of Arkansas Presbytery, which embraced the northern half of the State. The society had informal services prior to 1844, but, according to Dr. J. A. Dibrell, the society was organized probably during that year. It is thought that the first pastor, Rev. Aaron Williams, organized the church, among whose original members were Elder Calvin Phelps and wife, Elder and Mrs. Charles Stewart, Mrs. L. Gross, Mary Hinkle, Dorothy Davis, Mr. and Mrs. Cunningham, Mr. and Mrs. (?) Houck, Mrs. Mary Gross, Mrs. J. B. Ogden, Mrs. Abbott, Mrs. Pryor, Mrs. George W. Paschal, *et al.* The present church—which was the first—was built of wood and brick by the society in 1846 at a cost of $1,200. It was dedicated by the second pastor, Rev. W. K. Marshall, D. D. The membership reached its high-water mark about 1848, when they numbered sixty persons; but the organization of the Alma Church drew off a large number who lived there. It should be mentioned also that the acoustic properties of the church building were planned by the famous Washington architect, Mills, whose great equestrian statue of Jackson is so well known. The pastors that followed Dr. Marshall are Revs. Elizur Butler, Thomas Urmston, J. C. Kennedy, G. L. Wolfe, S. B. Irvin and W. F. Sample. The present membership numbers thirty persons.

The Alma Presbyterian Church is a member of Washburn (or Washbourne) Presbytery, and was organized in 1878 by Rev. J. C. Kennedy. The members constituting the first church were

R. M. and Mrs. Alexander, W. C. and Mrs. Bostick, A. C. and Mrs. Powe and others. The officers were J. K. P. Douglass and J. H. McNeely. The present edifice is a neat frame structure, the only one owned entirely by the society. It was dedicated in December, 1886, by Rev. W. F. Sample. The pastors have been Revs. J. C. Kennedy, S. B. Irvin and W. F. Sample, the present pastor. The church is in a prosperous condition, with a membership of sixty persons. Five elders and three deacons constitute the officers.

The Catholics.—St. Michael's Catholic Church at Van Buren is the only representative of this denomination in Crawford County. It is a member of the diocese of Little Rock, and was organized at an uncertain date. The chief event of importance in their history is the erection of a church on Broad Street, which was made possible by contributions of members of the local society, the congregation at Fort Smith and the citizens of Van Buren of various societies. The building is a frame edifice of a value estimated at $2,500, and was dedicated June 7, 1873, by the Rt. Rev. Edward Fitzgerald, bishop of Little Rock. The society has since prospered under the care of two successive pastors, Rev. M. Smith, and the Rev. Father Maurell, of Fayetteville, the present incumbent of the priestly office. Their organization has a membership of about 100 persons.

Missionary Baptists.—The Clear Creek Missionary Baptist Association is an offshoot of the Dardanelle Association, from which it withdrew to organize in 1871. About nine or ten churches, seven of which withdrew from the above-mentioned association, met at Concord Church, in Crawford County, and formed the present organization, which includes churches in Crawford County, and many north of the Arkansas River, in Franklin County. They chose for moderator a prominent organizer of the association, Col. M. F. Locke, of Alma, and Rev. W. R. McLain, as clerk. The moderatorship has been held by one or the other of these two gentlemen ever since, the former serving all but about two or three terms. In 1884 the association met at Mt. Zion Church, Franklin County; in 1886 at New Prospect Church, at Mulberry, and in 1877 at Alma, Crawford County. The present officers are Col. M. F. Locke, moderator; J. M. Lawrence, clerk, and M. H. Wagner, treasurer. They have 26 ministers, 5 licentiates and 27 churches. Total membership, 1,243.

Vine Prairie Missionary Baptist Church was organized June 3, 1882, by Rev. P. A. D. Smith, with thirteen original members. The first pastor was Rev. Nathan Adams, next Rev. Horace Meaddears (or Meadors) and Rev. Payne, the present pastor. They have a neat frame building 24x40 feet, built in 1886, costing about $200.

The Oak Grove Missionary Baptist Church, a member of Clear Creek Association, was organized January 22, 1882, by J. A. D. Smith, chairman; J. M. Kimberlin, secretary; M. Adams, J. E. Hicks, L. Scott and T. J. Davis. These, with J. E., G. W., Rosanah and Telitha Cox, S. L. Looney, S. A. Boggs, A. F. Looney and Mary M. Pendergrass, constituted the original membership, which has since increased to forty persons. Rev. M. Adams, the pastor, and Deacon G. W. Cox, church clerk, embraced all the first officers. Among those who are members of the society, J. A. D. Smith and J. M. Kimberlin are ministers; Mr. Adams and Rev. J. W. Richardson, the present pastor, have been the only ones in charge. The deacons are Messrs. Hicks, Scott and Davis. The society has so far been compelled to use a school-house for worship.

The Fine Spring Missionary Baptist Church was organized July 14, 1883, as a part of the Clear Creek Missionary Baptist Association. Rev. John O. Love was the minister. C. A. Heathcock and David Reed also took part in the organization. The society meets at a school-house three miles north of Alma. Their pastors have been W. M. Hicks, C. A. Gowin and Rev. Horace Meaddears (or Meadors). The original members were J. O. Humphrey, W. F. Flowers, Julia Flowers, Daniel Allen and sister and Mary A. O'Kelley. The present membership is thirty-four.

The Alma Missionary Baptist Church was organized in August, 1873, with the following members: Rev. F. L. and Mrs. Mary Seaward, with their two daughters, Misses Laura A. and Fannie; Dr. W. L. and Mrs. Jane R. Wynne; Col. M. F. and Mrs. N. A. Locke; three members of the Broome family, Mrs. M. A.,

T. W. and J. E.; C. C. Adams and Mrs. Nancy Hill. Rev. F. L. Seaward was their first pastor, and services were conducted in the public school building, which is elsewhere mentioned. They were the first of the four religious societies to withdraw from that building and erect a church. In 1878 Col. M. F. Locke, Rev. F. L. Seaward, Dr. Wynne and others began the work, and soon after that they were enabled to dedicate a neat wooden structure, which has cost them about $1,600. The pastors succeeding Rev. Seaward have been Revs. F. L. Kregel, M. O. Lucas, S. I. Lee and their present minister, Rev. E. Windes. Their present membership is about eighty persons. It might be of interest to note that the most prominent moderator, Col. M. F. Locke, of the Clear Creek Missionary Baptist Association, to which this church belongs, is a member of this society.

The Van Buren Missionary Baptist Church was not successful in forming an organization until 1885, and even then their membership was small, embracing only—among the male members— J. C. Clark, Mr. Reese, Mr. Hill, G. F. Stamps, T. Funk and James Lloyd. Elder John Mayes, of Fayetteville, and Deacon Clark organized the society as a member of Clear Creek Association. There is but little to record until the year 1887, when they erected their present frame church, at a cost of about $1,800. Their membership increased under the pastoral charge of Elders O. M. Lucas and Enoch Windes, the present pastor, until it has reached the number forty-one.

The Red Bird Missionary Baptist Church, a member of Clear Creek Association, is located two miles north of Belmont, Crawford County. It was organized the third Sunday in 1884, with the following members: C. W. Smith, Justin Smith, Josiah and Louisa Baird, C. W. and Sarah Bolton, J. S., Sr., Eveline, William, Rutha, J. S., Jr., and Nancy Smith and J. W. Cain. The officers were J. W. Cain, clerk; Deacon J. S. Smith, Sr., treasurer. The society have no building, but hold services in the school-house of the district. Their pastorate has been filled by Revs. T. R. Early, Horace Meadors and the present incumbent, J. M. Payne. The membership has been as high as 115 persons, but ninety-two is their present number.

Cedar Creek Missionary Baptist Church was organized in

1873 by Elder A. P. Whit, with E. Morris as moderator and Simon Whit as clerk. Among the members were Robert Reed, George Allen, Louisiana Morris, Albert Reed, Mary Burkett, Julia Reed, Amanda Allen, John Allen, R. Reed, William Allen, Mary Lewis, Mary Larue and J. B. Lewis. They first used a log school-house on the creek in Cedar Creek Township, but in 1876 a frame structure was erected at a cost of about $500. It was dedicated by the pastor, Elder C. A. Gowin. His successors have been Elders Simon Whit, Daniel Johns, J. H. Hill, E. A. Scott, S. L. Story, C. R. Johns, and C. A. Gowin himself. They have about fifty members. The Methodist and Christian Church people hold occasional services in this church.

Mount Moriah Missionary Baptist Church, a member of Clear Creek Association, was organized October 1, 1887, by Elders C. A. Gowin and John Brim, pastor. The society had no building, but their members held meetings about a mile north of Rudy. Among these members were W. H. Walker, deacon and clerk, M. A. Walker, Charles Baker and wife, Dilley Brim, John Lamson, B. Bruner, Sarah Bruner, James and Ann Howard, Mary Mullen, Caroline Jones and Elder Joseph Hudson. Rev. John Brim is the pastor, but Elder Hudson and Deacon Winfrey have officiated in various church duties at times. They have thirty-seven members.

Union Chapel Missionary Baptist Church was organized June 10, 1883, by Elders C. A. Gowin, C. R. Johns and E. Morris, with the following members: Mary A. Davis, Lizzie Service, Sarah Spangler, Isabel Richie, Nancy E. Pesterfield, S. J. Davis, A. K. Standridge and E. H. Hanner. The pastors have been Revs. C. A. Gowin, W. D. Cox and George F. Fatum. The present membership is fifty-eight.

Zoar Missionary Baptist Church was organized in 1859 by Elders Claborne, Jones and D. C. Harrison. Their first building was a log house, erected in about 1867, eight miles northeast of Van Buren. It cost about $100. They enroll about thirty-seven members at present. The original members were Elder Jones and wife, Elder Harrison and wife, C. C. Johnson, O. B. Wallace and Elizabeth Wallace, Sarah O'Neal and Phoebe Temple.

New Prospect Missionary Baptist Church No. 2, a member of Clear Creek Association, was formed August 18, 1883, by D. W. Chambless and J. M. Lawrence. The Oak Grove school-house and church combined, a two-story building, erected in 1882 at a cost of $1,100, is their present place of worship, located four miles southeast of Van Buren. The original membership embraces S. J. N., N. E., Jesse M. and Elder Daniel W. Chambless, E. W. Houston, W. L. H. Couch, Thomas A. Hill, Sarah E. Chambless, Eliza Lemley, Christina Lemley, Mary C. Shoemaker, M. E. Houston, Mary Couch, Martha E. Hill, Mary E. Couch, S. E. Houston and Mary E. Miller, but their number has grown to seventy-four, and prospects for the construction of a building, exclusively their own, are bright. Their present church was dedicated by the only pastor they have had, the Rev. Elder D. W. Chambless. N. E. Chambless is church clerk.

The Woman's Christian Temperance Union of Van Buren has been an important factor in both the social and political history of Crawford County. It was organized February 2, 1882, with twenty-eight members. The officers chosen were as follows: Mrs. Jesse Turner, president; Miss Mattie Southmayd, Mrs. C. M. Thompson, Mrs. W. H. H. Shibley, vice-presidents; Mrs. Lewis Bryan, recording secretary; Miss Fannie Thompson, corresponding secretary; Mrs. J. O'Connor, treasurer; Mrs. M. D. Garnett, librarian. In November of the same year the society made a vigorous fight for prohibition at Van Buren, under the "three-mile" law, and to all appearances succeeded. The validity of the proceedings was questioned, however, and the case was brought before the county judge. Attorneys Thomason, Turner and Brown appeared for the petitioners for prohibition, and Attorneys Neal and Huckleberry in behalf of the opposition. The petition was granted. In their efforts of a similar character afterward the society was unsuccessful, but their efforts have had a great influence on public sentiment. Mrs. W. H. H. Shibley succeeded Mrs. Turner. The present secretary is Miss Alice Brelsford, and the treasurer, Mrs. C. M. Thompson. They have a membership of about forty-five.

The Van Buren Young Men's Christian Association was organized November 27, 1887, at the Methodist Church in that city. State Secretary Bill, of the state organization of Arkansas, was present, and the following officers chosen: Gen. Hugh F. Thomason, president, and D. H. Miller, secretary. There were forty-two members at this meeting—a temporary organization; the permanent society was formed a week later, with Hon. B. J. Brown as president, G. C. Thayer and Dr. R. W. Quarles as vice-presidents, W. H. H. Shibley as secretary, and John Fritz as treasurer. The society holds weekly meetings. Its rooms are in the Edmondson Block.

POST-OFFICES AND FINANCES.

Post-offices.—The number of post-offices established in Crawford County, between the years 1829 and 1888 was fifty-eight, as follows, with names of postmasters and dates of appointment:

Akeville (late Oak Grove): T. I. Price, June 1848; discontinued September, 1849.

Alma: Alex. W. Griffin, June, 1871; George F. Bolling, April, 1872; discontinued March, 1873; re-established April, 1873, George F. Bolling; Bidkar P. Renfroe, March, 1875; William A. Britten, August, 1881; E. B. Hassett, June, 1882; Noble Bonlin, April, 1884; Hugh S. Lewers, April, 1885.

Andros: Henry H. Epperson, June, 1886.

Anna: Jeremiah M. Spencer, August, 1880.

Arkloe: Mary A. F. Bullock, April, 1880; Robert I. Glass, October, 1880; Josias B. P. Bullock, May, 1882; discontinued October, 1884; re-established July, 1885, Malissa Bullock; discontinued March, 1886.

Armada: Andrew J. Nordin, March, 1888.

Barcelona: Tom Comstock, October, 1888.

Belmont: John M. James, January, 1848; Hugh R. Frazier, July, 1852; William Steward, October, 1857; discontinued June, 1859; re-established January, 1860, Samuel S. Roberts; John R. Meaders, April, 1866.

Bidville: H. A. Hedding, September, 1883; F. S. Henry, May, 1884; re-appointed April, 1885; discontinued January, 1886; re-established January, 1880, John B. Harrison.

Britton: Harvey A. Hedding, September, 1883; Elijah J. Crider, September, 1886.

Cantonment Gibson: E. W. B. Nowland, November, 1832; discontinued July, 1839; re-established July, 1839, W. L. Wharton. Now in Cherokee Nation, Indian Territory.

Cedarville (late Spencer's shop): Henry C. Crowell, June, 1872; B. B. Thayer, September, 1872; James F. O'Bryan, February, 1874; G. B. Childus, February, 1875; George W. Crowell, July, 1875; Robert C. Crowell, January, 1876; Peter Hunt, June, 1878; Leonidas Neal, September, 1878; James Fears, August, 1881; Cornelius W. Neal, January, 1882; M. J. Purcell, October, 1887.

Cherokee Agency: Hercules T. Martin, January, 1840. Now in Washington County.

119

CRAWFORD COUNTY, ARKANSAS - BIOGRAPHICAL AND HISTORICAL MEMOIRS
****

Chester: James C. Wright, March, 1883.

Crawford (changed to Pleasant Hill): Alexander McLean, September, 1832.

Dora: Albert Hood, April, 1888.

Dripping Springs: George W. Matlock, March, 1870; discontinued June, 1870; re-established May, 1872, Wallace Deffbaugh; discontinued December, 1872.

Dyer: Walter A. Dyer, July, 1885; John W. Moss, July, 1886; Tilghman M. Layton, June, 1887; Robert N. Anderson, June, 1888.

Eads: William C. Eads, October, 1881; William A. Briscoe, July, 1882; re-appointed August, 1882; Francis M. Clawson, May, 1887.

Elm Springs: W. Barrington, July, 1850. Now in Washington County.

Fort Smith: John Rogers, October, 1829. Changed to Sebastian County March, 1851.

Frisco: Benjamin F. Strong, April, 1883; John W. Shaberg, January, 1888.

Frog Valley: Josiah Kester, August, 1879; Paton Peters, December, 1879; discontinued February, 1880.

Gotha: Rudolph R. Ueltzen, August, 1886; Lovelace Cliett, November, 1886; discontinued December, 1887.

Graphic: William B. Moore, March, 1883; Archibald Y. Killingsworth, October, 1883; John B. Meek, October, 1886; Frank Dyer, February, 1888.

Hale: Harrison B. Hale, May, 1888.

Hansen: Alex Thompson, June, 1881; Joseph C. Howell, September, 1883; discontinued November, 1885.

Harroldton: James F. Gooding, June, 1886.

James Fork: Jeremiah Hackett, August, 1847; Jacob W. Bender, May, 1850; changed to Sebastian County, March, 1851.

Lancaster: James F. Ferguson, November, 1882; re-appointed November, 1884; Samuel Steward, March, 1884.

Lee's Creek: Thomas Shannon, January, 1832; Sanford N. Elmore, February, 1835; George W. Duval, December, 1838; changed to Natural Dam March, 1839; re-established, Hiram Bradie, March, 1854; discontinued July, 1866; re-established, William Dudley, August, 1866; James A. O'Bryan, March, 1870; Andrew P. Simon, January 1871; Sibramer R. Cox, October, 1871; Richard C. Oliver, December, 1872; John J. Beale, January, 1887.

Leonardsville: Amasa Watson, December, 1879; Fred Sperry, April, 1882; discontinued September, 1882.

Lock: William F. Thornton, March, 1884; James K. P. Vaught, November, 1884; discontinued September, 1886.

Mine Prairie, changed to Vine Prairie: Thomas J. Davidson, October, 1876.

Mountainburgh (late The Narrows): Wesley H. Gilstrap, September, 1876; Henry Remy, March, 1878; Albert Simcoe, January, 1882; Anderson O. Gilstrap, June, 1883; John B. Wright, January, 1886; John L. Dement, April, 1886.

Mulberry: Thomas Moore, May, 1830; discontinued September, 1833.

Natural Dam (late Lee's Creek): Washington Duval, March 1839; Andrew Norton, November, 1845; Washington Duval, January, 1846; discontinued August, 1846; re-established April, 1847, James Farris; D. C. Price, September, 1847; Andrew Morton, December, 1850; discontinued May, 1860; re-established October, 1860, Andrew Morton; Jesse W. Branson, April, 1866; Mrs. Mary E. Oliver, April, 1867; discontinued, September, 1868; re-established August, 1872, James P. Babb; Nimrod P. Rice, February, 1875; discontinued November, 1875; re-established January, 1877, Henry King.

Oak Grove: James B. McPherson, February, 1844; changed to Akeville June, 1848.

120

CRAWFORD COUNTY, ARKANSAS - BIOGRAPHICAL AND HISTORICAL MEMOIRS
****

Ozark (now in Franklin County): William Hail, December, 1836; Samuel Evans, September, 1837.

Penny Witt: A. J. Harben, March, 1854; discontinued March, 185—.

Penultima: William H. Dillard, August, 1842; James W. Bates, December, 1843; dicontinued February, 1847.

Pleasant Hill (late Crawford, now in Franklin County): John Lasater, January, 1838.

Redtop: Benjamin Dyer, August, 1886; discontinued November, 1887.

Rudy: George H. Rudy, February, 1883; Douglas Allen, December, 1886; William D. Rutledge, December, 1887.

Sand Point: Lewis Keifer, June, 1879; Bartlett Irwin, April, 1880.

Short Mountain: Gilbert Marshall, February, 1830; Thomas Hixson, December, 1833; William Hull, December, 1835; Samuel Weaver, July, 1837; discontinued July, 1838.

Speir: John L. Speir, February, 1888.

Spencer's Shop: John Spencer, March, 1870; Henry C. Crowell, April 1872. Changed to Cedarville June, 1872.

Stattler: John P. Stewart, June, 1882; Vincent S. Vestal, November, 1883; Josiah R. Harden, April, 1886.

Steep Hill: Samuel B. Stephens, November, 1847; Isaac H. Parish, January, 1849; discontinued June, 1849.

Stop: Nathan W. Leach, June, 1884; William H. Leach, June, 1887.

Sugar Loaf: Giles S. Brown, August, 1847; George N. Brown, June, 1849. Changed to Sebastian County March, 1851.

Tarrytown: William J. Meadows, Jr., August, 1871; Cyrus Barrier, February, 1875; William J. Meadows, April, 1876; discontinued August, 1878; re-established, David H. Creekmore, February, 1883; W. F. Flowers, July, 1886.

The Narrows: William Howard, July, 1848; Asahel L. Orrick, July, 1856; William Russell, Jr., January, 1857; James G. Marlar, July, 1857; John L. Morgan, April, 1858; discontinued July, 1866; re-established May, 1867, Andrew I. Peters; Thomas H. Simcoe, December, 1867; James S. Bushong, July, 1869; Samuel L. Strong, December, 1871; William H. Peters, November, 1872; Samuel L. Strong, May, 1874; Wesley H. Gilstrap, March, 1875. Changed to Mountainburgh September, 1876.

Uniontown: Joseph C. Wood, April, 1881.

Van Buren: Thomas Phillips, March, 1831; John Drennon, December, 1836, Josiah W. Washbourne, October, 1844; George W. Clark, June, 1846; Cornelius D. Pryor, December, 1846; Nicholas A. Pryor, August, 1849; Davidson Dickson, April, 1852; Jonathan A. Eno, July, 1852; William B. Heard, December, 1855; James S. Bushong, October, 1865; Samuel D. Dougherty, April, 1867; Julius A. Nobles, March, 1873; Mrs. Lizzie Lockhart, March, 1874; James H. Huckleberry, October, 1879; re-appointed January, 1882; Alvis Smith, August, 1883; re-appointed January, 1884; James T. Stuart, January, 1886.

Vine Prairie (late Mine Prairie): Thomas J. Davidson, October, 1876; discontinued November, 1877.

Zenobia: William H. Cate, July, 1887; Charles M. Smith, March, 1888.

The number of post-offices in Crawford County now (November, 1888,) existing is thirty, as follows: Alma, Andros, Anna, Armada, Barcelona, Belmont, Bidville, Britton, Cedarville, Chester, Dora, Dyer, Eads, Frisco, Graphic, Hale, Haroldton, Lancaster, Lee's Creek, Mountainburgh, Natural Dam, Rudy, Sandy Point, Speir, Stattler, Stop, Tarrytown, Uniontown, Van Buren, Zenobia.

Finances.—The statement of the finances of the county for the year ending June 30, 1888, is as follows: Receipts, $22,650.95; expenditures, $24,374.50; outstanding scrip, $8,384.12. Thirteen out of eighty-eight districts, only, did not vote the five-mill tax.

CRAWFORD COUNTY.

William M. Alexander, farmer and stock raiser, was born in Williamson County, Tenn., in 1828, his parents being Alfred and Rebecca (Kerby) Alexander, natives of the same county, where they lived until 1837. They then started for Oregon, but stopping in Stoddard County, Mo., died there in 1881 and 1883, aged seventy-six and seventy-one, respectively. In religion they were Methodists. The grandfather, Thomas Alexander, was born in Buncombe County, N. C., was an early settler of Tennessee, a soldier in the Revolution, and died in Williamson County, aged one hundred and five. His father came to America from Ireland, and died in Tennessee, aged one hundred and ten, on the farm upon which our subject's father was born William M. is the eldest of a family of himself and six sisters, and was reared in Stoddard County, Mo., during the pioneer days, receiving but a very limited schooling. In 1856 he married Sarah M., daughter of John Edwards, and a native of Kentucky. Mr. Edwards was born in England. This union was blessed with six children, three sons now living. In 1872 Mr. Alexander moved from Stoddard County to his present farm, in Vine Prairie Township. He now owns eighty acres of well-improved land, all of which he has cleared. Having learned the cooper's and blacksmith's trades, he works at them in connection with his farming. He is always willing to aid any enterprise for the advancement of the county, and is known as one of its upright and well-to-do citizens. He cast his first presidential vote for Pierce, and with the exception of 1864, when he voted for Lincoln, has supported every Democratic candidate since. He is a member of the Producers' Trade Union, and Knights of the Horse. Himself and wife belong to the Methodist Church.

John M. Allen, farmer, was born in this county in 1845, and is the oldest son of William C. and Nancy (Lewes) Allen. The father was born in Roane County, Tenn., in June, 1806, and in 1832 immigrated to Washington County, Ark., by water, finally coming to Crawford County, and settling at Van Buren, when there was but one house in the place. In 1842 he married Nancy Lewis, who was born in Clark County, Ark., in 1821, and is a daughter of Hugh and Nancy Lewis, early settlers of Arkansas, and of English and German descent, respectively. Mr. Lewis was a farmer by occupation, and died in 1839. His wife died ten years previous. William C. Allen moved to Crawford County in

123

CRAWFORD COUNTY, ARKANSAS - BIOGRAPHICAL AND HISTORICAL MEMOIRS
****

1843, and there passed the remainder of his life engaged in farming. To himself and wife seven children were born: Celia E. White (of this township), John M., James S. (of Van Buren), Sarah J. (of this township), David F., Hugh L. and Mary Allen. The last three named are deceased. Mr. Allen died in 1881, and his wife in 1874. The grandfather, John Allen, was a native of Virginia, served in the War of 1812 and died about 1818. His wife, Celia (Oliver) Allen, was born in Tennessee, and died about 1810. On account of the unsettled state of the country during the war, our subject did not receive much of an education, and in 1870 began life for himself by farming, having been discharged from the army June 10, 1865. He enlisted in 1864, in Company F, under Capt. Joseph Crouch, Bryant's regiment, and was paroled by the Federal authorities. In 1870 he married Miss Catherine White, who was born in Germany in 1843, and is a daughter of Henry and Maria (Buschmann) White, who were born in Germany in 1810 and 1808, and died in 1863 and 1862, respectively. Mr. White was a farmer by occupation, and upon coming to America proceeded at once to Van Buren and located in this county. To Mr. and Mrs. Allen four children have been born: Nannie E., William Walter, Caroline L. and James W. Mr. Allen is a well-to-do man, and has served about three terms as school director. He has seventy-five acres of good land, thirty-five acres of which he cultivates. His farm is well improved, and he lives in a comfortable frame dwelling. He belongs to the Cumberland Presbyterian Church, and is a member of the Masonic fraternity. In politics he is a Democrat, and his first presidental vote was cast for Seymour, in 1868.

William M., James A. and Thomas Allen are sons of William and Elizabeth (Rose) Allen. William M. was born in Roane County, Tenn., December 8, 1846; James A., in Whiteford County, Ga., October 16, 1849, and Thomas, in Crawford County, Ark., March 16, 1854. The father was born and reared in Tennessee, and about 1847 immigrated to Georgia. He was a contractor on the L. T. V. & G. Railroad, and also engaged in farming. He came to Crawford County, Ark., in 1853. The mother is a native of Roane County, Tenn., and is related to the Tipton family. Of her five children four are living, our three subjects and Jessie F. John A. is deceased. The paternal grandparents were early settlers of Tennessee. Mr. William Allen died in this county in June, 1856, aged thirty-five, but the mother is still living and makes her home with her children. She is sixty-two years old. William M. received a common-school education during his childhood, and at the age of sixteen the main support of his mother and the children fell upon him. March 24, 1872, he married Sarah J. Carlisle, daughter of Alexander Carlisle. This union has been blessed with seven children: Mary A., Julia W., Ollie J., Jessie W., Emma M., John H. and James Thomas (deceased). Mr. Allen enlisted in Brooks' brigade, Confederate States army, in 1864, was taken prisoner at Clear Creek, and sent to Little Rock, where he was kept a prisoner until 1865. He then returned to Van Buren, where he farmed. In 1876 he engaged in milling, and in 1884 removed to the mill he now has in partnership with his two brothers. He is a Democrat, a close communion Baptist, and a member of the Agricultural Wheel. Thomas B. Allen was married December 27, 1887, to Florence Jackson, daughter of B. H. and Elizabeth Jackson, and is engaged in the above named mill. James A. is unmarried, and politically is a strong Democrat. The mill which Allen Bros. own was erected in 1870 by Wiley Bronson, and is a large three-story building, having cotton-gins, carding machines and a hominy and flour mill. Allen Bros. also own 160 acres, seventy being cultivated.

Martin Barker, farmer and stock raiser, was born in LaFayette County, Mo., in 1832, and is a son of John and Sarah (McFarland) Barker, who were born near Lexington, Ky., and East Tennessee, respectively, about 1810. When young they accompanied their parents to LaFayette County, Mo., where they were married. They lived in Platt, LaFayette, Johnson and Barry Counties, Mo., until about 1845, and then removed to Texas. The father died two years later when returning to Missouri, after which the family came to Crawford County, where the mother died. She was a devout member of the Presbyterian Church. Thomas Barker, the grandfather, and his wife, were of Dutch descent, and died in Texas and Missouri, respectively. Martin Barker is the eldest of three sons and four daughters born to his parents, and thus upon the death of his father the main support of the family fell upon him. He received but a meager education during his youth, and lived at home until twenty-one, when he was mar-

124

CRAWFORD COUNTY, ARKANSAS - BIOGRAPHICAL AND HISTORICAL MEMOIRS
****

ried to Mary Ann, daughter of Joshua and Lucretia Hargrove, natives of Georgia. Mrs. Barker was born in Tennessee, and in 1850 came to this county, where her mother died. To Mr. and Mrs. Barker six children have been born, of whom two sons and three daughters survive. With the exception of 1859, which was spent in Texas, Mr. Barker has resided in different portions of Crawford County, although he has lived upon his present farm since 1868, which, when he first located upon it, was in the midst of the forest. He now has seventy-five acres of cleared land and owns in all 220 acres. In politics he was formerly a Whig and since the war he has been a Republican.

Dr. Beal, colored, farmer and stock raiser of Richland Township, was born near Raleigh, N. C., in 1822, and is a son of Lewis Hinton, who was the property of William Hinton. The latter took them to Alabama, and there they were sold to John S. Beal, with whom our subject remained, after he obtained his freedom, until 1871. He then went to Lawrence County, Kas., and the following year came to Crawford County, Ark. He soon after homesteaded forty acres of his present farm, which now contains 120 acres in the home place and 150 acres of bottom land. He is one of the most successful farmers and well-to-do citizens of the township, and his property is all the result of his own labor and business ability. In 1872 he married Millie Smith, who was reared in Alabama and Texas, and died in 1878, leaving two children. In 1880 Mr. Beal married Ellen Stowe, who was born in South Carolina, and came to this county in 1875. Mr. Beal and wife are members of the African Methodist Church. He is also a member of the I. O. O. F., and in politics is a Republican, having cast his first presidential vote for Gen. Grant.

William R. Bolling, proprietor of the Alma Flour and Corn-mill and Cotton-gin, which he erected in 1880, and has since successfully operated, was born in Perry County, Ala., in 1841, and at the age of nine accompanied his parents to Choctaw County, Ala. In 1869 they came to Crawford County, Ark., where the father died in 1885. He, Thornberry Bolling, was a descendant of Pocahontas, was born in South Carolina in 1817, and was a well-to-do farmer and upright citizen. He was for many years a member of the Baptist Church and Masonic fraternity, and was the father of ten children. The grandfather, Samuel Bolling, was born in Virginia, and died in Perry County, Ala. The mother of our subject, Nancy B. (Radford) Bolling, was born in Perry County, Ala., and is now sixty-five years of age. The town of Radfordville, in Perry County, Ala., was named in honor of her father, William, who was a soldier in one of the early wars, and a wealthy planter. Our subject, William R. Bolling, received a common-school education, and at the age of twenty left his studies to join Company F, First Alabama, Tennessee and Mississippi mixed regiment of infantry. He was at the battle of New Madrid, was captured at Island No. 10, served six weeks at Camp Douglas, Ill., and from there went to Madison, Wis., at which place he was exchanged in September, 1862. He afterward served a short time in the Fifty-fourth Alabama Infantry, and after his discharge joined Company B, First Alabama Battalion, which was shortly consolidated with the Thirteenth Alabama, and known as the Fifty-sixth Alabama Cavalry until the close of the war. In October, 1866, Mr. Bolling married Carrie R., daughter of William S. and Sarah L. Horn, of Alabama. To them ten children were born, of whom six are living. In 1869 Mr. Bolling accompanied his parents to this county, engaged in farming until 1880, and since that time, with the exception of the year 1882, has been engaged in the above named business in Alma. He was for four years engaged in the mercantile business in Alma. Mr. Bolling is the owner of 1,000 acres of land, well improved, upon which he has built a fine residence. He is a man of good business ability, and his property is the result of his own industry to a great extent. He is a Democrat, and cast his first presidential vote for Seymour in 1868. He belongs to the Masonic fraternity and Knights of Honor. Mrs. Bolling and three children are identified with the Baptist Church.

Dr. Addison McArthur Bourland, of Van Buren, was born in Franklin County, Ala., in 1825, and is a son of John Bacon and Nancy (Hardwich) Bourland. The Bourlands were originally from Scotland, afterward moved to Ireland, and before the Revolutionary War located in South Carolina, where Ebenezer Bourland, the grandfather of our subject, was born, in 1768. He was a son of John Bourland, a native of Londonderry, Ireland. In 1817 Ebenezer moved to Franklin County, Ala., and in 1833 to Franklin County, Ark., locat-

125

CRAWFORD COUNTY, ARKANSAS - BIOGRAPHICAL AND HISTORICAL MEMOIRS
****

ing seven miles northwest of Ozark. He died in 1842. John Bacon was born in North Carolina in 1805, and when twelve went to Alabama. In 1824 he married Nancy Hardwich, who was of English descent, and born on Duck River, Tenn., in 1806. In 1833 he moved to Franklin County, Ark., and there died in 1840, and his wife in 1882. She was the mother of five children, five of whom are living, Dr. Addison being the eldest. He was reared upon the farm, and at the age of seventeen, having received a common-school education, taught for three years. In 1844 he began to study medicine in Barry County, Mo., with Dr. B. B. Clements, and in 1846 enlisted in Company D, Arkansas Mounted Volunteer Cavalry, for the Mexican War. He went as far south as Buena Vista, and served one year as hospital steward, afterward being engaged as dispenser at the United States Hospital at the mouth of the Rio Grande. After retiring he again taught school, and in 1857 entered the medical department of the university at Nashville, Tenn., graduating the same year. He resided in Franklin County until 1864, and then came to Van Buren, where he is one of the leading physicians. He is conversant with Latin, Greek and French, and has a medical library in the latter language. He is a member of the Van Buren Medical Society, also a member of the American Association for the Advancement of Science, and he is indeed a self-made man. In 1848 he married Susanna E. Davis, who was born in Tennessee in 1830, and bore him four children: Ellen Florine, wife of Christian Bruun, professor of music at Batesville, Ark.; Thomas D., merchant at Van Buren; William A., merchant in Port Townsend, W. T., and Othello M. The latter graduated from Vanderbilt University when a young man, and afterward at Bellevue, N. Y. He is his father's medical partner, and a member of the Van Buren Medical Society, secretary of the Crawford County Medical Association, and a member of the American Medical Association. Mrs. Bourland died in January, 1859, and in November, 1865, the Doctor wedded Bettie Williams, who was born in Kentucky in 1842, and has two children: Juanita A., wife of Burr K. Field, civil engineer and vice-president of East Berlin Iron Bridge Company, and Rosena Kate. Dr. B. has given his children all the educational advantages available, and is one of the leading and public-spirited men of the county. He is conservative in politics, voting for principles and not a party adherent, but is Democratic in his views to a large extent. His religious views are that pure religion is the noblest quality to which our nature can attain, and defines it thus: Pure religion is that inspiration resulting from a conscientious loyalty to truth which fills one with a sincere, earnest, abiding desire to adjust one's self wisely to the conditions of our being.

Capt. William Bowlin, retired citizen of Van Buren, is a native of Knox County, Tenn., a son of Noble and Catherine (Clift) Bowlin, and was born in 1832. After the death of Noble Bowlin in Tennessee, in 1835, the mother married John Barnes, who also died in Tennessee. In the fall of 1843 Mrs. Barnes, with her seven children, in company with her brother-in-law, Robert McCurry, floated down the Tennessee River, on the Mississippi, to the mouth of the Arkansas River, in a flat-boat, and then travelled to Van Buren by steamboat, landing March 10, 1844. The mother made Van Buren her home, then, until her death, in 1868, aged sixty-two. Four of her children are now living: James, of Little Rock, captain of a steamboat; Catherine, wife of William Johnson, of California; Sarah, wife of Jasper Culvert, residing near Troy, Kas., and William. The latter was about twelve when brought to Van Buren, and when eighteen began to work in a printing office, as apprentice, and for about eight years worked on the Arkansas *Intelligence*, which was published by Absalom Clark. In 1859 he established a family liquor and grocery store, and continued in that business until 1863. He then gave up the mercantile business, and entered the Federal army, Gen. Pleasanton's division of the Department of the Missouri, and Gen. Sanborn's brigade, and Col. John E. Phelp's regiment, which drove the Confederate Gen. Price from Missouri in the fall of 1864, and received his discharge at Memphis, Tenn. He then resumed his business, in connection with which, for the past ten years, he has also engaged in farming. He now has 1,000 acres of land, 700 being well cultivated. Capt. Bowlin began life with but little, but by close attention to business and economy has amassed a fortune, which places him among the first ranks of Crawford County's business men. He is a director and stockholder in the Citizens' Bank, and a man who always lends a helping hand to public enterprises and charities. In

126

CRAWFORD COUNTY, ARKANSAS - BIOGRAPHICAL AND HISTORICAL MEMOIRS
****

1852 he married Samantha Neal, a native of Missouri, who became the mother of the following children: Rebecca, wife of John Clark; Elizabeth, wife of James Lowery; Noble; Lillie, wife of LaFayette Wright; John, and Fanny, wife of John O'Brien. Mrs. Bowlin died in 1866, and in November of that year Capt. Bowlin married Miss Julia Barnes, of this place, of whose seven children but two are living: Gertrude and Troy James. In politics the Captain is a Republican, and in 1860 served as city marshal one year, afterward holding the position three years in succession. After the war he was appointed by the governor on the board of registration, and served until the completion of the work. Himself and wife hold to the faith of the Methodist Episcopal Church South, and he has been a member of the I. O. O. F. since 1857.

Mr. H. Boyd, a farmer of Lee's Creek Township, was born January 1, 1837, in Floyd County, Ky., and is a son of James and Mary (Wood) Boyd, natives of Virginia. The father has always been a farmer, and in 1835 moved to Kentucky, where he has since lived with the exception of about five years, which he spent in Crawford County, Ark. He is now a resident of Floyd County, Ky. The grandfather, William Boyd, was of English descent, and lived in Virginia. He served in the Revolutionary War seven years, and died in 1868. Our subject had but few educational advantages when a youth, but became a well-informed man. In 1856 he married Miss Lucinda M. Branham, daughter of Isham and Lucy (Hatcher) Branham, and born in 1836. This marriage has been blessed with nine children, five boys and four girls, all save one girl now living. Mr. Boyd farmed upon rented land until 1879, and then purchased his present farm, which contains 400 acres, upon which he has erected a cotton-gin, grist and saw-mill. One of the natural wonders of Crawford County is a natural dam upon this farm, which runs across Mountain Fork of Lee's Creek, and is of hard granite, eight feet high and seventy yards wide. The pond above is six feet deep at low water. Mr. Boyd has been a Mason for seven years. In politics he is a Democrat, and in religion a Methodist.

John Bradford, farmer and minister of Anna, Ark., was born September 30, 1828, in Henry County, Tenn. His parents, R. B. and Mary Ann (Bradshaw) Bradford, were born in Tennessee and West Virginia, respectively. The father was a farmer by occupation, and never immigrated west. Our subject spent his early life in Tennessee, and when of age began to farm on his own account. January 27, 1858, he married Mary Ann Ford, who was born January 17, in Hinds County, Miss., and is a daughter of Ferdinand and Elizabeth (Whitford) Ford. They were born in Virginia and Tennessee, respectively, and in 1844 settled in Crawford County, Ark., having previously lived in Virginia, Tennessee and Mississippi. His grandparents were Boaz and Frances Ford, and the former was a soldier in the War of 1812. Our subject left his native State in 1857, and March 4 of that year settled in Crawford County, having made the journey overland. May 14, 1862, he enlisted in Company A, First Arkansas Volunteer Cavalry, which was commanded by Col. E. L. Harrison, and served in the same as sergeant under Capt. Joshua S. Dudley. Operating in Southwestern Missouri and Arkansas, he participated in the battles of Cassville, Newtonia, Forsythe, Mo., Huntsville, Ark., three battles at Fayetteville and Cane Hill. He was with Gen. Blount when Price made his raid through Missouri, and assisted in driving him from that territory. Being captured at Huntsville, he was taken a prisoner to Fort Smith, and held for six weeks. He was then paroled, and afterward exchanged, when he returned to the army, and served until August 23, 1865, at which time he was mustered out and returned to Crawford County. Feeling that his mission was to preach in the Methodist Church, Mr. Bradford began his ministerial duties September 18, 1872, and has since had charge of churches in Benton, Washington, Madison, Franklin and Crawford Counties. He is successful in farming, and has 400 acres of land, sixty under cultivation and well-improved, and the remainder in timber land. He belongs to the A. F. & A. M. and the I. O. O. F., and has always voted the Democratic ticket, his first presidential vote being for Pierce in 1852.

J. H. Branson, farmer, was born in Crawford County, Ark., in 1856, and is a son of J. W. and Nancy (Francis) Branson. The father was born in Kentucky, September 21, 1829, but was reared in Missouri, where the mother was born, February 18, 1832. Mr. Branson immigrated to Crawford County, Ark., in 1854, and for several years served as justice of the peace. He was a farmer, miller and blacksmith, and now lives in Barton County, Mo. He served for

127

CRAWFORD COUNTY, ARKANSAS - BIOGRAPHICAL AND HISTORICAL MEMOIRS
****

three years during the war as saddler, in the Sixth Kansas Cavalry, and was in the battle of Camlin. He was once wounded through the thigh by bush-whackers. The grandfather, William Branson, was born in 1806, and was married in 1828, the following year moving to Missouri. In 1854 he accompanied J. W. Branson to Arkansas, and has since resided in Crawford County, with the exception of the war period, when he lived in Texas. The maternal grandfather, H. F. Francis, was of Irish descent. Our subject received a good education when young, and when of age began life for himself upon a farm. In 1877 he married Miss Margaret Snider, daughter of James and Talitha (Bethel) Snider, and a native of this county, born in 1861. Mr. and Mrs. Snider were born in Kentucky in 1831, and in Tennessee in 1839, respectively. In 1832 Mr. Snider came to Crawford County, where he afterward engaged in farming. He was a carpenter by trade, and for three years during the war worked for the Government at Fort Smith. He participated in the battle at Prairie Grove and in the skirmish at Cane Hill the previous day. Although he started in life without means, Mr. Branson has, by industry and economy, become the owner of forty acres of land, and has a stock of cattle and mules valued at about $600. He is a Republican, and as such is serving as justice of the peace. He is a member of the Agricultural Wheel, and his wife belongs to the Methodist Church. They have four children.

Mr. G. I. Briscoe, grocery merchant, at Cove City, Crawford County, was the son of Francis M. and Lucy (Tolle) Briscoe. The father was born in Lewis County, Mo., and was killed during the Rebellion. He was a school-teacher by profession. The mother was of Dutch-Scotch descent, and was born in Lewis County, Mo., in 1840. After Mr. Briscoe's death she was united in marriage, in Texas, to M. L. London. In 1868 she came to Crawford County, Ark., where she still resides. By her first marriage she was the mother of two children, and by her second marriage of six. Her oldest child, William A. Briscoe, is engaged in the grocery business at Van Buren, and her second son, G. I., is in the same business at Cove City, as above mentioned.

Charles Fox Brown, M. D., of Van Buren, was born in Virginia in 1820, and is a son of Henry and Mary (Brown) Brown. The father was also a native of Virginia, born in 1770, was a soldier in the War of 1812, and was of English descent. He died in 1823. The mother was a descendant of a different family of Browns, was born in Virginia, and died in 1835, aged forty-five. Our subject is the youngest and only living child of a family of ten. He lost his father when three years old, and when ten accompanied his mother to Louisville, Ky., where he attended school four years. He then entered the Baptist Seminary at Richmond, Va. He soon after accepted a position as clerk in a store there, and in 1840 commenced the study of medicine, at Fayetteville, Ark., under Dr. J. C. Pollard. In 1844 he entered the medical department of the Louisville University, and attended one course of lectures. In 1845 he located in Fayetteville, and for a year practiced with his former preceptor. Coming to Van Buren in December, 1846, he practiced some time, and in 1848 entered the Ohio Medical College, from which institution he graduated in 1849. He is with one exception the oldest practicing physician and surgeon in Van Buren, and has attained a high rank in his profession. He is a member of the Crawford County Medical Association, and has at times been president of the Crawford County Medical Society for the past fifteen years. He is a charter member of the State Medical Society. April 1, 1858, he married Helen M. Bostick, a native of Columbia County, Mo., born in 1839. To them five children have been born: Mary G., Charles F., John B., Ione F. and Guy. Dr. Brown is a Democrat, and in 1861 enlisted in Ray's battalion, serving as surgeon. He served four years, and it is to the practice obtained in the army that he attributes a large portion of his success as a surgeon. He was in the battle at Oak Hill, and was afterward transferred to the Mississippi department, and appointed to hospital service. He is a Mason, and a member of the I. O. O. F., and Mrs. Brown and all the children belong to the Christian Church.

Dr. Eliab M. Brown, a wealthy farmer and physician, was born in Anderson County, S. C., in 1831, and is a son of Joseph and Mary (Moore) Brown, who were born in Anderson County, S. C., in 1806 and 1811, respectively. They passed their entire lives in their native State, and died in 1838 and 1846, respectively. The father was a man of education and ability, and in 1826 graduated from the State University at Charlotteville, Va., in the law and literary department. His father, John Brown, was of English descent, and born in Maryland. When young he went to South Carolina, where he became one of the wealthist merchants and land owners of Anderson County. He died in 1853, aged eighty-four. Dr. Brown's mother was a daughter of Samuel Moore, a planter of South Carolina, and a soldier in the War of 1812, under Jackson. Her grandfather, Eliab Moore, served through the Revolutionary War, as first lieutenant, under his brother, Capt. Samuel Moore. Our subject is the second of five children, and received his early education at a common school and Anthons' Academy. After leaving school he took charge of some mills on his mother's property, and then spent some time traveling. When twenty-six years old he attended a course of lectures at the medical college of the State of South Carolina, at Charlestown, and in 1860 graduated from the Atlanta (Ga.) Medical College, in the month of August. Since that time he has practiced his profession, with the exception of the time spent in service during the war, when he commanded Company L, Second South Carolina Rifles, until the battle of the Wilderness, May 6, 1864. At that battle he was so severly wounded that he was disabled from further service. Upon first entering the army he served some time as second lieutenant in Company J, Fourth South Carolina Volunteers. After the war he resumed his practice, speculated largely in real estate, and after searching some time for a healthy place to permanently locate, he settled in 1882 on a bluff, three miles west of Van Buren, on Lee's Creek. Finding that place not all he desired he finally moved upon his present farm, which is situated six miles north of Alma, on "Georgia Ridge." As a medical practitioner Dr. Brown is widely and favorably known as one of the best in the State. Since the war he has become a large real estate owner, and now has 1,560 acres in several farms, almost all of which is Arkansas River bottom land. In 1855 the Doctor married Emily, daughter of Eliab Moore, a native of Anderson County, S. C., and now the mother of eight children, five of the sons now living. The second son, Robert A., is a physician, and the third also, although he has not yet graduated. Dr. Brown is a Democrat, and cast his first presidential vote for Pierce, in 1852. He has been a member of the Masonic fraternity since 1856, and is now a Master Mason of Alma Lodge No. 43. At the close of the war Rev. Capt. Moore was shot and killed by a notorious Tory, Bill Cunningham, but his death was afterward avenged in Florida by his brother, Lieut. Moore, killing Cunningham. Lieut. Moore afterward was a State senator, and uncle of the renowned judge, D. L. Wardlan.

Judge Benton Jackson Brown, president of the Citizens' Bank, of Van Buren, Ark., was born in Dickson County, Tenn., on February 19, 1836. His father, John B. Brown, was born in North Carolina in 1785, and while still a young man immigrated to Tennessee. There he married Sarah, daughter of Robert Huston, and settled in Dickson County, where he remained until Benton J., the youngest of his fourteen children, was above one year old, when he removed to Johnson County, Ark., locating seven miles east of Clarksville. He was one of the most influential of all the pioneers in shaping the destinies of the then infant State of Arkansas. He had served for many years as county and probate judge in Dickson County, Tenn., and after his removal to Johnson County, Ark., he filled the same position for many years more. He also represented Johnson County in the State Legislature in 1844. It was a very wild country then, and all the schools were taught as "summer schools" after crops were laid by. Young Benton J. Brown received as a boy only a rudimentary education in a pioneer log cabin for a school-house. The seed of learning was planted in good ground. Not content with the narrow field thus opened to him, young Benton saved enough of his hard earned money to attend the college in Cane Hill, or Boonsboro, Washington Co. Ark., for one year, when he secured the position of teacher of mathematics (for which he showed an early proficiency) in the "Wallace Institute" at Van Buren, and by this means he paid his board and tuition while he perfected his studies in other branches of learning. In 1858 he began the study of law under Gen. S. H. Hempstead, of Little Rock, but he soon after returned to Van Buren, where he finished his elementary studies in the office of Walker & Green. In 1860 he began the practice of law, and gained success almost from the beginning. His untiring energy and industry, his good judgment, and a thorough knowledge of human nature and men, as well as a knowledge of law books, enabled him to take his place at once among the leading members of the bar. In 1861, when

129

CRAWFORD COUNTY, ARKANSAS - BIOGRAPHICAL AND HISTORICAL MEMOIRS
****

the great war began, he enlisted among the first, and was soon after appointed quartermaster with the rank of captain by Mr. Davis. While still in the army the people of his judicial district elected him prosecuting attorney in 1862, but deeming his place of duty to be at the front, he remained in the service until the close of the war. When the war ended he spent one year in Texas. Some of his neighbors having trouble about some cotton seized by the Government at New Orleans, he was selected as the most capable man to entrust with the business of having it released. Large amounts of money being represented by the cotton, his full success gave him prominence among the business men of Shreveport, Jefferson and Northwest Texas. In 1866 he returned to his first love, Van Buren, where he resumed the practice of his profession. The Federal court, with its vast criminal business from the Indian Territory, was then stationed here. Judge Brown almost immediately became the most successful practitioner at the Federal bar, and had like success in the State courts. He was particularly successful later in commercial law, and was the trusted and confidential attorney of all the great wholesale establishments in Baltimore, Philadelphia, New York, New Orleans, St. Louis, Memphis and Louisville which did business here. He built up one of the most extensive and lucrative practices in Arkansas. When the Little Rock & Fort Smith Railroad received the patent for all its vast tract of land, Judge Brown was appointed attorney for the railroad and agent of the land department. Both as attorney for the railroad and as agent for this vast body of wild land he gained a good reputation. In 1873 Judge Brown was elected State senator, which office he held until shortly before the adoption of the Constitution of 1874, when he was appointed judge of the Fourth Judicial Circuit. In 1876, as elector, he was a member of the electoral college which cast the vote of Arkansas for the great statesman, Samuel J. Tilden, as President of the United States. In 1884, in response to calls from his friends in all parts of the State, he was about to enter the race for governor of the State, when ill health forced him to retire from active life. He has been a life-long Democrat, and has always the confidence of the people and has wielded a strong social and political influence. In 1885 he retired permanently from the practice of law. Unable to live in idleness, he bent his energies to organizing the Citizens' Bank, the largest and most successful institution of its kind between Fort Smith and Little Rock. He is interested in all of the public enterprises which are begun with the object of developing this great country. In addition to his other duties, Judge Brown was selected president of the Young Men's Christian Association, in which place he has wielded a good influence. In 1860 he was married to Miss Kate Rothrock, who was born in Cattahoula, La., in 1841. She is a woman of fine intelligence, great force of character and well read. Of this union eight children have been born, of whom only three are living, to wit: Lillian, wife of T. C. Finny, of Birmingham, Ala.; Eulle Kate, aged sixteen, now a student at the Augusta Female Seminary, at Staunton, Va., and Master Harold, a bright boy of fourteen, in whose honor the post-office and town of Haroldton, in this county, is named. Judge Brown has never been without farming interest. When his father died he took charge of his farm and ran it until he was of age, and since the war has had farms all the time, and now has the largest plantation in the county, and is one of very few lawyers who has made a success in running them. He cleared and put in cultivation more wild land than any man ever in the county. His father was sixty-seven years old at his death, his mother seventy, and although he was her fourteenth child she lived to see him married and settled in the practice of the law. Only two brothers and one sister of the family are living. As a citizen, lawyer and official, Judge Brown has always borne an untarnished record. His word in business is always taken with the fullest confidence that it will be performed. Among other possessions he will leave his family the most valuable will be that of a good name.

William D. Brown was born March 13, 1837, in Madison County, Ill., and is a son of John M. and Elizabeth (Vaughn) Brown. His parents depended largely upon him for assistance on the farm, and the school-house being ten miles distant, his education was necessarily very meager. He grew to manhood in his native county, and in 1861 married Susan Klein, daughter of Reuben Klein. Eleven children were born to them, the following eight now living: Mattie (wife of James Campbell), William M., Lulu (wife of William Daniel), Rosa, Wilburn, John, Emory, Riley, Katie and an infant. Those deceased are Charles, Mollie and Jessie. After his marriage Mr. Brown farmed in Illinois, and in 1862 enlisted in Company D, Fifty-ninth Illinois Volunteer Infantry, and during his three years service as private was in the battles of Pea Ridge, Corinth under Buel, Nashville, Stone River or Murfreesboro, Missionary Ridge, Dalton, where he was stationed two months, Marietta, siege of Atlanta, Jonesboro, Columbia, Duck River, seven charges at Franklin, and was discharged at Brownsville, Tex. His gallant services as a Union soldier were hardly surpassed during the war. He then farmed two years in Illinois, and then immigrated to Crawford County, Ark., in a two-horse wagon. He has since bought his farm of 200 acres, 100 of which he has successfully cultivated. He is a stanch Republican and a member of the G. A. R. Mrs. Brown and two daughters are active members in the Christian Church. Mr. Brown's father, John M., was born in Madison County, Ill., where he lived and farmed until over seventy years of age. Elizabeth (Vaughn) Brown, the mother, was born in the same county, and during her girlhood the Indians were so plentiful and troublesome that she was often obliged to seek shelter in the forts. She bore Mr. Brown nine children: William D., Joshua, Thomas, Franklin and Lucy, living, and Susan, James and two infants, now deceased. Mrs. Brown survived her husband a number of years, and died in 1877. Daniel S. Brown, the grandfather, was born in North Carolina, and was a pioneer settler of Illinois, where he died. His brother, John Brown, was a soldier almost his entire life, and is now a wealthy resident of Macoupin County, Ill. Eliza Vaughn, the maternal grandmother, was born in Illinois, and her husband, Josiah Vaughn, was of Indian extraction and a native of Kentucky.

Mr. J. W. Burrows, mercantile clerk at Armada, was born in August, 1856, in Washington County, Ark., and is a son of Reuben and Nancy M. (Gilstrap) Burrows, natives of Tennessee and Washington County, Ark., who died in 1862 and 1865, respectively. They immigrated from Tennessee to Arkansas in an early day, and were the parents of three children: J. W., Mary and Locky Jane. In 1861 the father enlisted in a regiment of infantry, which was operated in Western Kansas. He was killed in the battle of Prairie Grove. By occupation he was a farmer. The maternal grandparents, Isaac and Locky Gilstrap, came to Arkansas from Missouri, and died in 1877 and about 1873, respectively. The grandfather was born in 1800, and was a farmer. Our subject has spent his entire life in Washington and Crawford Counties, and at the age of thirteen started in life for himself as a farm hand. In 1877 he married Miss Phemy York, who was born in Kentucky in 1861, and is a daughter of James York and wife. Her father came to Crawford County, Ark., from Kentucky, in 1870, where he engaged in farming. He is the father of seventeen children in all, eight by his first wife and nine by his second. The union of Mr. and Mrs. Burrows has been blessed with five children: Mary Frances, Maud Ellen Sanford, Elasco and Effie Tennessee living, and one other now deceased. Mr. Burrows is a Republican, and cast his first presidential vote for James A. Garfield. He belongs to the Methodist Protestant Church and the Masonic and I. O. O. F. fraternities.

John F. Bushmiaer, farmer, was born in Prussia in 1832, and is a son of Henry and Margaret (Schnuky) Bushmiaer, also natives of Prussia. The father served in the Prussian army when quite young, being present at the battle of Waterloo and the capture of Paris. Some years after he became a government official. In October, 1847, he started with his family for the United States, and in the spring of 1848 landed at Van Buren, Ark., and soon after settled two miles south of the present site of Alma, where he died in 1849 and the mother in 1884. Both were members of the German Lutheran Church. John F., was the third of a family of five children, and while in the old country attended a common and graded school between the ages of seven and fourteen. He accompanied his parents to Crawford County, and is one of its oldest German pioneer citizens, as at the time of his arrival Van Buren was but a hamlet. The county seat had just been moved from the mouth of the Mulberry to Van Buren, and Sebastian was still a part of Crawford County. There are but few living here now who remember those days, and among those few is Mr. Bushmiaer. He being the oldest son, at the time of his father's death was left to care for the family. At the commencement of the war he joined Company C, of Col. Chas. A. Carroll's regiment of cavalry, and operated throughout the entire war in Missouri, Arkansas, Louisiana, Indian Territory and Texas, being in nearly all the engagements, and never being captured or wounded. The company was disbanded on Trinity River, in Texas. In 1868 Mr. Bushmiaer married Mrs. Caroline Smith, widow, whose maiden name was Winckly, a native of Virginia; she died, leaving three children. In 1883 he was married to Mrs. Catherine Ramsdan, a widow, and the sister of his first wife. Since 1849 Mr. Bushmiaer has lived upon the farm his father cleared, and he now has in all 340 acres of good land. He is an industrious farmer and stock raiser, and one of the well-to-do citizens of the township. He is an enterprising man, and has given his children all available educational opportunities. He is a Democrat, and cast his first presidential vote for Buchanan in 1856. He has been a member of the Alma Masonic Lodge since its organization, and is identified with the Lutheran Church. Mrs. Bushmiaer is a Baptist.

William H. Byers, loan and real estate agent at Alma, was born in Fort Smith in 1862, and is a son of W. H. and Ann C. (Williams) Byers, natives of Carolina and Tennessee, respectively, who were married in Nashville, Tenn. In 1855 they settled in Little Rock, Ark., and shortly after went to Fort Smith, where the father engaged in the shoe and tanning business until 1865, and then removed near Alma, where he died in 1885. He was of Irish descent, a strong Whig, and a member of the Masonic fraternity and I. O. O. F. The mother is still living. William H. Byers is the youngest of a family of six children, five of whom are living. After attending the common school he spent the winter of 1883–84 at Oxford, Miss., in a law school. He then taught school ten months in Crawford County, but has since devoted his attention to the practice of his profession in connection with the real estate business. He has been very successful, and in 1887 was elected mayor of Alma. He practices in the Crawford County Court and the United States Court at Fort Smith, and has bought a farm of 156 acres, near Alma, which is well improved and cultivated. In 1884 he married Rosie B., daughter of Josiah and Julia C. Foster, and by this marriage has one child. Mr. Foster was a pioneer settler of this county, who came here a poor young man, but steadily accumulated property until he became one of the wealthiest men in the county, owning 2,500 acres at the time of his death, in 1872. He was twice married, and Mrs. Byers is his twenty-sixth child. He was a life-long and zealous Democrat. Mr. and Mrs. Byers belong to the Missionary Baptist Church, and the former is a Mason.

L. B. Byars, senior partner of the firm of Byars & Co., was born in De Soto County, Miss., in 1842, and is a son of Abraham and Sarah (Moreland) Byars, natives of Rutherford District, S. C., who, after their marriage, went to Alabama. From there they went to Mississippi, and in 1874 came to Crawford County, Ark., where the father died in 1885, and the mother is still living, at the age of eighty-five. Mr. Byars was a son of Strippling Byars, who settled in Alabama in an early day. Our subject is the eighth of a family of nine children, and during his youth received a common-school education. In 1866 he married Nancy J. Cathy, also a native of De Soto County, Miss., in which county he farmed until 1870. After coming to Crawford County, at that time, he farmed here one year, and then engaged in the mercantile business with B. P. Renfroe for three years, after which he farmed five years and clerked one year. In 1883 he established his present business with L. T. Byars, his nephew, as a partner, but the firm, which is now known as Byars & Co., is composed of our subject and H. S. Lewers. They transact one of the largest businesses in the county, their stock being valued at $4,000, and their annual sales amounting to about $8,000. Their stock of general merchandise is well selected, and they are prosperous and leading men in the community. Mr. and Mrs. Byars belong to the Christian Church, and have had seven children, four of whom are living. Mr. Byars is a Democrat, and cast his first presidential vote for Seymour, in 1868. During the war he served in the Confederate army, in Company B, in Wirt Adams' regiment of Mississippi cavalry, operating in Kentucky, Tennessee, Mississippi, Alabama and Louisiana. He was present at the fights of Shiloh and Vicksburg, and participated in a number of skirmishes. He surrendered at Gainesville, Ala., in 1865.

Thomas T. Byars, chief of police of Alma, was born in what is now Tate County, Miss., in 1845, and is a son of Abraham and Sarah (Moreland) Byars. [See sketch of L. B. Byars.] He was the ninth of a family of ten children, and during his boyhood attended the common schools of the neighborhood. When but sixteen years of age he joined Company B, of Wood's regiment of Missis-

****

sippi cavalry, and was in active service nearly all the time until the close of the war, serving in Mississippi, Tennessee, Louisiana and Alabama. He surrendered near Gainesville, Ala., in April, 1865. In 1868 he married Blanche Cathy, of Mississippi, who died at Alma in 1871, leaving one child, also deceased. In 1876 Mr. Byars was married a second time, to Maty Byars, a native of Tennessee, who came with her parents to Fort Smith, Ark., prior to the war. To them four children have been born, all save one now living. Mr. Byars came to Crawford County, Ark., in 1870, and settled five miles southeast of Alma, where he lived seven years. He is now the owner of 160 acres of well-cultivated land, situated near Alma, which is all the result of his industry and business ability. Having farmed until 1887 his health became impaired, and he has since made his home in Alma. He is a Democrat, and cast his first presidential vote for Seymour. In 1888 he was elected chief of police, and is now holding that position. Since 1868 he has been a member of the Masonic fraternity and K. of H. He is a member of the Christian Church, and Mrs. Byars is a member of the Baptist Church.

John W. Cain is the only son of a family of five children born to Leonard C. and Minerva (Ross) Cain, natives of Whitely County, Ky., born in 1826 and 1829, respectively. The Cain family went from Virginia to Kentucky, and in the latter State the parents of our subject were married and engaged in farming. Mr. Cain was a Whig, and his death occurred in 1864. The mother belonged to the Missionary Baptist Church. She lived with her son John until her death, October 17, 1888. John W. Cain was born in Whitely County, Ky., June 25, 1848, and was reared upon a farm, receiving a common-school education. He lived with his parents until his marriage, September 3, 1871, to Olive K. Meadors, who was born in Crawford County, Ark., May 15, 1854. This marriage was blessed with seven children: Anna V., Crittie A. M., Pricie A. E., William L., James M., John M. and Lucinda E., who died September 28, 1888. Mr. Cain is a member of the Missionary Baptist Church, and his wife was a member of the same denomination. Her death occurred March 19, 1888. Four years after his arrival in this county Mr. Cain located on his present farm, which contains 320 acres of land, 150 being well cultivated. His property has been the natural result of about eighteen years of industrious work in this county. In politics Mr. Cain is a Republican.

Isaac A. Campbell, farmer and fruit grower, is the youngest of a family of five sons and three daughters of Isaac A. and Nancy C. (Blackwell) Campbell, natives of Tennessee and Virginia, respectively, and born in 1818. Some time after their marriage in Tennessee they came to Washington County, Ark., about 1850, where the father passed away in 1855. The mother came to Crawford County in 1860, and died here in 1882. The father was a farmer all his life, and both himself and wife were active members in the Christian Church. Isaac Campbell, the subject of this sketch, is a native of Washington County, Ark., and was born October 21, 1852. He received but a meager common-school education, as his youth was passed upon a farm, and the educational advantages in those days were few. He attended school but ten months all told. When twelve years old he began to work for himself, taking care of his mother; in 1860 he had accompanied her to Crawford County, being then but eight years old. September 29, 1872, he married Carrol A. Young, daughter of Zachariah Young, and a native of this county, born November 9, 1855. Mr. and Mrs. Campbell have had the following seven children: George M., Lee R., Carrie, Kate, Isaac A. (deceased), Charles and Cly. Mrs. Campbell is united with the Christian Church. Mr. Campbell rented land until 1877, and then bought forty acres of his present farm, to which he has added until he now owns 220 acres, of which some 110 are under cultivation. He is an enterprising man, and his property is the result of good management and economy. Politically he is a Republican, and he is a member of the I. O. O. F. and K. of P.

Silas M. Carney, farmer, was born June 30, 1850, in Rusk County, Texas, and is a son of William and Evaline (Sartain) Carney. He remained in Texas until five or six years of age, and then went to Pike County, Ill., by wagon, settling about thirty miles distant from Quincy. A year later he removed to Crawford County, Ark., within a mile of the place he now owns. He passed his younger days upon the farm, receiving a common-school education, and when nineteen married Martha Seagrave, daughter of Michael and Eliza (Crouch) Seagrave, natives of North Carolina and Tennessee, respectively.

133

CRAWFORD COUNTY, ARKANSAS - BIOGRAPHICAL AND HISTORICAL MEMOIRS
****

The mother was married in her native State, and afterward came to Arkansas, where Mrs. Carney was born, and where Mrs. Crouch now lives, aged seventy-three. Mrs. Carney was a schoolmate of her husband, and is now the mother of seven children: William M., Sarah E., Charles Mc, Laura R., James, Mary B. and Chester A. After their marriage Mr. and Mrs. Carney lived with Mr. Seagrave a year, and then homesteaded eighty acres of land, upon which they lived five years. They then sold the land and moved to a farm near by, which they made their home three years, and then settled upon their present place. Two years later they went to Washington County for a year, but then returned to Olliver Springs. Mr. Carney has always engaged in farming, and now owns a nice farm of 240 acres, 150 being well improved and cultivated. He is a well-to-do man, and politically is a Republican.

R. B. Carson was born October 15, 1828, in Haywood County, N. C., and is a son of Shadrick and Mary (Turner) Carson. The father was born in Tennessee before it became a State, and when eighteen went to North Carolina to live with relatives, where he afterward married. The mother was born in Haywood County, N. C., received a common-school education, and was a school-mate of Gen. Thomas, and of her thirteen children five are now living: Robert B., Lucinda, James, Joseph and Angeline. Those deceased are Martha, Adeline, Jane, Samuel, Margaret, William, John and Harriet. Mr. Carson was a man of means at the time of his death. He and his wife died in Georgia, but were buried in Tennessee. Robert Carson, the grandfather, was a native of France, who settled in Tennessee at an early day and there passed his life. His wife was born in Tennessee, and afterward married Sam Williams. She died in Nashville, Tenn. The maternal grandparents of our subject, Robert Turner and wife, were natives of North Carolina, where they passed their lives. Mr. R. B. Carson lived in Georgia until thirteen, being reared on a farm, and having but limited educational advantages. When nineteen he started to join the Mexican War, but was dissuaded by an uncle and returned home. July 27, 1849, he married Mary P. Louallen in Tennessee. This lady was born in North Carolina, and bore him six children, all save one now living: Shadrick M., Frank, Robert A., Charley and Martha. Hannah H. is deceased. Mr. Carson removed to Georgia from Tennessee, and twenty years after came to Arkansas, where he lost his wife in 1872. A year later he married Mrs. Eliza Fuller, by whom he has two children: Mary A. and Joseph H. Mrs. Fuller had one child, William, when she married our subject, October 30, 1873. Mr. Carson served six months during the war in Company G, Fifth Georgia Regiment, during that time experiencing all the hardships of war. After returning home he resumed farming and ran a dairy part of the time. When Mr. Carson first came to Arkansas he rented land for three years and then bought his present place, giving in part payment a span of mules. Since his second marriage he has lived upon his present place, which contains 310 acres, 130 being under cultivation. He has been a member of the Missionary Baptist Church for thirty-eight years, and his wife belongs to the Methodist Episcopal Church. Mr. Carson has served the community as constable, and is now director of the district schools. He is a Democrat in politics, and belongs to the Masonic fraternity, Knights of the Horse and Farmers' Alliance and Wheel.

Mrs. Matilda Jane Clonch was born in Crawford County, Ark., in 1841, and is a daughter of Henry and Martha (Swearingen) Hargrave. The father was born in Alabama, and when a boy came to Arkansas, which he made his home until 1849, then going to California, where he died the following year. For the life of the grandparents, John and Matilda Swearingen, see sketch of Mrs. Sallie Swearingen. Mrs. Clonch attended the country schools of Crawford County, and was reared in her native place. In 1861 she was united in wedlock to William Forrester, son of Solomon and Sadie Forrester, of this county. Mr. Forrester was born and reared in this State, where he farmed all his life, and died about 1862, and his wife about 1851. The husband of our subject was born and reared in Crawford County, where he received a common-school education. In 1861 he enlisted under Capt. Brown in the first company organized in this county, and was a participant in the "Oak Hill" battle. After his marriage he lived in Texas until his death in 1864. He was the father of two children, both of whom are deceased. In 1867 his widow married William Clonch, son of William Clonch and wife. He immigrated to Texas from Kentucky, and in 1869 came to Crawford County, living here until his death, October 26, 1873. He was a carriage-maker by trade, but after coming to this State engaged in farming. To Mr. and Mrs. Clonch three children were born, all of whom are now residents of Crawford County. They are Robert Henry, Sarah Francis Hull and Lucy Belle Clonch. Mr. Clonch was a member of the I. O. O. F. and the Cumberland Presbyterian Church, to which his widow also belongs.

William T. Coatney was born February 16, 1837, in Lafayette County, Mo., and is the son of George W. and Margeret (Smith) Coatney. The father passed his boyhood in North Carolina, and when sixteen immigrated to Kentucky, traveling the long distance on foot. In that State he married and engaged in farming, but later learned the tanner's trade. After his marriage he lived several years in Missouri, and then immigrated to Crawford County, Ark. He also lived a short time in Washington County, but died here June 20, 1888, aged eighty-three. The mother was born and reared in Kentucky, and like her husband enjoyed no educational advantages. She bore nine children, six of whom are living: James F., Elizabeth J., William T., Melinda C., Lucinda R. and Emeline; and Nancy A., Mary E. and Martha S. are deceased. Mrs. Coatney died October 12, 1887, being nearly eighty-two years old. William T. Coatney was born in Missouri, but was only a boy when brought by his parents to Arkansas. The county was so little inhabited that there were no schools at that time, and he was reared upon the farm. When eighteen he left the parental roof, and worked out for a year. When nineteen he married Elizabeth Cradduck, daughter of Presley M. and Sarilda (Lamb) Cradduck, natives of Kentucky. Mrs. Coatney was born in this county, and by her Mr. Coatney has seven children: Melissa E., Jonathan W., Elbert T., Sarah B., Lelah J., Katie P. and an infant who died unnamed. Mr. Coatney settled where he now lives in 1865, and he now has 120 acres of land, forty being well cultivated and improved. June 14, 1862, he was mustered into the Union service, and served three years, two months and ten days in Company D, First Arkansas Volunteer Cavalry, participating in the battles of Prairie Grove, Pea Ridge, Fayetteville, etc. He was discharged at the last named place in August, 1865. Mr. Coatney and wife belong to the Cumberland Presbyterian Church, in which the former is an elder. He is a Republican politically, and has served as school director.

Jesse P. Cole, farmer and stock raiser, was born in Monroe County, East Tenn., in 1840, and is a son of Andrew and Mary Ann (Robertson) Cole, natives of East Tennessee, born in 1802 and 1804, respectively. After their marriage they lived in Monroe County until 1845, and then moved to Tishomingo County, Miss., where the father died in 1873 and the mother in 1877. The former was a blacksmith by trade, and a successful farmer and stock raiser. The mother belonged to the Baptist Church, and her father, Joseph Robertson, was a soldier in one of the early wars. Jesse P. is the tenth child of a family of seven sons and seven daughters. He attended school but about one year, and accompanied his parents when they immigrated to Mississippi. In 1861 he joined Company C, Jefferson Davis' Legion of Cavalry, and served in Virginia until near the close of the war, when he was sent to North and South Carolina. He first served under Gen. J. E. B. Stewart and Wade Hampton, and participated in the battles of Seven Pines, Gettysburg, Antietam, Fredericksburg, the Wilderness, and many skirmishes. He surrendered at Raleigh, N. C. Although men were killed on all sides of him, he was never wounded, and was captured but once, when he was held a prisoner but two hours. Returning home he was married in December, 1865, to Barbara Ann, daughter of Thomas J. and Lucinda (Richardson) Moser, who went to Mississippi from Tishomingo County, Tenn., where Mrs. Cole was born. Mrs. Cole has borne twelve children, of whom six sons and four daughters are living. In 1867 Mr. Cole removed to Dyer County, Tenn., where he farmed until 1878, and then went to Washington County, Ark. The next year he came to Crawford County, and has since lived upon the farm he now owns, which contains 200 acres of land, and is situated three miles northeast of Alma. In politics Mr. Cole is a Democrat, and his first presidential vote was cast for Greeley in 1872. He has been identified with the Baptist Church since his youth, to which church his wife also belongs. He is a self-made man, and enjoys the respect of the community.

Zill Coleman was born in 1819, in Hickman County, Tenn., and is a son of Enos and Mary (Harrington) Coleman. The father was an early settler in Hickman County, where he spent the greater part of his life engaged in farming. He was an educated man, and served some time as constable. The

****

mother was born in North Carolina, and was nearly grown when she went to Tennessee, traveling there by wagon. She was the mother of ten children: John and Eliza (twins), Erzilla, Zill, E., Caledonia, Alexander and James (twins), Emeline and Caroline (twins). She and her husband died in Tennessee. The grandparents on both sides were natives of North Carolina, immigrated to Tennessee and died in the latter State. Mr. Coleman, our subject, grew to manhood in Tennessee, where he received a common-school education and worked upon the farm. After becoming fifteen he worked for wages three years, and when eighteen married Fannie Neal, who died in 1862, and was the mother of seven children, five now living: Enos, Young, Erzilla, Thomas and Sarah. Those deceased are Martha and McIlvina. Mr. Coleman was married a second time, to Mrs. Harriet (McCurdy) Lucas, daughter of Samuel and Rachel McCurdy, natives of Bedford County, Tenn. Mrs. Coleman was born in the same county, and when a young girl came to Arkansas. She is the mother of two children, Robert R. and Charles (deceased). By her first husband she also had two children, William F. and Samuel. Mr. Lucas died in California. Mr. Coleman came to Crawford County in 1841, and is now the largest tax payer in this section of the country, owning 1,040 acres of land, 200 acres being finely cultivated. He is a strong Republican. Two of his sons, Jasper and Young, served in the Confederate army, and Enos was a Union soldier. Having been a resident of this county so many years, Mr. Coleman enjoys the respect and esteem of the community, but although a public-spirited man has never wished to hold public office. He is a zealous worker in the Methodist Episcopal Church, to which Mrs. Coleman also belongs. He belongs to the Farmers' Alliance.

A. H. Colgrove, of the Van Buren Planing Mills, Manufacturers and Dealers in Lumber, Lath, Shingles, Lime, Cement and all kinds of Building Material. A full stock always kept on hand of Sash, Doors and Blinds. Stair work, Moldings, Brackets, Pickets, Turning, Dry Dressed Flooring, Ceiling, Siding and Finished Lumber a Specialty.

Samuel Collins, retail liquor dealer, of Van Buren, was born in Botetourt County, Va., in 1829, and is a son of John and Mary (Peery) Collins. The father was born in Lynchburgh, Va., in 1810, where he passed his entire life engaged in agricultural pursuits, and was killed in 1873, by the falling of a tree. The mother survived her husband but one year; she was a native of Virginia. Samuel Collins is the oldest of a family of eight children, and at the age of eighteen began to work at blacksmithing, at which he continued many years. In 1848 he moved to Searcy, White Co., Ark., and in 1851 went to Lewisburg, Conway Co., Ark. In 1860 he married Miss Lizzie L. Green, who was born in New Albany, Ind., in 1845, and is the mother of eight children: Pomp Lafayette, Mary M. (wife of Henry Whitaker, engineer on Fort Smith & Little Rock Railway), Willie Lee (wife of Louis Vogle, groceryman at Little Rock), Samuel C., Frederick D., Ernest C., Precious J. and Bennie E. During the late war Mr. Collins spent three years in New Albany, Ind. In 1876 Mrs. Collins started a boarding-house in Lewisburg, and in 1877 moved to Atkins, Ark., and established the Atkins Hotel. In 1882 they moved to Van Buren, where Mrs. Collins keeps a first-class hotel, known as the " Collins Hotel," and enjoys a liberal patronage. In January, 1887, Mr. Collins started the retail liquor business, in which he is now engaged. In politics Mr. Collins is a stanch Democrat, and he is a member of the K. of H.

Tom Comstock was born in Perry County, Tenn., and is a son of Ephraim and Nancy (Goodman) Comstock. His father was reared in Breckenridge County, Ky., and the mother in Graves County, Ky. Tom was born in 1838, and immigrated to McDonald County, Mo., in 1853, where he remained until nearly grown. When twenty years old he was married to Miranda Brown, daughter of Murphey and Rebecca P. Brown, of McDonald County, Mo. There he remained until the Rebellion, at which time he took his stand with the South, and became a noted element in the cause, not for cruelties or barbarity, but for the noble ambition of maintaining what he believed to be justice toward his people in the South. He was a private in Shelby's brigade of Missouri troops until the last year of the war, when he was transferred to an Indian special service regiment in the Indian Territory. Mr. Comstock during the war was always tender and merciful toward prisoners, women and children. At the close of the war he was disbanded in the Chickasaw Nation, near a place called Oichita; he then went to Lamar County, Tex., where he bought a small farm, on which he lived for over two years, then returning to his old neighborhood in Missouri, but not being satisfied there, he immigrated to where he now resides, in Crawford County, Ark., where has lived for about twenty years, most of which time he has been farming. He has now added the mercantile trade to his business, his qualifications for which are only a common-school education, with a reasonable degree of natural wit, humor and sociability. He has no desire to gamble, but being mixed with Indian blood he has a natural feeling for intoxicating beverages, but is not rude or quarrelsome when he is drinking, but full of love and kindness to his wife and children. He is in easy circumstances, and has a fine residence and a beautiful home on Lee's Creek, one and one-fourth miles from the Cherokee Nation line. He is well known in the country by the old familiar name of Uncle Tom. He delights very much in the comforts of the chase, and frequently he and his old associates, Att Ewing, Bob Lowe, Old Hardy Mattax, Jack Morton and others, go out in the Indian country on a camp hunt, which is a pride in the life of Uncle Tom, and the numerous stories and anecdotes he can tell of the wild forest, the beautiful grass, the rough hills, the jaggy rocks, the howling of wolves, the gobbling of turkeys, the lovely crack of the rifle, the hunter's equipage, the lonesome camp, the opportunity for contemplating the glory of nature, carries with them a love too extensive for utterance. Uncle Tom at times appears to be a little skeptical on the authenticity of the Bible doctrines, but he firmly believes in the power that rules, which he calls God; he does not believe that the devil, or all the devils in hell or on the earth, has ever changed God's course or interfered with His will or Divine planning. In following Uncle Tom's career we find in 1882 he engaged in politics for the first and only time, not solicited by friends, and seemingly no motive in view only curiosity, bringing his claims before the people as an independent Democrat. There were four newspapers published in his county, and they all opposed him; he asked his people to support him as their representative in the State Legislature; he was ably opposed by a statesman, who was the regular Democratic nominee and an able lawyer, and also an independent Republican, who was a lawyer, but, as events proved, he was the choice of his people by an overwehlming majority. While a member of the Legislature he did more for his county than any previous member, placing four leading measures into a law that was stubbornly opposed in the General Assembly, and which his county so strongly favored; these things alone make him a noted and popular man in his county. Uncle Tom is a devoted Mason, seeming to think Masonry gave him his best lessons; he has been several times master of subordinate lodges and often a member of the Grand Lodge of his State. He seems to give the Masonic business too much attention; he is often found in melancholy reflection, when apparently he should be lively and jubilant; he seems to believe in dreams at times and other times appears to be thinking about imaginary pursuits, and even brought to tears over these foolish persuasions.

James M. Comstock was born February 23, 1860, in McDonald County, Mo., and is a son of Thomas and Miranda J. (Brown) Comstock, natives of Perry County, Tenn., and McDonald County, Mo., respectively, After becoming of age the father immigrated to Missouri, living in McDonald County until after his marriage. He next engaged in farming in Texas three years, returned to McDonald County a year, and then came to Crawford County, renting land on Lee's Creek a year, and then buying his present place. To himself and wife nine children have been born, six now living: James M., Randolph; Minnie, wife of Edwin McCoy, of Sebastian County; Clinden, Cornelia and Hardy, living, and T. G. and Piney, deceased. James M. worked upon his father's farm during his youth, as his father needed his services, and thus received a very limited education. When twenty-three he began life for himself, and went to Kansas as agent for a washing machine. In a short time he went on to McDonald County, and six months later returned to Crawford County. He then engaged in the mercantile business in Uniontown, with Mr. Wood, for four years, and then, selling his interest, went into partnership with his brother. They now have an extensive stock of goods and enjoy a good patronage. Mr. Comstock married Lucretia E. Wood, daughter of Joseph O. and Letitia Wood, by whom he has had two children, Kennie M., and an infant, who died unnamed. Mr. Comstock has always voted the Democratic ticket, and is a school director.

Barnett C. Conley is a son of Mason S. and Rhoda (Cheatem) Conley, na-

137

CRAWFORD COUNTY, ARKANSAS - BIOGRAPHICAL AND HISTORICAL MEMOIRS
****

tives of Georgia and Virginia, respectively. When young they both went to Alabama, where they were married, in Jackson County, and lived until 1830. They then settled in what is now Carroll County, where the father was killed about 1837. The mother died in this county, when about sixty years of age. The father was a good blacksmith, by which trade he earned his living. The mother was a Presbyterian, and the mother of three sons and three daughters. Barnett C. is the third child, and was born July 20, 1828. He was reared on a farm, and received no literary education, as he was troubled with weak eyes, which prevented study. In 1850 he married Catherine Shepard, a native of Crawford County, who bore him the following children: William M., Serilda, Julia A., Mason S. Mrs. Conley died in 1857, and two years later he wedded Ann E. Mullen, who was born in Tennessee, December 3, 1838, and reared in Washington County, Ark. She is the mother of eight children: Henry J., James B., John F., Francis C., Mary C., George M., Lydia B. and Edie E. Mr. Conley's first wife was a Methodist, but he and his present wife belong to the Christian Church. Mr. Conley has lived in this county nearly forty years, and although he began life with nothing, he now has eighty acres of land, sixty of which he has cultivated. He is a Republican and Master Mason.

Nicholas F. Cornelius, dealer in merchandise and clothing, was born in Hanover, Germany, in 1838, and is a son of Gerhardt D. and Margeret D. (Jontzen) Cornelius, natives of Hanover, born in 1813 and 1811, respectively. The father was a merchant and farmer, and died in 1851, his wife surviving him but eight years. She had three children, two of whom are living: Augustus D., dealer in agricultural implements at Rochester, Ind., and our subject. He lived upon the home farm until fourteen years of age, and then worked in a dry goods store at Bremen until 1854 as an apprentice. He then immigrated to the United States, and for three months clerked in New York. He then went to Indiana and clerked in a dry goods store until 1857, and then went to St. Louis and from there to New Orleans. After a three months' visit to Hanover in 1858 he returned to America, and for one year dealt exclusively in clothing at Buffalo. He then went to New Orleans, and in 1861 established himself in business in Van Buren. During war times he passed twelve months in Rochester, Ind., but with that exception has since been a resident of Van Buren, where he is held in high esteem, and ranked among its prosperous business men. In 1865 he visited Germany again for six months. In 1863 he married Miss Annie Hodges, daughter of John Hodges, and who was born in Louisville, Ky., in 1838. Mr. and Mrs. Cornelius have five living children: Frederick Marion, Rosena, Benjamin Augustus, Augustus Claude and Edna Daugherty. Mr. Cornelius is a Master Mason and a Democrat. In religion he is a believer of the German Lutheran creed, and his wife is a Presbyterian.

Daniel R. Coryell, M. D., of Van Buren, was born in Jennings County, Ind., in 1857, and is a son of Charles J. and Jane (Johnson) Coryell. His great-grandfather was a native of Grand Duchy, Germany, his grandfather, Michael, of New York, and his father, Charles, was born in Seneca County, N. Y., in 1824. In 1839 the latter went to Jennings County, Ind., with his parents, where he was married and now resides, engaged in farming, although he learned the carpenter's trade when young. The grandfather was a soldier in the war with Mexico, and died in 1865. The mother of our subject was born in South Carolina in 1826, and had nine children, of whom Daniel is the fifth. He was reared on a farm, and received his early education at Vernon Academy. When twenty he began to study medicine with Dr. J. F. Mitchell, of Vernon, and in 1880 entered the Ohio Medical College at Cincinnati, from which he graduated in the spring of 1883. The same year he established himself in Van Buren, and with the exception of the year 1887, spent in the drug business at Hackett City, has made this place his home. He is now enjoying the good patronage his skill as a physician deserves. In 1885 he married Miss Josie Winters, daughter of Joseph Winters, of this county. Mrs. Coryell was born in Texas in 1866, and has one child, Ruby. Dr. and Mrs. Coryell belong to the Methodist Episcopal Church, South. The Doctor is a Democrat in politics. He is a member of the Crawford County Medical Society and of the K. of P.

Henry Clay Cradduck was born February 16, 1847, in Crawford County, Ark., and is a son of Presley M. and Sarilda (Lamb) Cradduck. The father was born in Callaway County, Ky., and there grew to manhood, married and engaged in farming. The mother was also born in Kentucky, where she was educated, and married when about eighteen years old. She bore thirteen children, nine of whom are living: Mary McCaslin, wife of John McCaslin, farmer; Elizabeth, wife of William T. Coatney; Henry C.; Emily, wife of Thomas Dotson; John W., James P.; Delphia P., wife of William S. Morrison; James Nathan B.; Josie E., wife of G. D. Gilstrap. Moses M., Elbert T., Ann A. and William are deceased. Mr. Cradduck came to this county over forty-six years ago, and died here in 1862, and was survived by his widow but four years. The grandparents were natives of Kentucky, who came here also about forty-six years ago. While in Kentucky the grandfather served as deputy sheriff. Our subject was principally reared upon a farm in this county, and until his parents' death remained at home, receiving in the meantime a good common-school education. He then, having the care of his younger brothers and sisters, worked as a farm hand a year, and in 1868 married Rachel E. McCurdy, daughter of William K. and Mary McCurdy, early settlers of Washington County, who, however, came to this county before the war. Mrs. Cradduck was principally reared in Crawford County, where she received her education. During the war Mr. Cradduck drove a team for the Government, but has now lived upon his present farm eleven years. He owns a nice little farm of eighty acres, half of which is well cultivated. He is a licensed exhorter in the Methodist Episcopal Church, and also officiates as class-leader, steward and trustee, and although he refused to accept a license to teach he is an active worker in the church, as is also his wife. In politics he is a strong Republican.

John W. Cradduck, farmer, is a son of Presley M. and Sarilda (Lamb) Cradduck, who came from Kentucky to this county about 1840. The father died in Fayetteville, while looking after his stock interests, when about fifty-six years of age, and the mother died four years later, in 1865, aged fifty. The father was a Whig during the days of that party, but afterward became a Republican, and as such held the office of constable in Kentucky. Both himself and wife belonged to the Methodist Church. John W. Cradduck is the ninth of a family of thirteen children, and was born November 10, 1852, in this county. He lost his parents when but a boy, and from the age of thirteen has been dependent upon his own resources. With the exception of four years spent in Missouri, his entire life has been passed in this county. Although he received a meager education during his youth, he is a prosperous farmer of 160 acres, fifty of which he has under cultivation. In March, 1873, he married Penelope Phillips, a native of this county, and the mother of the following children: Charles B., Ira (deceased), James N., Rosa A., Fred and Dovie J. Since his marriage Mr. Cradduck has resided upon his present farm.

Philip R. Craven, retail liquor dealer of Van Buren, was born in Randolph County, N. C., in 1851, and is a son of Isaiah K. and Mary (Snider) Craven. The father was born in the same county in 1830, and his father, also, in 1793. The latter was a farmer and distiller, named John R., and his wife, Charity (Lambert) Craven, was born in 1791 and died in 1834. John R. died in 1858. Isaiah K. Craven married the mother of our subject in 1850, and that marriage was blessed with ten children, seven of whom are living: Philip R.; Sarah J., wife of Henry Yeager; Charity, wife of George Bly; Ida, wife of John Bly; Levi, Solomon and Lydia A. In 1869 Mr. Craven moved to Oregon County, Mo., and in 1870 to Randolph County, Ark. Having been left a widower in 1873, he was married in 1875 to Miss Lucinda A. Bly. He died in Randolph County, Ark., in 1876. Philip R. was reared upon the farm, and engaged in agricultural pursuits in Randolph County until 1876, and from that time until 1881 resided in McDonald County, Mo. From 1880 until 1882 he sold goods in Indian Springs, and then went to Washington County, Ark. In January, 1883, he came to Van Buren, and in 1886 established his present retail liquor business. In 1872 he married Miss Tennessee C. Cooper, who was born in Henry County, Tenn., in 1849. Mr. and Mrs. Craven have seven children: Dahlia, Eli H., Serena, Almedia C., Margeret E., Isaiah N. (deceased), Grover A. and Joseph L. F. In politics he is a Democrat, and cast his first presidential vote for Tilden in 1876. He is a member of the K. of P., and his wife belongs to the Methodist Episcopal Church, South.

Hon. David H. Creekmore was born in Abingdon, Va., in 1817, and is the fifth child of three sons and five daughters born to Ballantine and Mary (Brown) Creekmore. They were born in North Carolina and Virginia, respectively, and after their marriage settled in Abingdon, where they lived until 1819, then

139

CRAWFORD COUNTY, ARKANSAS - BIOGRAPHICAL AND HISTORICAL MEMOIRS
****

removing to Whitley County, Ky. After our subject had grown to manhood they crossed the line into Tennessee, settling in Scott County, where the mother died during the war. The father was a shoemaker by trade, and died some time after in Kentucky. The Creekmore family, which is now scattered over the United States, is directly descended from two brothers, Robert and Ballantine, who came to America from Scotland prior to the Revolution, and served throughout that war. After the surrender at Yorktown they went to North Carolina, and afterward removed to Whitley County, Ky. Our subject is a grandson of Robert Creekmore. During his youth he attended school but three months, but having a desire for knowledge, and being of a studious mind, he became a well-informed man, often studying by the light of a blazing pine. In 1843 he was married in Whitley County to Elizabeth, daughter of John Meadors. Mrs. Creekmore died in 1866 in Crawford County, Ark., leaving one daughter and five sons, and the following year Mr. C. married Mrs. Hannah Edwards, daughter of John L. Peters, and a native of Alabama. She accompanied her parents to this county at an early day, and was here married to Silas Edwards, who was killed in the war. By his second wife Mr. Creekmore has had five children, of whom four are living. Upon the commencement of the war Mr. Creekmore was living at Huntsville, Tenn., and he immediately joined Company G, Second Tennessee Infantry, United States Army, in which he served three months and three days. After his discharge in Kentucky he returned to Huntsville, but his patriotic impulse again compelled him to join his old regiment in Kentucky. He next farmed in Parke County, Ind., for three years, and spent the following year (1865) in Allen County, Kas. In 1866 he came to this county, and the next year settled on his present farm, which he afterward purchased. He came to the county a poor man, but now owns 240 acres of good land, 140 of which are finely cultivated. In 1860 he took the census of Scott County, Tenn., in 1870 the census of Crawford County, and in 1880 of Alma and Richland Townships. In 1873 he served as one of the three men who constituted the county court, and in 1874, after the Constitution was changed, was elected county and probate judge, serving two years with great satisfaction. In 1878 he represented the county in the Lower House of the Legislature one term. While in Huntsville, Tenn., he held the office of justice of the peace for five years. Although a self-educated man, he filled the various public positions with great credit, and to the entire satisfaction of his constituents. He is an enterprising man and public-spirited citizen, and is an earnest helper of all educational projects. His first presidential vote was cast for Gen. Harrison in 1840, and since the days of the Whig party he has voted the Republican ticket. He is a member of the G. A. R., and himself and wife belong to the Missionary Baptist Church.

Thomas L. Daniel, member of the grocery firm of Reed & Daniel, was born in Mercer County, Ky., in 1850, and is a son of John S. and Mary E. (Coleman) Daniel. The father was born in Virginia in 1814, and when a young man went to Mercer County, Ky., where he married Mary E. Coleman. She was born in Kentucky and died in 1860. Soon after her death Mr. Daniel moved to Madison County, Ala., and there married Miss Kate M. Bronaugh, who was born in Alabama in 1840. About 1862 Mr. Daniel came to Van Buren, afterward resided a short time in Hempstead County, Ark., and for quite a number of years has resided ten miles north of the county seat of Crawford County. Thomas L. Daniel passed his youth upon a farm, and in 1872 married Miss Sallie C. O'Bryan, daughter of Arnold O'Bryan. Mrs. Daniel was born in Crawford County in 1857, and is the mother of four children: Arnold, Ella and Emma, twins, and John. Mr. T. L. Daniel farmed until 1885, and then engaged in street sprinkling in Van Buren two years. January 10, 1887, he went into partnership with James F. Reed and his brother, William R., in the grocery business, the firm now being known as Reed & Daniel. They are good business men and have a liberal patronage. Mr. Daniel is a stockholder in the Van Buren Ice and Coal Company, and is the owner of seven acres of land in Logtown and eighty acres near Van Buren. In politics he is a Democrat, and himself and wife belong to the Christian Church.

William R. Daniel, of the grocery firm of Reed & Daniel, was born in Hempstead County, Ark., in 1864, and is a son of John S. and Kate M. (Bronaugh) Daniel [see sketch of Thomas L. Daniel]. Mr. Daniel's early life was spent upon a farm, and he received an education which helped make him a

140

CRAWFORD COUNTY, ARKANSAS - BIOGRAPHICAL AND HISTORICAL MEMOIRS
****

good business man in after life. In October, 1887, he married Miss Lulu Brown, daughter of William Brown, and a native of Illinois. Mr. Daniel is one of the enterprising young business men of Van Buren, is a stockholder in the Van Buren Ice and Coal Company, and is held in general esteem. In politics he is a Democrat.

John S. Daniel, father of Thomas L. and William R. Daniel, was the son of John R. Daniel, and grandson of William M. Daniel, of Orange County, Va. John S. Daniel was born in Spottsylvania County, Va., June 4, 1814, and moved to Kentucky in 1829. He attended the Catholic school at Bardstown, Ky., after leaving which he worked for Samuel P. Weisigar, at Frankfort, Ky., and afterward for John Postlethweight, at the Phœnix Hotel, Lexington, Ky. After marrying he opened the Smiley House, in Bardstown, Ky., and kept it about four years. In 1860 he immigrated to Crawford County, Ark., which has been his permanent home ever since, with the exception of two years during the Rebellion, when he made his home in Hempstead County, Ark. He, like a great many other Virginians and Kentuckians, was on the losing side of the late unpleasantness between the North and South. In politics his first vote for President was for Andrew Jackson. In 1860 he voted for John C. Breckenridge, and in 1888 for Grover Cleveland.

Elisha Dean (deceased), formerly a farmer in LaFayette Township, was born in Pickens County, S. C., in 1810, and was a son of Elisha and Jemima Dean. Both parents were natives of South Carolina, where the mother died. The father was a son of English parents, who settled in South Carolina in an early day. His death took place in Mississippi. Elisha Dean, our subject, was married, about 1835, to Caroline, daughter of James and Elizabeth Parsons, and a native of Pickens County, born in 1814. In 1837 they moved to Alabama, and from there went to Mississippi about six years later, making that place their home until 1867. They then came to Polk County, but only remained there one year, removing subsequently to Crawford County, and after renting land two years purchased a large farm on the mountains five miles north of Alma, in LaFayette Township. Mr. Dean at once proceeded to improve the place, and engaged in farming there until his death in 1875. He was a successful and good citizen, and his property was the result of his own labor and good management. He had been a member of the Baptist Church many years, and in politics was a Democrat. To himself and wife ten children had been born, of whom five sons and three daughters are living: William J., James M., H. Pinckney, Frank (of Washington Territory), Elisha P., Emily C. (wife of William Davis), Sarah A. (wife of William Sutton) and Margaret (wife of C. A. Bulion). Three of his sons, William J., James M. and Thomas P., served in the Confederate army. The last was captured in Mississippi, and after being held a prisoner some months, died at his home at the close of the war from the effects of army exposure. Mrs. Dean is a member of the Baptist Church. Elisha P. Dean, a son of our subject, was married in 1879 to Jennie Hill, who died four years after. He remained a widower one year, and then married Bettie Overstreet, daughter of Mattison Overstreet, and a native of Mississippi. Mr. Overstreet served in the Confederate army, and about 1869 came to Crawford County, where he died. Mr. and Mrs. Dean have two sons. Mr. Dean's first wife was a daughter of Richard Hill, of Georgia, where she was born. Mr. Hill came to Crawford County in 1869, and lived here until his death. Mr. Dean is a successful farmer of 200 acres of good land, well improved.

James M. Dean, farmer and miller, and the son of Elisha and Caroline (Parsons) Dean, was born in Cherokee County, Ala., August 28, 1837. The great-grandfather Parsons was an Englishman, and was once shipwrecked and picked up. He was an heir to an immense inheritance, but always refused to return and make claim thereto. He was captain of a ship, and was on his first voyage as such when wrecked. Elisha Dean lived in South Carolina until his marriage, and then went to Alabama, where he conducted a farm six years, after which he lived twenty-five years in Mississippi. In 1868 he went to Polk County, Ark., and in 1869 bought land near Clear Creek, Crawford County, where he farmed until his death, May 20, 1875. He was born August 27, 1810. The mother was born November 1, 1814, in Pickens County, S. C., where she was reared, and married in her twentieth year. She is now enjoying a ripe old age, living with a son on her husband's farm in this county. She is the mother of ten children, eight of whom are living: William J., James M.,

141

CRAWFORD COUNTY, ARKANSAS - BIOGRAPHICAL AND HISTORICAL MEMOIRS

****

Emily C. (wife of William Davis), Sarah (wife of William Sutton), Margaret (wife of Mr. Bullion), Hosea P., Franklin P., Preston B. Those deceased are Mary A. and Thomas P. Elisha Dean, the paternal grandfather, was born in South Carolina, and when seventy years of age went to Mississippi, where he died in his ninety-ninth year. His first wife, whose maiden name was Jones, spent her entire life in South Carolina. He afterward married a lady whose maiden name was Heard. His maternal grandparents, James Parsons and wife, were born and died in South Carolina. He was a soldier in the War of 1812. James' great-grandfather Dean was an Englishman who immigrated to America about 1700. James M. Dean was reared upon a farm in Mississippi. He remained home until twenty-four years old, and in August, 1861, enlisted in Company B, Fourth Mississippi Volunteer Infantry, which was known as the "Yellow Jacket" Company, and during his engagement served in a number of important engagements, among which were the siege of Atlanta, Nashville, Franklin, siege of Vicksburg, Murfreesboro, Snyder's Bluff, Duvall's Bluff and Corinth. He was captured at Vicksburg, but was exchanged. In November, 1865, Mr. Dean married Naomi Mayfield, daughter of Pearson and Jane (Young) Mayfield, natives of South Carolina, where Mrs. Dean was born, October 10, 1843. She went to Mississippi with her parents when eight years old, and is the mother of two children, Virgie L., wife of Samuel A. Miller, of Van Buren, and Bettie May. Mr. Miller is the present senator from this district. Three years after his marriage Mr. Dean farmed in Mississippi, and in 1869 immigrated to Crawford County. He rented land the first year, and then bought land, which he has since improved. He now has 240 acres, seventy-five being well cultivated. Beside his farm Mr. Dean has a saw and grist-mill and cotton-gins. He is a strong Democrat. He is a member of the Missionary Baptist Church, and his daughters, Virgie and Bettie, belong to the Methodist Episcopal Church, South.

Ben Decherd was born in Franklin County, Tenn., in 1828, being a son of Peter Spyker and Frances Holder Decherd. The father was of German descent, born in Abingdon, Va., in 1800, and was a son of Michael Decherd, a native of Pennsylvania, and a hatter by trade. In an early day he went to Franklin County, Tenn., where he died about 1835. Peter S. was a young man when he went to Tennessee. He was there married in 1827, and after accumulating a handsome estate he moved to McLennan County, Tex., in 1854, where he owned large landed estates and many slaves. In 1869 he came to Western Arkansas, and spent his remaining days on a farm near Van Buren. He died in 1879. The mother of our subject was born in Kentucky in 1812, and died in 1868. She was the daughter of John W. Holder, and the mother of eight children, of whom Ben was the eldest. He was educated in the literary and law departments of Cumberland University, Lebanon, Tenn. In 1873 he located near Alma, Crawford Co., Ark., where he farmed on Clear Creek. In 1886 he was elected circuit clerk and *ex-officio* county clerk and recorder of Crawford County, by thirty-six majority, and in 1886 was re-elected by 160 majority, and is now filling the position satisfactorily. In politics he is a Democrat, and his first presidential vote was cast for Pierce in 1850. In 1852 he married Miss Mary McClain, a daughter of Josiah S. McClain, who was county clerk of Wilson County, Tenn., for forty years. Mrs. Decherd was born in Lebanon, Tenn., in 1830, and bore our subject three children, all of whom are deceased. Mrs. Decherd died in 1869, and in 1873 he married Mrs. Ada S. Barbour, *nee* Alexander, who was born in Mecklenburgh County, N. C., in 1838. Mrs. Decherd had three children by her first marriage: Edward A., now city attorney at Springfield, Mo.; Mary E. and Annie. Mr. Decherd is an elder in the Cumberland Presbyterian Church.

James A. Dibrell, M. D., was born in Nashville, Tenn., in 1817, and is a son of Edwin and Martha (Shrewsbury) Dibrell. The father was a descendant of a French Huguenot family which fled from France during the reign of Louis XIV into South Carolina, and later into Virginia. His father, Anthony, was a member of the Virginia Legislature. He was a soldier in the Revolutionary War, was wounded at Guilford, and carried off the field by a giant named Peter Francisco. He was a politician, and had some sparring tilts with John Randolph. For about twenty years Edwin Dibrell was recorder and *ex-officio* clerk of the mayor's court at Nashville. He subsequently conducted a tobacco commission house in Richmond, Va., and under President Polk was a clerk in the Federal treasury department. He was a self-educated man, and a stanch supporter of

142

CRAWFORD COUNTY, ARKANSAS - BIOGRAPHICAL AND HISTORICAL MEMOIRS
****

justice. He died in Richmond. Martha Shrewsbury Dibrell was of English descent, a native of Kentucky, and the mother of nine children. Our subject was chiefly educated in the University of Nashville, under the distinguished Dr. Lindsley. He was fond of the classics, and studied medicine in Nashville three years under Dr. Thomas R. Jennings, and graduated from the medical department of the University of Pennsylvania in 1839, and fifteen years later reviewed his studies at that place. Since graduating he has practiced continuously in Van Buren for forty-eight years, with the exception of four years spent at Little Rock during the war, whither he went for personal safety. For some time he was assistant surgeon of both armies. Dr. Dibrell has devoted his entire attention to his profession, and has performed a large number of difficult surgical operations. His eldest son, J. A. Dibrell, Jr., is professor of anatomy in Little Rock, and president of the medical college there. He is a man of sterling integrity. His profession yields him an annual income of about $3,000 a year, and he is one of the prominent physicians of this part of the State. In 1841 the Doctor married Miss Ann Eliza Pryor, who was born in Nashville, Tenn., in 1825, and died in 1854. She was the mother of the following children: Angela Medora, wife of Dr. Elias R. Du Val, a physician of Fort Smith; James A., M. D., graduate of the University of Pennsylvania, and resident of Little Rock; Ann Eliza, wife of George Sparks, of Fort Smith. In 1855 the Doctor wedded a sister of his first wife, Jane Emily Pryor, a lady of culture and beauty. This union has been blessed with four children: Sarah Susan, wife of Dr. George F. Hynes, of Fort Smith, Ark.; Edwin R., M. D., graduate of the State Industrial University of Little Rock, of the University of Pennsylvania, and post-graduate of New York, now a resident of Little Rock; Irene Griffith, wife of Albert Shibley, of Van Buren, and Matt. Shrewsbury, who is studying medicine under his father. Dr. Dibrell joined the Masonic Lodge No. 6 in 1841, has occupied all the chairs, and has been Master of the lodge several years. He is also a Knight Templar. He was medical examiner of the New York Mutual Life Insurance Company for several years, and in 1886 was president of the State Medical Society, of which he is a member. He is chairman of the county examining medical board, and a member of the American Medical Association. He has been a ruling elder of the Presbyterian Church since 1848.

James M. Dick was born in Wayne County, Ky., in 1851, and is a son of Thomas and Nancy (Foster) Dick, natives of the same county. The father is now eighty-seven years of age, and is engaged in farming in his native county in connection with stock raising. He has been twice married. John Dick, the grandfather, was born in Virginia, and in an early day went to Wayne County, where he died. He was a soldier in the War of 1812. The mother of our subject died about 1875. Her father, Fred Foster, was a native of Virginia, and an early settler of Wayne County, where he died in 1836. James M. Dick was the eldest of seven children, and during his youth received a common-school education. In 1871 he married Amelder, daughter of Cyrus and Zenovia Barrer, who came to Crawford County, Ark., from Kentucky in 1872 with Mr. Dick. He farmed on rented land in different parts of the county for some years, collecting a large herd of cattle in the meantime, and in 1883 purchased a tract of bottom land, which he proceeded to improve. He now has 220 acres of well-improved land, and is successfully engaged in farming and the lumber business, besides owning a cotton-gin. He has accumulated his property by industry and good management, and is one of the self-made men of the county. He is a law-abiding citizen, and has done good service as deputy sheriff and deputy United States Marshal in driving away lawless persons. In 1887 he was commissioned revenue detective, but on account of poor health resigned. In August, 1888, he was appointed agent of the "Lone Star Detective and Information Agency." In politics he is conservative, but cast his first presidential vote for Greeley in 1872.

Davidson Dickson was born in Trumbull County, Ohio, in 1821, and is a son of John and Sarah (Shields) Dickson, and of English and Irish descent, respectively. The father was born in Franklin County, Penn., in 1756; in 1798 removed to Washington County, and in 1800 went to Trumbull County, Ohio, where he died in 1826. He was a soldier in the Revolutionary War, and assisted in capturing the Hessians at the battle of Trenton. In connection with farming he engaged in merchandising. His third wife was the mother of our subject.

Her birth occurred in Pennsylvania about 1792, her death in 1850, and she was the mother of nine children, of whom Davidson was the sixth. He lost his father when fifteen years old, but continued to make his home with his mother until nineteen years of age. Having received a good common-school education, at the age of twenty-one he taught school two terms, and subsequently clerked in a store at Poland three years. He afterward made a trip through the Southern States, and April 25, 1844, came to Van Buren, where he established a grocery store, and engaged in business until 1846. In that year the Whigs elected him surveyor of Crawford County, and the following term he was re-elected. From 1850 until 1853 he served as deputy surveyor. In 1874 he was again elected surveyor, and has received the re-election each succeeding term. He has one of the best surveying outfits and the most copious field notes of any surveyor in Northwestern Arkansas, and fills the position with the utmost efficiency. He is the author of the map of Crawford County, which is skillfully done and finely executed. During the war Mr. Dickson served in the Confederate commissary department, his station being in Van Buren. In 1864 he began to clerk for C. C. Powell in his general store, and in 1866 he became a partner, but a year later resumed clerking. In 1851 he married Elizabeth Newland, who was born in Monroe County, Tenn., in 1829. This union has been blessed with five children: George (born April 12, 1852, died August 19, 1853), Albert (born April 5, 1855, in Union County, Oreg., and a saddler by trade), Belle Dora (born April 6, 1857, died January 12, 1880), Charles (born June 3, 1863, died February 12, 1883), and Homer (born October 3, 1870, and was drowned in the Arkansas River May 12, 1880). Mr. and Mrs. Dickson are members of the Methodist Episcopal Church, South, and the former is a Master Mason.

Robert L. Dillon was born in Rutherford County, Tenn., in 1842, and is a son of Allen and Lucy (Lafton) Dillon, natives of Virginia and Rutherford County, Tenn., respectively. They were married in the last named county, and some years after went to Sumter County, Ala., where the father died when our subject was quite small. The family then lived with Mrs. Dillon's father, in Tennessee, until Robert was ten years old, when they all removed to Jackson County, Ark., the grandfather dying soon after. Mrs. Dillon survived the death of her father but a short time, and then our subject came to Crawford County, Ark., with an aunt, with whom he made his home until the war. In 1862 he joined Company I (cavalry), commanded by Capt. J. F. Winfrey, which was afterward reorganized and made an infantry company in the nine months' service. He remained until the close of the war, and participated in the battle of Prairie Grove and many minor engagements. He surrendered at Fort Washita, I. T., and then went to Texas. In 1867 he returned to Crawford County, and rented land until 1878, after which he married Phoebe, daughter of Hon. Harvey and Agnes Steward [see sketch of W. T. Steward]. To this union six children have been born, of whom four are living. Since his marriage Mr. Dillon has lived upon his present farm, which is situated two miles above Rudy Station, and contains 160 acres, all of which Mr. Dillon has become the owner of by patient industry and economy. Politically he is a Democrat, and his first presidential vote wast cast for Seymour in 1868.

John H. Dougan, farmer and stock raiser, was born in Jefferson County, Ark., in 1850, and is a son of Thomas and Semiramis (Rogers) Dougan, natives of Tennessee and Alabama, respectively. He accompanied his parents to Saline County, where he was reared and married. The father died in Jefferson County, Ark., in 1863, and the mother is now living in Franklin County. She is a member of the Methodist Church, and her husband belonged to the Presbyterian. Being the second child and eldest son of a family of five sons and five daughters (two sons and two daughters now living), at the death of his father the main support of the family devolved upon our subject. He was educated in the common schools of the neighborhood, and lived with his mother in Crawford County until 1871, and in 1874 married Jane E., daughter of Richard M. and Nancy Thurston, and a native of Crawford County. This marriage has been blessed with three children. Mrs. Dougan's father served many years ago as justice of the peace, and was a native of Alabama. He served throughout the war in the Confederate army. His wife was born in Arkansas, and died about 1872, after which he was again married. Mr. Dougan owns 150 acres of land three miles east of Alma, and for some years has been running a sorghum mill Himself and wife are Methodists, and in politics he is a Democrat.

144

CRAWFORD COUNTY, ARKANSAS - BIOGRAPHICAL AND HISTORICAL MEMOIRS
****

M. W. Drewrey, brick manufacturer and contractor, was born in Princess Anne County, Va., in 1828, and is a son of Dr. Matthias and Frances (Wells) Drewrey. The father graduated from a medical college in Virginia, and was associated with Dr. Nash in Norfolk. He was of Scotch descent, born in 1800 and died in 1858. His father was John Drewrey, and his grandfather, Matthias Drewrey, came to the United States from Scotland at an early date. The mother of our subject was born in Virginia and died in 1830, and was the second wife of Dr. Drewrey, bearing him three children, of whom our subject was the eldest. Dr. Drewrey was three times married. M. W. Drewrey was but two years old when he lost his mother, and was educated in his native State, living in Norfolk, Va., until sixteen years of age. He then worked as an apprentice at the brick-mason's trade for five years, and in 1857 was employed in the Government navy yard at Norfolk for fourteen months. In 1861 he enlisted in the Confederate service, in Company A, Sixteenth Regiment Atlantic Guards, serving as first lieutenant for eighteen months. After the war he worked at his trade in Memphis, Tenn., and in 1869 removed to Van Buren, where he has since made his home. For the past eighteen years he has manufactured brick in Van Buren; the first year he made 600,000, and has averaged 300,000 per annum since, having made in all about 5,400,000. He has sold them for about $7 per 1,000, thus netting him the sum of $37,600. During these years he has erected a large number of the best buildings in town, among which may be mentioned the court-house, public school, Methodist Episcopal Church, South, and the business blocks of Wood & Southmayed, Creekmore & Lynch, etc. He has also erected a large college at North Fork and a public school at Paris, Ark. He is a good citizen, and has done more business in his line than any other man in the county. In 1857 he married Miss Amy Rainey, daughter of John S. Rainey, a native of Princess Anne County, Va., and this marriage has been blessed with two children, Maggie, living, and a son who died at the age of seven years. In politics Mr. Drewrey is conservative, but favors Republican principles. He is a member of the I. O. O. F., and himself and wife belong to the Methodist Episcopal Church, South.

Joseph Starr Dunham, editor and proprietor of the Van Buren *Press*, was born in Connecticut in 1823, and is a son of the late William H. and Frances (Starr) Dunham, he being the third of a family of five children. He was apprenticed to his uncle, William D. Starr, at the age of thirteen, thus learning the printer's trade, at Middletown, Conn. In 1859 he left Middletown and immigrated to Van Buren, where he established the Van Buren *Press* the same year, having purchased the materials for a printing office in Cincinnati. For a few years he was assisted in the management of the paper by his son, Joseph Starr Dunham (deceased), but with that exception has been the sole proprietor. He is a strong writer, a leading journalist of Northwestern Arkansas, and his paper is the oldest in the county, It contains the current news and has a weekly circulation of 550 copies. In 1846 he married Miss Mary C. Ward, who was born in Middletown, Conn., in 1825, and bore him four children: Frank Augustus (deceased), Mary Starr (deceased), Fanny Ingersoll, (wife of Phillip D. Scott, superintendent of ice factory at Van Buren), and Joseph Starr, Jr., who died June 23, 1888, in Van Buren, aged twenty-five. Mr. Dunham is a Democrat, and at the commencement of hostilities was for the Union, but afterward seceded with the State of Arkansas. He conducts the paper on strictly Democratic principles, and is a firm advocate of the nominees of that party. He supported Douglas in 1860, George B. McClellan in 1864, and all of the Democratic candidates in succession, to the present date. He also supported Baxter in the famous Brooks and Baxter quarrel, in Arkansas. He is a prosperous man, a stockholder in the Van Buren Ice and Coal Company, and a citizen of high standing.

Benjamin Dyer, farmer and stock raiser, was born in East Tennessee, near the Tennessee River, February 29, 1832, and when but a few weeks old was brought by his parents to Crawford County, which was then a vast wilderness inhabited by wild animals, game and Indians. He naturally had no educational opportunities when young, and his literary knowledge has all been obtained since by personal effort. He was married December 16, 1851, to Mary Ann Etherly, a native of Tennessee, who had just come to this county. She died in 1858, leaving two sons and one daughter, all of whom are now living near home. In 1859 Mr. Dyer married Sirviller, daughter of Sudeth D. and Sarah Turner,

145

CRAWFORD COUNTY, ARKANSAS - BIOGRAPHICAL AND HISTORICAL MEMOIRS
****

natives of Kentucky, who came to Arkansas in 1842, when Mrs. Dyer was but a year old. They first located in Washington County, but afterward went to Franklin County, where the father died in 1855. The mother died in 1873 in Crawford County. Mr. Turner served for some time as justice of the peace, and was surveyor of what is now Floyd County, Ky. To Mr. Dyer and his second wife ten children have been born, of whom four sons and five daughters are living. After his first marriage Mr. Dyer lived a year in Washington County. He then moved to Frog Bayou, but for twenty-nine years has lived on Little Mulberry, where he has a nice farm of 180 acres. For three years after his first marriage he engaged in blacksmithing, but since 1860 he has been engaged in fruit distilling. Before the war he was a Democrat, and cast his first presidential vote for Buchanan, but since then has been a Republican. He is a public-spirited citizen, and from 1864 until 1866 served as justice of the peace. He has belonged to the Masonic fraternity for nineteen years, and was formerly a member of the Pleasant Hill and Clear Creek Lodges; now, however, he is a member of the Graphic Lodge, No. 454. Himself and wife have been identified with the Baptist Church since 1855, to which church his first wife also belonged. During the late war Mr. Dyer served in 1864 in the Thirteenth Kansas as quartermaster, being stationed at Van Buren and Fort Smith, under Sidney Smith, in the quartermaster's department. Mr. Dyer's parents, Benjamin and Martha (Pogue) Dyer, were born in North Carolina in 1798 and 1806, respectively. They were married in their native State, and soon after went to Tennessee. In 1832 they came to this county, where the father died in 1835. He was a farmer, blacksmith and distiller, and it is thought he served in one of the early wars. The mother was a Baptist and a devoted Christian. Caleb Dyer, the grandfather, was born in North Carolina, and died in the East. His wife, Rebecca, came to this county in 1833, where she died in 1836.

Stephen M. Dyer was born in Washington County, Ark., in 1842, and is a son of Joel and Sarah Ann (Talkington) Dyer, natives of North Carolina and Kentucky, respectively. In 1836 Mr. Dyer's mother and nine children started for Arkansas, some traveling up the Arkansas River in a flat-boat and some crossing the plains with stock. They located where Mountainburg now is, when the country was a wilderness but sparsely settled. Joel soon after married, and lived in Washington County until 1850, when he removed to Dyer Station, in this county. He was of English descent, a well-to-do farmer, a stock raiser and blacksmith, and died in 1864. The mother died in 1881, and both belonged to the Presbyterian Church. Caleb Dyer, our subject's grandfather, was born in North Carolina, where he died when Joel was a boy. He was a soldier in one of the early wars. Stephen M. Dyer is the third child of a family of thirteen, six sons and six daughters living. He attended the log house subscription school-house of the neighborhood until seventeen, then attended a higher school in Washington County, and afterward went one term to Cane Hill College. Soon after the war began he joined a company of State troops, and afterward served in the First Arkansas Mounted Infantry under Col. Churchill. In June, 1862, he was transferred to the Twenty-second Arkansas Infantry, operating in the Trans-Mississippi Department. He was in active service during the entire time, and was never wounded or captured. He surrendered at Fort Smith. He accompanied Gen. Price on his raid through Missouri. In 1872 he married Elizabeth, daughter of Stephen Alsobrook, a native of South Carolina, who accompanied her father to this county in 1851. Mr. A. was a brigadier-general, and commanded the Crawford County militia at the battle of Elkhorn in 1862. Mr. and Mrs. Dyer have seven children, and since 1874 have lived adjoining the old homestead at Dyer Station, which was named in honor of the family. Mr. Dyer began life a poor boy, but is now comfortably fixed, and owns and operates a good cotton-gin by steam. He is a Democrat, casting his first presidential vote for Seymour in 1868, and has served as justice of the peace of Alma Township. He belongs to the Alma Masonic Lodge No. 43, and is a member of the new order "Palm and Shell." He is a Presbyterian and his wife is a Methodist.

Thomas R. Early was born in Whitley County, Ky., June 29, 1848, and is a son of Dr. James H. and Fannie F. (Hammond) Early. His great-grandfather was a soldier in the Revolutionary War, and his grandfather in the War of 1812. The father and mother were born in Whitley County in 1808 and 1809, respectively. Dr. Early represented his county in the State Legislature in 1844, and for forty years practiced his profession in his native county. In politics he was

146

CRAWFORD COUNTY, ARKANSAS - BIOGRAPHICAL AND HISTORICAL MEMOIRS
****

a Whig, and both himself and wife belonged to the Methodist Episcopal Church. Having lost his wife in 1859 he was wedded to Rebecca Sammons, *nee* Cummings, who had four daughters by her first husband. Mr. Early hád six sons and two daughters by his first marriage, and three sons by his second. Thomas R. was reared on a farm and educated at the common schools and Williamsburg Academy. At eighteen he began to teach in connection with farming, and has followed that profession since. January 12, 1871, he married Tempy Sammons, daughter of his step-mother. She was born November 21, 1851, in Whitley County, Ky., and is the mother of ten children: Randolph, James H., George W., William H., Willis, Samuel F., John F., Jacob, Fannie F. and Thomas S. Mrs. Early is a Methodist and her husband a Missionary Baptist. After living in Kentucky until 1880 they moved to Lamar County, Texas, and three years later came to this county. In 1863 Mr. Early enlisted in Company F, Thirty-second Kentucky Infantry, United States army, serving three months. On the day of his discharge he enlisted in Company G, Forty-ninth Kentucky Infantry, and served until December, 1864. Three brothers also served in the Union army. He is a Republican, served as justice of the peace in Kentucky, and holds the same office here. In 1888 he was the Republican nominee for representative, and ran ahead of his ticket, but was beaten sixty-nine votes. He owns 200 acres of land, 100 being cultivated, and has made his property by personal effort.

T. W. Edmondson, of the firm of Wood, Edmondson & Britt, Star Grocery House, was born in Fort Smith in 1857, and is a son of Samuel and Ann (Manning), Edmondson. The father was of Scotch-Irish descent, born in Tennessee in 1803, and when small went with his father, Thomas, to Macon, Ga. He was a lawyer, and when a young man located in Crawford County, at old Crawford Court House, but later moved to Fort Smith, where he was one of the first settlers. He devoted his attention to his profession and political affairs, and represented Sebastian County in the State Legislature two terms. He was one of the leading lights of the Fort Smith bar for a number of years. His death occurred in 1866. The mother of T. W. was Mr. Edmondson's second wife, who was born in Ireland in 1819. She came to the United States when about twelve, and is now a resident of Fort Smith. Two of her children are living: Samuel M., born in Fort Smith in 1853, and now justice of the peace, and our subject. His early education was received at the last named place, and when thirteen he clerked in a restaurant one year, and afterward in a bakery. In 1876 he came to VanBuren, and established a bakery and restaurant. In 1882 W. O. Girard became his partner, and in 1884 Mr. Edmondson sold his interest. In 1885 he worked for Shibley & Wood, and the following year Harry Wood and himself established a grocery, which they ran a year. He then sold out to Mr. Wood and started for himself, and in 1887 sold out to James Wood and Frederick Britt, but in March, 1888, bought a third interest in the firm. They have one of the finest and best stocks in Van Buren, and enjoy a large patronage. In 1879 Mr. Edmondson married Annie Wood, daughter of James M. and Sophronia Wood, and a native of this town, born in 1860. She is a member of the Christian Church, but he is a Catholic. He is a director and stockholder in the VanBuren Ice and Coal Company, and is treasurer of the same. Politically he is a Democrat, and his first presidential vote was cast for Hancock in 1880.

Leander Elkins, farmer, was born November 9, 1845, in Wayne County, W. Va., and is a son of D. K. and Lydia E. (Adkins) Elkins, also natives of the same State. The father moved to Vernon County, Mo., in 1856, and died the same year. In connection with farming he was a mechanic and cabinet maker, and worked at those trades. Eight of his eleven children are still living: Furibin, of Washington County; J. K., of California; Mrs. Nancy E. Kimes, of this county; Mrs. Phœbe Kimes, of this county; Mrs. Lucinda Reed, of Barry County, Mo.; Mrs. Louisa A. Kimes, of this county; Leander and L. W. Elkins, of Livingston, Ill. The grandparents, Jacob and Phœbe Adkins, were of English descent. The former was born in Jamestown Colony, Va., in 1758, and died in 1862, and the latter was born about 1768. They moved from Jamestown Colony to New River, and lastly to Wayne County, Va., where they engaged in farming. Our subject lived upon the farm in West Virginia until eleven years of age, receiving but a meager education, and then went to Missouri, and from Missouri to Arkansas in 1857, and at the age of twenty-one began life for himself by farming. In 1868 he married Marilda J. Kimes, who was born in Wayne

147

CRAWFORD COUNTY, ARKANSAS - BIOGRAPHICAL AND HISTORICAL MEMOIRS
****

County, Mo., in 1848, and is a daughter of Valentine and Martha (Stell) Kimes, natives of Virginia and Georgia, respectively. Mr. and Mrs. Kimes moved from Virginia to Wayne County, Mo., and in 1850 came to Crawford County. Seven of their children live in this county, and one resides in California. They are: Mrs. Louisa A. Lester, of California; F. M. Kimes, D. G. Kimes, James M., Mrs. Elkins, Hiram N. Kimes, Thomas H. Kimes, Mrs. Martha Tribble and Mrs. Mary Snell. Mr. Elkins enlisted May 14, 1864, in Company A, First Arkansas Cavalry, United States Army, serving under Capt. J. S. Dudley and Col. M. L. Harrison until discharged August 23, 1865. He operated in Northwestern Arkansas, Missouri and Indian Territory, participating in two battles at Fayetteville and nine guerrilla fights in Northwestern Arkansas. In politics Mr. Elkins is a Republican, and his first presidential vote was cast for U. S. Grant in 1868.

J. A. Farris, farmer of Alma, was born in Newton County, Mo., in 1840. His father, Jasper, was born near Chattanooga, Tenn., and after his marriage removed to Missouri, where he died, and his widow continued to live. Our subject and his brother were adopted by William Marrs, who came to Crawford County when Mr. Farris was about six years of age. He received but a limited education, and lived with Mr. Marrs until June, 1862, when he joined Capt. Carroll's company, and after the reorganization of the same served in Company C, Second Arkansas Cavalry, until the close of the war. He was on active duty nearly the entire time, and operated in Missouri, Arkansas and Texas until the company was disbanded at Marshall, Tex., in May, 1865. In 1859 he married Mahala Couch, who died in 1883, leaving six children. In 1885 he wedded Minda Warfield, a resident of Crawford County, but a native of Tennessee. Mr. Farris settled in Grayson County, Tex., after his first marriage, making that place his home until 1870, when he returned to Crawford County. He has since made his home near Alma, and by patient industry has become the owner of a nice farm of 240 acres. Politically Mr. Farris is a Democrat, and his first presidential vote was cast for Greeley, in 1872. Himself and wife belong to the Christian Church. Mr. Farris has no brother or sister living.

John Flanagin was born December 4, 1848, in Putnam County, Mo., and is a son of John and Ruth (Triplett) Flanagin. The father was born in Russell County, Ky., in 1810, and there learned the shoemaker's trade, which he followed about twenty years, part of the time in Jonestown, Ky. He immigrated to Missouri about 1845, and in 1868 came to Crawford County, Ark., where he died in September, of the following year. The mother was born in the same county as her husband, and bore him fifteen children, ten of whom are living: Elizabeth (wife of R. E. Spoon), William (of Montana), Millie (wife of Daniel Johns), Nathan, Anthony (of Sullivan County), John, Mary (also married), Nancy (wife of John Reed), Benjamin, Phoebe A. (wife of Clements Morton). Bryant, Lloyd and Charles died in prison at Alton, Ill., and Martha and Sarah are deceased. The paternal grandparents were natives of Ireland, and after their marriage immigrated to the United States, settling in Russell County, Ky., where they died. The maternal grandparents moved from North Carolina to Kentucky after their marriage, and subsequently went to Putnam County, Mo., where the grandmother died. The grandfather came to this county in 1866, returned again to Missouri, and died in Arkansas in 1880, aged eighty. Our subject's mother is now making her home with her son, Daniel, aged seventy-two, and in good health. John Flanagin lived upon the the home farm until his marriage, and received but a limited education during his youth. December 16, 1869, he married Martha E. Bogg, daughter of William T., a native of North Carolina, who went to Tennessee, from there to Texas, and then to Crawford County, Ark. Mrs. Bogg was born, married and died in Tennessee. Mr. and Mrs. Flanagin have had nine children, eight now living: Julia, Minnie, Emma, John, Robert, Katie D., Thomas Hendricks and Ruth. One child died unnamed. Mr. Flanagin continued to live with his mother one year after his marriage, and six years later bought his present place on Webber Creek, which contains eighty acres, sixty-five being cultivated. Mr. Flanagin is a Democrat, an admirer of Cleveland, and has served the community as justice of the peace, although he has never sought office. Himself and wife have been members of the Missionary Baptist Church for many years.

R. M. Flinn, farmer, was born on Mountain Fork, Crawford Co., Ark., in 1844, and is the oldest son of Hugh and Martha (Cottrell) Flinn. The mother was born in Virginia in 1806. The father was born in Ireland in 1802, and when

148

CRAWFORD COUNTY, ARKANSAS - BIOGRAPHICAL AND HISTORICAL MEMOIRS
****

young learned the stone-mason's trade. After coming to America, in 1837, he worked at his trade several years in Arkansas, Indian Nation and Missouri, and finally, in 1841, settled in Crawford County, Ark., with Alexander Graham and James Gregg. In 1875 he removed to Washington County, where he died February 14, 1881. Of his children, but two are living: our subject and J. R. Flinn (merchant and postmaster, of Evansville). R. N. Flinn received a common-school education during his youth, while living under the paternal roof. In 1869 he married Sarah Barker, daughter of John and Sarah (McFarland) Barker. Mr. Barker was reared in Missouri, where he afterward practiced medicine. In 1847 he came to Crawford County, and here died the same year; the mother survived him but four years. To Mr. and Mrs. Flinn four sons and four daughters have been born. In March, 1862, Mr. Flinn enlisted in Company B, Third Missouri Regiment, under Capt. Clark, Gen. Sterling Price's regiment, and participated in the battles of Elkhorn, Mo., Corinth, siege of Vicksburg, siege of Charleston, siege of Petersburg, Va., and others. He was wounded seven times: at Elkhorn, through the bowels; at Corinth, in the limb; at Grand Gulf, Miss., in the knee; at Vicksburg, had his thigh broken; at Charleston, in 1864, had his arm broken; and subsequently his thigh was again broken in the same place. He was taken prisoner first at Elkhorn, but was soon released; at Corinth he was captured, and taken to Alton, Ill., where he was kept until exchanged in 1864, and the third time was taken prisoner, and held until paroled at the close of the war. He then returned to Crawford County, where he has since lived engaged in farming. In politics he is a Democrat.

James A. Floyd, farmer and proprietor of cotton-gin, was born in Bedford, County, Tenn., in 1848, a son of James H. and Martha L. Lawrence, natives of Williamson and Rutherford Counties, Tenn., respectively. The father died in the last named county about 1849, and the mother in Bedford County in 1869. The grandfather, James Floyd, was born in Virginia, and died in Williamson County, Tenn., prior to the war. The grandmother was a native of North Carolina. James A. is the youngest of a family of three children, and receiving but a limited education during his youth, when of age he began life for himself by farming. In 1874 he married Maggie, daughter of J. G. Harrison, a native of Lincoln County, Tenn., where Mr. Floyd farmed until 1880. Since that time he has resided three miles from Alma, having now 160 acres of good land as the result of his labor and good management. Mrs. Floyd's father served as deputy sheriff of Lincoln County, Tenn., and in 1880 came to Crawford County, locating near Alma. Mr. Floyd is a Democrat, and cast his first presidential vote for Greeley, in 1872. He is a member of the Masonic fraternity, Alma Lodge No. 43, and belongs to the K. of H. He has one son and three daughters, and is united with the Methodist Episcopal Church, South.

Eugene N. Formby, farmer and stock raiser, was born in Newton County, Ga., in 1833, and is a son of Aaron and Elizabeth (Harvell) Formby, natives of Virginia, who went to Georgia when young and there passed their lives. The grandfather of our subject, Nathan, and his brother, Aaron, were the only ancestors who ever came to America. They came to fight in the Revolution under Gen. LaFayette, in which war Nathan was an officer. From these two men have descended the many families by the name of Formby which are now scattered over the United States. Both men were well-to-do planters and stock dealers and reared large families. Our subject lost his father when but seven years old, and his mother died in 1874. The maternal grandfather, Jackson Harvell, was of Irish descent and a native of Virginia. Eugene is the third of a family of six children, and having lost his father when so young his educational advantages were necessarily limited. His brother James enlisted in the Confederate army, and after a year's service died at Richmond, Va. Eugene served three years in the "Chatham Artillery," the first artillery company organized in the United States, which operated on the coast from Florida to North Carolina. During his entire service he never missed a roll-call, and the last year and a half served as wagon master. He was with Gen. Johnson at the time of the surrender at Greensboro, N. C. In 1855 he married Phœbe Ann, daughter of Jesse Birch, a native of North Carolina, and a soldier in the War of 1812. He removed to Georgia in 1836, and died during the late war. Mrs. Formby was born in Georgia in 1837, and is the mother of eleven children, all of whom reside near home. After his marriage Mr. Formby lived near Rome, Ga., until 1870, and then rented land in this county until 1872. He then began to clear his present farm in the wilderness, and he now has 500 acres of well-improved bottom land. He is one of the best farmers in the county and has a good steam cotton-gin. He had $600 when he came here and paid $1,200 for the home farm. The remainder of his property he has accumulated since. He is a Democrat, and in 1874 was elected justice of the peace, continuing to hold that office eight years. His first presidential vote was cast for Buchanan. He is a member of the Pleasant Hill Masonic Lodge No. 233, and himself and wife are Methodists.

Sterling Price Foster is a son of Josiah and Julia C. (Stewart) Foster. The father was born March 13, 1796, in Georgia, and when a young man went to Missouri, where he chose his first wife, by whom he had sixteen children, fourteen sons and two daughters. After her death he married the mother of our subject, who was born in Tennessee in 1824, and came with her parents to this county in 1840. Ten children, four sons and six daughters, were the result of this marriage. He first followed the plow when six years old, and beginning life with nothing became one of the largest land-holders in this county. He could neither read nor write, and his success was due to natural business sagacity and good management. He was by occupation a farmer, and was a successful trader in land and stock. He was a Democrat, and was a soldier in the Mexican War. He died December 21, 1870. The mother is still living. Sterling Foster, the youngest son, was born on the farm where he now lives on January 22, 1862. He lived upon the home place with his mother until 1887, and September 22, of that year, married Mary S. Alfred, who was born in Jackson County, Ala., April 22, 1862, and is a daughter of William and Jemima (Murray) Alfred, natives of East Tennessee and Georgia, respectively. When young the parents moved to Alabama, which was the State in which they were married. Mrs. Alfred died in 1862, and Mr. Alfred then married Jane Highfield. Five children were born of his first and eight of his second marriage. Mr. and Mrs. Alfred came to this county in 1880, where they are now living, both members of the church, as was the first Mrs. Alfred. Mr. Foster has always been engaged in farming, and has 220 acres, of which 180 are under cultivation. He is a Democrat, and his wife belongs to the Methodist Church, South.

Gillead J. B. Gideon, farmer and deputy sheriff of Whitley Township, was born in what is now Bartow County, Ga., in 1836, and is a son of Dr. Berry W. and Lillie (Park) Gideon, natives of Hall and Jackson Counties, Ga., respectively. They were married in Jackson County and died in their native State, where they had passed their lives. The father's death occurred in February, 1884, when he was eighty-two, and the mother died the following August aged seventy-two. He was a successful physician, and held a license which was given by the Legislature. During the Indian troubles in Georgia he commanded a company of volunteers. His father was a native of England. Our subject is the fourth child in a family composed of two sons and nine daughters. During his youth he received a common-school education while under the paternal roof. During the Civil War he served almost the entire time in Company K, First Georgia Infantry, State troops, known as "Joe Brown's Pets," guarding the bridges and railroads until the army entered Georgia, when he joined the regular service. He was discharged at Atlanta shortly before the close of the war, whereupon he returned home. In 1858 he married Margaret, daughter of William Mobley, who until 1870 lived in Georgia, and is now a resident of Johnson County, Ark. Of Mr. Gideon's ten children one son is in Tennessee and the remainder in Arkansas. Since 1870, with the exception of one year, Mr. Gideon has been a resident of Crawford County. In the meantime he spent a short time in both Franklin County and New Mexico, but finally located permanently upon his present farm in 1877. From a small piece of ground composed of forty acres, upon which he erected a log cabin sixteen feet square, he has been increasing his landed possessions until he now has 100 acres of cleared land, and is the owner of 240 acres of land in all in different tracts. He has given his children a good education, and for two years has been sheriff of the county. He has always been a Democrat, and his first presidential vote was cast for Breckenridge in 1860.

Alexander Gooding was born July 4, 1822, in Cocke County, Tenn., near Newport, and is a son of James and Elizabeth Gooding, natives of South Carolina. Of their five children our subject is the only one living. Those deceased are William, Francis, Andrew J. and Martin. Mr. Gooding immigrated to

Tennessee shortly after his marriage, and there died in 1823. The mother died in Crawford County in 1859, advanced in years. Alexander, when young, was left to care for his mother, and during his youth worked upon a farm, receiving a common-school education. When twenty-two years old he came to Crawford County, landing in Van Buren in 1844 $6 in debt. The first year he worked upon a farm, and then rented land for about six years. In 1844 he bought land near Dripping Springs, and in 1862 went to Texas. There he did frontier duty in the Confederate States army, under Capt. Toddie, for a few years, or till the surrender of Victoria Peak, in Texas. He once drove a government team as far as San Antonio, but participated in but one battle, Brushy Creek, Montague Co., Texas. In 1867 he left Denton County, Texas, and located upon his present place in Crawford County. He then bought 180 acres of land, to which he has added until he now owns 340 acres; 125 he has cultivated and devotes to farming and stock raising. January 9, 1851, he married Martha E. Collins, daughter of Dr. Dixon P. and Melvina (Cotterel) Collins, and a native of Alabama. To them eight children have been born, five of whom are living: James F., Alexander, Alice, Albert and Abbie. Those deceased are John D., Lee and an infant. Alice is now the wife of Richard J. Miller, of this county. Mr. Gooding, with four other citizens, founded a school at South Grove, paying the expenses thereof themselves; thus illustrating the interest he takes in educational matters. He is a Democrat, and has served as justice of the peace. He is a Mason, and himself and wife belong to the Cumberland Presbyterian Church.

James Greig (deceased) was born in Ayr, Scotland, in 1814. When a lad he was apprenticed to learn the stone-cutter's trade, which he afterward followed, and was considered a finished workman. When about twenty-one years of age he set sail for America, and, landing in New York, spent some years in the Eastern States. Working his way westward, in 1844 he came to Crawford County, Ark., and two years later married Lucinda Morton. This lady is a daughter of Andrew Morton, was born in Illinois in 1826, and came to this county with her parents in 1831. After his marriage Mr. Greig turned his attention to farming, in which he was reasonably successful. Although he enjoyed but very limited educational advantages during his youth, his fondness for books caused him to become a well-informed man, and in 1874–75 he was elected by the Democrats to represent Crawford County in the Legislature. He was a Methodist in religion, and a member of the Masonic fraternity. His death occurred in 1878. His wife also belonged to the Methodist Church, and to them the following children were born: Agnes, wife of W. S. Williams, a farmer of this county; Elizabeth (deceased), wife of D. E. C. Williams, farmer; J. Howard and William W., who now live at home; Martha A., wife of A. E. Lewis, a blacksmith; Hamlet, a farmer, husband of Julia Hainey. All of Mr. Greig's sons are stanch Democrats, like their father.

Judge Harrison B. Hale, a prominent citizen of Cedar Creek Township, was born in Washington County, Tenn., in 1840, and is a son of Benjamin and Nancy (Longmire) Hale, also natives of that State, born August 15, 1809, and April 3, 1808, respectively. Leaving their native State the parents first went to Barren County, Ky., then to Red River County, Texas. In 1859 they came to Cane Hill, Ark., in 1860 located in Crawford County, in 1874 went to Washington Territory, and in 1875 went to Oregon. In politics the father was a Whig, and in religion a member of the Missionary Baptist Church. He was a farmer by occupation, and while in Tennessee served as justice of the peace. He was twice married, and by his first wife had two children, one, Mesheck Hale, living near Warsaw, Mo. By his second marriage he had seven children, viz.: Our subject; Mrs. Hannah Martin, of Van Buren; Mrs. Mary J. Montgomery, of Barker Township, this county; Landon Taylor, of Montana; Joseph, Noah B. (deceased) and John (deceased). The grandparents, Joseph and Susannah (Hollin) Hale, were natives of Maryland, who immigrated to Tennessee. The paternal forefathers of our subject came to America from England with Lord Baltimore, settling in his colony, and the great-grandfather, George Hale, was a native of Maryland, and a soldier in the Revolutionary War. The maternal grandparents were of German descent and natives of Pennsylvania. Judge Hale passed his early youth in Tennessee, and attended the Fall Branch Seminary, in Washington County, of that State. He afterward went to Columbia College, Adair County, Ky., but his education was interrupted by the war. In 1862 he enlisted in Company E, and served under Capt. J. Winfrey. After being in Gen. Buster's

151

CRAWFORD COUNTY, ARKANSAS - BIOGRAPHICAL AND HISTORICAL MEMOIRS
****

cavalry, and participating in the battle of Pea Ridge, he was dismounted and joined Col. Clark's Ninth Missouri Infantry. He was present at the battles of Prairie Grove, La., Pleasant Hill, La., and Jenkins' Ferry. He received a slight wound in the head while in the Indian Nation, but served until the close of the war, being paroled at Van Buren in 1865. He was in an engagement at Newtonia, Mo., and in the northwest corner of this State, near old Fort Wayne, in the fall before the battle of Prairie Grove, Ark., being then under Gen. Cooper, of the Choctaw Nation. After the war he engaged in teaching, which he still continues to do, as he holds a first grade certificate. He made his home with his father until 1869, and October 17, of that year, married Ruth C. London, who was born in this county April 29, 1853, and is a daughter of John J. and Judith (Burnett) London. By this marriage Judge Hale has one child, Mollie J. Hale, born August 21, 1870. Mr. Hale is one of the successful and enterprising men of the county, and in September, 1878, was elected justice of the peace of the township, which office he held two years. In 1880 he was elected county and probate judge, and in 1886 was re-elected to the same office. This fall he was elected county surveyor, and he is now fulfilling the duties of his public offices with fidelity and zeal. He is a member of the Church of God, and is a Mason. In politics he is a Democrat, and his first presidential vote was cast for Seymour in 1868.

Moses Hall was born in Shelby County, Ky., July 13, 1826, where he lived upon his father's farm and received a common-school education. When twenty-six years old his father gave him a plantation, and in 1853 he married Mary E. Robison, daughter of William and Rebecca (Cunningham) Robison, natives of Kentucky. Mrs. Hall was born in Jefferson County, of that State, May 18, 1833. Mr. Hall came to Monroe County, Mo., in 1857, but returning to Kentucky in 1865, lived there until 1881. Coming to Arkansas he first located in Woodruff County, and in 1836 came to Crawford County, where he now farms upon 120 acres of land, ninety of which he has cultivated. Mr. and Mrs. Hall are members of the Presbyterian Church, and the parents of eight children, seven of whom are living: Benjamin L., William R., Elizabeth R. (deceased), Mary B., Virginia L., James T., George W. and Ella R. Mr. Hall is a Democrat in politics. He is a successful man, his property being the result of his own labor, and the property given him by his father was all lost during the war. Moses Hall, Sr., the father of our subject, was also a native of Shelby County, Ky., and his mother, Elizabeth P. (Crawford), was born in Greenbrier County, Va., but went to Shelby County with her parents when sixteen years old. The family on both sides have been Old School Presbyterians, and were of Irish descent. Mr. Hall was an extensive planter, a soldier in the War of 1812, and a Democrat.

Harrison D. Hammack, M. D., of Van Buren, was born in Smith County, Tenn., in 1837, and is a son of James D. and Martha Louisa (Richardson) Hammack. The father was born in Virginia in 1800, and was of Anglo-Saxon descent. Soon after his marriage, in 1824, he immigrated to Dixon Springs, Smith Co., Tenn. In 1858 he left for Madison County, Mo., and the last few years of his life were spent in Van Buren, Ark., where he died in 1887. His grandfather was with Gen. Jackson in the battle of New Orleans in the War of 1812. The mother of our subject was born in Virginia in 1806, and died in Madison County, Mo., in 1871. Harrison D. is the fifth of a family of eight children, and during his youth attended Arcadia College, in Missouri. After becoming nineteen he taught four years, and in 1861 went to Union County, Ill., where he taught one term. He next taught in Ramsey, Fayette County, and in 1863 began to study medicine under Dr. Alonzo Clark at that place. In 1867 he began to practice at Prairie du Rocher, Ill. In 1876, '77 and '78, he attended Bellevue College, in New York City, and graduated from that institution in 1878. During these years he studied surgery under Prof. Alexander B. Mott, from whom he received a surgeon's certificate, and in 1878 returned to Illinois and resumed his practice. In 1881 he came to Van Buren, where he is now well known and enjoying a lucrative practice, which is well merited. He has been married three times, his present wife having been Miss Jennie Parale Hurst, and a native of Texas. The Doctor has nine children: William A., Jacob W., Susan L., Aloysius, Rosalie, Olive, Regina, Stephen and Bessie. The Doctor and wife belong to the Methodist Episcopal Church, South, and to the Independent Order of Good Templars. He is a member of the American Legion of Honor; is inde-

152

CRAWFORD COUNTY, ARKANSAS - BIOGRAPHICAL AND HISTORICAL MEMOIRS
****

pendent in politics, and a member of the Southern Illinois Medical Association.

J. R. Harden, merchant and farmer, was born in Tennessee, near the eastern part of the Virginia line, September 1, 1826, and is a son of George and Elizabeth (Straup) Harden. The father was born in Virginia, of German parents, and was a farmer by occupation. In 1824 he immigrated to Eastern Tennessee, and nine years later went to Greene County, where he died. The mother was of Scotch-Irish parentage, and also born in Virginia, where she married Mr. Harden. Of their seven children, three are now living: Samuel, Sarah and Josiah R. Those deceased are Jonathan, Polly, Lemuel and an infant. The mother died in Tennessee. Our subject lived with his parents in Tennessee until seven years of age, and then ran away. He started to join a brother who was attending school at Richmond, Va., but was stopped by an uncle, and changing his course went to Bull's Gap, Greene Co., Tenn., where he lived with a man named F. W. Etter until grown, engaged in blacksmithing and farming. He then went to McMinn County, Tenn., and enlisted in Company B, Fourteenth Tennessee Regiment, commanded by Col. Trousedale, and served through the Mexican War. He served in every battle fought in the valley of Mexico, and was discharged at New Orleans. In August, 1848, he married Elizabeth Cox, in McMinn County, Tenn., of which she was a native. Her parents, William and Sarah Cox, were born and reared in Tennessee. To Mr. and Mrs. Harden five children have been born: Sarah, wife of J. H. Lowry, of this county; Harden, now a citizen of Chickasaw Nation; Andrew J. and Josephine, widow of R. E. Taylor, still living, and William C. and Emily J. (deceased). In 1849 Mr. Harden went to Greene County, Mo., and two years later went to Benton County, Ark. In the time of the war he took his family to Texas, but returned himself, and although he was opposed to secession, when the State seceded he took up arms in her defense, enlisting in the Home Guards. He then raised a company of which he was captain under Stan Watie. He afterward became a major, and served until the close of the war, participating in the fights at Wilson's Creek, Spring River, Newtonia and others. The company was disbanded in 1865, and he then passed two years in Texas and seven in Chickasaw Nation, where he erected the first mill. Two years after he came to Crawford County, where he is now engaged in the mercantile business, and has 160 acres of land, seventy-five being under cultivation. Since July 16, 1887, he has been an ordained minister in the Christian Church, to which his wife also belongs. In politics he is a Democrat.

Dr. Robert G. Harrison was born in Overton County, Tenn., June 24, 1828, and is a son of Richard H. and Elizabeth (Coons) Harrison. The father was born in Randolph County, Va., and when sixteen immigrated by wagon to Virginia, settled in Overton County, and worked upon a farm until a young man. He then practiced medicine, having devoted a large share of his leisure to study. During his latter life he farmed and taught school in Montgomery County, Ind., where he died. The mother was born in Roane County, Tenn., and was the mother of ten children, all, save one, now living: Harriet A. Woods, wife of Samuel Woods, of Darke County, Ohio; Rebecca J., wife of Jonathan Hale, of Mercer County, Ohio; Richard P.; James H., banker in Farmer City, Ill.; Richard W., Tuscola, Ill.; John C., M. D.; Benjamin F., of Evansville, Ind.; Sarah C., wife of Mark Harding, of Hillsdale, Ind., and Susan E., wife of James C. Weaver, of Fort Wayne. Thomas J. is deceased. Mrs. Harrison died at the age of seventy-eight, in Darke County, Ohio. The paternal grandfather of our subject was born in Randolph County, Va., from there went to Overton County, Tenn., was a soldier in the War of 1812, and died in Montgomery County, Ind., at an advanced age. His wife, Martha (Blair) Harrison, was born in Virginia, where she was married. She afterward accompanied her husband West, and died in Montgomery County, Ind. She was related to Gen. Blair. The maternal grandfather of our subject immigrated to the United States from Saxony when a young man, settling first in Overton County, Tenn., and died in Montgomery County, Ind. He was a man of fine education, having served in the German army before coming to America. His wife, Catherine, was born in Scotland, of German parents, was married in the United States, whither she had immigrated, and also died in Montgomery County. James Harrison, our subject's great-grandfather, was born near Richmond, Va., was a general in the Revolution, and died in Overton County, Tenn. His father

153

CRAWFORD COUNTY, ARKANSAS - BIOGRAPHICAL AND HISTORICAL MEMOIRS
****

was a Virginian, and lived and died in his native State. Benjamin Harrison our subject's great-great-great-grandfather, was born in Manchester, England, and was one of the signers of the Declaration of Independence. His father, Maj.-Gen. Harrison, was hung in Manchester for treason. Our subject, Dr. Harrison, passed his youth in his native county, where he received a common-school education. He subsequently studied under Prof. Thomas, and attended the Wabash College. He began the study of medicine in Crawfordsville, Ind., under Drs. Currie and McKey, and graduated from the University of Pennsylvania in 1854. He then practiced a few years in Montgomery County, Ind.; then in Montgomery County, Ill., and in 1856 went to Clinton County, Mo. He returned to Indiana in 1861, and in 1863 served as surgeon of the One Hundred and Twentieth Indiana Volunteer Infantry. He served until discharged at the close of the war, at Raleigh, N. C., and had charge of the First Division, Twenty-third Army Corps, under Gen. Scofield. He next went to De Kalb County, Mo., and in 1867 settled in Johnson County, Kas., but in 1880 came to Crawford County, Ark. He is a successful physician, and owns eighty acres of land, thirty-five being cultivated. February 23, 1868, he married Margaret Quinlin, a native of St. Louis County, and daughter of Patrick N. and Rachel Quinlin, natives of Ireland. Mr. Quinlin died in St. Louis County, and the mother is now living with her second husband in Iowa. Dr. Harrison is a strong Democrat, is now mayor of Cedarville, notary public, school director, and is in the United States signal service.

Charles F. Harvey, insurance and claim agent, and attorney at law, at Van Buren, Ark., was born in Prussian Saxony, Germany, in 1825, and is the son of William Harvey, a native of Saxony before its cession to Prussia. He served in the army of Napoleon I, and was with him in his disastrous Russian campaign, being present when Moscow was burned, and present in two of his great three-day battles. He immigrated to the United States in 1833, landing at Baltimore, Md., and crossing the Alleghany Mountains settled at Pittsburg, Penn. Six weeks after he lost his wife, she dying of cholera, which raged there at that time. About 1840 he moved to Harrison County, Ind., and died in Clark County, of that State, in 1878, at the age of seventy-seven years. He was a farmer by occupation and the father of seven children. Two died in Germany, two in this country, and three are still living, our subject being the fourth. He was brought to America when about eight years old, and his early education was confined to about nine months' attendance at a public night school. He lived with his father until he was twelve years old, when he was apprenticed to a manufacturer of window blinds at Pittsburg, and after serving out his apprenticeship he went to Nashville, Tenn., in 1843, and was a clerk in a store while there. In the fall of 1844 he went to St. Louis, and finding no steady employment at his trade, learned house and sign painting, and worked at that business there until 1846, when he enlisted in Col. Easton's regiment of volunteers to go to the relief of Gen. Taylor in Mexico, and served under his command until discharged. On his return to St. Louis he and his partner, Alexander McGrew, fitted up a flat-boat to find work during the winter along the lower river, and about twenty-five miles above Vicksburg their boat was wrecked in a great storm, and they barely saved themselves with their trunk. In 1849 he came to Louisville, Ky., and engaged in painting, and in 1854 lost his health, and the following year engaged in photography, traveling in the hope of regaining his health. In 1860 he came to Van Buren, where he has since lived. In 1866 he conducted a general store in connection with his photograph gallery, until 1881, and since 1868 has been interested in the insurance business, representing the Hartford, of Hartford, until they withdrew from the State at the beginning of the Brooks and Baxter war. Since then he has represented the Phœnix, of Hartford; New Orleans, of New Orleans; Pelican, of New Orleans, and Dakota, of Mitchell. He has served as justice of the peace for eight years or more, with credit, and since 1886 has been prosecuting claims against the Government. He is a Democrat in politics. In 1873 he married Miss Sallie M. Davidson, of Fayetteville, Ark., who was born at Monmouth, Ill., and died in Van Buren in October, 1873. In 1879 he wedded Mrs. Mattie G. Malone, a native of Alabama, who with himself is a member of the Methodist Episcopal Church, South, at Van Buren, of which church he is a steward and trustee. In 1869 Mr. Harvey was elected by the Arkansas Annual Conference a lay delegate to represent it at the General Conference that met at

154

CRAWFORD COUNTY, ARKANSAS - BIOGRAPHICAL AND HISTORICAL MEMOIRS
****

Memphis, Tenn., in 1870, and was again elected a lay delegate by the same conference in 1877 to represent it at the General Conference held at Atlanta, Ga., in 1878. Mr. Harvey is a Mason of the Council degree.

James D. Hawkins, sheriff, is a native of this county, and was born September 1, 1843. His father, Isaac, was born in Shenandoah County, Va., and for many years was a steamboat clerk. When a young man he came to Van Buren, and he married Susan M. Wasson, at Palmyra, Mo., where she was born. For some time he served as constable of Van Buren. He died in 1858, and his wife in 1881. They had five children, of whom four are living: James D., Josephine (wife of G. W. Wines), Harry and Holdena White. James D. was reared and educated in Van Buren, and was an apprentice at the harness and saddler's trade, at which he worked until the war. In 1861 he enlisted as private in Carroll's company, under Gen. Pierce, and after the company disbanded, subsequent to the battle of Oak Hill, he enlisted in Company G, Twenty-second Regiment Arkansas Infantry. He was wounded at Prairie Grove, December 7, 1862, and was disabled until the following March, but afterward was in the battles at Helena, Little Rock and Camden. June 9, 1865, he was paroled at Shreveport. Until 1868 he drove cattle in the Indian Territory, and then returned to his birth-place. In 1870 he married Sarah Mooney, daughter of W. B. and Nancy (MaLoy) Mooney. She was born in Texas in 1854, and bore him seven children: William, James, Gertrude, Maurice, Ella, Philip and George. From 1882 until 1886 he sold groceries in Van Buren, and was then elected sheriff of the county by a majority of 267. In September, 1888, he was re-elected by a majority of 327, which fully illustrates his capabilities as an officer. In April, 1886, he was elected mayor of Van Buren, and filled that position of trust in a faithful manner. He was elected sheriff in the following September, and resigned the office of mayor. He is a Democrat, and cast his first presidential vote for Greeley. His wife and children belong to the Methodist Episcopal Church, South, and the former is a member of the Ladies' Aid Society. He belongs to the K. of P., A. O. U. W. and American Legion of Honor. He is a prosperous business man, and a stockholder in the Van Buren Ice and Coal Company.

Henry Clay Hayman was born in Brown County, Ohio, in 1827, and is a son of Sampson and Elizabeth (Reeder) Hayman. The father was of German descent, and was born in Pennsylvania in 1787. He was a machinist and engineer by trade, and when young went to Kentucky, where he afterward married. He then went to Brown County, and his death occurred in 1837. The mother was born in Kentucky about 1800. She was the daughter of Simeon Reeder, who married Elizabeth Boone, daughter of the famous pioneer, Daniel Boone. Mrs. Elizabeth Hayman died in 1835, and was the mother of five children, of whom two are living: John Q. A., a wealthy miller of Lexington, Ky., and our subject. He lost his mother when eight years old, and his father when he was ten years of age, after which he was cared for by his maternal grandmother until he was twelve. He then accompanied his uncle near Flemingsburg, Ky., and there worked with his uncle, who was a miller by trade. When nineteen he left his uncle, and went to Cincinnati, Ohio, and with his twin brother, John Q. A., worked in a mill until 1852, when he came to Van Buren, where he has since resided, and has engaged in the milling business, more or less, ever since. In 1847 he married Miss Jane Casner, who was born in Hamilton County, Ohio, in 1827, and has borne him three children, all born in Cincinnati, Ohio; Simeon, engineer; Ella, deceased, and William, chief engineer of the Van Buren Ice Factory. In politics Mr. Hayman is a Republican, and after the cessation of the late hostilities, during the reconstruction was United States Military Registrar of Crawford County. He has served in the city council, at different times, thirteen years, and was a member of the school board a number of years. He is a Royal Arch Mason and a Past D. D. G. M. of the I. O. O. F. of Arkansas. His wife is a member of the Christian Church.

William Henry, superintendent of round-house at Chester, is a son of Thomas and Honoria (Morgan) Henry, natives of Ireland, who came to this country when young. For many years the father engaged in railroading, and having made his way to Franklin County, Mo., he bought land there and interested himself in farm life. He and his wife were members of the Catholic Church, and of their family our subject and a sister are the only children now living. William Henry was born in Franklin County, Mo., September 17, 1861, and attended school in Pacific, Franklin County, and the Washington University at St. Louis. In 1879 he was apprenticed in the St. Louis & San Francisco Railroad shops at Springfield, Mo., and after learning his trade served in the capacities of fireman, machinist, etc. In March, 1887, he took charge of the shops at Springfield, and in July of the same year became the superintendent at Chester, and has since filled that position with credit, to the complete satisfaction of his employers. June 5, 1887, he married Miss Bertha Duff, a native of Jefferson County, Mo., and is now the father of a son, James W. Both Mr. and Mrs. Henry are Catholics, and he is a member of the order of Catholic Knights. In politics he is conservative.

Wesley Hinson was born in Union County, N. C., September 3, 1843, and is a son of Jeremiah J. and Elizabeth Hinson. The father lived in his native State, North Carolina, until 1853, from that time until 1859 living in Saline County, Ark. He finally located upon a farm at the foot of the mountains, in Vine Prairie Township, Crawford County, and there farmed until his death in 1877, aged sixty-two years, with the exception of some time spent during the war in Texas. He was of Irish and Spanish descent, and for twelve years was an ordained minister in the Methodist Church. His father was also named Jeremiah J. Wesley Hinson was the oldest of three children, and when but a boy lost his mother. He came to Crawford County when nine, and at the age of eighteen joined the Second Arkansas Battalion. He operated in Virginia with Lee's army, and participated in the Seven Days Fight, the Seven Pines, Fredericksburg, Antietam, and at Gettysburg was captured. He was taken to Columbus, Ohio, and after taking the oath of allegiance went to Bedford County, Penn., and worked some time in a machine shop. In September, 1863, he joined Company D, Thirteenth Pennsylvania Cavalry, being mustered in at Harrisburg. After Lincoln's proclamation ordering all who had fought in the Confederate army to the Northwest, he went first to Minnesota and then to Ft. Wadsworth, Dak., remaining until September, 1865. He then went to Pennsylvania, and was discharged the following year, since which time he has lived in Crawford County. In December, 1866, he married Johanna, daughter of George and Hester Ann Ragsdale, who came here with her parents in an early day. She lost her mother when but a girl, but her father is now living in Washington County. He served two years in the Confederate army. Mr. Hinson first homesteaded forty acres of land upon coming here, but by patient economy and good management is now the owner of 160 acres of good land, and is one of the prominent citizens of the county. He is now serving his fourth term as justice of the peace, and has had but two cases appealed, which were both confirmed. He is an active member of the Methodist Episcopal Church, South, to which he has belonged since 1853, and of which his wife has been a member since 1867. He does a good work as Sunday-school superintendent. He belongs to the Pleasant Hill Masonic Lodge, No. 233; has served as Senior Deacon and Senior Warden, and is now Worshipful Master. He is also Worthy Patron of the Eastern Star Chapter No. 63, and Organizing Deputy of that order in the thirteenth district, which comprises Sebastian and Crawford Counties and the northern part of Franklin. In politics he is a Democrat.

Jeremiah J. Henson, farmer and stock raiser, was born in North Carolina in 1849, and is a son of Jeremiah J. and Elizabeth Henson [see sketch of Wesley Hinson]. He was their youngest child, and when young attended the neighboring subscription school, but his studies were interrupted by the Civil War, the last two years of which he spent in Texas with his father. In 1870 he left the paternal roof and married Mary, daughter of Jesse W. and Elizabeth Wallace, who were then residents of Lee's Creek, but now live in Texas, where Mrs. Henson was born. This union has been blessed with eleven children, of whom four sons and three daughters are living. Since his marriage, Mr. Henson has lived in Vine Prairie Township, with the exception of the year 1883, which he spent in Texas. His home farm contains 160 acres, which is well improved, with good buildings and a nice house. He also owns 200 acres of bottom land, sixty-five of which are improved, and all of which is the result of his industry and management. He began life owning but a horse, saddle and bridle, and has always engaged in agricultural pursuits. He is a public-spirited man and advocates all enterprises for the public good. He has given his children the benefits of good educations, and is well known as a respected and honest citizen. During the war he was a Union man, but not an abolitionist, and in politics he is a Democrat, his first presidential vote having been cast for Greeley. Himself and wife are members of the Methodist Church, and he belongs to Pleasant Hill Masonic Lodge No. 233.

John Henson, farmer, of Vine Prairie Township, was born in Saline County, Ark., in 1853, and is a son of the Rev. Jeremiah J. and Margaret (Hopper) Henson, natives of North Carolina, where they were reared and married. In 1853 they came to Arkansas, living first in Saline and Garland Counties, and in 1859 came to Crawford, their deaths occurring here in January, 1877, and 1882, respectively. Both belonged to the Methodist Church, in which for many years Mr. Henson was engaged as a local preacher. He was twice married, his last wife being the mother of our subject. He was captain of a company of militia at the commencement of the war. He was of Irish-Spanish and Scotch descent. John Henson was the eldest of four children, and his education was received in the common schools of Crawford County and at Cane Hill College, which he attended five months; he afterward taught several months. In 1875 he married Eliza J., daughter of Richard R. Wigley, who came here from Georgia soon after the war. This marriage has been blessed with eight children, five of whom are living. Mr. Henson has lived upon his present farm since 1881. This contains 160 acres of land, and the upper strata of earth seems to be underlaid with a fine quality of coal, which has been found in several places only a few feet from the surface. Mr. Henson began life a poor man, but is now comfortably fixed, and is one of the enterprising and worthy citizens of the township. He is a Democrat, cast his first presidential vote for Tilden in 1876, and for two years served his township as constable. Himself and wife are Methodists, and he is a member of the Producers' Trade Union. He has some Cherokee Indian blood in his veins.

Ben F. Hodges, of the firm of Meyer, Hodges & Co., of Van Buren, was born December 2, 1852, on a boat on the Ohio River, near Cannelton, Ind., and is a son of John and Ann (Medlicot) Hodges. The father was a native of England, there learned the butcher's trade, and before reaching his majority immigrated to America, locating in Louisville, Ky. He was married in 1852, soon after removing to Cannelton, Ind., and in 1852 came to Van Buren. He engaged in butchering throughout his entire life, and while in Van Buren packed and shipped pork to the southern markets. The mother was born in Dublin, Ireland, and came to the United States when a young woman. Both are deceased. Three of the children are now living: Mary, wife of Dr. Thomas Caster, of Ozark, Ark.; Harriet, wife of N. F. Cornelius, of Van Buren, and our subject. The latter was but six years of age when he was brought to Van Buren, and at the age of eleven began to clerk in a store. In 1865 he went to Rochester, Ind., to learn the baker's trade, and in 1869 returned to Van Buren, working at the business until 1871, when he again clerked. In 1879 himself, H. F. Meyer and J. W. Statler went into the general mercantile business. The last named gentlemen sold his share to the other two in 1885, and since that date the business has been owned by Messrs. Meyer & Hodges. They carry a complete and first-class line of goods and enjoy a large patronage. Mr. Hodges is a man of good business capacity, temperate habits and courteous manners. He is a Democrat in politics, and a member of Ivanhoe Lodge No. 27, K. of P.

Richard Holcroft, farmer, was born April 13, 1835, in New Castle County, Del., and is a son of Thomas and Margeret (Beaston) Holcroft. The father came to the United States from England when about five, and learning the cotton-spinner's trade in Philadelphia, followed that all his life, managing a number of cotton factories. He is now living in Chester, Penn., aged seventy-six, and enjoying good health. The mother was born in Delaware, of Swedish parents, and there grew to maturity and married. She was the mother of eight children, five of whom still live: Richard, John, William, Mary A. and Sarah. Those deceased are George, Alfred and Edward. The mother died in Chester, Penn., in 1869. Our subject passed the principal part of his youth in Philadelphia, Penn., receiving a good education and learning the blacksmith and machinist's trade, which he followed until two years ago. After leaving home, when sixteen, he served an apprenticeship of five years, and then worked as a journeyman in Toronto, Canada, two years. He then spent one year in Philadelphia, and October 4, 1856, enlisted in the United States army, going to Florida to quell the Seminole Indians. In 1857 he went to Kansas, and then crossed the plains to assist in settling the difficulty with the Mormons. Upon the outbreaking of the Rebellion he was ordered from Fort Randall, Neb., to

157

CRAWFORD COUNTY, ARKANSAS - BIOGRAPHICAL AND HISTORICAL MEMOIRS
****

Virginia, arriving there the day John Brown was hung. He served as United States artillery sergeant, and after his discharge re-enlisted as sergeant of ordnance, and served for three years, being engaged in but a few minor battles with the Indians. He next worked for the Government two years in the ammunition department, and some time later ran the engine in the *Public Ledger* paper-mills of George W. Childs for five years. After running an engine in Philadelphia thirteen years he engaged in the queensware business three years, and then bought eighty acres of land in Crawford County, Ark., which he now owns, and forty of which he has cultivated. October 10, 1861, he married Jane Stewart, a native of London, Canada, but a resident of New York City at the time of her marriage. Seven of their ten children are living: Ida, William, Sarah, Edward, Eliza, Samuel and Mattie. John, Charles and an infant are deceased. Mrs. Holcroft is a member of the Methodist Episcopal Church, and Mr. H. is a member of the K. of P., I. O. O. F., U. A. M. and G. A. R. In politics he is a Democrat.

Mrs. Catherine Hollis. James Little (deceased) was born in Georgia in 1801. When a young man he immigrated to Clark County, Ark., and there married Nancy Gentry, a native of Nashville, Tenn., born in 1802, who came with her parents to Clark County. After his marriage Mr. Little moved to Washington County, in 1828, and engaged in farming and stock raising. He was left a widower in 1840, with four sons and three daughters. He then married Elizabeth Franklin, who bore him two sons. He was a Democrat, and in religion was a Primitive Baptist, as was his first wife. Mrs. Little is still living, and is a Methodist. The death of Mr. Little occurred in 1844, and was much mourned by his friends and acquaintances. Catherine, the fourth child, one of his first wife's children, and the widow of the highly esteemed Luther N. Hollis, was born October 10, 1825, in Clark County, Ark. She was there united in marriage, in 1848, to Alex. A. Steward, who was born in Indiana in 1820. Mr. Steward came to Arkansas when a boy, and had been previously wedded to Esther Hinds, who lived but a short time. Mr. Steward was a shrewd business man, second lieutenant in the Mexican War, and a Democrat. He died in 1853. The following year his widow married Luther N. Hollis, who was born in Indiana in 1826. Having learned the tanner's trade when a boy he worked at that business in Cincinnati, Ohio, Cassville, Mo., and Fayetteville, Ark. Later in life he turned his attention to farming. He also served in the Mexican War, and upon the outbreaking of the Rebellion enlisted in the first Confederate company—Capt. Carroll's—that left Crawford County, serving as first lieutenant until the close of the war. He was twice taken prisoner and twice released. He died in 1877, lamented as a kind-hearted neighbor, loving father and faithful friend. Mrs. Hollis has but one living child, Miss Luther Maud Lee, who was born June 14, 1865, but she has cared for an orphan boy, Dick Hollis, who lives upon the farm. Mrs. Hollis owns 357 acres of land besides town property.

James K. P. Howell was born in Crawford County, Ark., in 1844, and is a son of William and Elizabeth (Cheneault) Howell, natives of Arkansas and Tennessee, respectively. The father was a farmer, and died in 1844. The mother was born in 1819, and died in January, 1870. Of her two children, our subject is the only one living. He grew to manhood upon a farm, and lived with his mother during her lifetime. During the latter part of the war he served nine months in Capt. Miles' company, Col. Wallace's regiment. In 1868 he married Mary C. Wilson, who was born in Buchanan County, Mo., in 1851, and now has six children: Emma, Henry F., Minnie, Tennessee, Mary Willie, and an infant daughter. Mr. Howell owns 287 acres of land on Lee's Creek, seven miles northwest of Van Buren, and until recently lived upon his farm. He then purchased a restaurant in Van Buren of Mr. Kronk, of which he has since been the proprietor. He keeps a first-class restaurant in every respect, setting a good table and having everything neat and comfortable. He is a Mason, and himself and wife belong to the Methodist Episcopal Church, South. In politics he is a Democrat.

Henry Howell was born December 20, 1847, in Greene County, Tenn., and is a son of Henry and Martha (Lowe) Howell. The parents were born in Tennessee, where they received a subscription school education and were reared and married. To them nine children were born, seven of whom are living: Andrew, Adam, Thomas, Henry, Margaret (wife of J. T. Morton), Catherine (wife of John Burchfield) and Emily (wife of Z. T. Waters). In 1850 Mr.

Howell immigrated to Arkansas on a flat-boat, settling first on Lee's Creek near Van Buren, where he lived five years. He was the founder of Uniontown, where he farmed until his death in 1884, aged seventy-two. He was constable and deputy sheriff. The mother is now eighty-one years old and enjoying good health. Philip Howell, the grandfather, was born in Tennessee, and a soldier in the Mexican War. His wife was also a native of Tennessee. Hugh Lowe, the maternal grandfather, was of Irish parentage, and died in Tennessee. Our subject received a common-school education, and lived with his father until after coming to this county. When sixteen he enlisted in the Confederate army, served under Capt. Brooks about one year, and participated in the battle of Fayetteville. After returning home and farming ten years, he engaged in the mercantile business, and is now doing a flourishing business in connection with his farming. He owns 160 acres, eighty of which he cultivates, and has also a cotton-gin, grist and saw-mill. In 1862 he married Sarah Jackson, a native of Illinois, and daughter of William Jackson. To them six children have been born, all save one now living: Rosa, Manta, William H. and Martha. Lillie is deceased. Mr. Howell is a Democrat and Royal Arch Mason. He is a public-spirited man, and interests himself in the educational advancement of the county.

Hon. James H. Huckleberry, attorney at law, was born in Jennings County, Ind., in 1840, and is a son of Silas D. and Lettice (Prather) Huckleberry. His great-grandfather, George Huckleberry, immigrated to the United States and located in Pennsylvania before the Revolutionary War. About 1800 he located in what is now Clark County, Ind. He fought in the Revolutionary War. His son, David Huckleberry, was born in Pennsylvania, and died in Indiana about 1844. Silas D. Huckleberry was born in Clark County, Ind., in 1814, and was a farmer by occupation. About 1837 he moved to Jennings County, Ind., and there served as constable several years. In 1854 he was elected sheriff of the county, and served the full time allowed by the State law. He belonged to Company I, Sixth Indiana Regiment, and served as captain of the same two and a half years. He fought in several skirmishes besides the battles of Stone River, Perryville, Ky., and Chickamauga. While in the army he contracted disease, from which he died in Jennings County in 1870. He was of Welsh-German descent. Mrs. Lettice (Prather) Huckleberry was of Scotch-Irish and English descent, and was born in Jennings County, Ind., in 1817. Her father was William Prather, who was born in Maryland in 1766. He was a descendant of two brothers who came to America before the Revolution, and about 1800, with nine brothers and two sisters, he settled near Utica, Clark Co., Ind., where they took up a large tract called Clark's Grant. Mrs. Huckleberry is still living. James H. is the oldest of eight children, and when young attended the Vernon public school, and spent two terms at Asbury University at Greencastle. In April, 1861, he left the freshman class to enlist in Company G, Fifth Indiana Regiment, for three months, and at the close of the Western Virginia campaign returned home and enlisted in Company I, of the same regiment, for three years. He was present at the fights at Shiloh, Tullahoma and Chickamauga, and was seriously wounded in the last named battle. He was discharged with his regiment at Indianapolis in September, 1864. In 1865 he entered the law school at Albany, N. Y., from which he graduated the following year. He began to practice in Vernon, Ind., and in 1868 located in Fayetteville, Ark. In 1869 he was appointed United States attorney of the Western District of Arkansas, by President Johnson, and, as the Federal court was held at Van Buren, he came here, and held the office until 1872. April 6, of that year, he was made circuit judge of the Fourth Judicial Circuit, and resided at Huntsville until 1874. Since 1876 he has resided in Van Buren, and from 1879 until 1883 was postmaster. In 1884 he represented Crawford County in the House of Representatives, and served on the railroad and judicial committees. In politics he is a Republican, and his first presidential vote was cast for Lincoln. In 1864 Mr. Huckleberry married Laura Barnum, who was born in Jennings County, Ind., in 1842 and died in 1866. October 21, 1870, he married Mattie L. Jarvis, who was born in 1844 near Williamsburg. Her great-grandmother was of Indian origin. Mr. and Mrs. Huckleberry have four children: James H., Jr., Malcomb L., Silas I. and Bessie L. M. Mr. Huckleberry is a Royal Arch Mason, an I. O. O. F., and has been a G. A. R. since 1866. He is a Methodist and his wife a Congregationalist. He is a prosperous business man and a director in the Crawford County Bank.

Andrew H. Huckleberry, M. D., was born in Clark County, Ind., October 5, 1844, and when three years old was taken by his parents to Jennings County, Ind., where he grew up on a farm, and received a common-school education. In May, 1864, he enlisted in Company I, One Hundred and Thirty-fourth Indiana Volunteer Infantry, and served 100 days. Soon after his return he began the study of medicine under Dr. C. H. Green, of North Vernon, Ind., and in 1870 attended a course of lectures at the Cincinnati College of Medicine and Surgery. The same year he came to this county, and has since been engaged in trading, farming and the practice of his profession. He is one of the energetic and enterprising men of the place, having accumulated his property by the exercise of industry and good management, and in his home place has 194 acres of land, of which some 140 are highly cultivated. December 25, 1873, he married Emily Mobly, daughter of Charles Mobly, an early settler of the county. Mrs. Huckleberry was born in Crawford County, July 4, 1853, and is the mother of the following named children: James A., Eva W., David, Jesse W. and Lettice M. Mrs. Huckleberry is a member of the Methodist Church, South. Dr. Huckleberry is a Republican in politics, and has served as magistrate. He belongs to the G. A. R., American Legion of Honor, Knights of Labor and Arkansas State Wheel.

Mrs. Lucinda (Meek) Hutchins was born in Henry County, Ky., October 6, 1824, and is a daughter of Jonathan and Catherine (Newhouse) Meek. The father was born in 1797 in Henry County, Ky., passed his life engaged in farming, and died in 1852. The mother was born in Kentucky in 1801, in 1850 moved to Illinois, and died in 1881. Her grandparents were Basil and Elizabeth Meek, and the former died in 1829. Our subject passed her youth in Henry County, Ky., with but few educational advantages, and in 1844 married A. C. Burgess. In 1849 they went to Illinois, and there engaged in farming until 1869. January 7, 1870, having made the journey by land, they arrived in Crawford County, where Mr. Burgess died, in 1882, aged fifty-nine. He was a Democrat, and while in Illinois served eight years as justice of the peace and four years as constable. He was a member of the Methodist Church, to which Mrs. Hutchins still belongs. In 1884 our subject was united in marriage to Henry B. Hutchins, who was born in Orange County, N. C., June 3, 1799, and died December 18, 1886. After leaving his native State he went to Tennessee, and in 1836 went to Texas, finally coming to Crawford County, Ark., in 1866. He served his township in the capacities of justice of the peace and constable for one term each, and by occupation was a farmer and stock raiser. He was a member of the Methodist Episcopal Church, South, and to him, by his first wife, eleven children were born, of whom three are deceased. John E., of Texas; James C., of Texas; Mrs. Samantha E. Felton, of Texas; Mrs. Nancy C. Stokes, of Texas; H. M. [see sketch]; W. M., of Washington County, Ark.; M. E., of this county, and G. B., also of this county, are the children still living. Those deceased are H. L., Samuel and Martha.

H. M. Hutchins, farmer, of Crawford County, was born in Texas in 1855, and is a son of H. B. and Julia A. (Bell) Hutchins. [For life of father, see sketch of Mrs. Lucinda Hutchins.] His mother was born in 1824, in Washington County, Ark., and died in 1882. Our subject lived in Texas until eleven years old, and then came to Arkansas. His educational advantages were limited, and at the age of twenty he began life for himself by farming. In 1877 he was united in marriage to Miss Harriet E. Nelson, who was born in Mississippi in 1858, and is a daughter of J. H. and Nancy (Lawhon) Nelson. Mr. Nelson was born in Georgia in 1811, and Mrs. Nelson in Alabama in 1819. The latter died in 1859. To Mr. and Mrs. Hutchins four children have been born, three of whom are living: Lena B., Zeluka D., Wiley Walker and Jimmie L. (deceased). Mr. Hutchins is a well-to-do farmer, owning 135 acres, which he has obtained by industry and good management. Eleven acres are devoted to farming. In politics Mr. Hutchins is a Democrat, and his first presidential vote was cast for Samuel J. Tilden, in 1876.

Robert S. Hynes is a son of William M. and Mary (Russell) Hynes, and was born in Canada in 1845. The father was born in Dublin in 1793, and received a classical education in England. In 1820 he immigrated to Canada, where he taught in the Lower Canada College at Montreal, and was superintendent of public schools for many years in Leeds County. He died in 1866. The mother was born at Old Johnston, N. Y., in 1812, and died in 1880. She was the mother

160

CRAWFORD COUNTY, ARKANSAS - BIOGRAPHICAL AND HISTORICAL MEMOIRS
****

of ten children, six of whom grew to maturity and four of whom are living. Robert S. was educated at Lower Canada College, and in 1864 came to the United States, passing the years until 1871 in various cities, and then locating in Bentonville, Ark. He then started the *Advance*, a successful paper, which he sold in 1877. He then bought the Reynolds Tobacco Factory. In 1879 he came to Van Buren, continuing the same business, but in 1884 sold his business and purchased the Crawford County Bank. In 1886 Hon. Jesse Turner and D. W. Moore joined him in making the bank a stock company with a capital of $50,000, and he was elected cashier. He was one of the original incorporators of the Van Buren Canning Company and the Van Buren Ice and Coal Company, is a stockholder in each and treasurer of the former. Mr. Hynes is an enterprising man, and has been closely identified with many of the chief movements which have made Van Buren what it is. He was one of the active spirits in securing the San Francisco Railroad to this town. In 1873 he married Kate Riley, daughter of Dr. Willshire Riley, a senator from Little Rock District and a man of prominence. She is also the granddaughter of Capt. James Riley, author and traveler. Her place of nativity was Toledo, Ohio, and she has three children: Willshire, Linzee and Robert S., Jr. Mr. Hynes owns a plantation of 800 acres of bottom land on the Arkansas River, which is considered one of the best in the county. In politics he is a Democrat, and himself and wife belong to the Presbyterian Church, of which he has been a ruling elder eight years.

William M. James was born on the farm where he now lives, in Rudy Township, Crawford Co., Ark., in May, 1846, and is a son of Robert and Elizabeth (Freeman) James, natives of Warren and Cannon Counties, Middle Tenn., respectively. In 1842 they immigrated to Crawford County, locating at Van Buren, and two years later moved upon the farm our subject now owns, which formerly belonged to Mr. James' brother, John. Robert and John were both carpenters, and built three of the first gins erected in the county. In 1849 Robert went to California, and mined for seven years, after which he was never heard of. The grandfather, William James, was of English descent, born in Carolina, and early settled in Warren County, Tenn., where he died. The mother of our subject was married a second time, in 1854, to Moses Ford, and died in November, 1885, aged sixty. She belonged to the Methodist Church. William M. is the third of five children. One of his brothers, Romulus, died in the Little Rock hospital of measles during the war while in the Confederate service. William remained at home until sixteen, and then began farming on his own account. Two years later he joined Company G, of the Sixth Kansas Battery, and a month later went to Texas, where he remained until the close of the war. He then returned home, and in December, 1866, married Millie, daughter of Jonathan and Rachel Fine, who were born in Tennessee, in 1814, and Kentucky, in 1819, respectively. They were reared and married in Washington County, Ark., and in 1858 came to Crawford County, settling at Fine Springs, where the father died in 1875, and the mother still lives. The paternal grandfather of Mrs. James was a pioneer of Washington County, Ark., where he died, and the maternal grandfather, Peter Mankins, was also an early settler of that county. He outlived four wives, and died a few years ago at the advanced age of one hundred and thirteen. Mrs. James was born in Washington County, Ark., and has borne our subject ten children, five sons and five daughters, all of whom are living in the neighborhood of their birth-place. Mr. James is a self-made man, and has 356 acres of land, 125 being in bottom land. He is a successful stock raiser, owns seven fine jacks, and spares no pains in the cultivation of his stock. He has a large number of Poland China hogs, and is one of the well-to-do men of the county. He has always been a Democrat in politics, and cast his first presidential vote for Greeley. He has given his children good educations, and one son is now attending school at Pea Ridge. Mrs. James belongs to the Primitive Baptist Church.

John D. James, general merchant, planter and stock dealer, was born near Alma in 1848, and is a son of Robert S. and M. E. (Freeman) James, natives of Cannon and Warren Counties, Tenn., respectively. In 1842 they came to Arkansas, and about 1849 Mr. James went to California, and has never since been heard of. He was of English descent, his grandfather having come to America with Lord Baltimore. Robert was a mechanic, and served in the war with Mexico. The mother died in 1885. John D. is the fourth child of a family of three sons and two daughters, and, after receiving a common-school educa-

161

CRAWFORD COUNTY, ARKANSAS - BIOGRAPHICAL AND HISTORICAL MEMOIRS
****

tion, began life for himself at the age of fourteen by farming and stock trading. During the latter part of the war he served about two years in Company A, with the Cherokees, in the Indian department, in the Indian Territory, Arkansas and Texas. In 1869 he wedded M. L., daughter of Harvey Steward, who was a native of Vermont. Mrs. James was born in this county, and is the mother of seven children. After his marriage Mr. James engaged in farming and trading until the foundation of Alma, when he built a hotel and livery stable, the first in the place, which he conducted several years. He is now one of the wealthiest and most prominent business men in the place, his stock being valued at from $25,000 to $40,000, and his annual sales amounting to about $100,000. He employs about eight clerks constantly, and his success is due to his business ability, as he has twice been burned out. About ten years ago he was shot in the street by a desperado, and for a long time was disabled. He owns 900 acres of land near Alma, and was one of the leading men in the upbuilding of that town. In politics he is a Democrat, and has served as chairman of the Democratic County Committee. His first presidential vote was cast for Tilden. He belongs to the I. O. O. F., and his wife is an earnest worker in the Christian Church.

J. M. Kerens was born in Ireland in 1839, of Irish parents. His father, Thomas, was born in 1812, and his mother, Elizabeth Gegerty, was born in 1819. After their marriage they left their native land, and sailing for America, landed at Montreal, Canada. They remained there but a few years, and then went to Rochester, N. Y., but the following year went to Chicago. In 1851 they left the latter place for Jackson County, Iowa, where they remained eleven years. They next removed to Kansas, where Mr. Kerens died August 10,1862, the mother afterward coming to Fort Smith, Ark., where she now lives. Mr. Kerens was by trade a tailor. The grandfather, James Kerens, passed his life in Ireland, but the grandmother, Margeret Kerens, accompanied her son to America, and died at Rochester, N. Y., aged eighty-seven. J. M. Kerens received a good education, and in 1857 began life for himself. During the war he was stationed at Fort Smith in the quartermaster's employ, and he participated in the battle at Cabin Creek. In 1875 he married M. J. Simpson, daughter of H. W. and Harriet (Hunter) Simpson. The father was born in Kentucky in 1802, and was married in 1832. The mother was born in Nashville, Tenn., in 1823, and in 1836 came to Washington County, Ark., where she is now living, having married S. F. Gray after the death of Mr. Simpson in 1862. He was killed by Indians. Our subject came to Crawford County several years ago, locating upon his present farm in 1884. This contains 280 acres of valley land, fifty of which are under cultivation. He has a family of three daughters and one son, and is a member of the Catholic Church. In politics he is non-partisan.

John B. Kibler, farmer, was born in Wurtemberg, Germany, in 1817, and is a son of Sebastian and Elizabeth (Miller) Kibler. The father was a baker, and died when our subject was but six years old. The mother afterward married, and coming to the United States, settled in Cincinnati, Ohio. John, who was the youngest of three children, attended school until fourteen years of age, and then spent three years' apprenticeship with a lock and gunsmith. He worked at that trade until 1839, when he came to the United States, landing at Baltimore. He then went to Philadelphia, where he soon after enlisted as a recruit, and served five years in the Sixth Infantry, in Florida, in the Seminole War. He was discharged as a member of Company E, in 1844, at Fort Gibson, Ind. T., and enlisted again for five years, at the close of which time, being discharged, he came to Van Buren, Ark. In 1845 he married Melinda Burk, who was born in Germany, and who was brought to the United States when two years old by her parents. She died in 1870, leaving a family of four children, three of whom are living. In 1872 Mr. Kibler married Mrs. Diana Bingham, *nee* Shaber, who died in 1880. His third marriage occurred in 1882, when he wedded Nellie Atkins, a native of Illinois, whose parents now reside in Joplin, Mo. In 1847 Mr. Kibler settled upon his present farm, which was then in the wilderness, with but two houses between it and Van Buren, a distance of seven miles. Mr. Kibler is the owner of a nice farm, which at one time contained 160 acres. During the latter part of the Rebellion he served nearly two years in Company I, First Arkansas Infantry, United States Army, operating in Arkansas. He and twenty-seven others were once attacked by about 2,000 Confederates, and after fighting bravely three hours they were captured, two men having been killed and two wounded. The enemy paroled them before daybreak for fear of being attacked by Unionists, but three men were missing and never heard from. The remainder rejoined their command at Fort Smith, and the rebels fled to Missouri. Mr. Kibler cast his first presidential vote for Polk. He is a member of the Lutheran Church, and one of the respected citizens of the township.

A. J. Kimbler was born in Texas in 1859, and is a son of Samuel and Elizabeth (Orey) Kimbler, natives of Virginia, born in 1818 and 1819, respectively. From Virginia they moved to Wisconsin, from there to Texas, and in 1866 came to Crawford County, Ark. The father was a farmer, and was a soldier in the Rebellion. His death occurred October 12, 1886, and that of his wife October 12, 1884. Of their eleven children, the following five are living: William Kimbler, Crawford County; Mrs. Rebecca Wheeler, Dardanelle, Ark.; Franklin, Chickasaw Nation; Mrs. Matilda Frances Bird, Washington County, Ark., and our subject. Mr. Kimbler's early ancestors were German. He passed his youth in Crawford County, attending school but little, but becoming a successful tiller of the soil. As a consequence he now owns 176 acres of good bottom land, eighty acres of which are in the home place and finely cultivated. He is a member of the Christian Church, as were his parents. In politics he is a Republican, and his first presidential vote was cast for James A. Garfield.

Francis M. Kimes, proprietor of the Van Buren Carding Mills, was born in St. Francis County, Ark., January 14, 1842, and is a son of Valentine and Martha (Stell) Kimes. The father was of German descent, born in Virginia in 1811, and when fifteen went to Overton County, Tenn., with his father, Valentine. In 1831 he moved to Wayne County, Mo., where the father died, and in 1839 went to St. Francis County, where the following year he married the mother of our subject, who was born in South Carolina in 1821. In 1843 he returned to Wayne County, Mo., and in 1851 located in the northern part of Crawford County, where he and his wife still live. They have nine children living: Francis M., David G., James M.; Jane, wife of L. Elkins; Hiram N., Thomas H.; Louisa A., wife of Mr. Lester; Martha, wife of Thomas Trible, and Mary, wife of James Snell. Our subject came to Crawford County with his parents when nine years old, and here grew to manhood. In 1862 he enlisted in Company A, First Arkansas Cavalry, United States Volunteers. Among others he was present at the fights at Fayetteville and Perry Grove, and was captured near Bentonville in October, 1864, being retained at Tyler, Tex., until the surrender, and was discharged August 23, 1865. September 15, 1865, he married Miss Louisa A. Elkins, who was born in Virginia in 1844. This marriage has been blessed with eight children: Ulysses S., Abraham L., John W., William S., Virginia, Francis M., Lizzie and Thomas. Mr. Kimes farmed until 1877, and then moved to Van Buren, and established the wool carding mills, which he has since operated with success, running them about eight months during the year. He received the patent of the Kimes Cotton Planter in 1881, and has since been interested in the manufacture of that article, having made about 300 machines, which give general satisfaction. In politics he is a Republican, and he has served as treasurer of Crawford County two years. He is a Mason, and himself and wife belong to the Methodist Episcopal Church.

H. P. King, general merchant, was born in 1837, in Tennessee, and is a son of Johnson and Minerva King, natives of the same State. The father was a farmer by occupation, and in 1838 immigrated to Southwestern Missouri. He died at Mount Vernon in 1862, being attacked and killed by bushwhackers. The grandfather, William King, was born in America. Our subject received but a limited education during his youth, and in 1850 began life for himself, and in 1853 immigrated West, crossing the plains with an ox team. He spent nearly six months on the road to the then Territory of Oregon, where he remained two years, then engaging passage on a sailing brig for San Francisco, Cal., where he arrived in March, 1855. He stopped in California with varying success until October, 1866, when he crossed the Pacific Ocean and returned via the Isthmus, Nicaragua, Central America and the Atlantic to Charleston, S. C., thence through the almost depopulated South, arriving at Van Buren about the 15th of December, 1866. In 1867 he was married in Crawford County, Ark., to Miss R. A. Howell, daughter of Philip and Eliza Howell. He was left a widower in 1876, and the following year married Miss R. E. Pendergrass, daughter of John and Jane Pendergrass, formerly of Tennessee. Mr. King

163

CRAWFORD COUNTY, ARKANSAS - BIOGRAPHICAL AND HISTORICAL MEMOIRS
****

engaged in farming from 1866 until 1876, since which time he has engaged in mercantile life, meeting with good success, and has since accumulated considerable property. In politics Mr. King is a strong Democrat, and greatly in favor of a reduction of the tariff. He is a member of the I. O. O. F. and A. F. & A. M., and himself and wife belong to the Cumberland Presbyterian Church.

James Kenner, farmer, was born January 27, 1834, in Hawkins County, Tenn., and is a son of Wiley B. and Elizabeth (Shanks) Kenner. The father was a native of Virginia, who in an early day started for Tennessee by wagon, where he engaged in farming in an unsettled country. He had but a limited education, and it was in Tennessee that he died in 1861. The mother was born in Hawkins County, Tenn., where she passed her entire life, dying upon the old homestead in 1887. She had ten children, seven of whom are now living: William, Hanson, Mark, Dock, Newton, Polly A. and James. Those deceased are Lucinda, Marian and Wiley R. Hanson Kenner, the grandfather, was a resident of Virginia, and engaged in trading with the Indians. The maternal grandparents were both natives of North Carolina, born of German parents, and in an early day went to Tennessee. Our subject passed his youth upon the farm in Tennessee, receiving only a common-school education, but learned the blacksmith's trade. When twenty-four years of age he left home and married Adeline Wells, daughter of Newton and Susan (Brewer) Wells. Mr. Wells was a soldier in the Mexican War. Mrs. Kenner was born and reared in Tennessee. To Mr. and Mrs. Kenner six children have been born, all save one living: Susan, Sallie, Minerva, Wiley and John. Polly Ann is the one deceased. During the late war Mr. Kenner enlisted in Company H, Eighth Tennessee Volunteer Infantry, First Brigade, Third Division, and served until the close, being mustered out in North Carolina. He was in the battles at Burnt Hickory, Atlanta Crossing and others, and, besides being on the raid through Georgia, participated in a number of other engagements. After the war he returned to Tennessee, and twelve years ago came to Crawford County, buying land on Cedar Creek, where he lived eight years. He then removed to his present farm, which contains 160 acres, forty of which he has finely cultivated. He is a member of the Missionary Baptist Church, and in politics is a Republican.

Peter Kuykendall was born in Buncombe County, N. C., June 7, 1814, and when about ten years old was taken by his parents to Georgia, and from there to McMinn County, Tenn. Four years later they went to Knox County, Ind., and in 1833 the family located opposite Memphis, Tenn., in what is now Arkansas, spending about two years in the southeastern part of the State, during which time Peter carried mail on horseback from the Mississippi River to Little Rock, then but a village. In 1835 the family moved to what is now Crawford County, where the father died in 1846, aged fifty-two, the mother living until her death after the war. Their names were James and Rebecca (Norton) Kuykendall, and they were both natives of Buncombe County, N. C. Mr. Kuykendall was of Dutch descent, and a successful farmer. For some years he served as justice of the peace. His father, James, was a Revolutionary soldier, and died in Georgia. The parents of our subject were for many years connected with the Baptist Church. Peter is the eldest of a family of eight children, only four of whom survive. He was given but a limited education during his youth, and in 1833 was married in Knox County, Ind., to Martha Tague, a native of North Carolina, who died in 1871, leaving seven children, all of whom have since died. In 1873 Mr. Kuykendall was united in marriage to Mrs. Frances Harris, daughter of Cader Woodard. Mr. Woodard was born in North Carolina, and after his marriage went to Alabama, living there until after the war, and then going to Texas, where he died. He served as justice of the peace in Alabama. Mrs. Kuykendall was first married, in Georgia, to Charles P. Harris, in 1856. Her husband served in the Confederate army under J. P. King, and, coming to Crawford County in 1861, died in 1872, leaving a widow and four children. Our subject has no living children, but has about sixteen grandchildren and several great-grandchildren. He has been a resident of the county over fifty-three years, having settled upon his present farm on Frog Bayou in 1836. He has accumulated his property since coming here, and now owns 380 acres, and is considered one of the substantial men of the county. He remembers when there was but one store in Van Buren, and when the few settlers were obliged to protect their property and lives against the wild animals which inhabited the forests. He endured all the hardships of pioneer life, and earned the money to

164

CRAWFORD COUNTY, ARKANSAS - BIOGRAPHICAL AND HISTORICAL MEMOIRS
****

buy the first horse he owned by making rails. For many years his corn was ground by hand in a stone mill, and rather than borrow his neighbor's horse Mr. Kuykendall used to take his chickens to Van Buren, walking the distance of ten miles. He is a Democrat, and has voted for every presidential candidate on that ticket since 1836, with the exception of war times. Mr. Kuykendall would never accept public office. He was a Southern sympathizer during the war. One son, James, was a private soldier in the war, and was captured at Helena, Ark., and was kept a prisoner at Alton, Ill., for two years. He served under Col. Wallace. His other son, Andrew J., served two years during the latter part of the war. Mr. Kuykendall's first wife belonged to the Baptist Church, and his present wife is a member of the Christian. When the family first came here from Knox County, Ind., they rowed in a flat-boat down the White River into the Wabash and Ohio, and thence to the Mississippi, landing opposite Memphis, where Mr. Kuykendall ran a ferry across the Mississippi River.

Samuel L. Larue was born in Kentucky in 1830. His grandparents, Samuel and Elizabeth (Waters) Larue, were natives of Virginia and of French and German descent, respectively. In 1806 they moved from Virginia to Kentucky. They were wealthy farmers and slave-holders, and died in 1840 and 1858. The maternal grandparents, James and Elizabeth (Waters) Castleman, were also natives of Virginia, who moved to Kentucky when young, and lived until their respective deaths in 1842 and 1854. They were also wealthy people, and owned a large number of slaves. The parents of our subject, Josiah and Mary (Castleman) Larue, were born in Virginia, in 1804, and in Kentucky, in 1810, respectively. When young the father moved to Kentucky, where he married and engaged in farming the remainder of his life. To himself and wife thirteen children were born, nine of whom are living, and two are residents of this county, viz., our subject and James Larue. Mr. Samuel Larue received but a limited education during his youth, and began life for himself when twenty-one years of age. He left Kentucky when forty-one years old and came to Arkansas. Since then he has by industry and good management become the owner of 300 acres of land, 110 acres being well cultivated and improved, with a good residence and out-buildings. There are three tenement houses upon the home place, and his fruit farm contains 1,000 apple trees besides a large number of peach and plum trees. In 1851 Mr. Larue married Mary Burdine, who was born in Kentucky in 1830, and is the mother of seven children, all, with the exception of Mrs. Letitia Hubbs, of Texas, being residents of this county. The other children of our subject are Mrs. Elvira Lowett, Mrs. Frances Rainey, Mrs. Grace Swearingen, Christopher C., Mrs. Elizabeth Cluck and Mrs. Martha Johns. Mrs. Larue's father, John Burdine, was born in 1802 and died in 1878, having been a farmer all his life. His wife, Rebecca Burdine, was born in 1812 and died in 1834. Of their fifteen children but two survive, viz.: Mrs. Larue and Mrs. Sarah Larue. Our subject, wife and four children are active members of the Missionary Baptist Church, and Mr. Larue belongs to the Masonic fraternity. Democratic principles were instilled in his mind when a youth, and he has always voted the Democratic ticket, his first presidential vote having been cast for Taylor in 1848.

James C. Larue was born in Hardin County, Ky., October 2, 1831, and is a son of Josiah and Mary (Castleman) Larue. The father was born in Virginia in 1805, and was an infant when taken by his parents to Hardin County, Ky., in an early day. Hardin County was afterward divided, one portion being named "Larue," in honor of his family. He received a collegiate education, but was a farmer by occupation. His death occurred in 1857. The mother was born in Hardin County, and bore Mr. Larue thirteen children, Samuel, James C., William, Jacob, David, Hardin, Thomas, Lydia and John still living. Those deceased are John, Squire, Sarah, Elizabeth and an infant. Samuel Larue, the grandfather, was born in France, and immigrated to Kentucky in 1810 from Virginia, in a wagon, with 100 horses and ninety negroes, he having been a man of means. Himself and wife died in Kentucky. James Castleman, the maternal grandfather, was born in Pennsylvania about 1810, of French parentage, and he also immigrated to Kentucky from Virginia. Elizabeth (Walters) Castleman was his second wife, and died in Kentucky. James C. Larue, our subject, lived with his parents during his youth, passing a large portion of his time upon the river. In 1853 he married and began life for himself by farming a year. He then went on the river again, and after teaming three years in Henderson,

165

CRAWFORD COUNTY, ARKANSAS - BIOGRAPHICAL AND HISTORICAL MEMOIRS
****

Ky., resumed his farming. Seven years after he sold out and went to Kansas, where he remained a short time before going to Texas. In 1866 he settled in Crawford County, where he now has 368 acres of land, 160 being under cultivation. August 19, 1853, he married Sarah M. Burdine, a native of Hardin County, Ky., and daughter of John and Rebecca Burdine, also natives of that county. To Mr. and Mrs. Larue twelve children have been born: William, Benjamin F., Jacob, Thomas, Robert E. L., Julia, wife of L. Cluck, and Rosa V. living, and David, Mary, Joshua and two infants deceased. Mrs. Larue has been identified with the Baptist Church over twenty years. Mr. Larue is a Baptist, but not identified with the church in Arkansas. He is a Democrat and a member of the I. O. O. F.

Francis Laurent, grocer of Van Buren, was born in France in 1844, his parents being Lewis and Mary (Gongon) Laurent, also natives of France. He is the only child, and when two years old was taken by his parents to Montreal, Canada, where his father taught him the shoemaker's trade. In 1862 he came to the United States, and during that year enlisted in Company H, Second New Hampshire Volunteer Infantry, serving until the close of the war. He was in the Army of the Potomac, and after the cessation of hostilities worked at his trade in Abingdon, Va. Four months later he went to Knoxville, Tenn., but soon went to Kingston, where he lived one year. His next place of residence was Lebanon, Tenn., and then he spent a year in Petersburg, Ky. In 1870 he went to Memphis, Tenn., from there to Corinth, Miss.; in 1881 went to Fort Smith, Ark., and finally, in 1884, became a citizen of Van Buren. Since 1871 he has been engaged in the mercantile business, and he is now a successful business man of this place. In 1868 he married Mrs. Clementine Fox, nee Gaines. This lady was born in Charlotte County, Va., in 1840, her parents being Richard W. and Annie (White) Gaines, born in 1781 and 1803, respectively, in Charlotte County, Va. Mr. Gaines died in 1847, and the following year his widow and four children went to Green County, Ky., and in 1850 moved to Trigg County, where Mrs. Gaines died in 1866. In 1859 Clementine married George Fox, who died in 1867. Mr. and Mrs. Laurent have an adopted daughter named Pearl, aged thirteen. Mr. Laurent is a member of the I. O. O. F. Lodge, No. 6, of Van Buren. He is an enterprising man, a stockholder in the Van Buren Ice & Coal Company, the Van Buren Canning Factory and the Building and Loan Association.

Mrs. Nancy G. Leach was born in Greene County, Mo., in 1842, and is a daughter of Simpson and Sarah (Hicks) Breedlove, who were born in Tennessee in 1817 and 1814, respectively. When grown they moved to Missouri, and were there married in 1839, soon after their arrival. In 1856 they removed to Johnson County, Tex., and in 1860 went to Washington County, Ark. The father served in the Mexican War, and afterward engaged in farming until the commencement of the Civil War, when he went away with the militia, and has not been heard of since. The maternal grandparents of Mrs. Leach, viz., John and Nancy (Haggard) Hicks, were born in Tennessee, and in 1838 removed to Greene County, Mo., where they engaged in farming the remainder of their lives, and reared a family of thirteen children. Mrs. Leach has three brothers and two sisters. She was married November 22, 1860, to Mr. Nathan W. Leach, son of Richard and Eliza (Hewitt) Leach, of Washington County, Ark., of which Richard Leach was a pioneer settler. Mr. Nathan Leach was a farmer and merchant, and held the office of postmaster. His widow's present farm is located upon the mountain, and contains 180 acres, half being cleared and well cultivated, with a good orchard and nice buildings. Mr. Leach departed this life April 14, 1887, leaving a family of five children, all, with the exception of Mrs. Alice Garrison, still living with their mother. Mrs. Leach is an active member in the Methodist Church, to which her husband also belonged.

Edward Lee, grocer, was born in South Carolina in 1822, and is a son of Henry and Lucy (Furlow) Lee, natives of the same State. From South Carolina they moved to Cherokee Nation, or what is now Alabama, in 1836, and in 1859 the father came to Crawford County, Ark., where he died in 1862, his wife having died in 1838. The father was a successful farmer, and the father of ten children, of whom but our subject and one sister are living. The grandmother of Mr. Lee, Sarah Lee, was a native of Ireland. When Edward was about thirteen, he accompanied his parents to Cherokee Nation, and on November 26, 1858, landed upon the present site

166

CRAWFORD COUNTY, ARKANSAS - BIOGRAPHICAL AND HISTORICAL MEMOIRS
****

of Chester, Ark., having made the journey hither by wagon. In 1843 he married Miss Sabrey Rankin, who was born in Tennessee in 1821, and bore him seven children: Martha, now Mrs. Clark, of Newton County, Ark.; Emeline, now Mrs. Simms, of this county; Mary, now Mrs. McClendon, of this county; Frances, now Mrs. Osborn, of this county; Decatur, Lucinda and an infant, deceased. Mrs. Lee died in 1875. Her parents were Moses and Sallie (Tombs) Rankin, who in an early day moved from Tennessee to Alabama. In 1877 Mr. Lee was united in marriage to Mrs. Margaret Miller, daughter of William H. and Terracy Runolds, who came from Alabama to Arkansas. This union has been blessed with three children, only one of whom survives, Margaret Alice. Until this year, when he went into the grocery business, Mr. Lee has been exclusively engaged in farming. He is a self-made man, and owns 240 acres, twenty-five of which he has cleared, besides being the owner of a good store at Porter. In 1863 he enlisted in Company D, First Arkansas Infantry, United States Army, under Col. Searle, and until the close of the war operated in Missouri and Arkansas. Among the battles in which he fought are Saline River and Prairie de Hand. Mr. Lee is a member of the Masonic fraternity and I. O. O. F., and in politics is a Republican.

Hugh S. Lewers, postmaster of Alma, was born in South Carolina, in Lawrence District, in 1841, and is a son of Thomas and Theresa (Sims) Lewers, natives of the same State, and born in 1817 and 1820, respectively. In 1845 they removed to De Soto County, Miss., where the father died in 1865 and the mother in 1849. Mr. Lewers was twice married. From August, 1861, until the close of the war, he was with Col. Wirt Adams' regiment of cavalry, and after commanding Company B two years, was made major. In 1864 he was made lieutenant-colonel, which position he held until the close of the war, being actively engaged, with the exception of thirty days. Among the important battles in which he participated were Shiloh, Nashville and Bowling Green. He was a stanch Douglas Democrat, and at first opposed secession, but afterward yielded. His grandfather came to America from Ireland before the Revolution. His father, Rev. Samuel B., was a Presbyterian minister, who lived in South Carolina until 1851, when he removed to Mississippi and died. He was a soldier in the War of 1812, and his widow is now living in Mississippi, aged ninety-four. Hugh S. Lewers was reared upon a farm, and in 1861 joined Company K of Col. J. G. Ballantine's regiment, Confederate States Army. Early in 1863 he joined his father and served with him until the close of the war, operating in Mississippi, Tennessee, Kentucky and Alabama. He was in active service the entire time, and surrendered at Gainesville, Ala., in May, 1865. In December, 1862, he was captured near Holly Springs, Miss., but paroled a few days later, at which time he joined his father. In 1861 he married Martha Atkins, a native of Alabama, who died in 1865, leaving one child. In 1869 he wedded Lizzie Liles, a native of South Carolina, who bore him one child, now deceased. In 1881 Mr. Lewers came to Crawford County, and until 1885 engaged in farming, but was that year made postmaster of Alma, and has since retained that position, although he still owns a fine farm of sixty-five acres of bottom land. Himself and wife belong to the Presbyterian Church, and he is a member of the Masonic fraternity. He has always been a Democrat, and cast his first presidential vote for Greeley in 1872.

Robert M. Littlejohn, freight agent of the St. Louis & San Francisco Railway, at Van Buren, since July, 1886, is a native of Louisiana, and was born in 1840. His parents, William and Jane J. (McAlpin) Littlejohn, were born in North Carolina and Mississippi, respectively. The father was a merchant, notary public and a member of the Presbyterian Church. He died in Louisiana in 1849, having lived there about fifteen years. The mother was a Methodist, and coming to Little Rock, Ark., about 1869, died at that place in 1879. William Littlejohn, the grandfather, came to America from Scotland in 1760, and settled in Edenton, N. C., where he died in 1817, aged seventy-seven. For forty years he was engaged as a shipping merchant. In 1771 he married Sarah Blount, daughter of Joseph Blount, who went to North Carolina before 1760, settling in Perquimans County, on the oldest land grant in North Carolina, made by the Yeophin Indians to George Durant in 1662. Robert M. Littlejohn is the oldest of a family of two sons and two daughters, and was educated at the S. P. Helen Institute at Shreveport, La. In April, 1861, he joined Capt. Flournoy's company, Second Louisiana Regiment, serving until after the Seven Days

167

CRAWFORD COUNTY, ARKANSAS - BIOGRAPHICAL AND HISTORICAL MEMOIRS
****

fight in front of Richmond, when he was transferred to Reef's cavalry, under Col. Monroe, of Arkansas, soon after being made quartermaster, which office he held until discharged at Shreveport, La., in July, 1865. He was married at Van Buren, in 1863, to Helen J., daughter of William F. and Mary A. England, natives of South Carolina and Virginia, respectively. Mr. England was a furniture maker, and in an early day came to Crawford County, where he died. His wife is still living. After the war Mr. Littlejohn was engaged as a bookkeeper in Van Buren a short time, and then farmed for ten years about ten miles below Van Buren. Returning to town, he then secured a position with the Little Rock & Fort Smith Railroad, and afterward became clerk with the freight agent at Little Rock. He then worked two years in Van Buren with the same company, and since that time has been with the San Francisco line. In politics he is a Democrat, although reared a Whig. He is a member of the I. O. O. F., and his wife belongs to the Presbyterian Church. Mr. and Mrs. Littlejohn have four daughters, one married and living in Florida, one in Little Rock and two at home.

James G. Lloyd is a son of Elder William B. and Mary E. (Hall) Lloyd. The father was born in Georgia in 1808, and when young was taken by his parents to Alabama, where he afterward married and lived until their removal to Noxubee County, Miss., where the mother died. She was a native of Alabama, and several years her husband's junior. Mr. Lloyd still lives in Mississippi, where he has engaged in farming, and preaching in the Missionary Baptist Church for over forty years. The mother of our subject was also a Missionary Baptist. Mr. Lloyd has always been a Democrat. By his first marriage he had six sons and one daughter, and by his second one son and one daughter. James G. Lloyd was the third child, and was born in Noxubee County, Miss., October 22, 1835, where he was reared upon a farm and educated in the old subscription schools. When twenty years old he began life on his own account as an overseer. In 1858 he married Elizabeth Sallis, a native of Alabama, by whom he had three children: William S. (deceased), Susan E. (deceased) and James H. Mrs. Lloyd died in 1866, and a year later he was married to Miss Mary C. Black, who was the mother of four children: Richard A., Lydia C., Durward P. and Carrie C. Having been left a widower a second time, in 1876, in 1878 Mr. Lloyd wedded Martha C. Garner, who bore him one child, Bettie L., and died in 1879. In 1880 Mrs. Fannie E. Pile, *nee* Mayfield, became his wife. She had three children by her first husband, viz.: Theodore, Wallace and Herschel. She and Mr. Lloyd are the parents of five, named as follows: Amzy B., Josie, Virgie E., Bonnie E. and Levie T. Mr. Lloyd and his four wives were all united with the Missionary Baptist Church. In 1874 Mr. Lloyd came to this county, and is now the owner of 120 acres of land, sixty being well improved and cultivated, and well fitted with good buildings. In the fall of 1861 Mr. Lloyd enlisted in Company C, Fortieth Mississippi Volunteer Infantry, and served in the Confederate army until the close of the war. He participated in the battle of Iuka, second battle of Corinth, and at Vicksburg was surrendered to the enemy, but afterward exchanged. He also went on the Georgia campaign. He was never wounded.

Col. M. F. Locke, planter, miller and merchant, of Alma, was born near Murfreesboro, Tenn., in 1826, and is a son of William and Margeret (Bowman) Locke. The parents were natives of North Carolina, where they were probably married, soon after removing to Rutherford County, Tenn., where the father died in 1831 and the mother in 1881, respectively. Mr. Locke's grandfather was of Irish descent, and his father commanded the "Murfreesboro Blues" at the battle of the Horseshoe Bend, in the War of 1812. The mother was a daughter of Col. Sam Bowman, of near old Jefferson, Tenn. Our subject, with an elder brother, was the main support of the family during his youth, and he consequently received but a common-school education. In 1849 he married Elizabeth Buie, who died in Texas in 1864, whither Mr. Locke had gone in 1850. The following year he married Narcissa A. Montgomery. By his first wife he had six children, all of whom are living. Mr. Locke is a Democrat, and cast his first presidential vote for J. K. Polk. In 1852 he was elected a member of the Lower House in the Texas Legislature, and served until 1859. In 1856 and 1857 he was speaker. In 1860 he was elected to the State Senate, but in 1861 resigned, and was made colonel of the Third Texas State Regiment Cavalry, nine months after being transferred to the Tenth Texas Dismounted Cavalry, Confederate

States Army, which he commanded until the close of the war. At the beginning of his service he had 1,200 men under his command, and at the end only sixty-five men were paroled. He participated in the battles at Farmington, Corinth, Richmond, Ky., Mansfield, Chickamauga, Mission Ridge, Dalton, and was through the entire Georgia and Atlanta campaign. His command was discharged at Meridian, Miss. In the winter of 1865-66 he came to Crawford County, Ark., and in 1868 purchased land upon the present site of Alma, which town he helped to found in 1872, and where he has been a prominent citizen ever since. For some years he was engaged in the mercantile business, and for a year and a half edited the Alma *Democrat*. He is now largely engaged in farming and the milling and gin business, having several cotton-gins and a flour and corn-mill at Alma. He is also the owner of 1,000 acres of land, and is considered one of the successful citizens of the county. He is a member of the Masonic fraternity, and belongs to the Alma Lodge, No. 43. His wife, who died in 1886, was a member of the Missionary Baptist Church, and he is also a member of that denomination. During the Mexican War he served in the First Mississippi Regiment under Jeff. Davis.

M. L. London was born in Tennessee in 1837, and is the second son of John J. and Juda (Burnett) London, natives of South Carolina and Tennessee, respectively. The parents were married in Tennessee, and in 1846 came to Crawford County, Ark., where they afterward resided engaged in farming. Four of their children are still living: R. H. London, of this county; Mrs. J. Barker, of Prairie Grove; Mrs. Ruth Hale, of this county, and our subject. Mr. and Mrs. London died in 1878 and 1877, respectively. The grandfather, John J., and his wife, were natives of Virginia, and wealthy farmers. The maternal grandfather, John Bernett, was born in Virginia, and in 1846 came to Crawford County, Ark., from Tennessee. He was a farmer and a soldier in the War of 1812. He died in 1872 aged one hundred and ten. The grandmother, Saldie Burnett, was born in Virginia, and died in Crawford County in 1872. Our subject received but a limited education, and when eighteen began life on his own account by stock raising. In 1855 he married Angeline R. Hargrove, who was born in this county in 1839 and died in 1858. She was the mother of two children, John Houston and Angeline Briscoe, both of whom still live in the county. She was a daughter of William and Angeline R. (Whitehall) Hargrove, natives of Mississippi. Mr. Hargrove assisted in driving the Indians into the Territory, and then came to Crawford County. Mr. London was afterward married in Denton County, Texas, to Mrs. Lucy (Tolle) Briscoe, who was born in Lewis County, Mo., in 1840, and is a daughter of Nimrod and Sidney (Mallory) Tolle, natives of Virginia, who went to Texas from Missouri in 1859. Mr. Tolle was a farmer, and in 1861 enlisted in Company E, Twenty-ninth Texas Cavalry, under Col. DeMoss. He was killed in Texas by bushwhackers in 1864. By his second marriage Mr. London has seven children, all of whom live in Crawford County. They are Ella Hargrove, Nathaniel W., Juda, Rose, Fanny, Samuel and Maude. In 1859 Mr. London went to Texas, but ten years after came to Crawford County, where he owns a farm of 364 acres on Cove Creek, 165 acres of which he cultivates. Cotton and corn are his principal productions. He also owns a store, grist and saw-mill, and a cotton-gin. He cast his first presidential vote for Stephen A. Douglas in 1860, and has since voted the Democratic ticket. In 1861 Mr. London enlisted in Company E, First Choctaw Regiment, commanded by Col. Walker, and for one year served under Capt. Welch. He was then transferred to the Twenty-ninth Texas Cavalry, commanded by Col. DeMoss, and served until discharged at Galveston in July, 1865. Among the battles in which he participated may be mentioned Elk Horn, Newtonia, Possahola, Saline River and Mark Mills. Mr. London belongs to the Masonic fraternity.

Rufus H. London was born October 30, 1840, in McMinn County, Tenn., and is a son of John J. and Juda (Burnett) London. The father was born in Virginia December 23, 1809, and died May 28, 1876. The mother was born September 28, 1813, in Roane County, Tenn., and died August 22, 1877. In early life they went to North Carolina from Virginia, and in 1830 went to Tennessee. They were married in Crawford County, Ark., January 3, 1847, and settling on Lee's Creek engaged in farming the remainder of their lives. Of their twelve children only five are living: M. L. London, Sr., our subject, R. C. (of Oregon), Mrs. Ruth C. Hale and Mrs. Juda L. Barker (of Prairie Grove, Ark.). The grandparents of our subject, John and Bethuna (Clarridy) London, were born in Virginia, and from there went to Burke County, N. C. The former enlisted in the War of 1812 under Gen. Jackson, and served twenty-three months, during that time receiving a wound in the shoulder. The grandmother died in 1836 in East Tennessee. The maternal grandfather, John Burnett, was born in 1765 in Roane County, East Tenn., and died in Crawford County, Ark., November 12, 1871, aged one hundred and six. His wife, Sarah (Oliver) Burnett, was born in Roane County, Tenn., in 1766, and died September 22, 1872. John Burnett accompanied John J. London to Crawford County in 1847. He was a farmer by occupation, and served throughout the War of 1812 under Gen. Jackson. Rufus H. London was seven years of age when his father settled in this county, and was reared when the school advantages were of little importance. November 12, 1861, he married Buena Vista Lewis, a native of this county, born April 13, 1847, and daughter of James M. and Catherine Lewis. Mr. and Mrs. Lewis were born in Kentucky and Tennessee, and died in 1854 and 1858, respectively. They were married in Arkansas, and their four children are residents of this county, viz.: Mrs. London, D. W. Lewis, J. B. Lewis and Mrs. Melissa Maxwell. Mr. London enlisted April 27, 1861, in Company A, Third Arkansas Infantry, Confederate States Army, and served until the surrender, June 7, 1865. He received a flesh wound in the hip at Honey Creek, and participated in the following battles: Oak Hill, Pea Ridge, Virdigris, I. T., Rabbit Ford, I. T., Poison Springs, Ark., Prairie De Hand, Ark., Moscow, Ark., and Saline River, Ark. Mr. London is a self-made man, and has 320 acres in his home place, 160 acres being well improved. He has a comfortable frame house, and owns 120 acres in Section 18. Himself and wife are members of the Methodist Episcopal Church, South, and are the parents of the following children: Marcus L., born in Denton County, Texas, in 1862; J. C., born in 1865; Ruth C., born August 20, 1867, now deceased; John J., born November 1, 1869; Mattie L., born July 29, 1871; Josephine, born October 5, 1873; Rufus H., born November 15, 1875; David B., born December 4, 1878; Lula F., born December 13, 1880; Juda B., born March 8, 1883; Jarvis L., born January 29, 1885, now deceased, and Willie P., born July 8, 1886. Mr. London is a member of the Dripping Spring Lodge No. 245 and the Farmers' Alliance, Lodge No. 1340. In politics he is a Democrat, and cast his first presidential vote for Stephen Douglas in 1860.

Rev. Dr. Elisha M. Lowrey, a Missionary Baptist minister, physician and surgeon of LaFayette Township, was born in Franklin County, Ga., in 1828, and is a son of Amos and Eliza Ann (Albrighton) Lowrey, natives of Wilkes County and Franklin County, Ga., respectively. They lived in Franklin County until 1835, and then went to what is now Gordon County, and later to Cobb County, where the mother died in 1860. Mr. Lowrey afterward married, and moved to DeKalb County, where he died in 1879, aged eighty-seven. He was a farmer by occupation, and had belonged to the Methodist Church from childhood. For several years he served as justice of the peace. The grandfather, Elisha Lowrey, was born in South Carolina, of Irish parents, and died in Georgia. He was a soldier in the War of 1812. Prior to the Revolution three brothers, Shadrach, Meshach and Abednego Lowrey, came to America from Ireland, and served in the above war. Meshach, the great-grandfather of our subject, settled first in South Carolina, but afterward went to Virginia. He was a minister in the Hardshell Baptist Church many years, and Dr. Lowrey remembers hearing him preach on the one hundred and sixth anniversary of his birth. Dr. Lowrey is the third of a family of seven children, and received his early education in an old log house, with a dirt floor and a fire in the center of the room. When seventeen years old he married Dorcas E., daughter of James and Rachel Stewart, of Cherokee County, Ga., who died in 1854, leaving three children, two of whom are living. In 1856 he was married a second time, Julia Ann, daughter of Moses M. and Elizabeth Ann Cantrell, becoming his wife. Her parents were born in South Carolina, but her birth-place was in Forsyth County, Ga. She has borne eight children, of whom six are living. After studying medicine four years our subject attended the Macon (Ga.) Botanic School, from which he graduated in 1859, although since 1854 he has practiced medicine with success. When ten years old he became a convert in the Methodist Church, and at the age of sixteen was licensed to preach, which he did for fourteen years. He then united with the Missionary Baptist Church, was immediately ordained, and has since been an earnest worker in that church, preaching with good results in his various places of residence. He preached and practiced medicine in the neighborhood where he was reared until the year 1870, when he came to Crawford County, and until 1880 lived upon forty acres of his present farm, which is situated five miles south of Mountainburg. He then engaged in the drug business at Alma until 1884, after which he lived in Choctaw Nation two years for his health. Since that time he has lived on the old place, which now contains 160 acres. He is widely and favorably known as a minister and physician, and in 1887 established a drug store at Graphic, which is now in the charge of one of his sons. During the war he served six months as surgeon in the Eighth Georgia Battalion. Since 1871 he has belonged to the Masonic fraternity, and is now a member of the Graphic lodge. His wife is a member of the Baptist Church, but was formerly a Methodist.

Michael Lynch, retired merchant, was born in Ireland in 1818, and came to the United States in 1840, settling in Van Buren in 1848. He followed mercantile pursuits for many years, and retired in 1882, and became identified with other enterprises, in which he is still engaged.

Thomas M. McGee was born in Van Buren in 1846, in the Collins Hotel, and is a son of Dr. Jonathan D. and Mary A. (Moore) McGee. Dr. McGee was of Scotch-Irish descent, and born in Kentucky in 1800. He was a graduate of the Lexington (Ky.) Medical College, and about 1818 came to Arkansas, locating about twenty miles below Van Buren, but being drowned out by an overflow, in 1833, moved upon the present homestead site. He was married in Arkansas, and visited his old home in Kentucky upon his wedding tour. He was one of the first white settlers in the county, and for a few years farmed in connection with the practice of his profession. He was a man of ability, and was for years the leading physician of the county, his practice extending as far as Fort Gibson. He died in 1862. The mother of our subject was born in Virginia in 1811, and died in 1878. She was the mother of seven children, three of whom are living: Mary (wife of H. A. Meyer), Lillie B. and Thomas M. The latter received his education in the Van Buren schools, and the Kentucky Military Institute, near Frankfort, Ky. After his education was completed he engaged in farming until 1874, and then dealt in fresh meats for two years. In 1881 he embarked in mercantile life, which he has since followed, and is now one of the substantial business men of Van Buren. In politics he is a Democrat, and in 1871 was Deputy United States Marshal. For two years he served as deputy sheriff of Crawford County, under Col. William L. Taylor, and he has been a member of the school board for a number of years. He has also been in the city council a number of terms. Mr. McGee owns about 350 acres of bottom land, and 235 acres of hill land, besides a number of town lots, and he is a stockholder in the Crawford County Bank. In 1861 he enlisted in the Confederate army, first in the Van Buren Guards, afterward becoming attached to Gen. Terry's regiment, which was stationed in Texas. He was in service during the entire war, and was present at the surrender at San Antonio, Tex. Mr. McGee belongs to the I. O. O. F., Lodge No. 6, and is an ancient member of the K. of P. Himself and wife are Episcopalians.

Frank R. McKibben, of the firm of McKibben & Pape, was born in Seneca County, Ohio, in 1843, and is a son of James and Caroline L. (McManigal) McKibben. The father was of Irish descent, and born in Center County, Penn., in 1808, where he farmed and merchandised. He was twice married, his second wife being the sister of his first wife. After the death of his first wife, in Seneca County, he returned to Pennsylvania, and after his second marriage located in Ohio, having traveled 400 miles on horseback to their destination. He was a large property owner and successful merchant, and died in Seneca County in 1856. The mother was born in 1812, and died in 1852. Frank R. McKibben was the fifth of a family of six children, and was left an orphan when a boy twelve years old, and reared by Henry Isabel, a carriage trimmer in Richland County, where he began to learn the trade at the age of fourteen. In November, 1861, he enlisted in Company A, First Ohio Cavalry, and participated in fifty-two engagements. He served under Gen. Garfield in Kentucky, Gen. Burnside in Tennessee, and Gen. Sherman in Georgia. He was discharged at Nashville in March, 1865. He was twice wounded, once at Morristown, Tenn., in the breast, and once at Smoky Mountains, in the limb. After the war he worked for his brother, David A., in the mercantile business at Fort Smith, Ark., until 1870, and then superintended Shaw's plantation. The following year

171

CRAWFORD COUNTY, ARKANSAS - BIOGRAPHICAL AND HISTORICAL MEMOIRS
****

he established a store in Van Buren, and in 1880 Henry T. Pape, a brother-in-law, became his partner. They have a handsome block, and carry a large line of general merchandise, hardware, clothing, furniture, etc. They carry the largest stock of general goods in Western Arkansas, and are gentlemen held in high esteem. In September, 1870, Mr. McKibben married Minnie E. Pape, daughter of Henry Pape, and a native of Cincinnati, Ohio, born in 1852. This union has been blessed with three children: Frank Pape, William Watson and Bertha Lucetta. Mr. McKibben is one of the most influential citizens of the place, and belongs to the Crawford Lodge No. 6, of the I. O. O. F. He is a member of the school board and town council, and is vice-president of the Van Buren Canning Company, and a stockholder and director in the Crawford County Bank at Van Buren. Mrs. McKibben is a member of the Presbyterian Church, and he is also a believer of that creed.

James W. McKinney, of the drug firm of McKinney & Kerr, was born in Sangamon County, Ill., in 1862, and is a son of Joseph and Jane (Erwin) McKinney. Joseph was a grain and lumber dealer, born in Jersey County, Ill., in 1833. In 1863 he moved to Girard, Ill., and engaged in the lumber business. He died July 13, 1871, while in the prime of life. The mother was born in Jersey County, Ill., in 1836, and is now living in Girard, Ill. She has three children: Edward, of Greeley, Colo.; James W., and Nona, wife of F. J. Lincoln, of Chicago, Ill., ticket agent of the Chicago & Alton Railroad. Our subject was reared in Girard, and at the age of eighteen began to clerk in a clothing store. In 1884 he came to Van Buren, where he and F. W. Langley engaged in the drug business. At the expiration of six months he purchased his partner's share, and in July, 1886, entered the firm, which has since been known as McKinney & Kerr. They have a fine trade, are careful and industrious men, and rank among our best citizens. May 27, 1885, Mr. McKinney married Miss Fannie A. Post, daughter of U. S. Post, of Girard, Ill. Mrs. McKinney was born in Macoupin County, Ill., in 1866. Mr. McKinney is a Democrat, a Mason and K. of P.

Frank G. Kerr, junior member of the above firm, was born in Saline County, Mo., in 1857, and is a son of John and Frances (Gault) Kerr. The father was of Scotch-Irish descent, and was born in West Virginia in 1825. When young he went to Saline County, where he married and passed his life. He was a machinist, and died in 1868. The mother was born in Virginia and died in 1875. She had three children: Frank G., Mitchell D., groceryman at Gilliam, Saline County, Mo., and James W., partner of Mitchell D. Frank G. was educated in his native county, and at the age of thirteen began to clerk in a drug store at Cambridge, where he remained about four years. He then clerked in Marshall, Mo., eight years, and in 1881 and 1882 took a course of lectures in pharmacy at St. Louis. Having attended the Philadelphia College of Pharmacy in 1882 and and 1883, he graduated from that institution in the latter year, and in April he and P. H. Franklin started a drug store at Marshall, Mo., under the firm name of Franklin & Kerr. In 1885 Mr. Kerr sold his interest to his partner, and in 1886, came to Van Buren. In July, 1886 he became a partner of Mr. McKinney, as above stated. Mr. Kerr is a Democrat, and cast his first presidential vote for Hancock in 1880. He belongs to the Masonic fraternity.

Col. James A. McNeely, mayor of Alma, was born in Rowan County, N. C., in 1820, and is a son of Alexander and Ann McNeely, natives of North Carolina, where they passed their entire lives. They were of Scotch descent. The father was a merchant by occupation, and served as paymaster during the War of 1812. Our subject lost his father when an infant. In 1845 he married Margaret Morrison, who died in 1855, leaving five children, only one of them now living. In 1857 he came to Arkansas, and the following year married Jane McCoy, by whom he has had two children, one of whom is living. In 1868 Col. McNeely removed to Stoddard County, Mo.; in 1876 went to Carthage, Mo., and in 1877 came to Arkansas, settling in Alma, where for some years he engaged in the drug business. During the years 1861 and 1862, and a part of 1863, he served in the Confederate army as major of the Thirteenth Arkansas Infantry, and after the battle of Shiloh was made colonel of the regiment. He resigned the office on account of ill health. In politics the Colonel is a Democrat, and his first presidential vote was cast for Polk in 1844. Prior to the war he served several years as postmaster of Greensboro, Ark., having a drug store at that place, and after the war he served as postmaster at Lakeville, Mo., where he kept a general store. In 1860 he took the first census of Craighead County, Ark., and for

172

CRAWFORD COUNTY, ARKANSAS - BIOGRAPHICAL AND HISTORICAL MEMOIRS
****

some time after the war was deputy clerk of that county. Since 1879, with the exception of two years, he has filled the office of mayor of Alma, his long term of office being sufficient proof of the satisfactory manner in which he has fulfilled the duties of the position.

Dennis Maddox (colored) was born in Tuscaloosa County, Ala., in 1839, and being the property of William Maddox was, upon the death of the latter, willed to his son, Benjamin Maddox. He accompanied his new master to Fayette County, Ala., and after having received his freedom by the general emancipation edict, remained with Mr. Maddox until 1869, when he came to Crawford County, Ark. He then rented land of William J. Neal for six years, when he purchased 160 acres of his present place, which now contains 280 acres. While with Mr. Maddox he was married, in 1865, to Maria Richards, a native of Tuscaloosa County, Ala., and owned by Robert Jamison, a wealthy man of that county. When he first came to this county Dennis Maddox was $25 in debt and had a sick wife and a small family of children. He made the journey to Crawford County in an old wagon drawn by an ox team, and despite the fact that he had many hardships to endure never lost his courage, and from a poor man grew to be one of the best farmers of the neighborhood in which he lived. In 1887 he and James Patton built a gin near Mr. Maddox's home, which they conducted one season, since which time Mr. Maddox has been the sole proprietor. Mr. Maddox is an enterprising man, and spares no pains to keep his farm and stock in good condition. There are five families living upon his place, all of whom he has assisted when times were hard. He never attended school himself, but has given his children the benefits of a good education, besides rearing and educating three orphans. Himself and wife belong to the Missionary Baptist Church, in which he has been a deacon for eighteen years. In politics he is a Republican, and he is a member of the I. O. O. F., belonging to Silver Rod Lodge No. 2,041, at Van Buren.

Hardy Mattax, a companion in hunting and friend of Tom Comstock, mentioned on a previous page, was born in Coweta County, Ga., in 1839, the son of H. H. Mattax. In 1841 the latter settled near White Plains, in Benton Co., Ala., where he lived until 1846, when his wife died, after which he returned to Georgia, Morgan County, the home of Hardy's grandfather. There our subject remained until nearly grown. In 1855, becoming possessed of a desire to see something of the world, he left home, and finally reached Cohutta Springs, Murray County, where some relatives were living, and here experienced the first pleasures of hunting, a pastime to which he has since been greatly devoted. Among his early successes was the killing of an immense bear, 600 pounds in weight, whose death only occurred after an exciting encounter. Entertaining a desire to attend school, he went to Benton, Shelby Co., Tenn., remaining as a scholar in schools there for six months. In 1859 he was occupied for a time in teaching penmanship at West Plains, Howell Co., Ark., subsequently resuming his teaching in a little primary school in Fulton County, where he went in 1861. When the war broke out he went to Memphis, Tenn., obtained employment until the Federals took the city, after which he lived near there until hostilities ceased. On the last day of 1870 he landed at Van Buren, Ark., removing from this vicinity, however, in 1873, to a place sixteen miles north, on Lee's Creek, and one mile from the Cherokee line, where was a good hunting ground. Here his early desires for the sport were again cultivated, and before long an acquaintance sprang up between Mr. Comstock and Mr. Mattax, which has since continued to the pleasure of each. It is impossible to give, in the space allotted in a work of this kind, a detailed account of all the experiences undergone by them in their numerous successful expeditions, howbeit they would be full of interest. Thrilling, humorous and enjoyable excursions have been made in the pursuit of this favorite occupation, in all of which peculiar success seems to have crowned their efforts. Both are well known throughout this community.

Benjamin F. Massey was born in Greenville County, S. C., November 29, 1832, and is a son of Clement and Annie (Jones) Massey. The father was born in Raleigh County, N. C., was a farmer by occupation, and a stone-mason by trade, and when young went to South Carolina, where he married Annie Jones. Mrs. Massey was born in South Carolina, and when a girl visited Kentucky, but returning was principally reared in her native State. To her and Mr. Massey were born ten children. Those living are Louisa, wife of William Howard,

173

CRAWFORD COUNTY, ARKANSAS - BIOGRAPHICAL AND HISTORICAL MEMOIRS
****

of Benton County, Ark.; Starling T.,of Illinois; Lavinia, widow of Abner Kent, of Illinois; Parthenia, widow of Thomas Gray, of Illinois; Benjamin F. and Enoch J., of Texas. Those deceased are Austin, John E., Irene White and Minerva Anderson. In 1837 Mr. Massey went to Georgia, and in 1851 immigrated by wagon to Montgomery County, Ill., and five years later went to Parker County, Tex. In 1866 he located permanently in Crawford County, where he died April 19, 1874, aged seventy-two years, seven months and twenty-eight days. Mrs. Massey died here December 11, 1876, aged seventy-seven years, six months and four days. Nathan Massey, the grandfather, was born in Maryland, immigrated to North Carolina, and afterward to Georgia. He was a Revolutionary soldier. He and his wife both died in Georgia. Enoch Jones and his wife, the maternal grandparents of our subject, were born in Maryland, and died in Kentucky and Illinois, respectively. Benjamin F. Massey was reared in Georgia from the age of five to nineteen, receiving but a common-school education. He is a carpenter by trade, and in 1851 accompanied his parents to Montgomery County, Ill. In 1854 he went to California by wagon, where he engaged in mining sixteen years, besides carpentering, milling, etc. In 1870 he settled near Cedarville with his father, and since that time has farmed. He moved upon his present place in 1871, and has 138 acres, sixty of which he has finely cultivated. December 21, 1876, he married Lavinia Vincent, daughter of Isaiah and Margaret Vincent, natives of Virginia and Bedford County, Tenn., respectively. Mrs. Massey was born in this county, and is the mother of four children: Charles L., born December 12, 1877; George F., born June 8, 1879; James B., born November 29, 1881, and Thomas A., born June 9, 1883. Mr. Massey and family are members of the Cumberland Presbyterian Church. Mr. Massey is a Democrat, and a member of the Masonic fraternity.

William A. Matlock, farmer, was born June 24, 1816, in Overton County, Tenn., one mile from the Kentucky line, and is a son of David C. and Martha D. (Armstrong) Matlock. The father was born in Buncombe County, N. C., April 4, 1793. He was a soldier in the War of 1812 under Andrew Jackson, whom he greatly admired, and participated in the battles of Talledega, Horseshoe and Tallahoochie. When young he went to Tennessee on pack-horses, and his father buying land of John Sevirs, they proceeded to make a home in the wilderness. From 1822 to 1845 he lived in Kentucky, working at the shoemaker's trade in connection with farming, and in 1846 he bought land in Crawford County, where Logtown is now situated, remaining until his death, at the age of seventy-nine. The mother was born in Surrey County, N. C., October 6, 1798, and when nine years old went to Cumberland County, Ky., by wagon. She was married in Overton County, Tenn., and died in Crawford County in 1865. Of her children these are living: William, Judah (deceased), married to Hugh McDougal, of Little Rock; Martha, widow of A. Smith, of Logtown; John, of Clarksville, Ark.; and David, Catherine, George, Jane, Harriet and Judah are deceased. When our subject's father settled in Arkansas, there were but eight houses in Jasper Township, west of the county road, and game and buffalo were abundant. William Matlock, the grandfather, was born in Henry County, Va., on Plumb Creek, from there went to North Carolina, and from there to Tennessee. He subsequently moved to Overton County, where he died. He was a soldier in the Cherokee War. Catherine Matlock, the grandmother, was reared in North Carolina and died in Overton County, Tenn. John Armstrong, the maternal grandfather, was born in North Carolina, and during the Revolution served as major, being a field officer in the battle of Saratoga, under Gen. Gates. He died in Batesville, Ark. His wife, Letitia, died in Tennessee. William A. Matlock was married in 1839 to Elizabeth Walthall, a native of Kentucky, who bore him one child, William J., now a resident of Lamar County, Tex. Mrs. Matlock died May 13, 1846, in New Orleans. Mr. Matlock came to Crawford County in 1846, and February 1, 1854, married Harriet, daughter of Jesse and Elizabeth Stewart [see sketch of John P. Stewart]. Mrs. Matlock has borne our subject ten children, all save one now living: Stephen T., Keturah, Martha Ellen, Edgar, Letitia, David, Hector, Lillie, Sidney and Elizabeth. Politically Mr. Matlock is a Democrat. He is the owner of a fine farm, and has been a successful agriculturist. He has now suffered with palsy for over twelve years, but was formerly the strongest man in the county, capable of lifting 950 pounds.

Nathaniel W. Matlock was born September 25, 1828, in Overton County,

174

CRAWFORD COUNTY, ARKANSAS - BIOGRAPHICAL AND HISTORICAL MEMOIRS
****

Tenn., his parents being Valentine and Mary (Bassett) Matlock. The father was born in Tennessee February 27, 1786, and the mother was born in the same State January 3, 1790. In 1839 they left their native State, traveling to Franklin County, Ark., by wagon. In 1840 they immigrated to Crawford County, Ark., where they lived until their respective deaths in 1868 and 1862. Mr. Matlock served in the Creek War, and was sheriff of Overton County, Tenn., for eighteen years. By occupation he was a farmer. Of his five children but two are living. Nathaniel W. Matlock is of English descent, and was but thirteen years old when he accompanied his parents to Arkansas, which was then unpopulated and in a wild state. His educational advantages were thus meager, and at the age of twenty-two he began life on his own account. November 6, 1873, he married Miss Rachel Mooney, who was born in this county in 1842, and is a daughter of William and Mary (Crawford) Mooney. Her father was born in North Carolina, and died in 1878. Her mother died in 1844. The following are their children who are still living: Mrs. Mary Shepherd, of Oregon; Mrs. Rebecca Baker, of Crawford County; George Mooney, of this county; Joel H. Mooney, of this county, and Mrs. Rachel Matlock. To Mr. and Mrs. Matlock seven children have been born, all of whom reside with their parents: Rebecca Lee, Harriet Lacy, William H., Rufus M., Charles M., George Franklin and Mary. In 1861 Mr. Matlock enlisted in the Frontier Guards, Confederate Army, under Col. Grashett and Capt. Brown, and served until the close of the war, participating in the following battles: Oak Hill, Honey Springs, Ind. T., Prairieville, Ind. T. Mr. Matlock is a successful farmer, owning 160 acres of land, forty of which he cultivates, and is also interested in stock raising. He is a member of the Methodist Episcopal Church, South, and belongs to the Masonic fraternity. In politics he is a Democrat, and his first presidential vote was cast for Pierce in 1852.

Joseph W. Matlock was born in Grainger County, Tenn., February 24, 1829, and is a son of George W. and Margaret (Bassett) Matlock. The father was born in Knox County, Tenn., and from there moved to Overton County, going thence after marriage to Grainger County, where he lived until 1847, enduring the hardships of pioneer life. He then located near Dripping Springs, in Crawford County, Ark., and improved land upon which he lived until his death May 18, 1875. The mother was born in Virginia, moved with her husband to Tennessee, and was the mother of six children: Joseph W., and Margeret E., wife of Sandy E. Winfrey, of this county, still living, and Valentine, Sterling, John and Martha, deceased. Joseph W. immigrated to Crawford County from Tennessee in 1847, journeying by water to Memphis, and thence up the Arkansas to Van Buren. He lived upon the home farm until of age, and October 10, 1850, married Martha J. Lester, daughter of William and Margaret E. Lester, natives of Kentucky and Missouri, respectively, who immigrated to Hempstead County, Ark., and from there to Washington County. The father died in Crawford County March 14, 1859, and the mother is now residing in California. Of their twelve children ten are living: Martha J., Sarah C., Mary S., Lavinia B., Nancy E., Cynthia E., Luvenia T., William S., Mark B. and Joseph P. Those deceased are Elizabeth and Thomas. To Mr. Matlock and wife nine children have been born: Margaret J., Sterling P., Henry P., Harriet S., Sarah A., William G., Joseph H., Andrew J. and Virginia P. (deceased). After his marriage Mr. Matlock farmed until 1857, then lived on Cedar Creek two years, and next rented land on Dripping Springs one year, or until the commencement of the war, during which time he lived in various places, and afterward returned to his present place. He owns 160 acres, about sixty being finely cultivated. Mr. Matlock is a Democrat, and in 1882 was elected county and probate judge, serving two years. Mr. and Mrs Matlock are members of the Methodist Episcopal Church, South, and among the respected citizens of the county.

John R. Meadors was born in Whitley County, Ky., October 7, 1826, and is a son of Jacob M. and Jane W. (Harman) Meadors. The former died in 1871 aged seventy-three, and the latter at the age of seventy-one. [See sketch of G. W. B. Meadors.] Jacob M. was a son of John Meadors, whose father was Jason Meadors. The latter married a Miss Mobley. John Meadors' wife was Delila Jones. and Jacob M. married Jane W. Harman, a daughter of Valentine and Sarah (Baken) Harman. The father of the latter, Thomas Baken, was a captain in Washington's army. and was killed in a duel with John Brown in South Carolina. In 1845 John R. Meadors married Susanna, daughter of Nathan

175

CRAWFORD COUNTY, ARKANSAS - BIOGRAPHICAL AND HISTORICAL MEMOIRS
****

Moore, who was the son of Thomas and Delila (Williams) Moore, natives of South Carolina, who went to Tennessee in 1825, and the same year settled in Whitley County, Ky. In 1856 they moved to Crawford County, Ark., where the father died in 1865 aged eighty-eight, the mother in 1877 aged seventy-three. Mr. Moore has been a class leader in the Methodist Church sixty years, and his wife had been a member for a long time. To the union of our subject and wife sixteen children were born, five sons and three daughters now living, and all married and residing in this neighborhood. In 1851 Mr. Meadors came to this county and purchased of the Little Rock & Fort Smith Railway a portion of his present farm, his deed, dated September 8, 1859, being the first issued by them. He has since added to his possessions until now he is one the largest land-holders in the county, owning 500 acres of good land, which is the result of his industry and business ability. He is a Republican now, but previous to the war was a Democrat. He is a leader of his party in this vicinity, and with the exception of six years has served continuously as justice of the peace since 1864. Since 1866 he has been postmaster of Belmont Post-office, and for nearly six years after 1868 was associate judge of the county court. He has never served on a petit jury, but has probably been on more grand juries, in both the federal and circuit courts, than any other man in the county. In May, 1878, a mercantile store, which he had been running, was burned, but in 1887 he again started a store on his farm, and is now doing business upon the old site. He is a public-spirited man, a member of the Farmers' Alliance, and himself and wife belong to the Christian Church.

George W. B. Meadors was born in Whitley County, Ky., in 1830, and is a son of Jacob M. and Jane W. (Harman) Meadors, natives of North Carolina and Tennessee, and born in 1799 and 1803, respectively. They accompanied their parents to Whitley County, Ky., where they afterward married and lived until 1851. They then came to Crawford County, where their respective deaths occurred in 1871 and 1872. For many years they were Missionary Baptists. The grandfather, John Meadors, was born in North Carolina, was a Revolutionary soldier, and in 1811 went to Whitley County, where he died. The great-grandfather came to America from Scotland when a young man, and lived in North Carolina until his death. The maternal grandfather, Valentine Harman, was born in North Carolina, served in the Indian wars and died in Whitley County, Ky. He was of Dutch origin. Mr. Meadors' great-grandfather, Capt. Thomas Baken, came to America from England, served in the Revolution, and afterward settled in South Carolina, and became a wealthy citizen. He was a member of the State Legislature, and met his death while fighting a duel with John Brown, a fellow colleague, friend and neighbor. George W. B. Meadors is the fifth of a family of thirteen children, and passed his boyhood near the Cumberland River among the Kentucky hills. His education was limited, as he attended school but a few months. From 1847 until discharged at Louisville in July, 1848, he served under Gen. Scott, in Company K, Third Kentucky Volunteer Infantry, going from Vera Cruz to the City of Mexico. He was run over by a wagon at the last place and severely hurt. In 1848 he married Lucy C., daughter of Nathan Moore, a native of Whitley County, Ky. Her parents came from South Carolina, and were early settlers of Kentucky. To Mr. and Mrs. Meadors seven children have been born, of whom two sons and two daughters are living. In 1851 Mr. Meadors came to this county and homesteaded forty acres, to which he has added until he now has 120 acres of well-improved land, upon which, since 1875, he has operated a good gin and corn-mill, all his property being the result of his own personal effort. He was formerly a Democrat, but since the war has been a Republican, and after 1868 served as deputy sheriff of the county for ten years. For five years after the war he held a captain's commission in the militia. Mr. and Mrs. Meadors are members of the Missionary Baptist Church. There are in this county eighty-three voters directly members of the Meadors family, and of these eighty-one are Republicans.

Hon. Samuel A. Miller, attorney at law and senator of the Twenty-fifth Senatorial District of Arkansas, was born in Van Buren, Ark., on November 28, 1857, and is a son of George E. and Mary A. (Shannon) Miller. The father was born in Powhatan, Va., in 1811, and in 1832 located two miles north of Van Buren, in Crawford County. He was a large land owner, having 1,000 acres in all, and for several years during the last part of his life was engaged in the mercantile business in Van Buren. He was assassinated by unknown parties in 1865. The mother was born in Batesville, Ark., in 1822, and was a daughter of William Shannon, whose brother Isaac introduced the "Shannon apple." Isaac was one of the first white settlers in Washington County, Ark., and there produced the apple. Mrs. Miller died in 1880, and of her thirteen children nine are now living: Maria J., widow of Gideon Lichlyter; Harriet E., wife of Hugh Morrow; Isabella, wife of Mariman P. Kilgore; William G., butcher; Alice, wife of James B. Johnson; Richard J., merchant; Lenora, wife of John Kilgore; Samuel A. and Lillie E. Samuel first attended the Van Buren schools, and later studied in the State University two years. He taught school two terms in 1875, and in 1879 began to study law under Hon. B. J. Brown, of Van Buren. In 1882 he was admitted to the bar, and he afterward became the partner of Judge William Walker, of Fort Smith, and subsequently of J. R. Reeves, but for the past year has practiced alone. In the fall of 1888 he was elected to represent Crawford and Franklin Counties in the State Senate, by a majority of 1,106. October 12, 1887, he married Miss Virgie Lee Dean, daughter of James M. Dean, and a native of Mississippi. They have one child, Dean M., and are active members in the Methodist Episcopal Church, South. Mr. Miller is one of the rising young attorneys of the county, and has the promise of a bright future before him. He is a member of the K. of P.

Thomas M. Mitchell was born in Crawford County, Ark., in 1857, and is a son of Thomas and Elizabeth (Stewart) Mitchell. The father was born in Middle Tennessee in 1813, when young immigrated to Jefferson County, Ark., there married, and afterward moved to Crawford County, locating six miles east of the county seat. About 1878 he moved to Johnson County, Ark. He served as justice of the peace for many years previous to the Rebellion, and died in 1881. His wife was born in Virginia in 1822, and died in 1873. She was the mother of nine children, five of whom are living: Robert M.; Mary, wife of W. L. Couch; Thomas M.; Nancy, widow of P. M. Huston, and J. Newton, operator in the Little Rock Railway office. Thomas M. lived upon the farm until seventeen, and then attended school at Hindsville, Ark. In 1876 he began to learn the marble cutter's trade at Bentonville, Ark., and worked as an apprentice three years. In the spring of 1880 Mr. Mitchell commenced business upon his own responsibility at Ozark, Ark., and in 1883 went to Bentonville, where he remained until March, 1886. He then returned to his native county, locating in Van Buren, where he is the only marble cutter of the town. He is a skillful workman, and has the monopoly of the trade of Van Buren. November 11, 1883, he married Miss Alice Mitchell, daughter of Zacharia Mitchell, and a native of Missouri. To them three children have been born: Claude, Annie and Charles. Mr. Mitchell is a Master Mason and a Democrat. Mrs. Mitchell belongs to the Methodist Episcopal Church, South.

Kindred Montgomery was born August 13, 1838, in Greene County, Tenn., and is a son of John and Nancy (Malone) Montgomery, natives of Virginia and Tennessee, respectively. The father was born in 1810, and in an early day went to Tennessee, and from there went to Washington County, Ark., in 1858. In 1861 he came to Crawford County, where he died in 1877, and Kindred came with his father to this county. Our subject never attended school, all his learning being received while at the plow. When eighteen he began life for himself, and in 1868 was united in marriage to Mary Hale, who was born in Tennessee in 1844, and is a daughter of Benjamin and Nancy (Longmeyer) Hale, of this county. Mr. Hale was born in Tennessee in 1809, and died in Oregon, and Mrs. Hale was born in the same State, and died in 1865. Kindred Montgomery has 400 acres of land in Crawford County, 280 on Lee's Creek and the remainder on Cove Creek, all of which he has accumulated by his own industry. In 1863 Mr. Montgomery enlisted in Company L, Fourteenth Kansas Cavalry, under Col. Haynes and Capt. Charles Harris, and served until discharged in 1865. In politics Mr. Montgomery is a Republican, and his first presidential vote was cast for Bell in 1860. Mr. and Mrs. Montgomery have had seven sons and three daughters.

D. W. Moore. Among the early settlers of Crawford County, Ark., should be mentioned the Moore family. Grandfather Benjamin Moore, a native of Virginia, came here with his family at an early day, and settled on the Sebastian County side of the Arkansas River, at what is known as Moore's Rock. His son, Benjamin L., was also born in Virginia, and came to this State with his parents. Upon arriving at man's estate he married Mary Walker, sister of

Judge C. W. Walker, and soon after settled in Crawford County, where he farmed for a time, and merchandised in Van Buren. The mother was a Methodist, and died when her only child, David W., was an infant. The father afterward married Emily H. Erwin, who became the mother of Benjamin L. Moore. The father was a Whig in politics. His death occurred when our subject was ten years old. David W. was born October 2, 1839, at Fayetteville, where his mother was visiting. He received as good an education as the times afforded during his younger days, his first teacher being Rev. Townsend, an Episcopal clergyman of culture, and his second the Rev. C. K. Marshall, a Presbyterian minister who taught in Van Buren. After his father's death he went to live with the family of Judge David Walker, of Fayetteville, remaining with them for ten years. At the age of sixteen, having nearly completed the course of the Arkansas College, he entered Princeton College, New Jersey, but left in eighteen months on account of ill health, returning to Fayetteville and living upon his uncle's farm. In May, 1861, he enlisted in Capt. Brown's company of Van Buren Frontier Guards for three months, and was appointed sergeant-major of Col. Gratiot's regiment. He was present during the fight at Wilson's Creek, and at the expiration of his service re-enlisted in Company G, of King's regiment of infantry, Confederate army, remaining until the close of the war. He participated in the engagement at Helena, and several others of minor importance. In 1863 he was adjutant of Stirman's battalion four months. He also served as quartermaster-sergeant. His command was disbanded at Marshall, Tex., and he then went to Little Rock from Shreveport on horseback. Arriving there he was made clerk of the quartermaster's office for nine months, and then for eight months held the clerkship on the steamer Argus, under Capt. Ed Noland. Then for a number of years he farmed in Crawford County, and subsequently secured an interest in the business of D. C. Williams, for whom he had kept books two years. Later the business was conducted by H. H. Shibley, George Wood and himself, under the firm name of Shibley, Moore & Co. Ill health, however, caused his return to farm life, which has since been his chief occupation. He is a stanch Democrat, and in 1872 was the Democratic nominee for representative of Franklin, Crawford and Sebastian Counties. May 27, 1875, he married Emma T. Johnson, a native of this county, and the mother of four children: David W., Thomas J., Benjamin L. and Mary W. Mrs. Moore is a member of the Episcopal Church. Mr. Moore owns 1,000 acres of land, and is a director of the Crawford County Bank.

Ex-Judge William T. Morgan, farmer and stock raiser, was born in Gibson County, Tenn., in 1843, and is a son of John and Susan (Basinger) Morgan, natives of Tennessee. The father was reared principally in North Carolina, but when grown returned to his native State. When our subject was about two years old his parents removed to Yell County, Ark., and when he was about eleven they went to Texas, where they lived until 1860. They then returned to Yell County, Ark., and afterward went to Missouri and Kansas. The father died in Crawford County in 1879. He served about eighteen months in Company E, Third Arkansas Cavalry, United States Army, in Arkansas, and participated in the battle at Prairie de Hand. The grandfather was of Dutch descent, a native of North Carolina, and a soldier in one of the early wars. Mrs. Morgan died in Yell County, Ark., and Mr. Morgan was afterward again married. William T. is the fifth of a family of eight children, and during his youth attended school but about eight months. When eighteen he joined the First Arkansas Cavalry, United States Army, and a few months later joined the First Arkansas Infantry, serving a year. He then served five months in the First Arkansas Cavalry, and in 1863 joined the Third Arkansas Cavalry, with which he remained until the close of the war, serving as sergeant. He operated in Arkansas, Missouri and Indian Territory, and participated in the battles of Prairie Grove and Pea Ridge, and a great many skirmishes. He was discharged at Louisburg in May, 1865. In 1869 he was married in Newton County, Mo., to Elizabeth, daughter of James Coats, and in 1886 married Mrs. Margaret Rance, daughter of A. B. Hudson, a native of Indiana, who died in Texas when Mrs. Morgan was a girl. Mr. Morgan has four living children by his first wife, and one by his second. In 1869 he settled upon his present farm, which was then in the midst of the wilderness, but which, with patience and industry, has become a fine farm of 560 acres of finely cultivated land. Mr. Morgan had but a team and $150 when coming to this county, and his property is the result of his own

178

CRAWFORD COUNTY, ARKANSAS - BIOGRAPHICAL AND HISTORICAL MEMOIRS
****

labor and management. From 1872 he served as justice of the peace of Richland Township about twelve years, and although several of his judgments were appealed, they were never reversed. In 1884 he was elected county and probate judge, and served two years. He is an active worker in the Republican party, and cast his first presidential vote for Lincoln in 1864. He is greatly interested in the educational advancement of the country, and has been school director many years. He is District Master Workman of the K. of L., and President of the K. of H. and F. A.

Jackson T. Morton was born May 4, 1835, in Madison County, Ky., and is a son of Samuel and Nancy (Burris) Morton. The father was born in Clark County, Ky., and was a farmer by occupation. Before coming of age he went to Madison County, having previously married Nancy Burris, a native of Clark County, and of one of the wealthy families. To them nine children were born, five of whom are living: Mary J., James W., Jackson T., Joseph and Samuel E. Those deceased are Elizabeth, Terrinda, Margaret and Dollie. Mr. Morton went to Adair County, Mo., in 1838, where he engaged in farming. Himself and wife died there in 1855 and 1859, respectively. Richard Morton, the grandfather, was born in Virginia, and when young immigrated to Kentucky, and was one of the pioneers of Tennessee. His wife, Mary (Nolon) Morton, died in Schuyler County, Mo., aged one hundred and twenty-five. Thomas Burris, the maternal grandfather, was an early settler in Kentucky, where he died, as did his wife, Elizabeth. John Burris, an uncle of our subject, served in the Mexican War, dying in Old Mexico. His brother-in-law, Frank Condon, also served, but survived the war and returned home. Jackson T. Morton was brought to Missouri when three years old, and there lived upon his father's farm, receiving but a common-school education. After his mother's death his father married Eliza Richardson, by whom he had one child, Nancy, who was noted for her beauty, and married a wealthy doctor of New Mexico. For some time after his father's death Jackson had the care of the family, but in 1863 he married Margaret Howell, daughter of Henry and Martha Howell. This union has been blessed with seven children: Martha E., wife of Cyrus Hindman; Mary E., wife of H. E. Miller; Lucy A., Armedia, Louana, Joe, Aggie and Thomas. In 1858 Mr. Morton came to Crawford County, Ark., living in various places. During the war he served one year in Company A, under Capt. Clarkson, and then went to Douglas County, serving in the State militia for some time. In 1867 he settled upon his present farm, which contains 120 acres, sixty being under cultivation. Mr. Morton is a stanch Republican, and has served as school director. He is a Mason, and his wife belongs to the Christian Church.

John W. Moss, general merchant at Dyer Station, was born in Carroll County, Tenn., in 1848, and is a son of William and Elizabeth (Montgomery) Moss. The mother was a native of North Carolina, who came to Randolph County, Ark., in 1868, and in 1870 removed to Crawford County, where she died in 1879, a believer in the Christian faith. John W. Moss made his home with his mother until his marriage, and has no living relatives to his knowledge outside of his wife and children. He had a sister who was burned to death when a child. His mother was twice married. He attended school but about six months during his youth, and at the age of fifteen began to work as a farm hand, after which he rented land until 1873. He then homesteaded forty acres in Alma Township, and by the practice of industry and economy is now the owner of 240 acres, 100 being bottom land, and all of it well situated. He farmed exclusively until two years ago, and then started a general merchandise store in the spring of 1886. He handles farm implements, and has a stock valued at $1,800, his annual sales averaging $6,000. He served during the war about eight months in the Twelfth Kentucky Cavalry, and being captured while at home in Carroll County, Tenn., was held a prisoner at Camp Chase until the close of the war, when he took the oath of allegiance. In 1867 he married Lucy C. James, who died in 1880, leaving three children. The same year he wedded Ursula Whittington, a native of Arkansas, by whom he has had four children, three of whom are living. Mrs. Moss' father was a native of Alabama. Mr. Moss is a Democrat, and for one year was postmaster at Dyer. He now fills the position of assistant postmaster.

Henry C. Mueller, shoemaker, was born in Hesse Darmstadt, Germany, in 1848, and is the son of Conrad and Anna Mueller. The father died in 1876, aged

179

CRAWFORD COUNTY, ARKANSAS - BIOGRAPHICAL AND HISTORICAL MEMOIRS
****

seventy-five. The mother died in 1878, aged seventy. Henry is the next youngest of eight children, five of whom reached maturity. At the age of fifteen he immigrated to America, and located at Portsmouth, Ohio, where he served three years as an apprentice at the shoemaker trade. In the winters of 1867 and 1868 he worked in Wheelersburg, Ohio. In January, 1868, he moved to Danville, Tenn., and worked there and at Erin, Tenn., until 1882, when he moved to Van Buren, Ark., and commenced raising fruit and vegetables. In 1884 he opened a shoe-shop, and works at his trade during the fall and winter months, giving attention to fruit farming in the spring and summer. He owns fifteen acres of land near the city, on which he lives, and has fourteen acres in strawberries, 2,100 peach trees, 400 plum, apple, pear and cherry trees and 1,000 grape vines. He owns 135 acres in all, in the vicinity of Van Buren. In 1868 he married Caroline M. Winkler, who was born in Wheelersburg, Ohio, in 1853, and is the mother of five children: Charles, Lillie, Nina, Arthur and Katie. In politics Mr. Mueller is a Democrat, and in religion he and his wife belong to the Cumberland Presbyterian Church. He is a Royal Arch Mason, and a member of the A. O. U. W.

Charles J. Murta, general merchant, was born in Ireland in 1855, and is a son of John and Catherine (Ward) Murta, natives of Ireland, born in 1828 and 1835, respectively. In 1865 they immigrated to the United States, and located at St. Louis, Mo. John served an apprenticeship at civil engineering in his native country, and afterward worked in England, Spain and Germany. After coming to the United States he was employed by the Iron Mountain Railway Company, and worked on the railroad from De Soto south through Missouri, Arkansas and Texas. Afterward he was on the Ft. Smith & Little Rock Railway from Clarksville, Ark., to Ft. Smith, and at present is working from Ft. Smith to Greenwood, being employed for the past twelve years by McCarty & Kerrgan. He is well known as one of the most skillful mechanics in his line in the country. Mrs. Murta died in 1865, and had three children: John, employe in the Memphis & Little Rock Railroad; Bryan, agent at Traskwood on the Iron Mountain Railroad, and Charles J. The latter was ten years old when brought to America, and was educated at St. Louis. When eighteen he began to engineer on the Iron Mountain Railroad, and afterward learned telegraphy, and from 1875 to 1885 was agent at Alma, Ark. In 1882 he bought 660 acres eight miles southeast of Alma, on the Arkansas River, had 550 under cultivation, and twenty-two tenement houses. It is one of the finest plantations in the county, and is now owned by Robert S. Hynes, to whom he sold it. In 1887 Mr. Murta began to merchandise in Van Buren, and in July, 1888, bought the hardware stock of Reynolds Bros., which he added to his former large stock. He is an energetic business man, and has one of the largest stocks of general goods in Van Buren. At one time he was engaged as book-keeper in the Exchange National Bank of Little Rock, and he is now a stockholder in the Van Buren Ice and Coal Company, and the Van Buren Canning Factory. In 1882 Mr. Murta married Miss Abbie Powe, a native of Alabama, and the mother of two children, John and Maggie. In politics Mr. Murta votes a national Democratic ticket, but in local affairs is independent.

Lee Neal was born August 30, 1847, in Van Buren County, Ark., and is a son of Joseph and Rosana (Robinson) Neal. The father was born in Chatham County, N. C., spent his youth in Tennessee, was married in Crawford County, Ark., and shortly afterward removed to Van Buren County, Ark. In 1859 he went to Texas; in 1861 he joined the Eleventh Texas Volunteer Cavalry, and served until discharged. He then re-entered the Confederate service, remaining until the close of the war, and participating in thirty-six different engagements, among which were Poison Spring, Helena, Jenkins' Ferry and others. Since the war he has lived in Crawford County, and is now sixty years old, and engaged in farming. The mother is a native of Tennessee, is sixty-two years of age, and is the mother of the following children: Lee, Melinda (wife of W. S. Lester), Seldon R., Dillis Neal, America, Laurana (wife of Marcus Lamb), Sarah J. and William E. The paternal grandfather of our subject spent his entire life in North Carolina. His parents were French, and left their native land on account of the religious intolerance there. Laurana (Arrington) Neal, subject's grandmother, was also born in North Carolina, and after her husband's death immigrated to Tennessee. She died in Crawford County, Ark. James R. Robinson, Lee's maternal grandfather, was born in Tennessee, when six-

180

CRAWFORD COUNTY, ARKANSAS - BIOGRAPHICAL AND HISTORICAL MEMOIRS
****

teen enlisted in the War of 1812, and about 1840 came to Arkansas. He died in Texas. His wife was born of German parentage, and was reared in Pennsylvania. Lee Neal accompanied his parents to Texas when ten years of age, received a good education there, and when seventeen served on post duty in the McGinnis regiment of Texas reserved corps. He afterward completed his education in Crawford County, Ark., and has since served the county six years as examiner of common free schools. For the past eight years he has been an ordained minister in the Methodist Protestant Church, and has charge of two churches. February 6, 1868, he married Serena T. Lester, daughter of William and Margaret Lester, and a native of this county. Her parents were both born in Hempstead County, Ky., and came to Arkansas in an early day. The father died here, but the mother is now a resident of California. Mr. and Mrs. Neal have three children: Edward J., born March 29, 1868; William A., born March 2, 1873, and Rosana Maud, born January 14, 1888. After his marriage Mr. Neal farmed and taught school until 1876, and has since that time been in the mercantile business in Cedarville, in connection with his farming. Mr. Neal is a public-spirited man, and has represented his county in the Lower House of the Legislature at Little Rock. He belongs to the Masonic fraternity and the Patrons of Husbandry. He is a large land owner in the township, and one of its best citizens. Mrs. Neal belongs to the Methodist Protestant Church.

Berkeley Neal, attorney at law of Fort Smith, was born in Crawford County, Ark., January 23, 1851, and is a son of William J. and Mouncy (Robinson) Neal. The father was born January 9, 1817, in Chatham County, N. C., and was a son of Younger and Susanna (Harrington) Neal, natives of the same county, born in 1778 and 1790, respectively. They moved to Hickman County, Tenn., in 1826, where he died in 1843 and she in 1867. Younger Neal served some time as sheriff of Chatham County. William J. was the third child, and when the Creek Indians came west in 1836 he was employed as cook for the officers, and went with them to Fort Gibson, Ind. T. After roughing it for some time he came to Van Buren, Ark., and in 1838 married Miss Mouncy Robinson, in Dickson County, Tenn., who was born in 1817. The following year he returned to Arkansas, and has since passed the remainder of his life in Crawford County. He has been a successful man, at one time owning a large tract of land, and still has in his possession 440 acres. He has seven children, all of whom are living and grown: Jonathan, probate and real estate agent; Francis M., justice of the peace; Elizabeth, Young, James, Berkeley and Willis H., attorney at law. Berkeley lived upon the farm until eighteen, and then clerked in a general store in Van Buren until 1872. He then began to study law under Benton J. Brown, and was admitted to the bar in 1873, subsequently practicing two years in partnership with his former preceptor. Mr. Neal soon became one of the leading members of the bar in the county, and about 1882 began to practice in the Federal court at Fort Smith, where he met with such success that January 2, 1888, he moved his office to Fort Smith, although he still retains an office in Van Buren, and spends two days a week in that place. In politics Mr. Neal is a Democrat, and although he has never sought office he was superintendent of the school board of Crawford County for two years. December 14, 1882, he married Miss Mary Edwards, daughter of Jesse Edwards, and a native of Crawford County. To Mr. and Mrs. Neal one child, Ollie May, has been born.

John Franklin Neal was born August 1, 1855, in Crawford County, Ark., and is a son of Palmer and Elmina (Neal) Neal, natives of North Carolina and Tennessee, respectively. The mother was born in Tennessee, and while on a visit to North Carolina was married to Mr. Neal, who was her cousin. They afterward spent about two years in Tennessee, and then immigrated to Crawford County, Ark., about three miles east of Cedarville. They had nine children, four of whom are living: Mary E., widow of John L. London; Miriam M., wife of William H. Maxey; John F. and Palmer H. Those deceased were James, Demarius, Julia A. (wife of William Larue), Cornelius W. and Virginia A. Mr. Neal farmed in this county from 1843 until 1875, and about 1877 went into the mercantile business, which he continued until his death in 1885, aged sixty-three. The mother survived him but a few days, and was sixty-two years old at her death. Mr. Neal was very poor when he came to this county, but succeeded in amassing property, and defended his possessions during the war by enlisting in the Confederate army, serving until the close of the war. He was one of the early settlers here, and with his wife endured many hardships during the pioneer days. He became the owner of large tracts of land, and was an extensive stock raiser. Our subject remained at home working upon the farm until of age, and received but a common-school education. He then went into the mercantile business with his father, and although he now owns considerable land and farms extensively he is still interested in mercantile life, owning a large stock of general goods, besides being a partner in the drug firm of Neal & Purcell. In October, 1878, he married Miss Naomi T. Crowell, daughter of Charles and Lavina Crowell, and a native of Benton County, Ark. This union has been blessed with four children: Princess Deborah and Rosa Belle, living, and William W. and Bertha G., deceased. Mrs. Neal is a Methodist, and Mr. Neal belongs to the Presbyterian Church, being superintendent of a Sunday-school. He is a very strong Democrat, and always votes a straight Democratic ticket. He belongs to the Masonic fraternity.

A. J. Nordin, merchant and minister, was born in Crawford County, Ark., in 1852, and is a son of Alexander and Betsey E. (Dodd) Nordin, natives of North Carolina and Tennessee, who died in 1863 and 1887, respectively. They were married in Tennessee, and in 1835 came to Crawford County and engaged in farming. Five of their children are now living: Mrs. Mary J. Townswell, Mrs. Arabella Seratt, Mrs. Ann L. Swinford, Mrs. Drueilla Furlow, of Barry County, Mo., and our subject, all save one being residents of this county. A. J. Nordin attended school in this county six months during his youth, and at the age of nineteen began life on his own account. January 22, 1871, he married Louisa Lane, daughter of Samuel P. and Nancy (Seratt) Lane. Mrs. Nordin was born in Illinois in 1849, and died in 1881, having borne five children: Francis Marion, Nancy Emeline, George Wesley, Mary J. (deceased) and William (deceased). December 22, 1881, Mr. Nordin was married to Miss Hannah Alice Arnold, daughter of Manuel and Mary (Anderson) Arnold, a native of Ohio. Mr. and Mrs. Arnold were born and reared in the same State, and from there went to Iowa, and afterward to Kansas, then to Benton County, Ark., then to Texas, then to Washington County, Ark., and finally located in Crawford County, where Mr. Arnold engaged in farming, blacksmithing and carpentering. He served in the war as a blacksmith. Four of his six children are living: Joseph Warren, Samuel Wayne, Mrs. Nordin and Mrs Elizabeth Kimes, all residents of Crawford County. Mr. and Mrs. Nordin are the parents of the following children: Obedience, Medy, Arthur, and Arrema (deceased). Mr. Nordin, although he began life poor, has accumulated a comfortable property, the most of which he has made by merchandising. He owns a one-half interest in a mercantile store, valued at about $3,000, and has 240 acres of land, seventy-five of which he has under cultivation. Since 1876 he has preached in the Methodist Protestant Church, his labors having extended over Missouri and Arkansas. He is a Republican and a member of the Masonic and I. O. O. F. orders.

William and John Obar have farmed in River Township since 1869, and own a large tract of land, situated in Crawford, Franklin and Sebastian Counties. In 1859 they located in the last named county, and there lived ten years, running a ferry across the Arkansas River. They then came to this county, and are now two of its wealthy citizens. William joined the New Mexico and Arizona brigade in Texas, and served two years in the army. In 1875 he married Mrs. Frances J. Mangram, by whom he has had eight children, five of whom are living. In politics he is a Democrat. John was drafted in the Confederate army, but after a few months' service joined the First Arkansas Infantry, United States Army, and served until the close of the war. He was married in 1862 the first time, and is now living with his second wife. Our subjects, William and John Obar, were born in Warren County, Tenn., in 1825 and 1828, respectively, their parents being Constance and Elizabeth (Tedford) Obar. In 1836 the family went to Hamilton County, Tenn., and in 1852 to Dade County, Ga., where they lived until 1858, at which time the mother, with our two subjects, came to Sebastian County, Ark., where the former died in 1865. The father had previously died while in Hamilton County. The grandfather came to America from Germany prior to the Revolution, and was killed in that war.

Richard T. O'Bryan, was born in Smith County, Tex., in 1848, and is a son of Arnold and Mary (Shepherd) O'Bryan. The father was born in Chatham

182

CRAWFORD COUNTY, ARKANSAS - BIOGRAPHICAL AND HISTORICAL MEMOIRS
****

County, N. C., in 1807, and was a son of William O'Bryan, a native of North Carolina, born about 1773. In 1810 he went to Wilson County, Tenn., and he died in Hickman County in 1828. He was a soldier in the War of 1812, and his father, William O'Bryan, was a brother of Daniel Boone's wife, Rebecca. Our subject's grandmother, Sophia Thomason O'Bryan, was born in North Carolina, and died in Maury County, Tenn., in 1816. She was the mother of six children, of whom Arnold O'Bryan was the second. He went with his parents to Tennessee when three years old, and was reared in Maury County, ten miles south of Columbia. In 1833 he left Tennessee, and came to Arkansas by boat and on horseback. He located in Crawford County, and was engaged by the Government to deal corn and beef to the Indians the first winter, and in the winter of 1834 to deal rations to the Cherokee and Creek Indians. July 6, 1837, he married Elizabeth Shepherd, who was born in Fluvanna County, Va., in 1820, and bore him eight children: Elizabeth Ann, died in 1855, aged seventeen; William D., accidentally drowned in Lee's Creek in 1858, aged eighteen; James A.; Mary Ellen, wife of George Yount; Richard T., John C., Robert S., and Sarah C., wife of Thomas R. Daniel, of Van Buren. After his marriage he farmed for seven years near Rudy Station, and then went to Fannin County, Tex. In 1846 he moved to Smith County, and in 1851 located near Sugar Loaf Mountain, Sebastian County. In 1853 he settled near the county seat of Crawford County, where he owned about 500 acres. He is one of the pioneer settlers of the county; for two years served as deputy sheriff, and in 1837 as constable. He lost his wife January 12, 1886, and now lives in Logtown. August 14, 1834, he was commissioned by Gov. John Pope captain of the militia of a Crawford County regiment, being the first man appointed to that position. He is a Republican, cast his first presidential vote for Jackson, and his wife was a member of the Christian Church thirty years. Our subject made his home with his father upon the farm until of age. In June, 1870, he married Miss Ann E. Williams, a native of Texas, who died in 1872. The next year he married Addie T. Hanson, who was born in this county, and is the mother of two children: Nettie and Bulila. Mr. O'Bryan is a well-to-do citizen of Van Buren Township. He has eighty acres of land, and is engaged in the grocery and liquor business in Logtown, which business he has conducted three years. He is a Republican, and for two years was marshal of Van Buren. His wife is a member of the Christian Church.

John C. O'Bryan, farmer and stock raiser, was born in Smith County, Tex., September 7, 1850, and is a son of Arnold O'Bryan. When about five years old his parents came to this county, he accompanying them, and it is here that his childhood was passed and his education received at the common schools of the neighborhood. June 9, 1870, he left the parental roof, having taken Harriet A. Young to wife. She was born in Washington County, Ark., January 21, 1853, but reared in Crawford County, and is the mother of five children: Renah I., Effie F., Wallace, Lela O., Eula B. After his marriage Mr. O'Bryan settled upon the place he still occupies, which contains 335 acres of land, 200 cultivated and improved. His success in life is largely due to his own personal efforts, and he is a good neighbor and citizen. In politics he is a Republican, and he belongs to the I. O. O. F.

Hon. John B. Ogden, Sr., was born in Cumberland County, N. J., July 3, 1812, his parents being Col. John B. and Sarah (Buck) Ogden, also natives of New Jersey. The father died in 1813, from the effects of a wound received at the battle on Jones Island, during the War of 1812. He was a speculator and trader interested in the products of the West Indies. The Ogden family is of English descent, and their original coat of arms represents a lion up a tree. The grandfather of our subject, Joseph Ogden, was a Revolutionary soldier, and was at the battle of Yorktown, under Gen. LaFayette. The mother of our subject was again married after Mr. Ogden's death, and lived until 1873. Her father, Joseph Buck, was also present at the battle of Yorktown, and commanded two brigades under Gen. LaFayette. Hon. J. B. Ogden was the only child, and was left fatherless when an infant. He received a common-school education, and at the age of seventeen began to study law with Gov. Elias P. Seeley, of New Jersey, a cousin of his mother. A few years later he began to practice, and in 1834 started westward. He located in Louisville, Ky., afterward going to Charleston, Ind. In 1843 he came to Van Buren, Ark., where he has since practiced his profession with great success. He has also done the largest

183

CRAWFORD COUNTY, ARKANSAS - BIOGRAPHICAL AND HISTORICAL MEMOIRS
****

collecting business of any one west of the Mississippi. In 1856 he was appointed United States Commissioner of the District Court, Western District of Arkansas, which also comprised all of the Indian Territory west of the Rocky Mountains, and held that office until the war, when he withdrew. In 1863 the Confederate States organized the Trans-Mississippi Department, and going to Shreveport to assist in the organization, he was given charge of the pay department, and served until August, 1864, when he resigned. He was then employed by private individuals in the removal of cotton and the collection of debts, and after peace was declared was tendered the position of clerk of the United States Court at Van Buren, but declined, as he could not conscientiously take the oath. In 1866 he was appointed Assistant United States District Attorney for the Western District of the State, and held the position six years. He has been identified with a large number of public enterprises, and is a stockholder in the Van Buren Ice and Coal Company. For the past four years, however, he has led a retired life. In 1835 he married Jane Sibley, daughter of Gen. John Sibley, of New Jersey. Mrs. Ogden was born in 1817, and died in February, 1866. The following four children were born to her: Charles (deceased), who was assistant secretary of State of Arkansas after the war; John B., Henry (deceased, October, 1886), Annie, wife of C. C. Colburn, editor of the Ozark *Democrat*, and Emma. In 1868 Mr. Ogden married Mrs. Susan H. Wing, *nee* Barron, of St. Charles, Mo. Mr. Ogden is a member of the I. O. O. F. and the Masonic fraternities.

R. C. Oliver, merchant and farmer, was born October 17, 1825, in Roane County, Tenn., and is a son of Eli and Aspasia (Ellis) Oliver, natives of the same State. In 1832 the parents removed from Tennessee to Washington County, Ark., and in 1842 came to Crawford County, where they died in 1846 and 1855, respectively. They reared a family of twelve children, two of whom now farm in Crawford County. The grandfather was John Oliver, and his wife, Julia, died in 1840. Our subject picked up what education he could, considering there were no public schools in those days, and at the age of twenty-one began to farm on his own account. In 1857 he married Mrs. Ellen (Redman) Behethland, a daughter of Hosea and Catherine (Barker) Redman. This lady died in 1864, and the following year Mr. Oliver married Mrs. Narcissa (Foster) Hargrove, daughter of Hocket and Zelika (Turner) Foster, and a native of Missouri, born in 1833. Mr. Oliver has three children, two sons and one daughter. Although he began life a poor young man, he has been successful in his farming and mercantile investments, until he now owns 800 acres of land, about half of which is under cultivation. He also has a grist and saw-mill and cotton-gin, and deals some in stock. In politics he is a Democrat, and his first presidential vote was cast for Lewis Cass in 1848.

Rev. Francis Marion Paine, a minister in the Methodist Episcopal Church, South, was born in Giles County, Tenn., July 4, 1822, and is a son of Gabriel Wilson and Mary (Hanners) Paine. The father was born in Hawkins County, Tenn., in 1801, and the mother in North Carolina in 1804. They were married in 1819, in Giles County, Tenn., where they had been brought up by their parents from early youth. The subject of this sketch removed with his parents to Hardin County, Tenn., in 1829, and in 1834 to Union County, Ill., where he grew up to manhood; and June 25, 1840, he was united in marriage to Miss Susanah Rich, youngest daughter of Thomas and Catharine (Noah) Rich. The grandfather of our subject, John Paine, was a native of North Carolina, a relative and great admirer of the noted skeptical writer, Thomas Paine. He was bold and adventurous, fond of the western wilds. In company with many of his relatives and personal friends, he crossed the Cumberland Mountains and made settlements at an early day on the rich lands of Elk River—now a part of Middle Tennessee. Having the advantage of a fair education for his day, he engaged in the service of capitalists as surveyor in locating Revolutionary soldier land warrants on the rich lands of the yet newer territory of West Tennessee, where he made his home later in life, and died at an advanced age. He and his wife were both of English descent. Mrs. Paine, wife of our subject, is of German extraction on her father's side; was born in Jackson County, Ala., February 24, 1824, and is the mother of eleven children, eight daughters and three sons, of whom four daughters and one son only are now living. Our subject, the eldest of nine children, had in early life only such educational advantages as were afforded by the common schools, first of Tennessee and later of Southern

Illinois. He engaged when quite young in teaching, and while teaching, in 1844, became a student of medicine. Through much self-denial and dint of energy and perseverance, he became a respectable scholar in the higher branches of the English classics. In 1854 he gave up his private school (Franklin Academy) in Sebastian County, Ark., to take charge of the Fort Coffee Academy, a mission school in the Indian Territory, under the auspices of the Board of Missions of the Methodist Episcopal Church, South. He continued his connection with the missionary work among the Indians, teaching and preaching—sometimes acting as general superintendent of a school and mission station. When the war came up, in 1861, he was superintendent of Fort Coffee and Newhope Academy, and had the pastoral charge of Fort Coffee and Newhope District as presiding elder. In 1863, on account of the desolations of the country from the war, he was necessitated to go to Texas with his family for safety and subsistence. He settled his family at Paris, Lamar Co., Tex., and engaged in the practice of medicine to support himself and family; in the meantime he became pastor of the Paris Station, Methodist Episcopal Church, South. At the close of the war, his father having died at Clarksville, Ark., it became necessary that he should take care of his aged mother. This eventuated in his removal back to Arkansas, which was consummated in 1867. This change, and the additional care of his mother, together with his large and expensive family, made it somewhat necessary for him to give up for a time the active pastorate, and become secular in his calling. His mother having died in 1871, he again entered the active pastorate of his church in 1872. In 1873 he was elected by the Arkansas Annual Conference one of the delegates to the General Conference, which met in the city of Louisville, Ky., in May, 1874. He was at that time presiding elder of the Dardanelle District. He served in this capacity for three terms, and then as station preacher in several charges. Finally, however, from the increasing infirmities of age, together with the effects of long and continued hard labor, he felt it his duty to ask the conference to permit him to retire from the activities of a Methodist itinerant minister, and occupy the less laborious position of a local elder in the church, which was granted him cheerfully by his conference. This was done at Ozark, Ark., in November, 1886. Our subject having homesteaded 160 acres of the Government, besides some other lands bought of private individuals, has settled on the 'Frisco line (St. Louis and Fort Smith branch) of railway, seven miles north of Van Buren, at Little Station, where he is now devoting his time and energies in the culture of fruits generally, but more especially that of strawberries, grapes and peaches; and having made the culture of these remunerative, and having considerable quantities of apples, pears, plums and cherries in young orchards coming on, it is but reasonable to conclude that, with the continuance of his present health and vigor of body and mind a few years longer, he will have a handsome yearly income from these to support comfortably himself and wife in their old age.

John E. Palmer was born in Jefferson County, Mo., November 28, 1827, and is a son of Samuel and Susan (Weidman) Palmer. Of German parents, the father was born in Pennsylvania, and when eighteen immigrated to Jefferson County, Mo., where he married, and farmed a number of years. He then went to Lamar County, Tex., and two years later went to Anderson County, where he died in 1867. The mother was born in Jefferson County, Mo., and had thirteen children, five now living, viz.: Catherine, wife of Henry Snow; John; Levi, of Anderson County, Tex.; Napoleon, of Brown County, Tex., and Sarah, of Anderson County. Mary, Samuel, Jane, and five smaller ones died. The paternal grandparents were natives of Pennsylvania, and there died. The maternal grandfather was an early settler of Jefferson County, Mo., and lived six miles west of Hillsboro. Our subject lived in his native county until fourteen, and as his father's attention was given to his mill, John was obliged to work a great deal upon the farm, but in leisure attended school. After becoming fourteen, he lived in Lamar County, Tex., two years, and then engaged in tanning and farming in Anderson County until the war. He then enlisted in Company I, Texas Infantry, for eight months, and afterward served two years and four months, or until the surrender at Hempstead, Tex., in 1865. Among others he was in the battle at Prairie Grove and Elk Creek, and while on picket duty at Fayetteville went three days without food. Returning to Texas, he settled in Lamar County, and then immigrated to Crawford County, where he has since

185

CRAWFORD COUNTY, ARKANSAS - BIOGRAPHICAL AND HISTORICAL MEMOIRS
****

lived. He has 160 acres of land, and has cultivated fifty acres. In 1848 he married Sarah Rooker, a native of Illinois, and daughter of Ransom Rooker. This marriage resulted in three children, two now living, Elizabeth and Ransom. After his first wife's death, Mr. Palmer was married, in 1872, to Polly Fears, of this county, who has borne him six children: Clarissa, Flora, Stella, Tommie, Frank, and an infant who died unnamed. Mr. Palmer is a Republican and a member of the Agricultural Wheel. Himself and wife belong to the Northern Methodist Church.

Henry Frederick Pape, junior member of the firm of McKibben & Pape, was born in Fort Smith, Ark., in 1854, and is a son of Henry and Elizabeth (Ziegenbein) Pape. The father was a contractor and builder of Hanover, Germany, and after his marriage immigrated to the United States in 1849, locating in Cincinnati, Ohio. In 1852 he moved to Fort Smith, where he died in 1866. He was a skillful workman, and erected a large number of buildings in that city. The wife was born in Germany in 1827, and is yet living and the mother of seven children: Minnie, wife of Mr. McKibben; Henry F.; Charles A.; Frank P., died in 1867, aged nine; William B.; and Annie M. and Ada D. (twins.) Henry received his education in Fort Smith and at the State University at Fayetteville. When his father died his partner in the mercantile business was A. Haglan, and Jacob Ziegenbein, his brother-in-law, then took charge. Four years later Mr. Z. died, and Charles A. Pape became the manager. In 1876 our subject took charge of the business, and held that position until 1880, when he became a partner of Mr. McKibben at Van Buren [see sketch of F. R. McKibben]. Mr. Pape is a prosperous business man, and is a stockholder in the Van Buren Canning Co. October 1, 1884, Miss Lucy S. Southmayd, daughter of L. C. Southmayd, became his wife. She was born in Van Buren in 1857, and is the mother of one child, Charles A. Mrs. Pape is an active member of the Methodist Episcopal Church, South. Mr. Pape is a Republican in politics.

Jesse Perkins was born December 23, 1828, in Warren County, Tenn., and is a son of Robert B. and Sarah (Norris) Perkins. The father was born in South Carolina in 1790, and after becoming of age went to Warren County, Tenn., traveling through unbroken country with a one horse and ox team. About twenty years later he went to Lafayette County, Mo., and farmed thirteen years. He had some nine negroes, two wagons and teams, besides other good property, which he sold for $35,000, and then spent a year in Washington County, where he made a crop, going in 1841 to Barry County, Mo., where he died in 1863. The mother was born in Warren County, Tenn., and had twelve children, half the number now living: Polly, widow of Robert Logan, of Missouri; Lavinia, widow of M. Logan; Martha, widow of James Mayfield; John B., Jesse and Robert. Those deceased are James, William, Jadida McWilliams, Jemima, Sarah Lee and Prudence A. The mother of these children was born in 1792 and died in Crawford County, Ark., June 11, 1884. Uto Perkins, the grandfather, immigrated to this country from England. He was a soldier in the Black Hawk War, and his wife, Sarah, was a native of South Carolina. David Norris, the maternal grandfather, was born of Irish parentage in the United States, and settled in Tennessee in an early day. His wife, Betsey, was a native of that State, and after her marriage moved to Lafayette County, Mo., where both she and her husband died. Jesse Perkins was brought to Missouri by his parents when an infant, and when fourteen went to Washington County, a year later going to Barry County. During the war he went to Texas, being in the Confederate service, but was discharged on account of disability. After living two years in Grayson County, he came to Crawford County, where he now has twenty-five acres under cultivation. In 1854 he wedded Lourena Hartley, daughter of Andrew and Lourena Hartley, of Benton County. Both parents were natives of Bedford County, where the mother died in 1837. Lourena then lived with her grandfather, Louis Heath. He originally came from North Carolina, and died in Benton County November 22, 1872. His wife, Elizabeth (Ray) Heath, was born in Tennessee in 1803 and died in Benton County in 1882. Louis Heath was a minister in the Missionary Baptist Church forty years, and for twenty-eight years had charge of a church in Bedford County. Mr. and Mrs. Perkins also belong to the Missionary Baptist Church, and in politics the former is a Democrat.

H. L. Pesterfield was born in East Tennessee in 1827, and is a son of David and Esther (Dunham) Pesterfield, both natives of East Tennessee, also. The father was by trade a cabinet-maker. The mother died in Washington County, Ark., in 1887. The grandfather, Henry Pesterfield, was born in Germany, and after coming to America passed his life in Illinois. He was a mechanic. Our subject obtained his education while working in the field, and in 1857 married Nancy Gant, daughter of John and Adeline (Dowsey) Gant. The marriage took place in Nashville, Tenn., while, with her parents, Mrs. Pesterfield was journeying from Tennessee to Texas. In 1866 they moved from Texas to Arkansas, where Mr. Pesterfield has since lived. To them four children were born: Esther A. Irwin, Sarah Ann Burgess, Mary Frances McAllister and Josephine Bacon, all of whom live near home. Mrs. Pesterfield died August 16, 1866, and in 1871 Mr. Pesterfield married Miss Susan McMaster, daughter of W. J. and Margaret (Harris) McMaster, who was born in North Carolina in 1850. Mr. and Mrs. McMaster were born in North Carolina in 1813 and 1827, respectively. In 1854 they left their native State and went to Missouri; in 1860 went to Texas, and in 1863 came to Arkansas. Mr. McMaster was a minister in the Methodist Church. Mr. and Mrs. Pesterfield have seven children, three being boys and four girls. During the days of the Whig party Mr. Pesterfield always voted that ticket, being strongly partisan, even at the tender age of ten, and since the organization of the Republican party he has been a stanch Republican.

Henry C. Pernot, proprietor of a livery, feed and sale stable and wagon yard, at Van Buren, was born in 1855, and is a son of Dr. Henry C. and Elizabeth A. (Sargeant) Pernot. Dr. Pernot was born in Thonars, France, August 1, 1820, his father being Denis Etienne Pernot, a professor of rhetoric and philosophy, and for many years inspector of colleges of the Royal University of France. Dr. Henry Pernot was educated at the Royal College of Poitiers, and at the Ecole de Medicine, Paris, from 1837 until 1847. In 1848 he published an important treatise entitled "Del 'Ipecacuanna dans le Fievre Pauperale." In 1847 he immigrated to America, and in 1851 graduated from the St. Louis Medical College. He then practiced two years in Prairie du Rocher, Ill., and three years in Ste. Genevieve, Mo. In 1851 he married Miss E. A., daughter of Dr. Ichabod Sargeant, of the latter place. This lady was born in Baton Rouge, La., is still living, and is the mother of three children: Minnie, wife of Rev. James Matthews, Episcopal minister in Mexico, Mo.; Henry C., and Sidney A., assistant cashier in Crawford County Bank. In 1852 Dr. Pernot came to Van Buren, where he passed the remainder of his days. In 1861 he was appointed surgeon in the Confederate army, being detailed for hospital duty until the close of the war. As a physician he ranked among the first, and as a public officer enjoyed the esteem and confidence of the community. He was a public-spirited citizen, philanthropic, and interested in art. He died in 1881, and had been a member of the city council of Van Buren many years. He also belonged to the school board, Masons and Odd Fellows, and was senior warden of Trinity Church. Our subject was educated in Van Buren, and in 1876 established a broom factory, which he conducted eighteen months. He then interested himself in photography, and in the spring of 1887 started his present livery business. He has a first-class stable, twenty-two horses and twelve vehicles, and is a well-to-do business man. In politics he is a Democrat, and in religion an Episcopalian. He belongs to the Masonic fraternity, I. O. O. F. and K. of P.

John H. Polly was born in Mississippi County, Mo., in 1840, and is a son of John and Mary (Hall) Polly, natives of Pennsylvania County, Va., where they were reared and married. About 1834 the father crossed the Blue Mountains in an ox-cart with his wife and family and located in Mississippi County, Mo. He then immigrated to Madison County, where his wife died when our subject was a small boy, after which he went to Wayne County, settling in Greenville, and again married. After running a hotel and blacksmith store some years at that place he moved upon a farm ten miles distant, and lived until his death. John H. is the youngest and only living child of a family of eight, and losing his father when he was about nine he was reared by his brother-in-law, Zedakiah Bedwell, in Greenville, receiving but little schooling. When he was twelve years of age his brother-in-law gave him a horse, which he sold, and with the money purchased an interest in a grocery house at Marble Hill. Two years later he started a general mercantile store in Wayne County, and two years after that engaged in the mercantile business at Poplar Bluff with increasing success until the war. He then sold out, and returning to Greenville, farmed one season, and then in 1862 enlisted in the Confederate army, in Capt. Holmes company of infantry. A few months later he was transferred to Company C, of Col. Reeves' regiment of Missouri cavalry, serving as sergeant-major, and being paroled as quartermaster at Jacksonport, Ark., at the close of the war, under Jeff. Thompson. He participated in a number of skirmishes, and did duty in Missouri and Arkansas. He then passed a year at Poplar Bluff engaged in blacksmithing, and also a year in Greenville. In 1869 he removed to Washington County, Ark., and since 1871 has been a resident of Prairie Township, Crawford County. He farmed exclusively until 1877, but since that time has been employed by the Singer Sewing Machine Company as agent and collector of Crawford and Franklin Counties. He is a man of good business ability, and although he began life for himself a poor boy now owns eighty acres of land and is a well-to-do man. He is a Democrat, and from 1882 until 1886 served as deputy sheriff. In 1860 he married Hannah, daughter of Thomas and Lucinda Hopkins, natives of North Carolina, who were married in Missouri. The father died when Mrs. Polly was but a girl, but the mother resides upon the old homestead in Wayne County, Mo. Mr. and Mrs. Polly are Methodists and the parents of six children, all save one now living. Mr. Polly is a member of the Pleasant Hill Lodge No. 233, A. F. & A. M. His first presidential vote was cast for Seymour in 1868.

P. M. Rains was born April 19, 1851, and is a son of Philip and Sarah (Webb) Rains. The father was born in North Carolina, and when a young man made an overland trip to Tennessee, where he engaged in farming until his death in 1851. The mother was born in Hamilton County, Tenn., and when twelve years old accompanied her parents to Sequatchie Valley, Tenn., living there five years. She then moved across the mountains, and finally came to this section of the country, where she married Mr. Rains. She is now living with her only child, our subject. The grandfather of P. M. Rains was born in North Carolina, and died in that State. The grandmother went to Tennessee at an early date, and after the death of her husband married John Nelson and settled near Batesville, Ark., where she died. The maternal grandfather of our subject was born in North Carolina, and about 1790 removed to Tennessee after a long and dangerous journey in a two-horse wagon. By his first marriage he had two children, Rhoda and Reggy, and his second wife, Sallie Flynn, was born in North Carolina, and was the mother of eight children: Matilda, Thomas, Mattie, Nora, Litt, Benjamin, Lucinda and Sarah A. He was an early settler of Tennessee, had to go eight miles to mill, and the nearest neighbor was about five miles distant. Our subject was born in Hamilton County, N. C., and having lost his father when an infant was obliged to support his mother, and thus was deprived of an education, his knowledge of books being acquired by personal effort. May 1, 1870, he married Martha Campbell, daughter of James Campbell, and the mother of five children, four of whom are living: Electra, Annie, Willie and Harry C. Ora is deceased. After farming two years in Tennessee, subsequent to his marriage, Mr. Rains settled in Independence County, Ark., and a year later came to Crawford County. He rented land for seven years, and then purchased his present farm, which contains 207 acres, 105 being finely cultivated. Mr. Rains always contributes to educational projects and anything which is for the advancement of the county. He is a stanch Democrat, and one of the best citizens of Cedarville Township. Mrs. Rains belongs to the Missionary Baptist Church.

Joseph L. Rea was born in McLean County, Ill., in 1851, and is a son of Thomas and Elizabeth (Ramsey) Rea, natives of Bedford County, Penn., and born in 1813 and 1822, respectively. The grandfather, Thomas Rea, came to the United States from Scotland about 1772, and located in Bedford County, Penn. Thomas Rea, Jr., lived in that county until 1848, and then moved to McLean County, Ill. In 1869 he went to Houston County, Tenn., and his death occurred in Gibson County, of that State, in 1880. He served in the latter part of the Civil War, on the Union side, and for a living followed farming in connection with blacksmithing. William Ramsey, our subject's maternal grandfather, came to the United States from Ireland previous to the Revolutionary War. Mrs. Rea died in 1876, and was the mother of five children: Lemuel R., of Van Buren; William, of Humboldt, Tenn.; Thomas L., of California; Nannie and Joseph L. The latter was educated at Urbana, Ill., and after leaving school clerked in a general store. In 1869 he opened a dry goods store in Humboldt, Tenn., sold goods for twelve years, and in 1882 came to Van Buren, being em-

188

CRAWFORD COUNTY, ARKANSAS - BIOGRAPHICAL AND HISTORICAL MEMOIRS
****

ployed by the Adams Express Company, and afterward by the Pacific Railroad and Southern Companies. He is now one of the young substantial business men of the place. In 1877 he married Miss Emma Hudson, daughter of William Hudson, of Humboldt, Tenn. Mrs. Rea was born in Alabama, and has one child, named Josie. She is a devout member of the Methodist Episcopal Church, and a lady of fine character. In politics Mr. Rea is independent. He is a member of the Masonic fraternity, of the Royal Arch degree, the A. O. U.W. and a K. of H.

Capt. David Reed was born in Orange County, Ind., in 1823, and is a son of Elias and Polly (Newjent) Reed, natives of North Carolina and Virginia. When five years old the father accompanied his parents to the Cumberland River country, Kentucky. After his first marriage he lived some time in White County, Tenn., and, his father having previously moved from Kentucky to Orange County, Ind., he immigrated hither in 1815, on a pack-horse. There he lost his first wife, and married Polly Newjent about 1821. In the fall of 1831 he started for Missouri, with two wagons, one six-horse and the other a four-horse vehicle, and the following spring located in Wayne County, Mo., when the country was a vast wilderness. He was a farmer, and a soldier in the War of 1812, and several of the Indian wars, although he did no active service. He departed this life in 1836, and his wife in 1851. The grandfather, Robert Reed, was a native of Ireland, and a soldier in the earlier Indian wars, previous to the Revolution. In the latter he fought in the battles of Camden, the Cow-Pens, Guilford Court-house, Eutaw Springs and others. He was a man of ability, and lived in North Carolina, Kentucky and Indiana. Going to Wayne County, Mo., in 1832, he died the same year. His wife also died in that county, aged one hundred years. David Reed was the second of ten children, and was educated at a subscription log school-house in Wayne County. At an early age he was left to help care for the younger children, and in May, 1847, joined Company I, of the Third Missouri Mounted Volunteers. Crossing the plains he served eighteen months in the Northwest and New Mexican army, and after fighting in the battle at Santa Cruz, returned overland, via Kansas City and St. Louis. He also served throughout the Civil War as captain of Company C, Second Missouri Cavalry, which he organized, having previously commanded Company B, of the State Guards of Missouri, three months. He was on the Price raid through Missouri and Kansas, and in the spring of 1862 operated in Mississippi and Tennessee, under Gens. Van Dorn, Price, Loring and Pemberton, participating in the battles of Corinth and vicinity, Tupelo, Miss.; Denmark, Tenn.; Iuka, Miss.; siege of Corinth, Franklin, Tenn., and surrendered at Jacksonport, Ark., in June, 1865, having never been captured or wounded. In 1865 he was married in Randolph County, Ark., to Mrs. Isabelle Brem, daughter of James Drake, and a native of Alabama. Her father was born in Kentucky, served under Jackson in the War of 1812, being in the battles of Horseshoe Bend and New Orleans, and died in Arkansas. Mr. Reed has had four children, two sons and one daughter now living. He settled in Crawford County, on his present farm, in 1868, and proceeded to make a home in the wilderness. He has a farm of eighty acres, and has made farming his principal occupation, although he is a blacksmith and wagon-maker by trade. He cast his first presidential vote for Polk in 1844, but from the time of the war until 1876 gave no other vote, since which year (when Tilden was his choice) he has voted for every Democratic candidate. He has refused to be a candidate for the Legislature, or to hold the office of sheriff, but served as justice of the peace eight years in Wayne County, Mo. He has belonged to the Baptist Church over twenty years, and his wife is also a member.

S. H. Reed was born in De Soto County, Miss., in 1837, and is a son of John and Ann S. (Rossel) Reed, natives of North Carolina and Virginia, respectively. When nine years of age Mr. Reed was taken by his parents to Hardeman County, Tenn., where he was reared. After his marriage in Alabama he settled in De Soto County, M's., where he died in 1849, and his wife survived him until 1853. James B. Reed, the grandfather, was born in North Carolina soon after his parents came to America, and was of Scotch-Irish descent. He died in Prairie County at the advanced age of one hundred and four. Our subject was the sixth of a family of nine children, and was educated at the neighborhood school-house and at Holly Springs, Miss. In September, 1861, he joined Company B, under Wirt Adams, serving throughout the war, although not on active

189

CRAWFORD COUNTY, ARKANSAS - BIOGRAPHICAL AND HISTORICAL MEMOIRS
****

duty except for two years, on account of disability. In 1858 he married Fannie E. Wilkerson, a native of Mississippi, who died July 15, 1886, leaving seven children. In August, 1887, Mr. Reed married Mary S. Day, who was born in Virginia and reared in Mississippi, where her father died. She came to Crawford County about 1878. Mr. Reed left the county of his birth in 1876, and coming to Crawford County, Ark., has since lived in Alma Township. He now owns sixty-five acres, two and a half miles east of Alma, and is a prosperous farmer. Mr. Reed belongs to the Methodist Church, and his wife to the Christian Church. He belongs to the K. of H., Alma Lodge No. 3,166. In politics he is a Democrat, and he cast his first presidential vote for Breckenridge, in 1860.

John D. Reinhardt, farmer and stock raiser, was born in Lincoln County, N. C., in 1834, and is a son of Michael and Maria A. (Allyn) Reinhardt, who were born in Lincoln County, N. C., in 1790, and New London, Conn., 1790, respectively. The mother was a teacher, and when a young lady had charge of an academy at Lincolnton, N. C. During the War of 1812 she lived at New London, and distinctly remembered the sight of the wounded men at that battle. Her father, Robert Allyn, was born in Connecticut, served in the Revolution, and was a member of the famous Cincinnati Society, composed of Revolutionary officers. The grandfather, John Allyn, came from a prominent English family, and in an early day located in Massachusetts. In 1837 he went to New London, Conn., and his death occurred there. He was a son of Robert Allyn, of England. His grandson, Capt. Francis Allyn, was a soldier in the War of 1812, and owned the vessel which brought Gen. LaFayette to the United States in 1824. Michael Reinhardt was twice married, and by his first wife, Mary (Moore) Reinhardt, he had five children. He married Miss Allyn in 1829, and died in 1852. She died in 1867. He and his wife belonged to the Presbyterian Church. He was a farmer by occupation, and lived in Marshall County from 1846 until his death, in 1852. He served in the War of 1812 as captain under Gen. Jackson, and when young represented Lincoln County, N. C., in the State Senate for several years. Christian Reinhardt, his father, was born on the Rhine, in Germany, and when a boy, after the death of his father, accompanied his mother to America. He was a descendant of the nobility in Germany. He served as stationary quartermaster in the Revolution, and died in Lincoln County, N. C. Our subject was the youngest of three children, attended the common schools of the neighborhood when a boy, and at the age of twelve went with his parents to Mississippi, where he lived thirty-three years. In 1856 he was married in Lagrange County, Tenn., to Sallie M., daughter of Joel and Anna Sledge, natives of North Carolina and Alabama, respectively. The father was of Welsh extraction, and died in Texas. The mother was a cousin of D. H. Hill, ex-president of the university at Fayetteville, and she died in Mississippi. Mr. Reinhardt has had eight children, of whom three sons and one daughter are deceased. In 1862 he joined Company K, Thirty-fourth Mississippi Infantry, Benton's regiment, and served as commissary, operating in Kentucky, Tennessee, North Carolina, etc. He fought at Perryville, Ky., Chickamauga, Lookout Mountain, went through the Georgia and Atlanta campaign, and accompanied Hood back to Nashville, Tenn., and Franklin, and surrendered with Gen. J. E. Johnston at Hillsboro, N. C., then returning home on foot. He has always been engaged in farming, and served two years as justice of the peace in Mississippi. In 1880 he came to Crawford County, where he has a farm of 600 acres, and deals extensively in stock. He makes a specialty of Holstein cattle and Essex hogs, and has a fine thoroughbred Lexington horse. He also owns a saw-mill at Dora. He is one of the foremost and most enterprising men of the county in all enterprises undertaken for the advancement of the same, and has greatly assisted in improving the stock of the county. He has been a life-long Democrat, casting his first presidential vote for Buchanan, and is a member of the Farmers' Alliance. Himself and wife are highly respected people, and active members in the Presbyterian Church. Both Mr. Reinhardt's paternal and maternal ancestors were people of note, and he has in his possession a coat-of-arms which belonged to the Allyn family in England over 400 years ago. Several of the Allyn family were massacred at the capture of Fort Griswold, Conn., during the Revolution, and Point Allyn, near New London, was named in honor of the family. Mr. Reinhardt possesses an heirloom in the shape of a violin, bearing the date of 1700, which his great-grandfather Reinhardt brought from Germany.

190

CRAWFORD COUNTY, ARKANSAS - BIOGRAPHICAL AND HISTORICAL MEMOIRS
****

B. P. Renfroe, general merchant, was born in Summerville, Tenn., February 15, 1833, and is a son of Marcus H. and Patsy (Perryman) Renfroe, natives of Alabama and Virginia, respectively, who immigrated to Tennessee and from there to Northern Mississippi, where they died in 1880 and 1869, respectively. The father was of Scotch descent and a farmer by occupation. For thirty-five or forty years he was a successful preacher in the Baptist Church, and he was the first treasurer of De Soto County, Miss. During the war he raised and commanded a company under Gen. Forrest, in the Confederate army. Bidkar P., our subject, received a common-school education during his youth, and in 1857 married Margaret E. Cathey, by whom he has two children: Thomas H. and Locke. When young Mr. Renfroe taught school one term in Texas, but since his marriage has been merchandising in connection with his farming. During the war he served in Company B, Wirt Adams' company, Confederate army, participated in the battle at Shiloh, siege of Vicksburg, the battles at Jackson and Meridian, Miss., but was the greater part of the time on detail service at headquarters. He was elected to the Mississippi Legislature in 1868, but the Legislature did not meet. Since 1871 he has been engaged in the mercantile business in Arkansas with great success, and is also the owner of a 160-acre fruit farm, seven miles northwest of Alma, and is considered one of the leading citizens of the town. In politics he is a Democrat, and his first presidential vote was cast for Buchanan, in 1856. Mrs. Renfroe is an active member of the Christian Church.

Elisha H. Robinson (deceased) was born in Wayne County, Tenn., in 1820, and when thirteen years old accompanied his parents to this county. He received a good education during his youth, and made his home with his parents until 1844, when he was united in marriage with Sarah, daughter of Younger Neal, and a native of Hickman County, Tenn., born in August, 1830. When fourteen years of age she came with her parents to this county, and after her marriage went to live upon Mr. Robinson's farm, which continued to be their home with the exception of three years, which were spent in Texas. In 1862 Mr. Robinson left his farm to join the Confederate army, in which he served until the cessation of hostilities, then returning to his farm work and stock raising. He became the most extensive farmer in his immediate community, and died in 1884, leaving a wife and nine children. The children are Melissa, Serena, Lilburn, Una, Gillie, Marshall, Francis, Kirby and Albert. Mr. Robinson was a faithful member of the Christian Church, to which his widow is also united. Mrs. Robinson is a highly respected lady, of more than ordinary business ability, and owns 200 acres of land, all under cultivation.

Joseph John Savage was born near Norfolk, Va., in 1833, and is a son of James and Charlotte (Smith) Savage. The father was of English descent, born in Nansemond County, Va., in 1806, and was a farmer by occupation. He was married in Edgecombe County, N. C., and soon after moved to that county. In 1848 he moved to Arkansas, and for a year lived at Pine Bluff, and then located in Bradley County. In 1859 he located five miles below the county seat of Crawford County. He died in 1862. The mother was born in Edgecombe County, N. C., and had six children, four of whom are living: Dr. M. T., of Halifax, N. C.; Henrietta, wife of Dr. William Grady, of Corsicana, Tex.; Della A., widow of J. M. Wright, of Alma, Ark., and Joseph J. The latter was reared upon a farm in Arkansas, and in 1859 came to Crawford County. In 1862 he enlisted in Capt. Wallace's company, Col. King's regiment, participated in the battle at Prairie Grove, and was afterward captured in Sebastian County and taken to St. Louis and from there to Alton. He was retained eighteen months in all, and discharged in March, 1865. March 4, 1866, he married Elizabeth Amanda Driver, daughter of William and Nancy (Franklin) Savage, and born in Washington County, Ark., in 1844. To them twelve children were born, of whom seven still live: Nettie, Moses Thomas, James William Benjamin Franklin, Lottie Jordan, Lee Constant, Walter Sumner and Russell Alexander. After his marriage Mr. Savage lived two years in Halifax County, N. C., and then returned to Crawford, locating on the old plantation five miles east of Van Buren. In 1872 he bought the property, now owns 400 acres of bottom land, and is a well-to-do citizen. Himself, wife and five children belong to the Presbyterian Church, which he joined in 1882. His grandfather was a Methodist preacher, and would never accept remuneration for his preaching. In politics he is a Democrat, and his first presidential vote was cast for Buchanan in 1856.

John W. Schaberg, station agent and telegraph operator at Porter, was born in Missouri in 1858, and is a son of John W. and Lizette (Dreameyer) Schaberg, who are now engaged in farming in Jackson County, Mo. The father was born in Femme Osage, Mo., and the mother in Warren County, Mo. Of their eleven children nine yet live, our subject being the oldest. The remaining ten are: Mrs. Mary Stock, of Jackson County, Mo.; Laura; Mrs. Lizzie Shroer, of Napoleon, Mo.; Hermann, George, Walter, Paulin, Carrie, William (deceased) and Garrett (deceased). William Dreameyer and wife, the maternal grandparents, were born in Germany, and died in 1872 and 1867, respectively. They came to America and settled in Missouri when that country was a vast wilderness, and Mr. Dreameyer served in the War of the Rebellion. John W. Schaberg made his home in Warren County, Mo., until twenty-two years of age, and until he was fifteen attended such common schools as the country afforded. He then attended the Central Western College, at Warrenton, Mo., for three years, and about 1867 graduated from the classical course of that institution. He subsequently, in 1880, took a course of book-keeping and telegraphy at the Bryant & Stratton Business College at St. Louis, Mo., after which he clerked a short time in Sullivan, Mo., and then for two years worked there as night operator. He then passed eight months in St. Clair, Mo., and for nine months was employed by the Iron Mountain Railway as relief agent. In 1885 he went to Van Buren, Ark., and in 1886 permanently located in Porter Township, where he has taken his place among the enterprising and prosperous citizens. In September, 1883, he married Miss Linda Rowland, who was born in Sullivan, Mo., in 1865, and is a daughter of Burl and Sarah (Riddle) Rowland. Mr. Rowland was born in Pulaski County, Mo., in 1844, on September 18, and Mrs. Rowland was born May 30, 1843. The following eight of their family of eleven children are now living: Mrs. Linda C. Rowland, J. W. Rowland; Pete Wiley, of St. Louis; Allie W., of Sullivan, Mo.; Minne Lee, Lilbern C., Charles B. and Ruth Alberta. Those deceased are Lorena Belle, Cynthia and Orie Nettie. To Mr. and Mrs. Schaberg two children have been born: Jessie Jewell, and L. Charles (deceased). Mrs. Schaberg belongs to the Missionary Baptist Church, and Mr. S. is a Mason. He belongs to the United Labor party, but in 1880 voted for James A. Garfield.

Philip Drennen Scott, secretary of the Van Buren Ice & Coal Company, was born here October 22, 1855, and is a son of Charles G. and Caroline (Drennen) Scott. The father was born in Galena, Kent Co., Md., in 1817, and was a son of Dr. Edward Scott, a native of Kent County, Md., born in 1778. He graduated from a medical college in Pennsylvania, and was a son of John Scott, who came to America from Scotland at a very early date. Dr. Edward Scott's wife, Annie Maria Comeygs, was born in Kent County, Md., in 1783, and died in 1857. Dr. Scott died in 1840, and was the father of thirteen children. Charles G. Scott came to Van Buren in 1836, and engaged in the mercantile business until the war. He was one of the original stockholders and directors of the Fort Smith & Little Rock Railway, and was president of the road fully ten years. From 1863 until 1874 he sold goods in Little Rock, and then returned to Van Buren, where he passed the last of his life in retirement. He was a successful business man, influential citizen, and highly esteemed person, and died in 1882. The mother of our subject, Caroline L. Drennen, was born in Nashville, Tenn., in 1825, and is a daughter of John Drennen, an early settler of the county. Mrs. Scott is still living, and of her seven children, four still survive: Emma A. (wife of James Lawson, of Little Rock), Fannie M., Philip Drennen and James Stuart (captain of a ferry boat at Van Buren). Philip D. attended St. John's College at Little Rock during his youth, and in 1874 went into the milling business with Thomas Gilham, in Van Buren. Two years later he sold his interest, and for five years was in the hardware business. In April, 1887, he became secretary of the Van Buren Ice & Coal Company, which position he has since filled. He is a good financier, and looks after his mother's interests, besides managing the ferry at Van Buren, and is a well-to-do man. September 28, 1880, he married Fannie I. Dunham, daughter of J. S. Dunham, editor of the Van Buren *Press*. Mr. and Mrs. Scott are members of the Episcopal Church, and have two children: Drennen and Dunham. Mr. Scott is a Democrat, and member of the K. of P. Besides being secretary of the Van Buren Ice & Coal Company, he owns stock in that and the Van Buren Canning Factory.

John Sharp, cotton planter, of River Township, was born near Little Rock, in Pulaski County, Ark., in 1851, and is a son of James M. and Nancy (Temple) Sharp, natives of Tennessee and Mississippi, respectively. They were married in the latter State, and moved from there to Pulaski County, Ark., and when our subject was but an infant went to Tipton County, Tenn., where the father died in 1856. The mother afterward returned to Arkansas, married, and is now living at Little Rock. The grandfather, John Sharp, was born in North Carolina, and died in Tipton County, Tenn., in 1868. Our subject was the second child of a family of four, and was educated at the Tabernacle in Tipton County, Tenn. He began life for himself by farming when fourteen in Pulaski County, and in 1880 came to Crawford County and took charge of the farm he now owns, which was then the property of D. E. Jones, of Little Rock. Four years later he purchased the plantation, which contains 873 acres of the finest bottom land, and is one of the best known and finest plantations in this section of the county, as well as the oldest. Although Mr. Sharp came to the county a poor man, he is now one of its rising citizens, his success being due to his business sagacity and industry. He has 600 acres of land under cultivation, and has twenty-six families on the plantation. He raises on an average 300 bales of cotton annually, does his own ginning and shipping, and also raises on an average 200 acres of corn. In 1886 he married Ella R., daughter of G. N. and Martha Wright, of Rome, Ga., by whom he has one son. Mr. Sharp is a Democrat, cast his first presidential vote for Greeley, in 1872, and since 1886 has been justice of the peace of River Township. He is a member of the K. of H., and himself and wife are Methodists.

William Henry Harrison Shibley, of the firm of Shibley, Bourland & Co., was born in 1840 in Ralls County, Mo., and is a son of Henry and Eliza Ann (Boyd) Shibley. Some time previous to the Revolutionary War John Shibley immigrated to America from Switzerland and settled in New York. He was the father of Henry Shibley, who was born in 1762 and died in 1853. In 1788 he married Elizabeth Shoults, and in 1792 moved to Montgomery County, settling upon land which is now owned by his descendants. His son, Jacob B. Shibley, was born in 1793; in 1814 he married Elizabeth Parks, and in 1818 moved to Luzerne County, Penn. In the winter of 1835 he went to Ralls County, Mo., and in 1843 moved to Adair County, where he died in 1872. His son, Henry, the father of our subject, was born in 1815, in Montgomery County, N. Y., in 1839 married Miss E. A. M. Boyd, and reared a family of seven sons and one daughter, all of whom are married. He is the grandfather of thirty-three children. In 1840 he moved to the northwestern part of Adair County, and commenced merchandising at Shibley's Point, in connection with which he engaged in milling. In 1860 he located four miles east of Van Buren, and is now the owner of 120 acres. For fifteen years he was a teacher in this county. Having lost his wife in 1883, he has since made his home with our subject. Mrs. Shibley was born in 1818, and was the mother of eight children: W. H. H., John S., M. D., of Paris; Lemuel S., farmer, of Green Forest, Carroll County; Edna E., wife of James M. Baxter, deputy sheriff; George W., of Van Buren; Albert B., of Van Buren; David P. and Jacob I., farmers, near Van Buren. Our subject accompanied his parents to Crawford County in 1860, and in 1862 enlisted in the Confederate army as a private, in Company G, Twenty-second Regiment Arkansas Infantry. He served three years, and participated in the battles at Prairie Grove, Saline River and Helena. He was made second lieutenant after the last named battle, then first lieutenant, and at the time of the surrender at Fort Smith was acting adjutant of the regiment and commanding his company. In 1866 he married Esther A. Cook, who was born in Dearborn County, Ind., in 1843, and is the mother of the following children: Harry B., David C. W., Mary E., William A. and Leah A. Mr. and Mrs. Shibley belong to the Cumberland Presbyterian Church, of which he has been ruling elder one year. Mr. Shibley was the chief clerk of Mr. D. C. Williams in his store for ten years prior to 1868, the firm then becoming Shibley, Wood & Co. In 1887 Mr. Shibley sold his interest to Wood Bros. & Southmayd, and in February, 1888, became president of the Van Buren Canning Company. He was the prime originator of the company and is its general manager. July 1, 1888, the company of Shibley, Bourland & Co. succeeded T. D. Bourland & Co. in the wholesale grocery and commission business. Mr. Shibley is one of the first business men of Van Buren, is stockholder in the Van Buren Ice and Coal Company, and a director and stockholder in the Crawford County Bank, having

193

CRAWFORD COUNTY, ARKANSAS - BIOGRAPHICAL AND HISTORICAL MEMOIRS
****

assisted in the organization of both enterprises. He is also treasurer of the Van Buren Building and Loan Association and the Van Buren Land and Improvement Company. He is a Democrat in politics, and has frequently been a member of the city council and school board. He is a member of Van Buren Lodge No. 6, F. & A. M., and Van Buren Chapter No. 3, R. A. M., and is High Priest of the latter; and Grand Master of Second Veil in the Grand Chapter of Arkansas. Both Mr. and Mrs. Shibley take an active interest in temperance, and are usually found with the most earnest workers in the promotion of this commendable virtue. The Sunday-school, too, receives a full share of their attention and encouragement.

Thomas Simco is a native of Crawford County, Ark., born in 1853, and is a son of Thomas and Sarah (Pope) Simco. The father was born in 1824, located in Crawford County about 1836, and died in 1871. Mrs. Simco was born in Tennessee in 1828, and was the mother of nine children, three of whom are living and residents of this county: William, Albert and Thomas. Marion and Rebecca Pope, maternal grandparents of our subject, came to this county from Tennessee, and were engaged in agricultural pursuits. Thomas Simco passed his youth here in Crawford County, receiving but a limited education, and in 1872 married Miss Rebecca Meadows, a native of the county, born in 1854, and a daughter of Samuel and Martha (Pope) Meadows. Mr. Meadows was born in Kentucky in 1832, and his wife in Tennessee in 1833. They both left their native States for Crawford County, Ark. In 1859 they went to Missouri, but returned to this county in 1867. Nine children were born to them, all of whom, save one, live in Crawford County: Mrs. Nancy Teague, Mrs. Rebecca Simco, John W., of Texas; Mary A., Sarah D., Andrew J., Martha, George L. and Ida B. Mr. Simco is a prosperous citizen, almost his entire property having been made by farming. He owns 120 acres of land, sixty-five of which are well improved and cultivated. Among the improvements may be mentioned three fine orchards. To Mr. and Mrs. Simco two children have been born, Sarah and William Allen. Being a Republican, Mr. Simco cast his first presidential vote for Rutherford B. Hayes, in 1876. He is a Mason, and a member of the I. O. O. F.

Albert Simco was born April 1, 1861, and is next to the youngest of nine children born to Thomas and Sarah (Pope) Simco. The father was born in Ohio (went to Illinois when small) in 1824, and the mother in Middle Tennessee in 1829. The father came to this county when a boy, and the mother with her parents when a girl. After his marriage Mr. Simco settled in the neighborhood of Mountainsburg, and although his chief occupation was farming, he also practiced medicine and merchandised to some extent. He and his wife were members of the Missionary Baptist Church. Albert Simco, the subject of this sketch, had six brothers, only two of whom are living; his two sisters are also deceased. He passed his boyhood upon the farm, receiving a common-school education, and at the age of fourteen took charge of the farm, and has been devoted to farm work since, although in 1879 he went into business with Jacob Yoes, but in thirteen months was obliged to return to his farm on account of his health. June 16, 1878, he married Mary C. Wright, a native of this county, and daughter of J. B. Wright. She parted, leaving one child, Josephine M. Mr. Simco's second wife was Violena J. Sims, daughter of B. F. Sims, and she has also borne Mr. Simco one child, Rubie. Mr. Simco is a Republican, and has been Worshipful Master of the Blue Lodge of Masonry, and Noble Grand of the I. O. O. F. Mr. Simco is a successful man, the owner of 260 acres of land, 110 of which are cultivated, and is one of the respected citizens of the township.

J. W. Simpson was born in Washington County, Ark., in 1844, and is a son of Hugh W. and Harriet T. (Hunter) Simpson [see sketch of J. M. Kerens]. The former was born in Kentucky, and was murdered in the Indian Territory. His wife was also a Kentuckian. The grandfather, James Simpson, was born in Kentucky, and served in the War of 1812, and his wife, Margret, accompanied her son to Arkansas. The maternal grandparents were natives of Tennessee, where they were reared. They immigrated to Washington County, Ark., in an early day, and afterward went to Texas, where Mrs. Hunter was killed by Indians. She was born in Tennessee, and moved to Arkansas after her marriage in Kentucky. Her husband, Dr. William Hunter, a Virginian by birth, went to Kentucky and lived there after his marriage until moving to Ar-

194

CRAWFORD COUNTY, ARKANSAS - BIOGRAPHICAL AND HISTORICAL MEMOIRS
****

kansas, going thence to Texas, where he practiced medicine. He served as a physician in the Mexican War, and participated in the battle of Baneras Pass. Three of his sons, John, Joseph and William, also served in that war. Our subject was attending school when the peace of the country was disturbed by the war, and consequently his studies were interrupted. In 1868 he began life for himself as a farmer, and in 1870 married, in August, Miss Margaret Graham, who was born in Crawford County in 1852, and is a daughter of Alexander and Isalima (Cross) Graham. Mr. Graham was born in Scotland, and was by trade a stone mason. After traveling all over the United States he finally located in Crawford County in 1844. Mrs. Graham was of English descent, and was born in Kentucky. After living some time in Indiana she came to Arkansas, where she was married at Bentonville. To Mr. and Mrs. Graham three children have been born: James J. (deceased), Daniel S., of this county, and Mrs. Margaret Simpson. To the latter seven children have been born, three boys and four girls. Mr. Simpson moved to Crawford County in 1879, and in 1881 bought his present farm of 160 acres, of which he has fifty under cultivation. In politics he is a Democrat, and his first presidential vote was cast for Greeley in 1872.

George W. Sims is only six months and ten days the junior of the Nation itself, having been born January 14, 1777, in the "Old Dominion." His father, Briggs Sims, was also a native of Virginia, and his mother, Frances (Duke) Sims, was born in North Carolina, whither Mr. Sims went when a young man and was married. Some time after his marriage Mr. Briggs and wife moved to Tennessee, and there engaged in farming, and reared a family of seven sons and seven daughters. Of this family, Mr. George W., the oldest, and Mr. Burl Sims, the youngest, are the only survivors. Mr. Briggs Sims was an active member of the Primitive Baptist Church, and died in 1840, his wife having passed away in 1836. Both the paternal and maternal grandfathers, Zachariah Sims and Burl Duke, were born in America, of English parents. The latter and his wife, Frances Duke, were early residents of Warren County, Tenn., where George W. passed his early life. At the age of twenty-one Mr. Sims started in the world for himself, and was soon united in marriage to Rachel McWreath, daughter of Michael McWreath. This union was blessed with seven children, the following four of whom survive: Mrs. Elizabeth Eddy, of this county; Mrs. Clerrinda Rankin, of this county; Mrs. Nancy Price, of Missouri, and Mr. Benjamin F. Sims, of this county. In 1854, having lost his first wife, Mr. Sims married Miss Nancy Hamblin, who was born in Hardin County, Tenn., in 1826. This lady is a niece of ex-President John Quincy Adams, and daughter of William and Elizabeth (Crosslin) Hamblin. The father was twice married, and by both marriages had twenty children, of whom but four live. Of these Mrs. Nancy Sims is the eldest. The others are: Mrs. Elizabeth Miller, of Washington Territory; Mrs. Jane Miller, of this county, and Uriah Hamblin, of Newton County, Mo. Mrs. Sims' father was a mechanic by trade. Mr. George Sims is a living representative of the War of 1812, in which he served as a private in Capt. Jones' company under Col. John Williams. About a year ago he was the recipient of a pension from the Government of $866, back dues, and $8 per month bounty for said services. Mr. Sims is one of the early settlers of this county, having long ago homesteaded his present property, from which he has never moved. He owns 160 acres of land, and although nearly one hundred and twelve years old, and becoming feeble physically, his strength of mind is wonderful for one of his advanced years. Mr. Sims was once an active member of the Masonic fraternity, but for many years now has attended none of the lodge meetings. He is non-partisan in politics, casting his vote for issues and not men.

Alfred Smith, farmer, of Lee's Township, Crawford Co., Ark., was born in Hawkins County, Tenn., and is a son of John B. Smith and Jane (Gallahorn) Smith. The father was born and reared in Hawkins County, and about 1837 immigrated to Arkansas, settling first in Washington County, from there coming to Crawford County in 1846. He was a soldier in the War of 1812, and died in the year 1847. The death of the mother occurred in 1846. Alfred Smith received but a limited education during his youth, and at the age of eighteen began life on his own account, as a farm hand. In 1855 he married Miss M. A. Williams, daughter of Thomas N. and Kansas (Moberly) Williams, of this county. Mrs. Smith bore him one child, and died in 1865. The following year he was united in marriage to Miss Melissa C. Brown, who left no children. His

195

CRAWFORD COUNTY, ARKANSAS - BIOGRAPHICAL AND HISTORICAL MEMOIRS
****

third marriage occurred in 1875, when Mrs. Lucretia Jane (Finnan) Morris, daughter of Alexander Finnan, of Tennessee, became his wife. Mr. Smith is a successful farmer, and the owner of 160 acres of land, about forty-five of which he has under cultivation. He is non-partisan in politics, but during the war served in the Home Guards under Capt. Oliver. His wife is a member of the Methodist Church.

Leonard Clay Southmayd is of English ancestry, and a descendant of Sir William Southmayd, of Kent County, England (to whom arms were granted June, 1604). He is a native of Connecticut, born at Middletown June 17, 1822, being a son of William and Sarah F. Southmayd (*nee* Dunham). The descendants of Sir William, early in 1600, left England and located in Essex County, Mass. The father of our subject, who is also named William, and is the seventh generation of Sir William, was born in Middletown, Conn., November 19, 1792 (now living), and married in 1818; he passed the most of his life in his native town, as a merchant and in commerce, and was moderately successful. His father, the sixth William, a native of the same town, was born in 1763 and died in 1856. He was by trade a saddler, and was a soldier and artisan in the American Revolution. Sarah F. Southmayd (*nee* Dunham) was born in 1794 and died in 1867, leaving four children, now alive, viz.: Leonard C.; Sarah F., widow of Elliott Savage, Meriden, Conn.; Mary D., widow of Chauncey Scranton, also of Connecticut, and Horace, a merchant residing in Hartford, Conn. Leonard attended the common schools of his town and completed his education at the preparatory school of the Wesleyan University. At the age of fifteen he entered his father's store as clerk, and remained until September, 1845, when he located in Van Buren, Ark., where he has permanently resided. From 1845 to 1851 he was in the employ of Wallace & Ward. From 1851 to 1856 he was a member of the firm, under the style and name of Wallace, Ward & Co. In 1856, Mr. Wallace retiring, the business was continued under the style of Ward & Southmayd until, in 1863, the vicissitudes of the war suspended all business operations. In 1878 he was elected to the position of circuit and county clerk, serving three terms, when, his private affairs requiring his personal attention, he declined a renomination, and has since devoted his time to his planting interests. In December, 1850, he was married to Susannah R. Howell, a native of Kentucky, born in Hardin County, April, 1832. She is a daughter of Laban C. Howell. They have four living children: Laban H., of the firm of Wood Brothers & Southmayd; Martha W.; Sarah E., wife of George R. Wood, president of the Citizens, Bank at Van Buren and a member of the last-named firm, and Lucy S., wife of Henry F. Pape, of the firm of McKibben & Pape. He is a Mason, and his wife is a member of the Methodist Episcopal Church, South.

Deweese Spencer, farmer, was born February 25, 1839, in Boone County, Ind., and is a son of Elijah and Elizabeth (Deweese) Spencer. The father was born near the Blue Ridge Mountains, Virginia, when ten years of age accompanying his father to Kentucky, where he grew to manhood upon the farm, and received his education; he also there married Elizabeth Deweese, who was born in Natchez, Miss., and when small went to Kentucky, while the country was a wilderness, inhabited by game and wild animals. She bore Mr. Spencer twelve children, eleven living to maturity, and six now living: Melinda, John, Johanna, Deweese, Sarah E. and James M. Those deceased are Mary, Nancy, Browning, Lewis, Andrew J. and an infant. John Spencer, the grandfather, was a soldier in the Revolution, and an early settler of Kentucky, where he died in 1851, at an advanced age. The grandmother, Johanna Spencer, also died in Kentucky, about 1854. The Deweese family is of French descent, and the mother of our subject was a relative of the physician Deweese of Philadelphia. When seven years old Deweese Spencer came to Crawford County, Ark., and at the age of twelve had attended school but six months. He remained at home until nineteen, and then worked ten months at $10 per month. He then drove a freight team for a year in the Indian Nation, after which he farmed some time on rented land. He served in the Union army throughout the war, eighteen months as a citizen scout, and during the commencement of the war as a recruiting officer. After farming a short time where he now lives, he passed two years in Greene County, Mo., and then farmed ten years on Lee's Creek. At the expiration of that time he sold out, and bought his present farm. In 1860 Mr. Spencer married Elizabeth Bowman, who bore him one child, William H., and died December 19, 1862. July 1, 1864, he married Caroline White, daughter of Henry White, both natives of Germany, and by his last marriage is the father of seven children: Elizabeth, Elijah W., Johanna, Sarah C., Lee C., Maud and John H. (deceased). Mr. Spencer is now providing a home for his mother, who is eighty-four years of age, and a member of the Cumberland Baptist Church. Mr. Spencer, the father, died in 1877, aged seventy-nine. Our subject is a well-to-do man, and the owner of 160 acres of land, 100 of which have been finely improved, almost all the improvements having been made by himself. He has been a minister for twelve years, is a Republican, and is a member of the Masonic fraternity and Agricultural Wheel. For ten years he has been a school director.

Wilborn Augustus Speir was born August 16, 1860, and is a son of John and Sarah A. (McWharton) Speir. The father was born in Tennessee, and when young went to Alabama and then to Georgia, and before leaving that State assisted in gathering the Cherokee Indians into one section, prior to their removal to the Indian Territory. He was married in Georgia, where his common-school education was acquired, and in 1869 came to Arkansas. The mother was born, reared and married in Georgia, and to her and Mr. Speir twelve children were born, all save two now living: William L. S., Elenore S., Seaborns S., Wilborn A., John L. S., Sarah M., Temperus U. and Thomas U. (twins), Mary C. and Charles W. Those deceased are Melvin C. and Franklin D. Our subject, Wilborn Speir, was born in Walker County, Ga., and since the death of his father, in 1883, has cared for his mother and sisters. He received but a limited education during his youth, and until nineteen years of age worked upon the home farm with his father, then working on the farm for himself three years. He then went to Uniontown, and, in partnership with two brothers, operated a grist-mill and cotton-gin for three years, when the mill was destroyed by fire. In 1885 he returned and purchased his present mill. He now owns 120 acres of land, forty-five of which he cultivates, and in connection with his milling has a blacksmith shop, and is engaged in the mercantile business with his brother. Politically Mr. Speir sympathizes with the Democrats, and he is a member of the Masonic fraternity.

P. E. Stafford, farmer, was born in De Kalb County, Ala., in 1847, his parents being Pleasant and Margaret (Reed) Stafford, natives of South Carolina and Tennessee, who died in 1865 and 1874, respectively. The father was a farmer, and was married in Alabama. To them eight children were born, of whom three yet live: Isaac, of this county; George W., of Washington County, and our subject. The grandfather, William Stafford, was of Irish descent, and served in the War of 1812, under Gen. Jackson. The maternal grandmother, Nancy Reed, was of English descent. P. E. Stafford received a limited education during his youth in Washington County, Ark., and when young began life for himself. In 1872 he came to Crawford County from Washington County, and in 1875 went to Texas. He remained there eighteen months, and then returned to Arkansas. In 1878 he purchased his present valley farm, which contains 280 acres, fifty of which are nicely cultivated, and improved with good buildings and an orchard. Mr. Stafford is a Mason, and in politics a Democrat, having cast his first presidential vote for Seymour. In 1872 he was united in marriage to Miss Rachel Gibson, a native of Madison County, Ark., born in 1853, and daughter of Joel and Rachel (Gilber) Gibson, natives of Kentucky. Mr. and Mrs. Gibson came to Madison County, Ark., from Kentucky about 1850, and there died when Mrs. Stafford was quite young. They reared a family of twelve children, eight of whom are living, and all residents of Crawford County but two. They are Mrs. Susanna Pope; Mrs. Martha Williams, of Texas; Lizzie Gibson, Mrs. Sarah Bushong, Mrs. Stafford, Mrs. Rhoda Stokee, and Mrs. Roxana Bolinger, of Madison County. Mr. and Mrs. Stafford are the parents of the following ten children, all of whom reside at home: Mary Jane, Rhoda C., Louie Emma, Luella, Nancy, Lena, William, Alice, Thomas and Jessie.

William C. Stevens, farmer, was born December 7, 1840, and is a son of Joseph B. and Tilda (Hawkins) Stevens. James B. was born in Kentucky, and when a boy went to Alabama, in 1831, at the age of eighteen. He settled in this State, where Fayetteville now stands, before even a court-house was built there. Four years later he went to Madison County, and from there to Carroll County. At the commencement of the war he went to Texas, and four years later settled in this county. A year and a half later he went to Little River County, Ark., where he now lives at the age of seventy-six. The mother was born in Tennessee, and when about grown went to Madison County, Ark., where she was married. To her seven children were born, four of whom are living: Amanda, Victoria, Arbelle and William C. Those deceased are Jack, Parthenia and Fidelia. The paternal grandparents went to Kentucky from Albemarle County, Va., about 1800, and from there went to Alabama, where the grandmother died, her husband afterward going to Texas, where he died, aged eighty-six. The maternal grandparents immigrated to Arkansas from Tennessee, and died in the former State. Our subject was born in Madison County, Ark., reared principally in Carroll County, and attended school but a short time at Berryville, as the country was but sparsely settled and schools were seldom taught. June 9, 1861, he enlisted in the Fourth Arkansas, Col. Walker's regiment, Pierce's brigade, State troops, and after two months' service went to Missouri and took part in the Oak Hill battle. Returning to Arkansas, the company being disbanded, he re-enlisted in the Confederate service in McBride's brigade (a Missouri brigade, six months troops), and at the expiration of the term of service the conscript law was passed, and Mr. Stevens joined an Arkansas regiment of the Confederate army for three years, or during the war. In November, 1863, he was wounded in the right arm, and remained in the Carroll County mountains four months before being able to again enter the service. In the spring of 1864 he joined Company I, of Gen. Joe Shelby's brigade, Hunter's regiment, under Capt. Ricketts, and was with that command four months, or until Price's raid to Missouri. While with Shelby he was in the White River swamps, in the northeast part of Arkansas, fighting the Federals. After leaving the service he went to Texas, and in 1866 he came to Arkansas, but returning to Texas remained until 1868, when he settled in Crawford County. In 1870 he married Jane Spoon, daughter of John Spoon, who has borne him two children: Mary A. and Amanda, both of whom are living. Mr. Stevens has 120 acres, thirty being cultivated, and located upon this place in 1881. Mrs. Stevens belongs to the Christian Church, and Mr. Stevens belongs to the Farmers' Alliance.

Samuel Stevenson is the second child of a family of eleven of James G. and Jane (Wadkins) Stevenson. The father was born in South Carolina, and when about twelve years old, having received a whipping from his step-father for some trivial offense, he ran away from home, and arriving in this State carried mail to and from Clarksville. Later he found his way to Cape Girardeau County, and there married the mother of our subject, who was born in that county, and was two years younger than himself. Soon after they traveled on mules to the northeastern part of Arkansas, finally settling in Lovely County, but after the Government survey, their property being on the Indian reservation, they moved to Washington County, there remaining until 1837. They then passed the remainder of their days in Crawford County, dying in 1865 and 1888, respectively. Both were members of the Christian Church. Mr. Stevenson was formerly a Whig, but afterward became a Republican, and served one term in the State Legislature. He was fond of hunting during the early history of the county, and often killed ten deer per day. Later he gave his time exclusively to farming. For several years he was justice of the peace in Washington County. Samuel Stevenson was born September 8, 1826, in Northeastern Arkansas. When twenty years of age he left his father's farm. For ten years he engaged in freighting in the Indian Territory, and then two years on the plains for the Government. He then began to farm, and has since continued engaged in that occupation with the exception of the time spent in service during the war. He now owns 240 acres, of which about 120 are cultivated, and his property is the result of his own industry and good management. In 1846 he married Susan West, a native of Kentucky, and now the mother of the following children: James G., Maria J., William, Amanda and Robert A. Mrs. Stevenson belongs to the Christian Church. In 1863 Mr. Stevenson enlisted in Company L, Second Arkansas Cavalry, Federal army, and served until the close of the war. He was in the battles of Wilson's Creek and Pea Ridge.

John A. Stevenson was born November 29, 1828, in the Indian Territory, a son of James G. and Jane (Wadkins) Stevenson [see sketch of Samuel Stevenson]. He was taken by his father when a month old to Washington County, Ark., reared on a farm there until twelve years old, and then came to Crawford County, schools then being almost unknown, and consequently he did not attend over four months. In 1850 he left home and went across the plains to

California, where he mined for three years. In 1861, having returned home, he enlisted in an independent company of the Arkansas State troops, and fought in the battle at Wilson's Creek. The company was then ordered to enlist in the regular Confederate service, which he refused to do, and in 1863 he joined Company L, Second Arkansas Cavalry, of the Federal army. He was discharged at St. Louis at the close of the war, and has since farmed and built cotton-gins. He now owns 172 acres, 120 being finely cultivated, and is a successful man. In 1853 he married Elizabeth White, who was born in Tennessee January 28, 1831, and accompanied her parents to this county when a girl. Jackson White and his wife, Elizabeth (Rider) White, were among the early settlers of the county. Mr. and Mrs. Stevenson have five children: William W., James G., Augusta M., Robert A. J., and Elizabeth F. A. Mrs. Stevenson is an active member of the Christian Church. Mr. Stevenson is a Republican in politics, a Mason, I. O. O. F. and K. of P.

Samuel Steward, of the firm of Steward Bros., general merchants, was born in Lancaster in 1842, and is the fifth of nine children born to William and Melissa (Dickerson) Steward, natives of Massachusetts, born in 1786, and of Kentucky, born in 1817, respectively. The father was taken to New York by his parents when two years old, and during the War of 1812 served in Gen. Scott's division in a New York regiment. He was wounded at the battle of Chippewa. Two years after the war he married Phœbe Dean, who died in Indianapolis, Ind., in 1830, where they had lived some time. In 1834 Mr. Steward married the mother of our subject. In 1835 he came to Crawford County, and built the first shanty and sold the first goods where Van Buren now stands. The next spring he moved on Frog Bayou, just south of the present site of Lancaster, at which time there were but two settlements above him and but a few between there and Van Buren. There he erected a saw and grist-mill, which he operated until his death, and which was the first mill in the county. He was one of the men who helped the progress of the neighborhood materially by his enterprise, business ability and labor. He built several mills and cleared a number of farms, besides being a successful mechanic and trader. His father, John Steward, came to America from Scotland prior to the Revolution, and was a mill-wright and mechanic. He spent his latter days in New York. Being reared during the pioneer days of Crawford County our subject received but little education during his youth. At the age of eighteen he joined Company I, Third Arkansas Infantry, Confederate Army, enlisting as a private under Capt. J. T. Steward, but soon becoming third lieutenant upon the reorganization of the company. In 1862 the Fourth Arkansas and Fifth Missouri companies united and formed the Ninth Missouri Infantry, in which he served as first lieutenant. After September, 1862, he held the office of captain of Company I during the remainder of his service. He was in the battles at Oak Hill, Mo., at Pea Ridge, Prairie Grove and other minor skirmishes in Missouri, Arkansas and Louisiana. He surrendered at Camden, Ark., May 28, 1865, four years from the date of his enlistment. After spending two years in Texas he returned home in 1867, and, purchasing the old homestead, has since lived upon the place of his birth. July 18, 1863, he married Elizabeth J., daughter of G. W. and Ellen F. Marshall, formerly of Alabama, where Mrs. Steward was born. Mr. Marshall died in 1873, but the mother is still living. Mrs. Steward came to this county in 1858, and since July, 1859, has been a member of the Missionary Baptist Church. She is the mother of seven children, five of whom are living and have received a good education. Mr. Steward has 236 acres of land, which he has himself improved, having been exclusively engaged in farming and milling until 1882. He then sold goods one year on the farm, and in 1883, with his brother John, established a general store at Lancaster. They carry a well-selected stock of goods, valued at $5,000, and their annual sales amount to about $10,000. Mr. Steward is a Democrat, and cast his first presidential vote for Douglas in 1860. Since 1884 he has been the postmaster of Lancaster.

William T. Steward, farmer and stock raiser, was born in this county, at Lancaster, in 1845, his parents being Hon. Harvey and Delilah (Ratliff) Steward. The father was a man of influence in the county, who, although he attended school but one month, studied at home under his father's direction and became a well-informed man. He engaged in blacksmithing, wagon-making and cotton-ginning, and by hard work and economy became the owner of considerable property. He worked as a general mechanic in Crawford County, Ohio, and

199

CRAWFORD COUNTY, ARKANSAS - BIOGRAPHICAL AND HISTORICAL MEMOIRS
****

also erected and operated a gin mill, which was the first in the county. He passed nearly his entire life in this county, dying about ten years ago, and he was three times married. He served three years during the war as a captain in the Confederate army, being stationed at Galveston Island. He was a Democrat, and as such represented the county from 1850 until 1852 in the Lower House of the State Legislature. The grandfather, William, was a soldier in the Mexican War, and for many years lived near Lancaster. He was a pioneer of this county, and built and operated the first water, grist and saw mill. He was thrown from his horse and killed during the war. Our subject was left motherless when three days old, and when nine years old he went to Texas with his grandfather, Thompson Ratliff, by whom he was reared. At the age of seventeen he joined Company D, of the Thirtieth Texas Cavalry, and was in active service in Texas, Indian Territory, Arkansas, Missouri and Louisiana until disbanded in Texas in the fall of 1865. He then returned to the home of his grandfather and engaged in freighting between Dallas, Austin, Milligan and Bryant City. He made one trip to Eagle Pass, on the Rio Grande, hauling cotton, hides and dry goods. In 1869 he married Johanna Johnson, who was born on the farm where Mr. Steward now lives, and where Mrs. Steward's father died. This union has been blessed with eight children, six of whom are living. Mr. Steward was married in Texas, and the same year returned to Crawford County, and has since lived upon his present place. He owns 176 acres near Alma, and in 1878 erected a steam corn mill and cotton-gin, which he now operates. He is a Democrat, and cast his first vote for Greeley in 1872. He is a Mason and a member of Alma Lodge No. 43, and himself and wife belong to the Christian Church.

William H. Stewart was born June 23, 1844, and is a son of Jesse and Elizabeth (Stockhouse) Stewart. [See sketch of John P. Stewart.] He attended the old-fashioned subscription schools during his boyhood, worked upon the home farm until fifteen, and then served a two-years' apprenticeship in a cooper shop. Upon the breaking out of the Rebellion he enlisted in Company K, Sixth Volunteer Kansas Cavalry, United States Army, having run away in order not to serve in the Confederate army. He enlisted October 8, 1863, and served until discharged at Leavenworth, Kas., in November, 1865. He participated in thirteen regular engagements in all, such as Prairie Grove, Cone Hill, Honey Springs, Cherokee Nation, Webber's Falls (where he was wounded), Fort Smith, Spadry Bluff (where he was again wounded), Marck's Mills, Jenkin's Ferry, Roseville, Prairie de Hand, Poison Springs, Princeton and others. He then farmed in Van Buren one year, and worked at the carpenter's trade in the city one year. After traveling over several counties in Texas he returned to Crawford County, and in 1867 married Sarah Ann, daughter of Rev. Pleasant and Matilda Bassham, natives of Tennessee, who upon coming to Arkansas settled in Boone County, where Mrs. Stewart was born. They afterward settled in Evansville, where Mr. Bassham was a missionary to the Indians. Mr. and Mrs. Stewart have five children: Wallace P., Powell E., Ida H., Ada and Beulah. After marriage Mr. Stewart located upon his present farm, which contains 160 acres of cultivated land. He is a strong Republican, served six years as road overseer, and is now serving his sixth year as school director. He ran for justice of the peace last election, and was defeated by only six votes in a Democratic township. He is adjutant of the G. A. R. Post, No. 15.

John P. Stewart, farmer, was born near Dripping Springs, this county, January 22, 1850, and is a son of Jesse and Elizabeth (Stockhouse) Stewart. The father was born in Pennsylvania, there received a common-school education, and learned the carriage-maker's trade, and when about grown went to Indiana, and after spending some years there and in Ohio, also engaged in distilling, he came to Crawford County, Ark., in 1835. He stopped at Van Buren, the place then only having a few houses, he at first being obliged to live in a tent. He soon erected a church. He lived here until his death. The mother was born in Crawfordsville, Hamilton Co., Ind., and was there reared and educated. She is now living in Crawford County, aged seventy-four. To her the following children were born: Francis M., Harriett, William H., Sarah, Melissa, Jesse, Nancy, John P., James I. and Taylor (deceased). Two of her sons were in the Confederate service. William was a Union man, served in the Sixth Kansas, and participated in the battle at Prairie Grove. Our subject remained at home until twenty-two, making his home with his mother, and then married Madeline A.

200

CRAWFORD COUNTY, ARKANSAS - BIOGRAPHICAL AND HISTORICAL MEMOIRS
****

Turner, daughter of William and Permelia Turner, natives of Tennessee. Mrs. Stewart was born in this county, where she received a good education, and when sixteen married Mr. Stewart, she having been born in 1856. After his marriage Mr. Stewart farmed upon the home place one year, and a few years later purchased his present home. In politics he is a Republican, and in religion his wife is a member of the Cumberland Presbyterian Church.

B. F. Strong, druggist, of Porter, was born September 14, 1810, in Ohio County, W. Va. His father, Samuel Strong, was a shoemaker by trade, and served in the War of 1812 under Capt. Reaves, dying in January, 1815, from the effects of exposure. The mother, Elizabeth (Huffman), was born in Ohio County, W. Va., in 1790, and died in 1862. William Strong, the grandfather, was born in Germany, and came to America in the colony founded by William Penn. He located in West Virginia, where he engaged in farming until his death, in 1830. His wife was also a native of Germany. The maternal grandparents, Benjamin and Sarah Huffman, were natives of Germany, who settled upon the Potomac after coming to America, and engaged in farming. Mr. Huffman died in 1833. Our subject is the only living child of a family of three. In 1840 he moved to Illinois, and from there went to St. Louis, Mo., in 1845. Two years later he went to Iowa, and the next year went to Mercer County, Mo. In 1869 he settled in Crawford County, where he has since resided. The years from 1850 to 1853 were spent by Mr. Strong in California. In 1863 he enlisted in the United States Militia, under Capt. Smalley, operating in Northern Missouri until discharged in 1863, after six months' service. Mr. Strong is a carpenter and mill-wright by trade. He is a well-to-do citizen, and besides his drug business owns five lots in Porter and three good houses. He belongs to the Masonic fraternity, and in politics is a Republican, though his first presidential vote was cast for Andrew Jackson in 1828. December 26, 1833, Mr. Strong was united in marriage to Miss Sarah Antill, who was born in Ohio on October 2, 1814, and is a daughter of James and Elizabeth (Guess) Antill. Mrs. Strong is the only living child of a family of eleven, and is the mother of four children living and five deceased. Those living are George W., Mrs. Sarah Elizabeth Ballew, Mrs. Emeline Lane and Mrs. Ellen Rankin. Those deceased: Samuel Strong, James M., William H., Thomas J. and Benjamin. James Antill and his wife, Elizabeth, the parents of Mrs. Strong, were descendants of William Penn, and died in 1876 and 1852, respectively. The father was born January 1, 1790, and was a mill-wright by trade. From Maryland he immigrated to Ohio, and from there to Virginia.

Mrs. Sallie (Cox) Swearingen was born in Kentucky in 1825, and is a daughter of Burwell and Rebecca (Moberly) Cox, natives of Kentucky and South Carolina, who were born in 1795 and 1802, and died in 1874 and 1876, respectively. The father was a farmer by occupation, and in 1830 moved to Arkansas with his family, where he passed the remainder of his life. The paternal grandfather, Capt. John Cox, was born in Virginia, and the maternal grandfather, Isaiah Moberly, was from South Carolina. The latter served throughout the Revolution, and was twice wounded. The battle of Cow Pens was fought upon the farm of our subject's great-grandfather. The grandmother, Frances (Coleman) Moberly, was born in South Carolina, and died in July, 1844. Mrs. Swearingen attended school but little during her girlhood, as there were no public schools in the neighborhood. In 1842 she married Samuel Swearingen, who was born in 1818, in Cooper County, Mo., and was a son of John and Matilda (Riddle) Swearingen, natives of Maryland, who moved to Missouri in 1817, and to Arkansas in 1839, settling in Crawford County. In 1847 they went to Texas, where Mr. Swearingen died in 1859 and his wife in 1861. Mr. Samuel Swearingen was a blacksmith by trade, and he became a well-to-do man through successful farming and blacksmithing. His widow now lives upon the home farm of 208 acres, of which seventy-five acres are under cultivation. In 1863 he enlisted in the Confederate service, under Col. Brooks, but was captured soon after, at Huntsville, and kept a prisoner at Rock Island, Ill., until exchanged in January, 1865. He then remained in service until the close of the war. His death occurred in 1871, at which time he had been a resident of this county for over nineteen years. To Mr. and Mrs. Swearingen eleven children were born, eight of whom live in Crawford County: Robert Swearingen; Thomas, farmer and teacher; Oscar; Philip, physician; Sarah Frances; Mrs. Elizabeth Dial, of Idaho; Claudius, Clarence and John. William and Edward died in 1878 and

1886, respectively. In politics Mr. Swearingen was a Democrat, and cast his first presidential vote for Martin Van Buren, in 1840.

R. E. Swearingen is the oldest son of Samuel and Sallie N. (Cox) Swearingen, and was born in Crawford County, Ark., in 1844. [For life of parents, see sketch of Mrs. Swearingen.] During his youth Mr. Swearingen had no educational advantages, public schools being then unknown in this part of the country. In 1872 he was united in marriage to Miss Susan Hargrave, who was born in this county in 1853, and was a daughter of Benjamin and Narcissa (Foster) Hargrave. Mrs. Swearingen died January 26, 1875, leaving one son and one daughter, and January 29, 1879, Mr. Swearingen was married to Miss Grace Larue, who was born in Kentucky in 1862, and is a daughter of Samuel and Mary (Burdine) Larue, also natives of Kentucky, who settled in Crawford County in 1870. By his last marriage Mr. S. is the father of three boys and one girl. May 12, 1861, he enlisted in Company G, Third Arkansas Infantry, for six months, in which he served till the following fall, when the regiment was disbanded. In July, 1862, he enlisted in Company G, Twenty-second Arkansas Infantry, in which he served till the close of the war, participating in the battles of Oak Hill, Prairie Grove, Helena, Ark., and Saline River, Ark. Mr. Swearingen has made all his property since starting in life for himself in 1870, and is now the owner of 234 acres of good valley and bottom land; 110 acres are in the bottom, and are cultivated and improved; he living in a nice house himself, and having one tenement house on the home place, besides good outbuildings. Mr. S. is a Democrat and cast his first presidential vote for Seymour in 1868. He is a Mason, and his wife belongs to the Methodist Church.

John Swearingen was born October 2, 1848, in Crawford County, Ark., and is a son of Samuel and Sallie (Cox) Swearingen [see sketch], and a brother of R. E. and P. B. Swearingen, whose sketches also appear in this book. He was not able to attend school until after the war, and at the age of twenty-three began farming on his own account. In 1873 he married Miss Susan Clonch, who was born in Texas in 1856, and is a daughter of William and Margeret (Bailey) Clonch. They were born in Kentucky in 1832, and were married in their native State in 1853. From Kentucky they went to Texas, and from there came to this county, dying in 1874 and 1865, respectively. Mr. Clonch was a mechanic and carpenter by trade. To Mr. Swearingen and wife seven children have been born, four boys and three girls. In politics our subject is a Democrat, and his first presidential vote was cast for Horace Greeley. Mr. S. is a well-to-do farmer and respected citizen.

Philip B. Swearingen, M. D., is a native of this county, born in November, 1861, and is a son of Samuel and Sallie N. (Cox) Swearingen. [See sketch of latter for ancestors.] He passed his boyhood and youth in his native county, attending the common schools and receiving instruction at home from an elder brother, Edwin, who is now deceased. He began life for himself by farming one year in 1880, and the following year taught school. He then traded in cattle until 1883, after which he became the agent of a nursery until some time in 1884, when he began to study medicine. In the fall of 1885 he entered the Missouri Medical College at St. Louis, from which institution he graduated March 3, 1887, his college expenses having been paid by the money earned by teaching school during vacations. After graduating he continued teaching for eight months, and then permanently established himself in Cove City, where he has practiced his profession successfully since 1887. June 6, 1888, he married Miss Letta Beale, who was born at Evansville, Ind., in September, 1864, and is a daughter of William and Julia (Prosky) Beale. Mr. Beale was born in Pennsylvania, was a ship carpenter by trade, and died in September, 1869. Mrs. Beale was born in 1832, and still resides at Evansville, Ind. Dr. Swearingen is a Democrat in politics, and cast his first presidential vote for Grover Cleveland in 1884.

Pleasant M. Tarpley was born in Carroll County, Tenn., in 1837, his parents being Thomas W. and Susan (Harvey) Tarpley, natives of Tennessee. In 1860 they left their native State and went to Greene County, Ark., where the father died in 1862, and the mother in 1875. The father was of Dutch descent, and was born in Giles County, Tenn., about 1800. In religion he was a Baptist. Pleasant M. is the sixth child of eleven sons and five daughters born to his parents, and is the only one living in this county. He only attended school two

202

CRAWFORD COUNTY, ARKANSAS - BIOGRAPHICAL AND HISTORICAL MEMOIRS
****

months, and when of age engaged in farming. He had previously worked four years on the railroad, and had learned the milling business, which he has followed at times ever since in connection with farming. He accompanied his parents to Arkansas, and at the opening of the war joined Company D, of the Fifth Arkansas Infantry, Confederate States Army, and served in the Army of the Tennessee four years lacking fifteen days. He fought at Berryville, Ky., Murfreesboro, Mission Ridge, Chickamauga, Kenesaw Mountain, Perry, Jonesboro, Ga., and Decatur, Ala. He was captured at the last named place in October, 1864, and imprisoned at Camp Douglas, Ill., until May, 1865. He served the greater part of the time under Gen. Hardee, and at the battle of Kenesaw Mountain was wounded in the right hip. After the war he returned to Greene County, Ark., and in 1866 married Sallie J. Childers, a native of McNairy County, Tenn., by whom he has had six children, four now living. Mr. Childers was a native of Virginia, and there served as justice of the peace for several years. Mr. Tarpley is a good farmer, and owns eighty acres of land. He is an enterprising man, and favors everything conducive to the public good. He belongs to the Pleasant Hill Masonic Lodge, No. 233, and the Producers' Trade Union. He is a Democrat, and cast his first presidential vote for Douglas in 1860. His wife belongs to the Methodist Church.

William Logan Taylor was born in DeKalb County, Tenn., in 1839, and is the son of William Walton Taylor and Ann Pratt Taylor. The father was the son of Joseph Taylor, and was of Welsh and Irish descent, born in Georgia in 1793; the mother was born in Alabama in 1797. Soon after their marriage, in Alabama, the parents removed to Tennessee, where they remained until 1840, when they removed to Ste. Genevieve County, Mo., living there until 1853. Then they went to Grayson County, Tex., where the father died in 1858; the mother died in Benton County, Ark., in 1877. William L. is the youngest of twelve children, only four of whom are now living. He was educated at McKinzie College, at Clarksville, Tex., entering that institution in September, 1858, where he remained until 1862, except one year he was employed as principal teacher in Colbert Institute, Chickasaw Nation. From 1863 to 1866 he was principal of the schools at Whitesboro, Sherman and Gainsville, Tex. He was clerk of the district court of Grayson County, Tex., but resigned that office in October, 1868, and moved to Van Buren, Ark., where he has been in active business ever since, in the law and claim business, except six years of the time, when he was sheriff of Crawford County, elected as a Republican. He now devotes most of his time to his farming interest, although he does a selected law practice. Mr. Taylor was a Whig before the war, and since has been a Republican. In 1864 he married Priscilla Steurt Williams, by whom he has five children: Charles E., Clara, Alice, George W. and Steurt, all living. Mrs. Taylor is a native of Arkansas, a member of the Methodist Episcopal Church, and devotes much of her time to church matters and attending the sick.

Francis M. Temple, farmer, was born June 2, 1830, in Williamson County, Tenn., and is a son of Roderick and Mary (Lee) Temple, natives of Virginia. The father immigrated to Tennessee alone when a young man, and located in Williamson County, and after his marriage moved to Davidson County, where he died in 1849. The mother went to Tennessee by wagon when a girl. She bore Mr. Temple eleven children, three of whom are living: Narcissus, Francis M. and William. Hubbard, James, Alexander, Mary, Eliza, Maria, Frederick and one other are deceased. Mrs. Temple died in Arkansas July 30, 1884, aged eighty-five. The maternal grandparents of our subject were early settlers of Tennessee, and there passed their lives. Francis M. Temple was reared upon a farm in Tennessee, and attended school but six months. He had a natural gift for mechanics, but has engaged in farming principally. After his father's death he cared for the family, and September 28, 1854, married Mary Roselle, who bore him two children, James M. and William A. Mrs. Temple died June 15, 1857, and March 29, 1863, he married Minerva Lewis, daughter of Henry and Jane A. (Hobaugh) Lewis, natives of Kentucky and Missouri, respectively. Mrs. Temple was born in Texas County, Mo., and when eight years of age came to Arkansas. She is the mother of seven children: Mary T., Francis M., Charles H., Sarah E., Narcissus I., Thomas Ivy and Edna. Mr. Temple enlisted in the United States army in 1862, joining Company D, First Arkansas Volunteer Cavalry, and being discharged at Fayetteville in 1865. Among other

203

CRAWFORD COUNTY, ARKANSAS - BIOGRAPHICAL AND HISTORICAL MEMOIRS
****

battles he was present at Prairie Grove, Fayetteville and Elkhorn. Mr. Temple came to Crawford County in 1850, settling near Flat Rock, and three years later moved near Ollivar Spring, where he lived three years. He then lived two miles north of this place for several years, and then settled where he now resides. He owns 160 acres, seventy-five of which are cultivated. He is a public-spirited man, and has given a lot on which to erect a school building. Himself and wife are members of the Methodist Episcopal Church. He is a Republican, and a member of the G. A. R.

Thomas J. Testerman, merchant of Porter, was born November 4, 1848, in Hancock County, Tenn., and is a son of Manoh and Polly Ann (Leversy) Tester-man, who were born in North Carolina and Hancock County, Tenn., in 1819 and 1827, respectively. The father was a man of good education, and left his native State to go to Tennessee. In 1854 he went to Missouri, and engaged in farming until his death in 1858. He was of English descent, and of his six children our subject is the only one living. Thomas J. passed his early life in Missouri, and in 1872 left Newton County, of that State, and came to Arkansas. He farmed until 1881, and then established his present mercantile business at Porter. He is a successful business man, and owns eighty acres of land, besides a house, lot and general store in Porter. Upon first coming to Arkansas he settled in Benton County, from there went to Washington County, and in December, 1882, permanently located in Crawford County. He is a Democrat, and his first presidential vote was cast for Horatio Seymour. He belongs to the I. O. O. F., and is one of the respected citizens of Porter Township. August 18, 1876, he married Miss Alice Clark, who was born in McDonald County, Mo., in 1856, and bore two children, Herbert Lee and Grace (deceased). Mrs. Testerman was a daughter of Jackson and Mary (Etres) Testerman. May 24, 1888, Mr. Testerman married Miss Madeline Kelley, a native of Washington County, Ark., and daughter of William and Abbie Kelley, who were born and reared in Arkansas.

John A. and George C. Thayer, editors and proprietors of the Van Buren *Argus*, are natives of Hillsboro, Ohio, sons of Barnabus B. and Sarah W. (Cowne) Thayer, and were born in 1847 and 1852, respectively. The father was of French descent, and born in Massachusetts in 1817. He was a shoemaker by trade, was married in Fredericksburg, Va., and afterward moved to Hillsboro, Ohio. In 1869 he immigrated to Van Buren, Ark., where he died in May, 1879. The mother was born in Fredericksburg, and is yet living. Three of her six children are living, viz.: John A., Mary B. (wife of John O. Cass, of Danville, Ill.) and George C. John A. and George C. were educated at the public schools of Hillsboro, the former becoming a carriage trimmer and the latter a printer. In 1871 George came to Van Buren, and worked for J. S. Dunham on the Van Buren *Press* as a journeyman, and in 1875 established the Van Buren *Argus* with his brother-in-law, John O. Cass. He bought the latter's share in 1878, and in 1880 sold the paper to John A. Thayer, who had become a citizen of the county in 1874. He then edited the Alma *Independent*, at Alma, for twenty-two months, at the expiration of that period returning and again becoming a proprietor of the *Argus*, which has since been conducted by the Thayer Bros. These gentlemen are men of strong principles and convictions, of courteous address, and their paper now has the largest circulation of any in the county, its weekly subscribers outnumbering 1,100. It is Democratic in politics, and devoted to the interest of Crawford County. George C. Thayer is a member of the Methodist Episcopal Church. May 2, 1864, John A. Thayer enlisted in Company H, One Hundred and Sixty-eighth Regiment Ohio Volunteers, and served until September 8, 1864, when he received his discharge at Camp Dennison, Ohio.

David Thompson (deceased) was a native of New Jersey, born on April 4, 1796. He early became a citizen of Little Rock, Ark., and in 1835 located two miles below where Van Buren is now situated. In 1836 he and John Drennan purchased 265 acres of land, and laid out the town of Van Buren. Mr. Thompson was a land speculator and trader, and also engaged in the general mercantile business. March 17, 1818, he married Miss Loretta Dedrick, at Jonesboro, Tenn., who was born in 1801 and died in 1837. She was the mother of eight children, of whom three are living: Frances M. (widow of James A. Scott), Calvin M. and Julia (widow of William P. Denkla). Calvin M. Thompson was born in Nashville, Tenn., in 1833, came to Crawford County with his parents, and after their deaths was reared by John Drennan. January 15, 1857, he

204

CRAWFORD COUNTY, ARKANSAS - BIOGRAPHICAL AND HISTORICAL MEMOIRS
****

married Miss Rebecca Wilcox, daughter of Hon. Henry and Sarah P. Wilcox. This union has been blessed with one child, Sarah F. (wife of Lewis Bryan). Mr. Thompson merchandised until the war, and has since been engaged in agricultural pursuits. In politics he is a Democrat, and his wife is a member of the Episcopal Church and a lady of fine character.

Henry Thompson was born June 9, 1823, in Anderson County, Tenn., and is a son of Joharda and Margaret (Green) Thompson. The father grew to maturity in North Carolina, and after his marriage settled in Anderson County, Tenn. He then lived in McMinn County five years and in Cherokee Nation one year, after which he spent forty years in Georgia and then came to Arkansas with his son, where he died in Franklin County, April 29, 1872, aged eighty. He served in the War of 1812, as private, under Gen. Jackson. The mother was born in Rutherford County, N. C., and had eight children, three of whom are living: Mary, wife of Henry Mullens, of Kentucky; Henry, and Amanda C., wife of David McClure, of Texas. William, Thomas, John, Coswell and Andrew are deceased. The grandfather, William Thompson, was born in North Carolina, and was an early settler in Tennessee, where he died. He participated in the battle of Orleans. His wife, Mary (Tabor) Thompson, was born in America, of Irish parents, and passed the greater part of her life in Tennessee, where she died nearly one hundred years of age. The maternal grandparents of our subject were of Irish parentage, and spent their lives in North and South Carolina. Henry Thompson lived in Tennessee until eight years old, but was principally reared in Walker County, Ga., where he grew up upon a farm and received a common-school education. He began life for himself as a wagon-maker and mill-wright, and in 1871 emigrated from Georgia to Arkansas, living in Franklin County five years, and then moved on his present place, which contains 465 acres, 150 being cultivated and finely improved. Mr. Thompson is a Republican, and when in Georgia served as bailiff and notary public. Since coming to Arkansas he has retired from political life. October 28, 1846, he married Mary Williams, daughter of Alexander and Margaret Williams, who bore him five children: William C., Cicero and James A., living, and Alexander and Margaret, deceased. Mrs. Thompson died October 2, 1858; she was a native of South Carolina. Mr. Thompson afterward married Ann Cobb, daughter of William and Ann (Wilson) Cobb, natives of South Carolina, who immigrated to Hall County, Ga., where Mrs. Thompson was born. To Mr. and Mrs. Thompson seven children have been born: Martha E., Orra A., Richard V., John F., Robert H., Rhoda J. and Amanda C. Mr. Thompson has been a member of the Missionary Baptist Church over forty-five years, was a member of the first church in Walker County, Ga., and Mrs. Thompson is also a member of the Missionary Baptist Church. Mr. Thompson is an earnest advocate of educational advancement, and a public-spirited man.

John Trewhitt was born in Putnam County, Mo., January 27, 1854, and is a son of James M. and Mary A. (Guffey) Trewhitt, natives of Tennessee. The father immigrated to Missouri in 1820, when there were more Indians there than white men. He afterward moved to Tennessee, making the journey in a one-horse cart, and settled on Blackbird Creek upon 160 acres. About 1860 he moved to Jasper Township, Crawford Co., Ark., entered 160 acres and cultivated twenty acres. He joined the State militia during the war, but was never called into active service, He lived in Kansas from 1863 until the close of the war. He then returned to Arkansas, and farmed upon the old place until his death, February 11, 1888, aged seventy-two. He had been a minister in the Presbyterian Church for fifty-five years. She was married in her native State, and had twelve children, seven now living: Elizabeth, wife of William Ails, of Kansas; Polly A., wife of Luke Stinnell, of Missouri; Ephebia, wife of Stephen Bachelor, of Arkansas; Martha, wife of A. McComb, of this county; Benjamin B., John and William. Sarah A., James M., Jesse, Melinda and Henry are deceased. Subject's grandfather, Jesse Trewhitt, was a physician, born in North Carolina, and in an early day went to Tennessee. In 1820 he came to Missouri, with subject's father, and afterward went to Arkansas, where he died at the age of seventy-eight. His wife, Elizabeth, was born and married in North Carolina, and was seventy-five years of age when she lost her husband. Henry Guffey, the maternal grandfather, was born in Maryland, afterward moved to North Carolina, from there to Tennessee, and died in Putnam County, Mo., aged one hundred and six. He served in the War of 1812, under Jackson. His wife, Lila, was born,

205

CRAWFORD COUNTY, ARKANSAS - BIOGRAPHICAL AND HISTORICAL MEMOIRS
****

reared and married in Tennessee, and died in Putnam County, Mo., aged seventy-six. Our subject lived with his parents until eighteen, and, being obliged to help support the family by working on the farm, had little schooling. He then started in life for himself, first renting land. When twenty years old he married Marilla A. Capps, daughter of Callaway and Hovia Capps, and a native of Missouri. She is a member of the Missionary Baptist Church, and the mother of four children: Biddie M., Rosa M., Minnie A. and Naomi A. After his marriage Mr. Trewhitt farmed for a year, and then learned the stone-mason's trade, at which he worked ten years. He worked on the San Francisco Railway two years, and then opened a blacksmith shop near Cedarville. Two years later he removed his business into Cedarville, where he is now employed. He is a stanch Republican, never having voted any other ticket, and is a member of the Masonic fraternity and the Farmers' Alliance.

Winfield S. Truitt was born in Putnam County, Mo., March 10, 1849, and is a son of Mary Truitt, now Mrs. Mulkey. Mr. Truitt spent the first ten years of his life in his native county, attending school as much as possible. His mother was dependent upon him to a great extent, however, so that his education was limited. After coming to Crawford County, Ark., he worked upon farms when he could, finally trading in land until he was able to buy his present farm. After the Civil War commenced he continued to farm about two years, and then enlisted in Company H, First Arkansas Volunteer Infantry, United States Army, under Col. Johnson, and served until discharged at Fort Smith at the close of the war. His company was almost exclusively engaged in frontier and border duty, so that he was subject to many hardships, and often attacked by Indians. He participated in several small engagements, and was in the battles at Camden and Saline River. After the war Mr. Truitt returned to Crawford County, and resumed his farming. He now has eighty acres, twenty of which are cultivated, and all the result of his own hard labor and industry. December 12, 1867, he married Miss Eliza Ewing, daughter of Alfred and Evaline Ewing, and a native of this county, where she was reared. Her father was born in Missouri, and her mother in Kentucky. Mr. Truitt had six children by his first wife, two now living: George W. and Nancy E. Those deceased are Mima, Anderson and two infants. Mrs. Truitt died March 19, 1879, and December 2, 1884, Mr. Truitt married Mrs. Mary Copps, nee Spenser, and a native of this county. Her father and mother were born in Indiana and Kentucky, respectively. To Mr. and Mrs. Truitt two children have been born: Iva and Aura (deceased). Mr. Truitt is a strong Republican, and although he has never sought public distinction has served as road overseer. He is a member of the Agricultural Wheel, and one of the county's respected citizens.

John B. C. Turman was born October 29, 1836, and is a son of James W. and Jane (Copps) Turman, natives of Tennessee. The father left his native State about 1822, and engaged in the stock business in Missouri, driving stock to St. Louis. In 1843 he immigrated to Carroll County, Ark., engaged in farming, and in 1846 represented the county in Congress. In 1848 he came to Crawford County, and engaged in the mercantile business near Van Buren until his death in 1870. To Mr. and Mrs. Turman nine children were born, eight of whom are now living: William F., John B. C., Carroll A., Mary J., Alfred W., Miranda, Austin C. and Nimrod. James is the one deceased. Mrs. Turman came with her husband to this county during its early history, and died here in 1870. Bright Turman, the grandfather, was born in Tennessee, came to Carroll County, Ark., in an early day, and died in 1846. After his death his wife, Mary, went to Texas, and died there in Scott County. Matthew Copps, the maternal grandfather, went from Tennessee to Missouri by boat, and died in 1843. His wife, Sallie, went from Ripley County to Lawrence County, where she died in 1855, aged seventy. She also was a native of Tennessee. Our subject came with his parents to Carroll County, Mo., when six years old, and until 1857 lived at home, acquiring but a common-school education, and having to travel three miles to the school-house. In 1862 he went to Missouri and enlisted in Company D, First Arkansas Volunteer Cavalry, as private. Eleven days later he was made sergeant, and in February, 1863, became second lieutenant in Company M, of the same regiment, and June 11, 1865, was made captain. He was with Gen. Seafield on his advance into Arkansas, and participated in the battles of Fayetteville and Piney, Ark., among others. After the war he returned to farming in Arkansas. In December, 1866, he married Sarah J. Snow, daughter of Randolph and Nancy (Walker) Snow, natives of Tennessee and Alabama, respectively. Mrs. Turman was born in this county July 4, 1842, and is the mother of seven children: Alice R., Emma F., Nancy J., Ollie B. and Lillie M., living, and Ward B. and an infant, deceased. In 1868 Mr. Turman was chosen to represent this county in the Lower House, which he did for two years, since which time he has been engaged in farming. He is clerk of the Legislation Board, and is now holding his second term as justice of the peace, having been elected on the Republican ticket in a Democratic township. His farm contains eighty acres, twenty-five of which are cultivated. He is a member of the G. A. R. and Wheel.

The Hon. Jesse Turner was born in Orange County, N. C., October 3, 1805, and is a son of James and Rebecca (Clendenin) Turner, and is of Scotch-Irish descent, both on the paternal and maternal side. More than 200 years ago his ancestors immigrated from Scotland to County Down, in the northern part of Ireland, and about 1750 came to America, settling in Lancaster County, Penn. Among this party was his grandfather, James Turner. James Turner, Jr., the father of Jesse, was born in Lancaster County, but his grandfather removed to North Carolina about the year 1762, taking his son James with him, and settled in Orange County (Hawfields), where the subject of this sketch was born. The father, James Turner, was a Revolutionary soldier, and fought under Gen. Greene at Guilford Court-house, and was an active participant in many other engagements with the Tories. He was finally take prisoner by the notorious Tory partisan, Col. David Fannen, in September, 1781, at Hillsboro, N. C., with Gov. Thomas Burke and many other Whig soldiers, all of whom were marched to Wilmington, and shipped thence to Charleston, where they were all detained as prisoners of war (except Gov. Burke, who made his escape) until the close of hostilities. The father, James Turner, died in 1856 at the age of ninety-eight years. The mother, Rebecca Clendenin, was born on Haw River, Orange Co., N. C., about 1765, and died in 1863 at the age of ninety-eight years. Of their nine children three are still living. David, farmer and hotel-keeper at Pittsboro, N. C.; Joseph, the youngest, living near the old homestead in North Carolina, and Jesse, the subject of this sketch, who received a good academic education, which has been very greatly improved by self-culture. At the age of eighteen he taught school, and at nineteen was a law student in the office of his early friend, William McCauley, Esq. In May, 1825, he was admitted to the bar at Ashboro, Randolph Co., N. C., and at once commenced the practice in the county court, and the following year he was admitted to practice in the supreme court. In 1830 he immigrated to the western country, stopping for a few months at Bellefonte, Jackson Co., Ala. In the spring of 1831 he continued his journey westward to the Territory of Ark., when he finally located at Van Buren, the seat of justice of Crawford Co., soon after becoming one of its most influential citizens. The first wife of Judge Turner was Violet P. Drennen, a native of Allegheny County, Penn., born in 1817. This lady survived her marriage less than one year. In the year 1855 the Judge married Rebecca J. Allen, a native of Warwickshire, England, but reared at Pittsburgh, Penn. This marriage has been blessed with one son, Jesse Turner, Jr., an attorney who was partly educated at Pittsburgh and Van Buren, Ark. His more advanced studies were pursued at Kenmon High-school, Amherst Court-house, Va., and at the University of Virginia. He is a young man of marked ability, and is now his father's law partner. Judge Turner was an ardent admirer of Mr. Clay, and an active and conspicuous Whig politician from the early formation of the Whig party until it ceased to exist as a distinct political organization. In the terrible struggle between the North and the South, growing out of the slavery agitation, he was opposed to the secession of the Southern States from the Union, because not authorized by the fundamental law of the Government, and because otherwise impolitic and ruinous to the best interests of the South. But when the war was over he sincerely desired a restoration of harmony and union between the lately warring sections. He therefore was opposed to the Government's policy of reconstruction, because he believed it calculated very greatly to estrange and embitter the sections, and utterly unworthy of the magnanimity and generosity of a great and powerful government in the hour of its triumph over a prostrate and helpless people. In 1838 he was elected a member from the counties of Crawford and Franklin to the House of Representatives of the Arkansas Legislature, and in 1840 he took a very active part in the canvass of that year, which resulted in the election of William Henry Harrison to the presidency. In 1841 he was appointed, by the Secretary of War, one of the committee to attend the examination of cadets at West Point, and in 1851, upon the establishment of the Western (Federal) District of Arkansas, was appointed United States Attorney for that district. In 1861 he was elected a member, from the county of Crawford, of the famous convention that ultimately passed the ordinance of secession. In 1866–67 he was a member of the State Senate, and took an active part in the deliberations of that body; was chairman of the judiciary committee, and in 1874–75 he was again a member of the State Senate from Crawford and Franklin Counties, when he again took an active part in the proceedings of that body, contributing his full share in building up the prostrated credit of the State. In 1878 he was appointed by Gov. Miller a judge of the supreme court, to fill the vacancy created by the resignation of Judge David Walker. Judge Turner has always been a steadfast friend to every public and private improvement looking to the up-building and development of the State. He has been connected officially with the Little Rock & Fort Smith Railway for many years, and is also connected officially with the Kansas & Arkansas Valley Railway, both of which enterprises are doing much, and will do a vast deal more, toward building up and adding to the wealth and prosperity of all Western Arkansas. Judge Turner's personal integrity, his high sense of honor and rare intellectual ability are recognized, not only by the community in which he lives, but throughout the State of his adoption. For more than fifty-seven years he has been a resident of the State of Arkansas, and during the greater part of this time has been engaged in the practice of the law in the Western counties of the State, including the United States Court for the Western District of Arkansas and the supreme court of the State. He deservedly stands high in his chosen profession of the law, not only for ability and learning, but for his bearing and deportment at the bar, which is worthy of all praise. Touching his religious impressions he is a firm believer in the immortality of the soul, and in reward and punishment here and hereafter, corresponding to our actions in this life, and though not a member of any church, he is a very liberal and generous contributor to all charities.

Henry Varbel, farmer of Lancaster Township, was born in Oldham County, Ky., in 1831, and is a son of Daniel and Elizabeth (Walker) Varbel, natives of Kentucky, where they lived until about 1835. They then removed to Buchanan County, Mo., and from there to Platt County, where the father died about 1844, and the mother about 1870. They were members of the Methodist Church, and were engaged in agricultural pursuits all their lives. Henry is the second child of a family of seven, and when young received a common-school education. In 1851 he married Catherine Richardson, of Platt County, Mo., who died in 1862, leaving two children. In 1865 he married Mary E. Goodman, by whom he has had twelve children, ten of whom are living. After his first marriage Mr. Varbel went to Bates County, Mo., and the following year went to Kansas, where he remained nine years. He then returned to Platt County, Mo., and after 1865 spent three years in Iowa. He then returned to Missouri, and in 1872 came to Crawford County, Ark., settling upon his present place, which then contained but five or six acres of cleared land, but to which he has added until he now has eighty acres. In 1881 he built a gin and corn mill, which he operated five years in connection with his farming. He is a member of the Five Springs Masonic Lodge, and is one of the enterprising men of his township. In politics he is a Democrat. His wife is a member of the Christian Church.

Dr. Vincent S. Vestal was born in Andrew County, Mo., December 7, 1850, and is a son of Daniel and Mary J. (Snelling) Vestal. The father was born in North Carolina, and in an early day immigrated to Platt's Purchase in Northwestern Missouri. This occurred when he was twenty-one years of age, he having been born September 9, 1815, and emigrating in 1835. In 1849 he went to Andrew County, and there died February 24, 1865, from the effects of army exposure. He was a soldier in the Union army. The mother was born in Kentucky April 20, 1823, and when very young went to Buchanan County, Mo., where she was reared and married. She is now living in St. Joseph, Mo., at the advanced age of sixty-five. To Mr. and Mrs. Vestal eleven children were born, nine of whom are living: Margaret E., Sarah F., Adelia E., Mary H., Vincent S., Elvira B., Daniel M., William H. and Dora H. Those deceased are David and Martha E. John Vestal, the grandfather, and his wife, Margaret, were natives of North Carolina, and died in 1830 and 1848, respectively. Vincent Snelling, the maternal grandfather, immigrated from Northwestern Missouri to Oregon in 1851, and died November 7, 1855. Our subject was reared in Andrew County, Mo., received a good rudimentary education in his boyhood at Rochester, Mo., and after 1868 completed his academic course at McGee College, Macon City, Mo. In 1871 he began to read medicine with F. H. Simmons, of St. Joseph, Mo., and two years later commenced to practice. In 1880 he went to Northwestern Medical College, St. Joseph, Mo., from which he graduated in 1881. Dr. Vestal first came to Arkansas in 1875, living at Evansville, Washington County, until 1877, and then moved upon his present place. He is now engaged in farming upon 283 acres, ninety of which he has cultivated, in connection with his medical practice, which is quite extensive. In 1882 Dr. Vestal was married to Miss Nannie E. Pride, youngest daughter of Dr. Samuel E. and Letitia J. Pride, natives of Tennessee. Mrs. Vestal was born in Crawford County. Dr. Vestal is the father of three children: Dora V. (deceased), Mary L. and Grace B. Mrs. Vestal belongs to the Cumberland Presbyterian Church, and the Doctor to the Missionary Baptist. The latter is a Democrat, and a member of the I. O. O. F.

Isaiah B. Vinsant was born February 26, 1842, in Crawford County, Ark., in the house where he now lives, and is a son of Isaiah and Margaret (Shinault) Vinsant. The father grew to manhood in his native State, Virginia, and about 1830 immigrated to Crawford County, Ark., before Van Buren was founded. He was by trade a tanner, shoemaker, cabinet-maker and wheel-wright, and engaged in all of them after coming to Arkansas. He came here upon the first keel-boat that ever navigated the Arkansas River, and died in this county March 4, 1862, about fifty-six years of age. He was a successful business man, well educated, and was the owner of a large tract of land. The mother, Margaret (Shinault) Vinsant, was born in Bedford County, Tenn., about 1826, and there received a common-school education. Upon reaching maturity she came to Arkansas, where she married and became the mother of eight children, all now living: James M., Isaiah B., Thomas J., Margaret, Andrew J., Tennessee, Elijah A. and George. Mrs. Vinsant is now living in Paris, Lamar Co., Tex. Her husband was a prominent politician of the county in early days, served two terms as probate judge, and was for a number of years justice of the peace. The paternal grandparents were natives of France, who immigrated to the United States in an early day, and passed the remainder of their lives. The maternal grandparents were pioneers of Tennessee, who late in life immigrated to Crawford County, where they died. The grandfather was a soldier in the War of 1812. Our subject was reared on the home farm, receiving a common-school education and also studying some of the higher branches. When eighteen he enlisted in the first company formed in the county, which was known as Company G, Third Arkansas Volunteer Infantry, and served in the Confederate army until the close of the war. The most important battles in which he fought were Wilson Creek, Prairie Grove, Poison Springs, Saline, Helena, evacuation of Little Rock and Prairie De Hand. After the surrender at Shreveport, La., he was paroled, and then made his home in Hunt County, Tex., until the following December, since which time his home has been in Crawford County. He is a successful farmer, owning 360 acres of land, 175 of which are well cultivated and improved. September 15, 1870, Mr. Vinsant married Sarah N. Foster, daughter of J. S. and Susan Foster, natives of Kentucky, who were reared in this county. Mrs. Vinsant was born here, and has borne our subject seven children, all save one now living: Minnie J., George W., William B., Othello M., Albert and Myrtis. Andrew is deceased. Mr. Vinsant is a strong Democrat, and as such has served two terms as county assessor.

W. K. Walker, M. D., was born September 17, 1847, and is a son of William and Frances (Miller) Walker, who were born October 16, 1808, in North Carolina, and February 12, 1809, in South Carolina, respectively. The former was a farmer by occupation, and died in 1875. In politics he was a Democrat. The mother died September 7, 1861. The grandfather, Wesley Walker, was born in Virginia in 1781, and during the War of 1812 served under Gen. Jackson. He engaged in farming for a livelihood, and died about 1834. The grandmother, Sarah (Cherry) Walker, was born in Pennsylvania in 1781, and died in 1876. The maternal grandfather, William Miller, was also a soldier in the War of 1812 under Gen. Jackson, and engaged in farming. He was a native of South

209

CRAWFORD COUNTY, ARKANSAS - BIOGRAPHICAL AND HISTORICAL MEMOIRS
****

Carolina, and died in 1840. His wife, Barbara (Rose) Miller, was of Dutch descent. Our subject began life for himself in 1866, as a carpenter in Atlanta, Ga., having passed his boyhood in the northern part of that State. He afterward farmed until 1878, when he began the study of medicine. He read medicine under Dr. B. M. Stephens, of Searcy County, Ark., and in 1882 received a certificate from the medical examiners of that county, of which he had become a resident in 1876. In 1883 he went to Logan County, and the next year located at Cove City, where he has since been actively engaged in the practice of his profession. In 1867 he married Miss Matilda Honnicutt, who was born February 22, 1852, and died October 25, 1881. Her parents were M. J. and Locky (Webb) Honnicutt, natives of North Carolina, who were born in 1818 and 1815, and died in 1886 and 1875, respectively. During 1862 Mr. Honnicutt enlisted in the Eleventh Georgia Regiment, commanded by Col. Anderson, and served under Capt. Welsh. In 1882 Dr. Walker married Mrs. C. J. Woodard, who was born in Kentucky, in 1848, and is a daughter of John and Vienna Evans, natives of North Carolina, who were born in 1814 and 1824. They moved to Kentucky from North Carolina in 1845, and in 1851 went to Georgia. In 1867 the father died, and in 1870 the family moved from Georgia to Arkansas. Mrs. Walker is the mother of four children by her first husband, J. B. Woodard, viz.: Mrs. Vienna London, James I. Woodard, Mary E. Woodard and Benjamin Woodard, all residents of this county. To Dr. Walker three children were borne by his first wife: Mary F., Benjamin S. and Jack Walker. Dr. Walker is a Democrat in politics, and cast his first presidential vote for Seymour, in 1868. He is now serving his third term as justice of the peace, and is a member of the Blue Lodge in Masonry, and is also a Chapter Mason.

William T. Wallace, retail liquor dealer, was born in Johnson County, Ark., February 10, 1849, and is a son of Vincent and Ruth (Suggs) Wallace. The father was born in Benson County, N. C., in 1815, and was a farmer and minister of the Methodist Episcopal Church, South. The great-grandfather, William Wallace, was a Revolutionary soldier, and according to the family tradition was of Scottish parentage. He was twice married. His second wife became the mother of several sons, who went West, and settled perhaps in Tennessee. His first wife's maiden name was Ferguson, who became the mother of two sons: Orren and Robert, the latter of whom was the grandfather. On account of real or imaginary mistreatment by his step-mother he left home as soon as he became large enough to find employment, and went to work for daily wages. He had had the benefit of but two weeks' education at school, but during leisure hours acquired sufficient education to transact such business as pertained to his occupation. His energy in business and faithfulness to his employers soon gave him a reputation as a farm manager, and his services were sought and liberally paid for by such men as Jesse Dickens and James Paine, wealthy planters of Person County, N. C. Feeling the embarrassment of a limited education he made an extra effort to send his children to school, of whom there were twelve of one mother, whose name before marriage was Jane Smith Daniel. Her father, Mathew Daniel, came from or near Petersburg, Va. His mother's maiden name was Smith. Her mother's maiden name was Rachel Satterfield, whose mother was a Jay. After Rachel's death Mathew Daniel married a lady whose name was Agnes Marr. She had first been married to a Mr. Perkins, and after his death became the second wife of Dr. Paine, the father of James Paine, of Person County, N. C., who was the father of the late Robert Paine, bishop of the Methodist Episcopal Church, South. The children of Robert and Jane Wallace were Elizabeth, Lucy, Greene, Vincent, Orren, Emily, Rachel, Jane, William, Robert, Jr., Martha and George. Robert, Sr., is said to have been a kind and indulgent father, though firm in his family government. A man of ready wit, who took delight in repartee. He died October 8, 1846, being about seventy-two years of age, and was a member of the Missionary Baptist Church. He left to his family some lands, nine slaves, and other property, which were divided among his children. Greene died in childhood, George when nine years old, and William when twenty-one years old. Vincent married Elizabeth Philips, Orren married Jane Gill, of Person County, N. C., and Robert, after coming to Arkansas, married Ann E. Porter, daughter of Judge David Porter, of Johnson County. Elizabeth was married to Bently Gray, Lucy to William Hamlin, Emily to Loften Walton, Rachel to Mathew Griffith, Jane to Carter Daniel, and Martha to S. B. Cazort, all of Person County, N. C. About the year 1840 Vincent Wallace and William Hamlin arrived in Arkansas, having left North Carolina a year or two previously, and stopped awhile in Tennessee, perhaps one or two years. Vincent's wife died in Carroll County, leaving one son, John, who died a prisoner of the war between the States, having been captured by the Federal troops. After the death of Vincent's wife he married Ruth Suggs, who was born in Alabama in 1825, and moved near Clarksville, where he reared a family, the surviving members of which now reside in Van Buren, Ark. He obtained a fair common-school education, and taught school in North Carolina, Tennessee and Arkansas. His chief occupation, however, was farming. He was also a minister of the Methodist Episcopal Church, South. He represented Johnson County in the Ninth General Assembly of the State, and, as is understood, was the only Whig ever elected to the Legislature from this county, which shows the high esteem in which he was held by his fellow citizens. About the last day of the year 1863 he was brutally murdered at his home, in the presence of his family, by three unknown men, who assigned no cause for the atrocious deed, except that in answer to their question, "Are you not afraid," he referred them to Matthew x, 28, when immediately they began shooting him, saying "We will make you fear us." He lived a few hours, long enough to admonish his children and friends to live Christian lives, and died in Christian triumph, his last words being, "The physical pain is intense, but my mind is at rest." Orren and Robert Wallace and Loften Walton left Carolina in the fall of 1848, and arrived at Clarksville, Ark., about the 8th of January, 1849. Orren Wallace resided in Johnson County until 1873, when he sold his Johnson County farm to Cazort Bros., and moved to Morrilton, in order to be near his river farm in Perry County, where he still resides, being over seventy years of age. While residing in Johnson County, without soliciting the office, he was repeatedly elected justice of the peace of Pittsburg Township. He was very hospitable to all, had a great many visitors, loved a joke, took a lively interest in the political affairs of his county, was positive in his convictions, and spoke his sentiments so freely that they were sometimes not appreciated by those who entertained different views. He was liberal to all church and school enterprises, and though a member of the Missionary Baptist Church was one of the chief contributors to the building of Ewing Seminary, a Cumberland Presbyterian school, and furnished one-third of the money to buy for church and school purposes the land and house known as the Pleasant Grove school-house, near Lamar, Ark. Mrs. Ruth Wallace is still living, and three of her seven children survive: William T., Matthew Vinant and Thomas Loftin. William T. Wallace was reared upon a farm, and in 1875 married Miss Lizzie Smith, daughter of Alvis Smith, of this place. Mrs. Wallace was born in Crawford County, and has seven children: Vincent Alvis, Sidney Orren, Carrie May, Thomas L. (deceased), Sallie Smith, infant son (deceased) and William T., Jr. In 1876 Mr. Wallace came to Van Buren, and for four years attended bar for his father-in-law, at the end of which time he established a retail liquor store of his own. In politics he is a Democrat. In 1869 the subject of this sketch taught one of the first schools under the free school system ever taught in Johnson County, Ark. He was then but twenty years of age; he continued to teach until 1875, the year of his marriage at Van Buren, Ark.

Dr. T. M. Warden was born in Madison County, Ky., January 19, 1809, and is a son of James and Jemima (Thorp) Warden. The father was born in Culpeper County, Va., about 1784, and in 1794 immigrated to Kentucky, traveling from Pittsburgh in a flat-boat and landing where Maysville now stands. He was reared upon a farm, received a common-school education, and died there in October, 1839. The mother was born in Madison County, Ky., in 1793, where she was married to Mr. Warden at the age of fifteen. She died in Missouri, where she went after her husband's death, her death occurring in 1873. She was the mother of eight children, only two of whom are living: Tillett M. and Thomas. Those deceased are Tarlton, Tilson, Tilman, Roxana, Mourning and Nancy. Nathan Warden, the grandfather, was born in England, and with two other brothers served in the Revolution, shortly after going to Culpeper County, Va., and subsequently to Kentucky, where he died. The mother was of Scotch parentage, and died in Kentucky. Thomas Thorp, the maternal grandfather, was born in Virginia, and there married Elinor Jackson, a relative of Gov. Jackson, of Missouri. They moved to Kentucky in an early day, and there passed their lives. Our subject was reared upon his father's

211

CRAWFORD COUNTY, ARKANSAS - BIOGRAPHICAL AND HISTORICAL MEMOIRS
****

farm in Madison County, receiving a good education, and after becoming of age spent three years in travel. He then began to study medicine under Samuel Brown, of Brandenburgh, Ky., and later attended the Louisville Medical Institute for two years, graduating in 1841. After spending some time in Leavenworth, Ind., he returned to Madison County, and next went to Milliken's Bend, La. After remaining in Vicksburg one year he came to Crawford County in 1846, where he has practiced his profession since, and is actively and successfully engaged, although eighty years of age. February 24, 1840, he married Mrs. Eliza Bartlett, a native of Bristol, England, and daughter of William Amas, a native of the same place. Mrs. Warden has borne seven children, six now living: Marian W., Mortimer, Isabella, Lillie, Clarence N. and Fannie W. Another child, Mortimer, is the one deceased. Mrs. Warden died March 8, 1885, aged seventy. Dr. Warden owns 130 acres of land, twenty-five of which he cultivates, and upon which he lives with his daughter Lillie. In politics he is a Democrat.

Andrew C. Wardlaw was born in Anderson County, S. C., in 1837, and is a son of H. H. and Betsey (Harris) Wardlaw, also natives of that State, where they passed their entire lives, dying in 1869 and 1851, respectively. Mr. Wardlaw was a farmer by occupation, and served as justice of the peace for thirty-eight years. The grandfather, James, also passed his life in South Carolina, that probably being his native State, and served as sheriff of Pendleton County for many years. The great-grandfather was one of the first settlers of Upper South Carolina, and came to America from Ireland. Our subject lived at home until after his father's death, during which time he received a common-school education. He served four years in the Confederate army, enlisting in Company J, South Carolina Infantry. In 1862 he was transferred to Company E, Sixth South Carolina Cavalry, being stationed most of the time in Virginia. He participated in the battles of Bull Run, Gaines' Mill, Gravely Run, Savage Station, Nance's Shop, Williamsburg, Seven Pines, Cold Harbor and many skirmishes. After Johnson's surrender he returned home, and in 1867 married Mary, daughter of William and Matilda Smith, of Andrew County, S. C. This union has been blessed with six children, all of whom are living. One is a telegraph operator in Chicago. Mr. Wardlaw remained in Anderson County until 1886, and then came to Crawford County, Ark., where he bought a farm of 160 acres, located six miles north of Alma, and engaged in farming, which has always been his occupation. In politics Mr. Wardlaw is a Democrat, and he has been a member of the Masonic fraternity since 1861. His wife is a Baptist, and they are enterprising people, who have given their children all the advantages of a good education. Mr. Wardlaw's grandfather and his two brothers, Andrew and Robert, were prominent jurists of South Carolina years ago, having been on the supreme bench for a number of years.

Col. J. M. Weaver was born in Pickaway County, Ohio, in 1836, an is a son of Isaac and Sarah (Fetters) Weaver, and of German descent. The father was born in Virginia in 1800, and when about twenty went to Pickaway County, Ohio, where he married and engaged in farming. He died in 1884 in Circleville. The mother was born in Fairfield County, Ohio, in 1807, is yet living, and was the mother of nine children, all save one now living. Our subject was the fifth child, and received his education at Lancaster, Ohio, and then engaged in farming. In April, 1861, he enlisted in Company A, Twenty-seventh Ohio Regiment Infantry, in six months was made captain, and was then promoted from time to time, until finally commissioned colonel. He was discharged at the close of the war at Columbus, Ohio, and had participated in the battles at Corinth, Resaca, Marietta and Atlanta, and was with Sherman on his march to the sea. July 4, 1864, he received a wound in the right thigh, which disabled him for three months, but as soon as he was able he rejoined his command. In 1865 he went to Pana, Ill., and there engaged in the hardware and real estate business, and in 1873 went to Charleston, Ark., and was made general agent of the Little Rock & Fort Smith Railroad, with which railroad he has been connected ever since. About 1881 he settled in Ozark, and in 1883 became a citizen of Van Buren, and has since erected one of the finest dwellings in the town. He is a business man of high esteem, and deals in farm and city property in Crawford County. He is a stockholder in the Van Buren Canning Factory, the Van Buren Ice and Coal Company, and is a director and stockholder in the Crawford County Bank. In 1858 he married Miss Mary A. Wells, daughter of Isaac Wells, and born in Pickaway County, Ohio, in 1835. They have three children: Isaac Newton, of Pana, Ill.; Martin L., secretary of the Van Buren Canning Factory, and John M., Jr., loan and real estate dealer of this place. Col. Weaver was once a Republican, but has since joined the Prohibition ranks. Himself and wife are members of the Methodist Episcopal Church, South, he having joined the church over twenty years ago, and now being steward and president of the board. He is an active worker in church matters, is a fine speaker, and is elector of the Fourth Arkansas District on the Prohibition ticket.

Mrs. Jeanette Webb was born in Hamilton County, Tenn., and is a daughter of George W. and Jeanette (Cloyd) Clingan. George W. was in all probability born and reared in Ohio, and emigrated from that State to Tennessee in 1825, when that part of the country was still a wilderness. He lived in Tennessee until his death, August, 1830. The mother, Jeanette Cloyd, was born in Ohio, and coming to Tennessee died in the same week that her husband did. The paternal grandfather was twice married. His first wife died in Tennessee, and the second in Clark County, Ark. The maternal grandparents were both natives of Ohio, where they passed their entire lives. Mrs. Webb, the subject of this sketch, was born April 20, 1827, and passed her early days with an uncle on the Hiwassee Purchase. After living two years among the Indians in the Indian Nation, she was taken to Hamilton County, and made her home with Joseph Roark until her marriage, in 1847, to Benjamin Webb. She is the mother of eleven children, all but three of whom are living. Mrs. Webb resided in Tennessee until 1871, and then lived one year in Missouri. Since that time she has lived in Crawford County, and since the death of her husband, July 22, 1881, has continued farming on the old place. She is a lady of more than ordinary business ability, and is an active member of the Missionary Baptist Church.

John L. Webb, farmer, was born July 25, 1851, in Hamilton County, Tenn., and is a son of Benjamin and Jeanette (Clingan) Webb. When a boy the father went to Tennessee, and was there reared upon a farm without enjoying many educational advantages. He was married in Tennessee, and in 1871 immigrated to Crawford County, Ark., but stopped on his way in Polk County, Mo., and there passed a year. He first settled six miles northeast of Dripping Springs, and four years later removed to the Richmond place, there dying in 1881, aged fifty-nine. The mother was probably a native of Hamilton County, Tenn., where she was married. She is now living upon the farm in this county, and has the same cultivated. During the war Mr. Webb was employed by the Government in making saltpetre. To Mr. and Mrs. Webb eleven children were born, eight of whom are living, viz.: Sarah E., John L., George W., Jerusha, Mary E., William J., Joseph T. and Samuel Z. Those deceased are Nancy A., Merida and an infant. John L. Webb, our subject, passed his youth upon the farm in Tennessee, but on account of the war was unfortunately deprived of educational advantages. When a young man Mr. Webb left home, and for two years was engaged in handling sheep in Kansas. Having previously gone to Missouri in 1871, and coming to Arkansas from there, upon leaving Kansas he returned to Arkansas, and engaged in farming. December 25, 1878, he married Mary E. Winfrey, daughter of Samuel E. and Margaret (Matlock) Winfrey, who came to Arkansas from Alabama in an early day. Mrs. Webb was born in this county, and is the mother of five children: Neta, Homer, Margaret J., Frances Cleveland and Sarah A. (deceased). Mr. Webb settled upon the place he now occupies in 1879, and, in partnership with a brother, owns 400 acres of land, 125 being finely cultivated. Mrs. Webb is an active member of the Missionary Baptist Church. Mr. Webb is a stanch Democrat, and, although he has no desire for political distinction, has served as school director and filled several small offices.

Jacob F. Wells was born in Newton County, Ark., in 1842, being a son of Jacob and Rosanet (Newcomb) Wells. The father was probably born in Illinois, and came to Newton County from Missouri in 1838. In 1844 he came to Crawford County, settling upon the farm subject now owns, and dying in Van Buren in 1865, at which time he was living with his second wife, subject's mother having died soon after coming to this county. The father was of Irish descent, and both himself and wife belonged to the Baptist Church. Jacob F. is the youngest of a family of ten children, nine now living, and all save one residents of Crawford County. His brother, Thomas, served from June, 1862,

213

CRAWFORD COUNTY, ARKANSAS - BIOGRAPHICAL AND HISTORICAL MEMOIRS
****

until the battle of Prairie Grove, where he was killed, in Company G, Twenty-second Arkansas Infantry. Jacob spent three years of active service in the same company, with the exception of six months, when he was disabled by gunshot wounds in his right side, received at the battle of Helena. He fought at Prairie Grove and Saline, and participated in every engagement that this brigade fought in, operating in Arkansas, Louisiana and Texas. He surrendered at Fort Smith on June 10, 1865. In 1866 he married Jane Yerton, who died in Texas in 1875, leaving four children, and in 1878 married Martha J. Chastain, also a native of this county, who died in 1887, he having thus lived with his first wife nine years, three months and twenty-eight days, and with his second nine years, three months and twenty-nine days. December 22, 1887, he was married a third time, Mrs. Sarah C. Dover, *nee* Rozell, becoming his wife. She also is a native of Crawford County, and is a Methodist. Mr. Wells and his first two wives many years ago united with the Baptist Church. Mr. Wells is a blacksmith and wood-worker by trade, and has a nice farm of 162 acres, upon which he has lived fifteen years. He has been engaged in blacksmithing eighteen years. He is a Democrat, and cast his first presidential vote for Greeley. In 1888 he was elected justice of the peace of Vine Prairie Township, and he has filled the offices from Junior Deacon to Worshipful Master in the East, in Pleasant Hill Masonic Lodge No. 233.

Zachariah Wells, editor and publisher of the Van Buren *Graphic*, is a native of Pine Bluff, Jefferson Co., Ark., and was born in 1855. He is a son of Zachariah and Elizabeth (German) Wells. The father was born in Mobile, Ala., in 1828, and during his youth learned the printer's trade. In 1850 he immigrated to Pine Bluff, where he established the Arkansas *Republican*, the first publication of that place. He edited the paper seven years, and passed the remainder of his life in Jefferson County, serving as county judge six years. He died in 1869. The mother was born in Pine Bluff in 1835, and died in 1871. She was the mother of six children, five of whom are living, our subject being the second. He was left an orphan when young, and at the age of fourteen began life as an apprentice in a printing office. He served there five years, and the next ten years worked as a journeyman at Pine Bluff, Little Rock and Memphis, among other places in several of the Southern States. In January, 1887, he became a citizen of Van Buren, and March 12, 1888, assumed the editorship of the Van Buren *Graphic*, which is a Republican paper, with a weekly circulation of 900, and is rapidly becoming one of the best papers in the county. In 1879 Mr. Wells married Miss Fredonia Rutherford, who was born in Upion Springs, Ala., in 1860, and is the mother of one child, Frederick Clyde.

John Q. West was born April 13, 1843, in Crawford County, Ark., and is a son of Miram H. and Mary A. (Stevenson) West. The father was born in Kentucky, and when a young man came to Washington County, Ark., and farmed until 1840, when he came to Crawford County. In 1842 he married Mary A. Stevenson, daughter of James G. and Jane Stevenson, pioneer settlers of the county, who came here about 1830. To Mr. and Mrs. West six children were born: John Q., James G., Miram H., Lavinia J., wife of L. W. Thomas, of Indian Territory; Anna, wife of Louis J. Keifer, of the same place, and Susan, wife of Fred Keifer, Peru, Kas. Mr. West represented the county in the House of Representatives in 1856. He died in 1860, and his wife in 1887, she being sixty-one years of age. James Stephenson, the maternal grandfather, came to Crawford County from Cape Girardeau, Mo., represented the county in 1865, and was also justice of the peace. He died December 1, 1865, and his wife in 1888, at the age of eighty. Our subject attended the log cabin school-house during his youth, but has since become well informed by study and observation. When twenty-five years of age he left the paternal roof and enlisted in Company L, Second Arkansas Volunteer Cavalry, United States Army, as quartermaster-sergeant, serving two years. The most important battles in which he participated were Booneville, Big Blue, Upshaw, and Jefferson City. He was discharged at LaGrange, Tenn. In 1865 Mr. West married Mary E. Campbell, daughter of Anderson and Nancy C. Campbell, and a native of Lawrence County, Ark. This union was blessed with ten children, seven now living: James W., Nettie, Florence, Etta, Benie, Bessie and Fannie. Nannie, Louella and Nora are deceased. After his marriage Mr. West began farming, and in 1875 was ordained in the Christian Church, although he had preached prior to his ordination. He has been of great assistance in building up that denomina-

214

CRAWFORD COUNTY, ARKANSAS - BIOGRAPHICAL AND HISTORICAL MEMOIRS
****

tion in the county, and has charge of the Antioch, Van Buren and Philadelphia Churches. In 1882 he was elected assessor on the Republican ticket in a Democratic county, and held that office four years. He is a Republican, but also a worker in the Prohibition cause. He is a member of the I. O. O. F. and A. O. U. W., and his wife and two children have become identified with the Christian Church. For two years he served as justice of the peace.

Dr. Luther C. White (deceased), of Van Buren, was born in Woolwich, Me., February 16, 1810, and was of Scotch descent. He lived upon a farm until nearly grown, and then clerked in a drug store in New York City for a short time. He then began the study of medicine, and graduated from the Bellevue College, after which he went to Wilkesbarre, Penn., and commenced to practice. About 1851 he removed to Stephenson County, Ill., and about 1857 became a citizen of Van Buren, where he died April 5, 1888. He was three times married. His first wife, Harriet Dyer, was born in Maine, and died July 4, 1844. In 1848 he married Miss Aseneth C. Dodson, daughter of Joel Dodson, of Wilkesbarre, Penn. This lady was born November 11, 1819, in Luzerne County, Penn., and died August 31, 1872, in Stephenson County, Ill., while on a visit. February 9, 1874, Dr. White wedded Emily H. Moore, *nee* Williams, who died in September of the same year. Dr. White had four children by his second wife: Annie Caroline (born in Columbus, Luzerne Co., Penn., September 23, 1849, died in Chicago June 19, 1865), Henry Kirk (born at Hazelwood, Stephenson Co., Ill., September 29, 1853, and died at Savannah, Ill., August 12, 1857), George Melvin (born at Van Buren April 8, 1858, died at Polo, Ill., September 30, 1859) and John D. (born at Van Buren February 18, 1861, and educated at the State University of Arkansas). Dr. White was a strong Union man during the war, and served as United Sates Marshal of the Western District of Arkansas four years, being appointed by President Lincoln. He was a stanch Republican, and in 1872 represented the Eighth District in the State Legislature. Dr. White was a skilled physician, and a man held in universal esteem. He was a member of the State Medical Society, a charter member, director and stockholder in the Citizens' Bank of Van Buren, and a stockholder in the Van Buren Canning Factory. His son, John D., is one of the enterprising citizens of the town. Dr. White was liberal in his religious views.

Hon. Henry Wilcox (deceased) was born near Utica, N. Y., in 1800, and having been left an orphan at a tender age, was educated in Hamilton College of that State. In 1826 he was engaged as private instructor in the family of ex-Gov. Floyd, of Virginia, and in 1828 went to Marion County, Mo., to teach. In 1829 he married Miss Sarah P. Pettus, daughter of Thomas and Rhoda (Dawson) Pettus, natives of Virginia. Mrs. Wilcox was born in Green County, Ky., in 1812. Mr. Wilcox taught a few years after his marriage, and then conducted the Western Hotel, at Palmyra, for two years. In 1843 he began the study of law, and in 1845 came to Van Buren, and was soon admitted to the bar. He devoted his entire attention to his profession, and was one of the legal lights of Northwestern Arkansas for over twenty years. For several years he was school commissioner of Crawford County. His death occurred in 1864. To himself and wife four children were born: Granville (deceased), Rebecca, wife of C. M. Thompson; Juliette E., wife of A. H. Lacy, and Antoinette, wife of F. W. Schaurte, of St. Louis. Granville Wilcox was educated at the Ozark Institute, and when the Rev. Robert Graham organized the Arkansas College, at Fayetteville, he followed him to that place, and remained under his instruction five years. He graduated from Princeton College at the age of twenty, and then began to study law at home under his father. He was admitted to the bar when twenty-three, and served as prosecuting attorney of the Western District of Arkansas one term. He was political editor of the Van Buren *Argus* nine years, and in 1866 and 1867 was a member of the State Legislature. He died in 1886, aged fifty. He was, like his father, a man of unblemished reputation, and a man of extraordinary legal ability. He was known as the "Little Giant" of Arkansas. During the war he served in the Confederate army, entering as third lieutenant, and leaving lieutenant-colonel. He was also quartermaster in the Indian Department. Henry Wilcox was an I. O. O. F., and Granville belonged to the Masonic fraternity. Mrs. Wilcox is enjoying a ripe old age, and makes her home with her daughter, Mrs. C. M. Thompson.

W. S. Williams, farmer, was born in this county in 1844, his parents being T. N. and Candas (Moberly) Williams, natives of Kentucky, born in 1806 and

****

1816, respectively. After 1832 they made their home in Crawford County, where the father died in April, 1875, but the mother still lives. The paternal grandfather, David Williams, was a resident of Kentucky, and the maternal grandfather, Clem Moberly, and his wife, came from that State to Arkansas in an early day. The subject of this sketch was reared in his native county, receiving but few educational advantages, and at the age of twenty-two began life for himself. In 1867 he married Miss Agnes Gregg, daughter of James and Lucinda (Morton) Gregg, and born in this county in 1847. Mr. James Gregg was born in Scotland in 1815, and his wife was born in 1826. He was a stone-mason and farmer, and upon coming to Arkansas assisted in the building of the fort at Fort Smith. Mr. and Mrs. Williams are the parents of two boys and two girls. During the war Mr. Williams drove a Government team in the year 1862, in Gen. Blunt's army, and he was present at the battles of Saline River and Fayetteville. He has always followed agricultural pursuits, and although he began life a poor man, now owns over 400 acres, and has 185 acres under a fine state of cultivation. He is a member of the Masonic fraternity, and is a Republican.

Dr. L. J. Wilson, practicing physician and surgeon of Alma, was born in Lincoln County, Tenn., in 1836, and is a son of James and Elizabeth J. (Bourdon) Wilson, natives of Dinwiddie County, Va., born in 1791 and 1794, respectively. They were married in the same county, and then went to Maury County, Tenn., later settling in Lincoln County. When our subject was five years old they went to Marshall County, Miss., where the father died in 1871, and the mother in 1862. Mr. Wilson was a farmer, and served a short time in the War of 1812. His father, Robert, came to America from England at an early day. Dr. Wilson is the ninth of a family of ten children, and although his youth was passed upon a farm he received a good academic education. At the age of eighteen he began to read medicine, and graduated from the Jefferson Medical College, at Philadelphia, in 1859, which was then the foremost medical institute in the United States. Having practiced to some extent in the meantime, he immediately began to practice in De Soto County, Miss., but upon the breaking out of the war raised Company G, First Mississippi Regiment, and served as first lieutenant until captured at Fort Donelson; a week later he made his escape, and returning home organized Company D, Second Mississippi Volunteer Infantry, and thereupon went to Virginia, serving as first assistant surgeon until the close of the war in the Army of Northern Virginia. After the surrender at Appomattox he resumed his practice in Tate County, Miss., and in 1883 removed to Alma, Ark., where he now enjoys a liberal patronage. In 1860 he married Elizabeth C. Skipwith, of Memphis, Tenn., great-granddaughter of Gen. Nathaniel Green. Her father, Gray Skipwith, was for many years a prominent physician of Jackson, Miss., and there died of yellow fever. He was for many years a lieutenant in the United States Navy. Dr. Wilson has had seven children, three of whom are living. In politics he is a Democrat, and he cast his first presidential vote for Bell in 1860. He is a member of the Masonic fraternity, and himself and wife belong to the Presbyterian Church.

Capt. John F. Winfrey was born in Monroe County, Miss., February 22, 1823, and is a son of John F. and Mary Ann (Cottrell) Winfrey, natives of Buckingham County, Va. They went to Madison County, Ala., with their parents, when young, where they were afterward married, and lived until 1829, with the exception of 1822 and 1823, which they passed in Monroe County. They then came to Crawford County, when the country was an unbroken wilderness, with only a few white settlers. Mr. Winfrey purchased a small piece of improved land of Stephen Coose, where Lillie is now situated, but after raising one crop removed to what is now known as the Shaw farm, and is owned by John Sharp. This is situated on the river bottom, and in 1833 the water rose so high that he was obliged to move upon Frog Bayou, just above Rudy, where he farmed until his death, in December, 1860. He was a Whig in politics, and fought in the War of 1812. His father, Henry Winfrey, was a man of good education, who often drew up public documents, and died in Northern Alabama in 1818. He was of English descent. The mother of our subject was a daughter of Maj. Richard Cottrell, who was born in England, and when young came to the United States with his parents, being reared in Virginia. He located in Crawford County in 1854, where he lived until his death. He was twice married. His first wife, the grandmother of our subject, died in Alabama. John F.

Winfrey is the fourth of a family of eight children, and being reared, as he was, in the wilderness, he received a very meager education. When twenty-five he left home and obtained a position as watchman on a steamboat running from Little Rock to New Orleans. He soon purchased the bar, conducting it for a year and a half, but in 1850 went to California with 106 others, and spent five years in mining, with the exception of a short time in 1852, when he returned home by water for a visit. In 1858 he married Margaret E., daughter of William and Elizabeth Snyder, natives, respectively, of Virginia and Kentucky, and early settlers of this county, where Mrs. Winfrey was born. Mr. and Mrs. Snyder lived on Mountain Fork of Lee's Creek, in Lee's Creek Township, for many years, and there died. To Mr. Winfrey and wife eleven children have been born, three sons and one daughter now living. Richard B. is now serving his second term as assessor of Crawford County. Mollie is the wife of T. E. Cathey. William E. and Sandy E. are the two youngest. Since his marriage Mr. Winfrey has lived upon his present farm of eighty well-improved acres. Before the war he was a Whig, but is now a Democrat, and after being elected sheriff in 1874 filled that position satisfactorily for four years. He served in the Confederate army four years. The first three months he was with Capt. Stewart's State troops, and the remainder of the time commanded Company E of the Third Arkansas Cavalry, operating in Cherokee Nation and Arkansas, and participating in the battles of Wilson's Creek, Prairie Grove and many skirmishes. He and his wife are active members of the Methodist Church, South.

Thomas A. Wood, planter and prominent citizen of Alma Township, has been a resident of Arkansas for fifty-one years, was born in Northeast Georgia in 1829, and is a son of Enoch and Jane (Lovelady) Wood, natives of Carolina. The left their native State for Georgia, and in 1837 moved to Pope County, Ark., where the mother died in 1855 and the father in 1859. Mr. Wood was of Scotch-Irish descent, and a farmer by occupation. The grandfather, John Wood, was a Revolutionary soldier. Our subject was the youngest child of nine, and being reared in Arkansas during the pioneer days, received a meager education. When about twenty years of age he crossed the plains to California with an ox team, and there spent about eight years mining and trading. After remaining about two years he made a short visit home, and returned by the usual water route. He was financially successful, his home trip being made with some stock. In 1859 he married Matilda Howard, who died in 1860, leaving one child. In 1861 he married Julia, daughter of Silas Wright, of Johnson County, Ark. This union was blessed with six children. Mr. Wood was among the first to enlist in the Confederate army in Pope County. He joined Company A, Col. Jack Williamson's battalion, and operated in Arkansas, Tennessee, Mississippi and Georgia. The company was reorganized at Corinth, Miss., in 1862, and was transferred to the Third Arkansas Cavalry, participating in the battles of Chattanooga, Shiloh, Corinth, Murfreesboro and many minor engagements. Mr. Wood was captured near Nashville in the winter of 1863–64, taken to Cairo, Ill., and while on the way to Vicksburg, Miss., made his escape at Milliken's Bend. He immediately crossed over into Arkansas, and attached himself to Gen. Shelby's command, with whom he remained until the close of the war. He accompanied him on his raid through Missouri, and was present at the surrender at Clarksville, Ark., in May, 1865. Mr. Wood then made his home in Pope County until 1873, when he came to Crawford County, Ark., and settled on bottom land in River Township, where he still owns a good farm. He also has a fine farm of 200 acres near Alma, owning 700 acres in all. Mr. Wood is one of the enterprising and wealthy citizens of the county, and is largely engaged in stock and cotton raising, having an annual yield of from 150 to 200 bales of cotton. He has been a Democrat all his life, and cast his first presidential vote for Pierce in 1852. He has for twelve years been a member of the Masonic fraternity, belonging to the Alma Lodge No. 43. Mrs. Wood is a Methodist. Mr. Wood has always had a disposition not to be outdone in any respect. He is fond of sport, such as hunting, and especially shooting on the wing, for which purpose he makes frequent visits to the Indian Territory, with good success.

Joseph C. Wood was born November 21, 1841, and is a son of William M. and Mary C. (Winkler) Wood. The father was born and reared in Madison County, Ky., and when twenty-four went to Missouri, where he bought and sold land until 1840, when he married the mother of our subject, who bore him two children, Joseph, and William (deceased). September 12, 1852, Mr.

Wood went to Benton County, Ark., and a few months later bought land near Uniontown, Crawford County. A year later he went to Schuyler County, Mo., again returned to Crawford County, and in 1864 went to Iowa until the close of the war. Two years after the death of his first wife, in Arkansas, he married Susan M. Biswell, a native of Adair County, Mo., who bore him seven children: John W., Martha, George, Minnie, Charles, Lee and Lavinia (deceased). Mr. Wood farmed in Douglas County, Kan., a short time after the war, and then returned to Crawford County, where he died in 1882, aged sixty-seven. The mother of our subject was a native of Madison County, Ky., and died in Crawford County. Thomas Wood, the grandfather, was born in Pennsylvania, of English parents, immigrated to Kentucky, and died in Madison County, aged sixty-two. He was a mechanic and stone-mason. His wife, Agnes (Kinkaid) Wood, was also born in Pennsylvania, of Scotch-Irish parents, and died in Kentucky. William Winkler, the maternal grandfather, was born in Germany, there became a shoemaker, and immigrated to Kentucky, where he married Mary Nolan, a native of Kentucky, of Irish descent. He died in Kentucky, and she in Missouri. Matthew Wood, the great-grandfather, was a cabinet-maker in London, England, who immigrated to Pennsylvania in an early day. The maternal great-grandmother, Sarah Nolan, died in 1853, in Schuyler County, Mo., aged one hundred and thirty, and her husband was a Revolutionary soldier. Joseph C. Wood, our subject, was born in Adair County, Mo., and when twelve came with his father to Crawford County, afterward accompanied him to Iowa and Kansas, and after returning to Crawford County engaged in farming. He gained the greater part of his education by burning the midnight oil, and when of age enlisted in the Confederate army, under Capt. Duncan. He remained in this company about three months, and fought in the battles at Pea Ridge and Sugar Creek. After the evacuation of Fort Smith he worked on train duty in the Federal army three months, and then on the ferry at Van Buren. He served until May, 1864, after which he lived in Kansas two and a half years. After returning to Arkansas he farmed until 1865, and has since enjoyed a good mercantile trade at Uniontown. In February, 1860, he married Letitia Maybery, a native of Virginia, and daughter of Charles and Ellen Maybery. To Mr. and Mrs. Wood ten children have been born, eight now living: Thomas F., Lucretia E., Andrew B. C., Antoinette, Nancy, Walter M., Ola, Omega, and Zellie. Charles W. and Dora E., are deceased. Mr. Wood is a Democrat, and has served two terms as justice of the peace. He is the postmaster of Uniontown, and a Mason. His wife belongs to the Missionary Baptist Church, and he to the Christian.

George R. Wood, senior member of the firm of Wood Bros. & Southmayd, general merchants, was born in this county and town in 1853, and is a son of James M. and Sophronia (Clyman) Wood. The father was born in Sevier County, Tenn., attended the State University of Georgia two years, and in 1849 came to Crawford County, Ark. In 1851 he married, and then farmed until 1854, when he embarked in the mercantile business, continuing in the same until his death, in 1880. He was the mayor of Van Buren two years, and one of its successful business men. The mother was born in Danville, Vermilion Co., Ill., in 1834, and is a daughter of Bennett H. and Matilda (Lancaster) Clyman, natives of Virginia, born in 1793 and 1799, and who died in Van Buren, in 1849, and Danville, Ill., in 1840, respectively. Mr. Clyman was a packer, who came to Van Buren in 1845. George R. Wood is the eldest of a family of ten children, seven of whom are living: G. R., Margaret E., Anne E. (wife of T. W. Edmondson), James M. (of the firm of Wood, Edmondson & Britt), John J. (of the firm of Wood Bros. & Southmayd), Henry C. (of the same firm) and Norma. Our subject first attended school at Van Buren, and then passed two years at St. John's College, in Little Rock. He then worked in his father's store until 1878, when W. H. H. Shibley, D. W. Moore and himself became partners in the general mercantile business. Mr. Moore sold his interest in 1880, to Shibley & Wood, and in January, 1887, the firm began business under the firm name of Wood Bros. & Southmayd. They carry one of the largest stocks in Van Buren, and occupy a building 30x115 feet, two stories high. In 1876 Mr. Wood married Sarah E., daughter of L. C. and Susan R. Southmayd. Mrs. Wood was born in Van Buren in 1854, is a member of the Methodist Episcopal Church, South, and the mother of five children: Susan, Clyman, James, Mattie and Annie. Mr. Wood is a Democrat, casting his first presidential vote for Samuel J. Tilden,

218

CRAWFORD COUNTY, ARKANSAS - BIOGRAPHICAL AND HISTORICAL MEMOIRS
****

and in June, 1888, was a delegate from his congressional district to the National Convention held at St. Louis. He is a good business man, and has very recently been elected president of the Citizens' Bank, of this town. He is also president of the Van Buren Ice and Coal Company. He is a Master Mason and K. of P.

Franklin Wright was born in North Carolina in 1829, and is a son of James H. and Polly (Brooks) Wright, natives of the same State, where they were reared. After their marriage they lived in Tennessee until the war, when they removed to Kentucky. A few years later they went to Indiana, and there the mother died in 1884, aged seventy-seven, and the father in 1885, aged eighty-three. They were people of good standing, and had for many years been members of the Baptist Church. In occupation the father was a farmer. The great-grandfather Harrison was a soldier in the Revolution. Our subject was the second child in a family of five sons and seven daughters. William, one brother, served in the Confederate army until the surrender of Vicksburg, when he was paroled. He is now living at Nemeha, Neb. James H., another brother, died at Knoxville, Tenn., while in the Confederate service. Franklin attended a common school in North Carolina, and was there married, in 1854, to Charity, daughter of Abraham and Mary Church, all natives of North Carolina. The father died in that State, and the mother died in Tennessee in 1876. The date of Mrs. Wright's birth is January 9, 1833. To herself and husband ten children have been born, of whom two sons and three daughters are living. Mr. Wright lived with his parents in Tennessee and North Carolina, and in 1858 removed to Hancock County, Tenn. In 1863 he went to Kentucky, and in the same year, in July, enlisted in Company A, Forty-seventh Kentucky Volunteer Infantry, serving eighteen months in the United States Army. He was stationed in Kentucky, and was honorably discharged at Lexington, December 26, 1864. In 1868, after his return home, he went to Madison County, Ind., and four years later went to Madison County, Ark. In 1874 he went to Franklin County, and kept a boarding-house for railroad hands at Mulberry. He now lives upon a nice farm of 160 acres, seven miles north of Mulberry, upon which he moved in 1876. At that time the place was nothing but a wilderness, but by hard labor he has converted it into a well-inproved piece of land. He is an enterprising man, who takes an interest in public affairs, and believes in educating his children. His son James received his education at Ozark College. In politics he was once a Whig, but after the days of that party became a Republican. Himself and wife are active workers in the Baptist Church, to which they were united when young.

Capt. James C. Wright, merchant and postmaster at Chester, is a son of Isham and Mary (Shepherd) Wright, natives of Kentucky and Alabama, respectively, who came to this county during their youth. The mother having returned to her native State, she was there married to Mr. Wright, and in 1841 they returned to Crawford County, settling upon their present place. He is a farmer, and in politics a Jackson Democrat, and is now seventy-six years of age. She is a member of the Methodist Church, and seventy-eight years of age. Capt. Wright is their eldest son, and was born July 3, 1830, in Jackson County, Ala. He was educated in the old-time schools, and when eighteen began the battle of life for himself. In 1850 he married Maria J. Marlar, a native of Giles County, Tenn., who came to Crawford County in 1843. She died in 1858, leaving one son, William, and the same year he married Sarah C. Lester, a native of this State, by whom he has one daughter, Lulu S. Capt. Wright belongs to the Methodist Church, with which both his wives were united. While the war was in progress, having taken part in the fight at Wilson's Creek, he returned and organized Company E, Thirty-fourth Arkansas Infantry, Confederate States Army, of which he was elected captain in May, 1862, holding that office until the close of the war. January 2, 1863, while home on recruiting service, he was captured by the enemy, but was exchanged ten days later, after which he returned to his command. Upon the close of the war he engaged in farming until 1883, and then built a small store, which he stocked with goods, and his business venture has been so successful that since then he has built himself a more commodious house. He is a self-made man, a Democrat, Royal Arch Mason, and a member of the Knights of Labor.

Gabriel N. Wright, of the firm of W. A. Bright & Co., planters, ginners and millers, was born in Paulding County, Ga., in 1835, and is a son of Henry and Elizabeth (Goddard) Wright, natives of South Carolina and Georgia, respectively. They were married in the latter State, and there passed the remainder of their lives, the father being drowned when our subject was an infant. He was a farmer by occupation. Gabriel Wright, the grandfather, was born in South Carolina, and was a soldier in the Revolution. He was a descendant of a prominent Quaker family, whose many offsprings are now living in various States. The great-grandfather of our subject came to America from England in an early day, and settled at Charleston. Mrs. Wright was married to Howard Barbara after the death of her first husband. Gabriel N. lived with his mother and step-father until about six years old, and then with his grandmother and step-grandfather until sixteen, receiving but a limited education, and then passed four years learning the bricklayer's and contractor's trade. He followed the above business with remarkable success until a few years ago, having erected many prominent buildings in Arkansas, such as the university building at Fayetteville, store buildings in Fort Smith and the Presbyterian Church at that place, which was his last work in that line. He has also built many public buildings in Georgia and Alabama, among which are the college building at Jacksonville, Ala., and court-house at Gadsden, Ala. He began life for himself a poor boy, and at three different times met with severe losses, but by perseverance and industry has now become a wealthy citizen. His cotton-gin has a capacity of sixteen bales per day, and he and W. A. Bright own 1,000 acres of bottom land, about 550 being under cultivation, making this place one of the best farms in the county. During the war he did not go upon the battle-field, but served his country by being engaged in nitre and mining works. He had a contract to furnish the Confederate army with nitre and potash, and his works were located in various parts of Georgia and Alabama. In 1865 he was captured in Alabama, but was paroled the next day. At the commencement of the war he assisted in raising two military companies for service, and was tendered the position of adjutant, but found his services would be more valuable at home. In 1860 he married Martha R. Woodruff, a native of Georgia, whose parents were from North Carolina. Mr. and Mrs. Wright have had seven children, five of whom are living, and have received a good education. From 1870 until 1877 Mr. Wright lived at Fort Smith, and then removed to a store of his in the country, thus laying the foundation for the town of Levaca. There he engaged in farming, merchandising and milling until 1885, when he established the above described business in River Township. He has taken all the degrees in the Masonic fraternity, having been a member since twenty-one years old, and is also a member of the K. of H. Himself and wife belong to the Methodist Episcopal Church, South. He has always been a Democrat, and his first presidential vote was cast for Buchanan.

M. L. Wright, grocer and liquor dealer, was born in Johnson County, Ark., in 1854, and is a son of Dr. J. M. and Vienna (Miller) Wright, natives of Tennessee and Georgia, respectively, who, when young, accompanied their parents to Arkansas. The mother died in 1865, and the father is now living with his third wife. Before his marriage he attended lectures at the Missouri Medical College in St. Louis, afterward practiced his profession, and during the war served as surgeon in the army. For the past fourteen years he has practiced law in Crawford, Sebastian, Logan, Franklin, Johnson and Pope Counties, with his office at Alma. He has for ten years been justice of the peace in this county, but now resides in Franklin County. He is of Scotch-Irish and English extraction. His father, Silas C. Wright, came to Arkansas from Virginia when it was still a Territory, and served as sheriff of Johnson County. He died in Pope County in 1872. Our subject spent his boyhood at home, where he received a common-school education, and at the age of seventeen began life for himself by farming. In 1876 he went into the grocery business at Alma, and in 1877 into the liquor business. Selling out in 1878, he clerked in a general store for eighteen months, and in 1881 and 1882 was in the liquor business at Van Buren. Returning to Alma he established a grocery store. In 1883 he started another saloon, and a year ago also engaged in the grocery business again. His stock is valued at about $5,000, and he is a prosperous citizen. He is a Democrat, cast his first presidential vote for Tilden, and in 1868 was elected clerk of Crawford County, serving two years. He was chief of police in Van Buren four years, and has also held that position in Alma. When a young man he edited one of the first papers published in the county, at a time when Van Buren was built of log cabins, and has been one of the leading men of that place, having been in business there for about thirty years. He now owns about fourteen dwellings there, and has two business houses and one residence in Alma. He is one of the directors of the Crawford County Bank. April 13, 1879, he married Lillie B. Bowlin, who was born in Van Buren April 2, 1860, being a daughter of William and Lemantha Bowlin; she is the mother of one child. During the war Mr Bowlin served in the Federal army in the First Arkansas Infantry, being the commander of Company A, and operated in Arkansas, Tennessee, Mississippi and Louisiana.

Dr. William L. Wynne was born in Wake County, N. C., in 1821, and is a son of Allen S. and Elizabeth (Thompson) Wynne, natives of the same county and State, born in 1800. In 1841 they went to Shelby County, Tenn., where their respective deaths occurred in 1865 and 1885. The father was a Missionary Baptist minister for the last fifteen or twenty years of his life, and by occupation was a farmer. His father, Major William Wynne, was also a farmer, and was born in Virginia. Our subject is the oldest of four brothers, and during his youth attended the common schools of the neighborhood and Wake Forest College in North Carolina. After teaching school three years he read medicine two years in Memphis, Tenn., and then spent one year at the Memphis Medical College. He next practiced ten years in Marshall County, Miss., and in 1859 graduated in his profession from the above named institute, after which he resumed his practice in Marshall County. In 1862, owing to the excitement of war times, he went to Gilmore, Tex., where he practiced with success until 1871, at which time he came to Alma. He soon established himself here, but for the past few years, owing to poor health, has been obliged to confine his visits to the town and neighboring country. In 1851 he married Rebecca Jane, daughter of Samuel and Elizabeth Montgomery, natives of South Carolina, which was Mrs. Wynne's native State. In 1836 the family removed to Northern Mississippi, and in 1854 went to Tennessee, where Mr. Montgomery died in 1856, and the mother in 1878. Dr. Wynne and wife have had eight children, four of whom are living. Dr. Wynne owns ninety acres of land near Alma and is comfortably fixed. In politics he was formerly a Whig, and his first presidential vote was cast for Clay in 1844. Since the war he has been a Democrat. Himself and wife belong to the Missionary Baptist Church.

William M. Wynn, farmer, was born in Washington County, Ark., in 1836, and is a son of Josiah and Harriet (Turner) Wynn, natives of Kentucky and Tennessee, respectively, who settled in Washington County in an early day. When our subject was about twelve they came to Crawford County, Ark., and located one mile north of the present site of Alma, where the mother died. The father was twice married, was a farmer by occupation, was a member of the Masonic fraternity, and for many years served as justice of the peace in this county. His father was Harmon Wynn. William M. is the youngest child of nine born by his father's first marriage, twenty-three children having been born by both marriages. He attended school but about three months, and in 1856 married Martha Cumpton, of Hempstead, County, Ark. This union was blessed with nine children, four of whom are living. Mrs. Wynn has now been dead thirteen years. During the war Mr. Wynn served four years and two months in the Confederate army, in Capt. Winfrey's company, serving in Arkansas and the Indian Territory, and being in active service nearly all the time. He rode his own horse and bore his own expenses, never being reimbursed by the Government. After the war he moved upon his present farm, which contains 160 acres, and is located near Alma. Mr. Wynn has now been a resident of the county over forty years, and distinctly remembers when it was a wilderness, inhabited by wild game and Indians. In politics Mr. Wynn is a Democrat. Mrs. Wynn was a member of the Baptist Church.

Mederith Yancy was born July 11, 1803, in Pendleton County, S. C., where his parents, Silas and Sallie (Smith) Yancy, were born and reared. The father was a farmer, and in 1819 moved to Tennessee, where Mrs. Yancy died in 1820. Mederith received a common-school education, and when of age started out in life for himself. In 1833 he married Polly, daughter of Burgess and Elizabeth (Mayo) Wit. Mr. Wit was born in 1766, and in 1781 enlisted in the army, serving until the close of the war under Capt. Carouse. He died in 1842. Mrs. Wit was born in 1776. Mrs. Yancy is a native of Tennessee, where she was born in 1810. In 1851 she went to Washington County, and in 1858 came to Crawford County. She is the mother of the following children: William Brownlow, of

Washington County; Hezekiah, of this county; Elizabeth Watson, who now lives at home, and Filmore, also of this county. Mr. Watson came to Crawford County, Ark., in 1878, with his mother, from Perry County, Ark., and was here married. He was born March 19, 1844, and in 1863 enlisted in the war as a private in Company C, Third Arkansas Cavalry, serving first under Capt. Gates and afterward under Capt. Matthews, Col A. H. Rhyan commander. He received his discharge June 22, 1865. His marriage occurred September 3, 1882. Mr. Yancy owns 157 acres of land, sixty acres of which he has cleared. He is a successful farmer and fruit grower, having an orchard of 140 apple trees besides other fruits. He was a member of the Methodist Church until it was disorganized. In politics he is a Democrat, and his first presidential vote was cast for Andrew Jackson in 1824.

Jacob Yoes, a leading business man of the county, is the oldest but one of a family of six children born to Rev. Conrad and Kizey (Bloyd) Yoes, and was born September 3, 1839. His grandfather came from Germany and located in Virginia, where his father was born in 1804. When young he came west, and for some time lived in Missouri, and then in the western part of Arkansas Territory. That part of the Territory being given to the Cherokees, he moved to Washington County, and there married Miss Bloyd, who died when our subject was about ten years old. He then married Wilsie Hanse, with whom he now lives in Mountainsburg, and who has borne him two daughters. For more than forty years he has been a minister in the Methodist Church, with which both of his wives were united. He was formerly a Whig, but is now a Republican. Jacob Yoes passed his childhood on a farm near the West Fork of White River, in Washington County, and, owing to the scarcity of schools, received a very meager education. When seventeen years old he started to make his way in the world, with but $2 and his clothes. His father's parting advice was "Pay all your debts, be truthful, be honest," and his financial success has been based on these cardinal principles. His first contract was to work "three dry months" at three bits per day. After spending some time in the Granby lead mines of Missouri, and some time in Kansas, he returned to Washington County, and in 1858 married Mary A. Reed, a native of the county. He farmed until June, 1862, and then enlisted in Company D, First Arkansas Cavalry, United States Army, serving three years, three months and twenty days. He was on detached duty the greater share of the time, and the only battle in which he participated was at Prairie Grove. May 24, 1863, he was fired on by a posse of Confederates, one shot taking effect in his right hip, one in his left, and a third breaking a bone in the left limb. He was taken prisoner to Van Buren, a distance of fifty miles, and held until exchanged in August of 1863, after which he served until the close of the war. In 1864 he was commissioned first lieutenant, but would not accept. He was discharged at Fayetteville in August, 1865. He was elected sheriff of Washington County during his absence, and upon his return assumed the duties of the office. In 1867 he was appointed to the same position, and served another year. In 1868 he represented the county in the State Legislature, and in 1870 took the Government census. The same year he opened a country store twenty-five miles south of Fayetteville, which he still owns. He is a successful man, owns a large store at West Fork, a flouring-mill, hotel, and has a controlling interest in a canning factory. At Chester, Crawford County, he has a large store and hotel, and at Mountainsburg another store. Then he owns stores at Woolsey Switch, Walker Switch, and at Graphic. He has about 100 acres of land in the county, and has made all his money himself, his only inheritance being $33. He is a Mason, and a member of the I. O. O. F. and G. A. R. He is a Republican, and his wife is a member of the Christian Church. They have had eleven children: William C., Lydia J., Francis M., James J., George A., John W., Gilham C., Thomas D., Mary B. and Matilda and Daisy, deceased.

William C. Yoes, son of Jacob Yoes [see sketch], and his business manager at Chester, Ark., was born September 25, 1859, near Winslow, Washington Co., Ark. He received a rudimentary education at the common schools of the county, and then spent a term at the Arkansas Industrial University. When about fifteen years of age he entered his father's store as salesman, and has been in the mercantile business ever since. His father had charge of the Mountainsburg House, and William clerked for him until the spring of 1881, when he was sent with a stock of goods to Winslow, and he continued in this business until August, 1887, since which time he has occupied the position he

222

CRAWFORD COUNTY, ARKANSAS - BIOGRAPHICAL AND HISTORICAL MEMOIRS
****

now holds.   September 14, 1884, he wedded Miss E. Frances Beakley, a native of this county.   Mrs. Yoes is a member of the Methodist Church, and the mother of the following three children: Bertie C., John D. (deceased) and James F.   Mr. Yoes is possessed of good business qualifications and holds a responsible position.   He does business in a large two-story brick building, 47x100 feet, of which 22x100 is devoted to mercantile purposes, and the remainder used as a hotel.   He also has a grocery department adjoining.   He employs four clerks, and is one of the prominent business men of the place. He is a stanch Republican, and a Royal Arch Mason.

243

444